Revolution and the Transformation of Societies

Revolution and the Transformation of Societies

A Comparative Study of Civilizations

S. N. Eisenstadt

THE FREE PRESS
A Division of Macmillan Publishing Co., Inc.
NEW YORK

Collier Macmillan Publishers
LONDON

The Free Press
A Division of Macmillan Publishing Co., Inc.
866 Third Avenue, New York, N.Y. 10022

Collier Macmillan Canada, Ltd.

Library of Congress Catalog Card Number: 77–5203

Printed in the United States of America

printing number

1 2 3 4 5 6 7 8 9 10

Library of Congress Cataloging in Publication Data

Eisenstadt, S. N.
    Revolution and the transformation of societies.

    Includes index.
    1. Revolutions. 2. Social change. I. Title.
HM281.E37   301.6'333   77–5203
ISBN 0-02-909390-2

To *Kalman Silvert,*
Lover of Liberty,
Sympathetic and Skeptical
Observer of Revolutions

Contents

PREFACE   xv

CHAPTER 1   **Revolutions and Social Change—**
                     The Problem   1

1. The Modern Revolutions and the Study of Social Change   1
2. The Image of Revolution: Violence, Discontinuity, and
   Totality of Change   2
3. The Persistence of the Image of the True Revolution   3
4. Common Assumptions of Studies of Revolution and of
   Evolutionary Approaches to Social Change   4
5. Basic Assumptions of Studies of Revolution   5
6. Major Approaches to the Study of Revolution   5
7. Weak Points in the Approaches to the Study of Revolution   7
8. Implications of the Weaknesses of the Approaches to the
   Study of Revolution   8
9. Toward a New Approach   9

CHAPTER 2   **Protest, Rebellion, Heterodoxy, and**
                     Change in Human Societies   19

1. The Sociological Approach to Change   19
2. Analysis of Change in Contemporary Sociological
   Theories   23
3. Theoretical Convergences: Symbolic and Institutional
   Dimensions of Social Organizations—The Ground
   Rules of Social Interaction   27
4. The Symbolic Dimension of Human Activities: Contents
   of the Ground Rules of Social Interaction and of the
   Parameters of Social Order   29
5. The Institutionalization of the Ground Rules of
   Social Interaction   31

6. The Interweaving of the Symbolic and the Organizational
   Aspects of Social Action. Setting up Ground Rules for
   the Major Institutional Spheres   34
7. The Construction of Societal Centers and of the
   Major Types of Collectivities   36
8. The Interaction of Existential Codes, Social Codes,
   and Symbols of Collective Identity. Institutionalization of
   Codes and Social Division of Labor as Source of
   Tensions, Conflicts, and Contradictions   39
9. Themes of Protest Generated by the Institutionalization
   of Codes and the Social Division of Labor   42
10. Protest, Rebellion, Change, and Violence   45
11. The Variability of Change   45

CHAPTER 3   Change in Traditional Societies—
            A Brief Overview   52

1. Change in Primitive Societies   52
2. Major Characteristics of Archaic and Historical
   Civilizations. The Dimensions of Societal
   Differentiation   54
3. Traditional Legitimation. Institutionalization, Tensions,
   and Contradictions   56
4. Rebellion, Heterodoxy, and Political Struggle in
   Traditional Societies   58
5. The Variability of Traditional Societies.
   The Evolutionary Perspective   60
6. A Preliminary Critical Analysis of the
   Evolutionary Perspective   65
7. The Problem of Revolution in a Comparative
   Analysis of Social Change   68

CHAPTER 4   Patterns of Change in Traditional
            Societies   73

PART 1   *Patterns of Change*   73
1. Introduction   73
2. The Pattern of Segregative Change. Patrimonial,
   Tribal, and City-State Regimes   75
3. Coalescence of Protest Movements and Ideological
   Articulation of Political Struggle in Segregative Change   77
4. Conflicts and Contradictions in Segregative Change   79
5. The Pattern of Coalescent Change. Imperial and
   Imperial-Feudal Societies   80
6. Coalescence of Protest Movements and Ideological

Articulation of Political Struggle in Imperial and
Imperial-Feudal Societies   82
7. Conflicts and Contradictions in Imperial and
Imperial-Feudal Societies   83
8. The Pattern of Change in Exceptional City-States
and Tribal Federations   84

PART 2 *Development of Patterns of Change*   85
1. Introduction   85
2. Structure of Centers. Center-Periphery Relations
and Strata Formation in Imperial and Imperial-Feudal
Regimes. Structuring of Collectivities   86
3. Cultural Orientations of Imperial and
Imperial-Feudal Societies   89
4. Structure of Centers. Center-Periphery Relations
and Strata Formation in Patrimonial Regimes. Structuring
of Collectivities   90
5. Patterns of Incorporation of Social Units in
Patrimonial Regimes   93
6. Cultural Orientations Prevalent in Patrimonial Regimes   94
7. Structure of Centers. Center-Periphery Relations and
Patterns of Conflicts, Contradictions, and Transformability
in Imperial and Patrimonial Systems   94
8. Structure of Centers. Center-Periphery Relations and
Strata Formation in Exceptional City-States and
Tribal Federations   97
9. Cultural Orientations of Exceptional City-States and
Tribal Federations   99

PART 3 *Analytical Conclusions*   100
1. Cultural Orientations. Symbolic Articulation. Institutional
Structure and Patterns of Change   100
2. Organization and Autonomy of Institutional
Entrepreneurs and Elites. Cultural Orientations.
Institutional Structure. Patterns and Directions
of Change   102

CHAPTER 5 The Variability of Patterns of Change and
Transformation in Traditional Societies—
Some Selected Cases   114

PART 1 *Patterns of Change in Patrimonial Regimes*   114
1. Variability of Cultural Orientations. Types of
Entrepreneurs and Patterns of Change   114

2. Change in Patrimonial Regimes. Buddhist Societies   115
3. Change in Otherworldly Civilizations. India   116

PART 2   *Patterns of Change in Imperial and
         Imperial-Feudal Systems*   122
1. Introduction   122
2. The Russian Empire   123
3. The Byzantine Empire   127
4. The Chinese Empire   128
5. The Islamic Civilization   134
6. Western European Civilization   139
7. A Comparative Note. Japan   143

PART 3   *Analytical and Comparative Conclusions*   145
1. Symbolic Articulation. Structure of Elites.
   Patterns of Change   145
2. Cultural Orientations Influencing Patterns of Change.
   Commitment to the Cosmic and Social Orders   147
3. Cultural Orientations Influencing Patterns of Change.
   Perception of Tension between Cosmic and Mundane
   Orders. Otherworldly Foci of Salvation   147
4. Cultural Orientations Influencing Patterns of Change.
   This-Worldly Foci of Salvation   150
5. Cultural Orientations, Ecological Conditions, and
   Patterns of Change. Compact and Crosscutting Markets   152
6. Dependence on External Markets and Patterns of
   Change. City-States and Tribal Federations   154
7. Multiplicity of Patterns of Change in Traditional
   Societies. Revision of the Evolutionary Perspective   155
8. Symbolic and Structural Premises of Traditional Societies.
   Their Effects on Patterns of Change   159

CHAPTER 6   Modern Revolutions and the Revolutionary
            Premises and Symbolism of
            Modern Civilization   173

1. Characteristics of Modern Revolutions   173
2. Restructuring of Themes of Protest in Modern
   Revolutions. The Modern Revolutionary *Erlebnis*   175
3. Outcomes of Modern Revolutions. Modern Social
   Structures. The Civilization of Modernity   177
4. Revolutionary Premises of Modern Civilization   179
5. Expansion of Modern Civilization. The International
   Systems   182

6. Revolutionary Symbolism in Modern Civilization. The Spread of Socialism   183

7. Contradictions of Modern Civilization and the Spread of Socialism   185

8. Carriers of Modern Revolutionary Symbols   187

9. Differential Spread of Radicalism, Socialism, and Revolutionary Imagery   188

CHAPTER 7   The Social and Historical Conditions of the Modern Revolutions   **195**

1. Conditions behind the Development of Modern Revolutions. The Different Approaches   195

2. The Sociocultural Setting of Modern Revolutions   198

3. The Historical Setting of Modern Revolutions   201

4. Social, Cultural, and Historical Conditions behind Later Revolutions   201

5. Social, Cultural, and Historical Frameworks. Preconditions of Revolution   204

6. First and Later Revolutions. Similarities and Differences   205

CHAPTER 8   Variability of Revolutionary Patterns and Outcomes   **215**

PART 1   *Modernization, Discontinuity, Violence, and Institutional Expansion*   215

1. Approaches to the Study of Outcomes of Revolutions   215

2. Criteria of Institutional Change in Post-revolutionary Societies   217

3. Conditions behind Different Revolutionary Outcomes. Existing Approaches. Economic Backwardness. Class Structure   219

4. Criticism of Existing Approaches   220

5. Structure of Centers and Elites. Solidary Relations in Revolutionary Societies   222

PART 2   *Comparative Case Studies of the Outcomes of Revolutions*   223

1. The Revolutionary Process and Outcomes in Europe   223

2. The American Revolution and the Revolt of the Netherlands   227

3. The Revolutionary Process and Outcomes in China   228

4. The Revolutionary Process and Outcomes in Russia   231

5. The Revolutionary Process and Outcomes in Turkey   232

6. Continuity in Cultural Codes, Symbols of Identity, and Institutional Structures ... 233

7. Restructuring of Tradition ... 236

PART 3 *Analytical Conclusions* ... 239

1. Structure and Closure of Centers. Patterns of Revolutions and of Social Transformation. Discontinuity and Dislocation ... 239

2. Closure of Centers. Solidarity, Dislocation, and Coercion in the Restructuring of Postrevolutionary Societies ... 243

3. Autonomy and Solidarity of Elites. Restructuring of Institutional Complexes ... 245

4. Restructuring of Ruling Classes. Transformation of Traditions and of Orientations of Protest ... 246

5. An Illustration. The Chinese Revolution ... 247

6. The International Setting and Revolutionary Outcomes ... 249

PART 4 *Comparative Excursus* ... 251

1. Revolutionary Tendencies in Nineteenth- and Twentieth-Century Europe ... 251

2. Transformative and Revolutionary Tendencies in Jewish Tradition and Society ... 253

3. Japan. The Meiji Restoration and Nonrevolutionary Transformation ... 261

CHAPTER 9 Beyond Classical Revolutions—Processes of Change and Revolutions in Neopatrimonial Societies ... 273

1. Introduction ... 273

2. Incorporation of Patrimonial Societies in the Modern International Systems ... 274

3. Structural Characteristics of Neopatrimonial Societies. Center-Periphery Relations and the Political Process ... 276

4. Processes of Change in Neopatrimonial Societies. Social Mobilization. Restructuring of Elites, Institutional Spheres, and Social Hierarchies ... 279

5. The Noncoalescent Pattern of Change in Neopatrimonial Societies ... 280

6. Restructuring of Elites and Populist Incorporation ... 281

7. Continuity of Patrimonial Center-Periphery Relations ... 282

8. Persistence of Patrimonial Orientations ... 283

9. Structure of Elites in Neopatrimonial Societies. Embedment, Lack of Autonomy, and Dissociation ... 285

10. Variations in Neopatrimonial Societies ... 286

11. Structure of Rebellions, Movements of Protest, and
    Political Struggle in Neopatrimonial Societies   287
12. Fragility of Neopatrimonial Regimes   289
13. Coercion, Repression, Expansion, and Stability in
    Neopatrimonial Societies   289
14. Revolutionary Movements in Neopatrimonial Societies   292
15. International Factors   292
16. Revolutions and Revolutionary Regimes in Neopatri-
    monial Societies: Mexico, Bolivia, Cuba, Portugal   293
17. Summary   298

**CHAPTER 10   Beyond Classical Revolutions—
                Revolutionary Movements and Radicalism
                in Late Modern Societies   311**

1. The Expectation of Revolution   311
2. Structural Transformation. Institutionalization of
   Revolutionary Symbolism. Changing Relations among
   State, Society, and Economy   314
3. Segregation of Political Struggle and New Patterns of
   Conflict. From Revolution to Revolt   316
4. Changing Foci of Protest   317
5. Revolutionary and Radical Groups. Student Revolt   320
6. The Weakening of Revolutionary Transformation.
   The Shifting Premises of Modern Civilization   322

EPILOGUE   329

1. Introduction   329
2. Incorporation of Revolutionary Symbols in
   Modern Societies   329
3. Conditions behind the Incorporation of
   Revolutionary Symbols   331
4. Analytical Conclusions   334
5. Analysis of Revolutions and Criticism of
   Sociological Theory   335
6. The Need for Further Research   336

INDEX   339

Preface

In this book I attempt to put the analysis of revolution in what seems to me to be a new framework. I do not attempt to add anything new to the analysis of the causes of revolutions whether interelite or class conflict, frustration of rising levels of expectation, and the like. My interest is a question that has been neglected in the literature: in what circumstances, under what conditions, do such causes give rise to what have been called revolutions and revolutionary transformations? A closer look at the list of these causes shows that in some cases they give rise to the decline and disintegration of regimes or empires; in others they give rise to far-reaching social change and transformation but not in the revolutionary mold. In other words, while social conflict, heterodoxy, rebellion, change, and transformation are inherent in society, that combination of components of social action that comes under the rubric of pure, true, or classical revolution constitutes a unique process through which social change and transformation takes place.

Hence, the central task of this book is to analyze under what conditions and in what historical circumstances do revolutions and revolutionary transformations occur.

This approach puts the problem of revolution in the framework of the comparative study of civilization, a study in which I have been engaged for many years. My first treatment of this problem appeared in *The Political Systems of Empires* (New York: Free Press, 1963). *Political Sociology* (New York: Basic Books, 1970), especially the introductions, also dealt with comparative analysis, as did an earlier work on modernization, *Modernization, Protest, and Change* (Englewood Cliffs: Prentice-Hall, 1966), and a subsequent volume, *Tradition, Change, and Modernity* (New York: Wiley, 1973), which included far-reaching revisions of the different approaches to modernization. These books necessitated the reappraisal of many central problems of sociological theory, the first step of which task was published in *The Form of Sociology: Paradigms and Crises* (with M. Curelaru; New York: Wiley, 1976).

It was through this reappraisal of sociological theory that I grew dissatisfied with existing analyses of the causes of revolution, as analyzed in detail in Chapters 1 and 7 of this volume, explanations that for the most part rest on class analysis. In this book I attempt to go beyond these approaches without denying their partial validity. The theory that informs my analysis of revolutions is spelled out in Chapter 2.

In the preparation of this work I have been helped and stimulated by many colleagues. My interest in revolution was largely reawakened by discussions with Theda Skocpol about her own work on revolutions. Although, as indicated in this book, I do not agree with several of her interpretations, I do think that her and Kay Trimberger's writings on revolution represent advances in this area.

I have lectured on the subject of revolution and discussed this phenomenon in different places and with various colleagues—especially in Jerusalem, Harvard, and Pittsburgh. I would like to acknowledge an intellectual debt to Nur Yalman, Mike Fisher, Jorge Dominquez, and Al Craig at Harvard University, to Rainer Baum and James Molloy at the University of Pittsburgh, and to James S. Coleman of the University of Chicago. Jan Heesterman of the University of Leiden helped me greatly in the analysis of the dynamics of Indian civilization and Sherif Mardin in the analysis of revolution in Turkey. Al Craig read and commented in detail on the short section on Japan. Yehuda Elkana and Yaron Exrachi commented extensively on earlier versions of various parts of this volume.

My work on the dynamics of civilization in general has been supported by the Ford Foundation; research support for work conducted in Jerusalem was provided by the Harry S. Truman Research Institute and was greatly facilitated by the Jerusalem Van Leer Foundation.

My initial idea for the book crystallized in 1975 when I was a visiting professor in the Department of Sociology and the Center for Middle Eastern Studies at Harvard University. The first outline of the book was completed in the spring of 1976, when I stayed at the Bodmerhouse of the University of Zurich and enjoyed the facilities of the Institute of Sociology. Marie Therese Ficnar and Marie Hofflinger are especially to be thanked for their help. Most of the final draft was written while I was lecturing at Harvard in fall 1976.

The various drafts of the manuscript were typed by Raya Inbar, Moshe Levi, and Judy Kissos in Jerusalem and by Cally Abdulrazak at the Department of Sociology and Mona Campanella at the Center for Middle Eastern Studies at Harvard. Moshe Levi typed the final draft. To all of you I am greatly indebted. Katty Levin and Sonia Herzberg worked on the footnotes and Jerry Michalowicz helped me in the earlier stages of the work in the analysis of the theoretical literature on revolutions. Madeleine Sann did a wonderful job copyediting the manuscript and Elly Dickason at The Free Press supervised all the stages of preparing the work for print. Claire Davis helped in proofreading.

Revolution
and
the Transformation
of Societies

Chapter 1.   Revolutions and Social Change—The Problem

1. THE MODERN REVOLUTIONS AND THE STUDY OF SOCIAL CHANGE

The great revolutions that ushered in the modern era—the Great Rebellion (1640–1660) and the Glorious Revolution (1688) in England, the American Revolution (ca. 1761–1776), and the French Revolution (1787–1799)—and those events that carried the revolutionary message throughout the world—the European revolutions of 1848, the Paris Commune (1870–1871), and above all the Russian (1917–1918) and Chinese (1911–1948) revolutions—profoundly influenced the self-image of modern societies. These phenomena likewise shaped revolutionary symbolism and imagery and became part and parcel of political and ideological symbolism and thought in the modern world. They also greatly influenced the development of sociology. It is not only that modern sociological thought and analysis emerged out of ideological and intellectual trends closely associated with the various revolutionary experiences that shaped modern society or that the understanding of modern society, with its revolutionary origins and experiences, as a unique type of society has constituted the principal focus of modern sociological and political analysis.[1] But also, these revolutionary experiences, as they were perceived in the major intellectual trends of modern society, gave rise to some of the basic assumptions of modern sociopolitical thought in general, and of sociological analysis in particular, about the nature of society and, above all, about social change and the transformation of societies.[2]

The persuasiveness of these assumptions resulted in the adoption of the European revolutionary experience as a model for other societies. Accordingly, sociologists have often analyzed historical situations in light of categories and assumptions that may be inappropriate to them.

However, it is not easy to challenge these assumptions because in large part they are only implicit. Even theories and approaches associated with such scholars as Daniel Lerner and Gabriel Almond, the various theories of modernization, and the so-called neo-evolutionary approaches

1

initially formulated by Talcott Parsons and Robert N. Bellah have been identified as ideologically antirevolutionary by more radical social theorists. Indeed, many of the accusations that have been leveled at these approaches—their inapplicability to non-Western societies (specifically, the latter's modernizing experiences), their Western bias, and their social determinism—have been directed at assumptions they share with ideologically radical analyses of revolutions.[3]

Just as the complex social realities of modern and modernizing societies have in many ways refuted the initial model of modernization, which was developed in the fifties, so also the great variety of so-called revolutionary situations and the fact that few of them corresponded to the image of social transformation derived from the European (or classical) revolutionary experience call for revision of contemporary approaches.

2. THE IMAGE OF REVOLUTION: VIOLENCE, DISCONTINUITY, AND TOTALITY OF CHANGE

The very forceful image of revolution developed in part by revolutionaries and in part by modern intellectuals and sociologists in particular has several components: violence, novelty, and totality of change. These dimensions apply to the revolutionary process—to its causes and effects alike.[4]

The process of revolution is seen as the most intense, most violent, and best articulated of all social movements. It is seen as an ultimate expression of autonomous will and of deep emotions, encompassing formidable organizational capacities as well as a highly elaborated ideology of social protest, especially of a utopian or emancipatory image based on symbols of equality, progress, and freedom and on the central assumption that revolutions will create a new and better social order.[5]

Similarly, the causes of revolutions are not identified as merely temporary or marginal frustrations or disturbances. Revolution is held to be rooted in fundamental social anomalies or inequities—above all, in inter-elite struggles; in the combination of these struggles with broader or deeper social forces such as class conflict; and in the dislocation, social mobilization, and political organization of broader (especially newly emerging) social groups.[6]

The outcomes of revolutions have been envisaged as manifold.[7] First is the violent change of the existing political regime, its bases of legitimation, and its symbols. Second is the displacement of the incumbent political elite or ruling class by another. Third are far-reaching changes in all major institutional spheres—primarily in economic and class relations —leading to the modernization of most aspects of social life, to economic development and industrialization, and to growing centralization and participation in the political sphere. Fourth is a radical break with the past (Alexis de Tocqueville of course pointed out the relativity of such discontinuity).[8] Fifth, given the strong ideological and millenarian orientations of revolutionary imagery, it also has been assumed that revolutions will bring about not only institutional and organizational transformations but also moral and educational changes, that they will create or generate a new man. These five dimensions constitute the image of the pure revolution as it developed in the public consciousness and in the literature.

3. THE PERSISTENCE OF THE IMAGE OF THE TRUE REVOLUTION

As we have seen, the image of the pure (true, real, or classical) revolution emerged out of the interpretation of the historical experience of the great revolutions.[9] This image was systematically analyzed first by Tocqueville,[10] Lorenz von Stein,[11] and Karl Marx,[12] although intellectuals from the eighteenth century onward have concerned themselves with it. Important twentieth-century students of revolution include Emil Lederer, Gustav Landauer, Theodor Geiger, and Eugen Rosenstock-Huessy.[13] It permeated even the formal sociological discussions about revolutions in that period.[14] Most of these scholars (while not necessarily identifying themselves with revolutionary causes) presented this image both as depicting the nature of the European revolutionary experiences and as pointing the way for future, universal revolutions. The latter tendency was strongly reinforced by the spread of revolutionary ideologies and of socialist and Marxist movements and ideologies in particular.[15] Although the Marxists dismiss bourgeois revolutions as merely political in the sense that such revolutions affect only the political sphere and the bourgeoisie, they attribute their occurrence to a broad combination of social forces and see them as leading ultimately to total societal transformation. Thus, all these classical approaches assume that convergence among certain important societal components is a precondition of total social transformation.

The image of revolution as encompassing the elements of totality of change, discontinuity, and novelty (and violence) is also sustained in most recent analyses or definitions of revolution. Thus, according to Carl Friedrich:

> Revolution, as Eugen Rosenstock-Huessy has written, brings on the speaking of a new, unheard of language, another logic, a revolution of all values. . . . Political revolution, then, may be defined as a sudden and violent overthrow of an established political order.[16]

Eugene Kamenka writes:

> [R]evolution is a sharp, sudden change in the social location of power, expressing itself in the radical transformation of the process of government of the official foundation of sovereignty or legitimacy and of the conception of the social order. Such transformations, it has usually been be-

lieved, could not normally occur without violence, but if they did, they would still, though bloodless, be revolution.[17]

Finally, Samuel P. Huntington defines revolution as "a rapid, fundamental, and violent domestic change in the dominant values and myths of a society, in its political institutions, social structure, leadership, and government activities and policies." [18]

The more systematic sociological approach of Chalmers Johnson, influenced by Neil Smelser's earlier work on collective behavior, is based on similar assumptions, as are many more recent works on crises of regimes.[19] Even the more cautious definitions of revolution proposed by Charles Tilly [20] and Volker Rittberger [21] (and to some extent Kamenka's definition quoted earlier),[22] which confine the concept of revolution to the political sphere, acknowledge the notions of totality of change, novelty, and discontinuity in this restricted context. They also subscribe to the assumption that such revolutions are closely related to social transformation.

4. COMMON ASSUMPTIONS OF STUDIES OF REVOLUTION AND OF EVOLUTIONARY APPROACHES TO SOCIAL CHANGE

The assumptions about the nature of social change implicit in the image of the true revolution are most fully articulated in the conceptual framework central to classical and modern sociological analyses of macrosocietal change—namely, that of stages in the evolution of human society.[23] The very idea of stages suggests a noncontinuous transition from one stage to another, and advocates of this scheme assume that all spheres of social life will proceed through the same or parallel stages. This process is regarded as the most fundamental and significant in the development of human societies by classical evolutionists, Marxists, and neo-evolutionists alike.[24]

Needless to say, these schools variously identify the central forces that shape broad societal changes and the ultimate emancipatory goals of social evolution. They differ also in assessing the importance of violence in the transition from one stage to another.[25]

Although Max Weber accepted the evolutionary perspective in part, he questioned the concept of stages and particularly the inevitability of progress.[26] Perhaps for this reason he did not sytematically analyze revolutions as such or total social transformation. Weber's major contribution to the study of social change was that he showed how different features of social order have autonomous dynamics and patterns of change, which may coalesce in distinct ways in various settings. Accordingly, one of the major challenges facing sociologists is to confront the classical approaches to revolution with the type of analysis of social change pursued by Weber. In this process we may overcome certain weaknesses of the classical approaches to the study of social change—weaknesses that can be seen most clearly in analyses of revolution.

5. BASIC ASSUMPTIONS OF STUDIES OF REVOLUTION

The classical approaches assume that in any instance of real transformation, the various components of social change subsumed under the image of revolution will necessarily come together. Any situation lacking such convergence is seen as anomalous or aberrant.

Moreover, movements of change and their outcomes generally have been measured against the ideal-typical revolution. Thus, the literature on revolutions and social movements has focused on the distinction between real, total revolutions and incomplete processes of societal transformation such as coups or dynastic changes. The latter are held to occur in the absence of deep-rooted social conflicts.[27]

Many studies of social movements and especially those of peasant rebellions therefore distinguish between conditions that lead to rebellions or coups and those that lead to real revolutions. They do not inquire into the conditions under which the manifold elements of pure revolutions may be combined in different ways to generate diverse types of social transformations.[28]

Truly enough, in close relation to the ideological and political discussions that reformists and revolutionaries began having in the late nineteenth century, some attention was paid in the literature to the distinction between conditions that account for social transformation through revolution as against the conditions under which such change may be achieved without revolution. But even here relatively little systematic research was done, and the suspicion lingered that changes effected through reforms are not as true, deep, or real as those effected through revolution.[29] Only relatively recent works—for instance, Sherif Mardin's analysis of the Kemalist Revolution and Kay Trimberger's studies of elite revolutions [30]— have attempted to construct a typology of revolutionary experiences to analyze the conditions under which different types of revolutionary processes and social transformations are engendered.

6. MAJOR APPROACHES TO THE STUDY OF REVOLUTION

The weaknesses of the approaches that take the image of the pure revolution for granted is most evident in various types of analyses specifically concerned with the causes, processes, and consequences of revolution.[31]

Analysis of the natural history of modern revolutions is the first such approach that we shall consider. It is best represented in the works of Lyford P. Ewards, George S. Pettee, and Crane Brinton.[32] This approach tries to identify typical stages in the process of revolution as well as common social-psychological characteristics of the process of revolutionary upheaval. In the twenties the natural history approach became closely related to the study of crowd, or mass, behavior,[33] later, it was associated with the study of collective behavior and social movements and the study of violent outbreaks and their place in social life and in the political process.[34] The most fruitful of such works examined sources of discontent and violence,[35] the structural dynamics of social movements and their influence on existing social and political structures,[36] and the possibilities of revolution in the Third World.[37] A recent outgrowth of the natural history approach has been concerned with the revolutionary *Erlebnis* (experience).[38]

Another major approach focuses on the preconditions of revolution. This approach has taken three directions. The first, in Theda Skocpol's words is "the search for aggregate psychological theories which attempt to explain revolutions in terms of people's motivation for engaging in political violence or joining oppositional movements.[39] The principal focus of this psychological or psychosocial approach is the identification of stages or conditions of dissatisfaction that may lead to tension and to political violence, presumably culminating in a revolutionary outbreak. This approach identifies perceptions of deprivation on the part of different groups as the most important such condition.[40]

The second direction is the study of crises of regimes and of internal wars. The study of crises of regimes is concerned mostly with the identification of the broader structural conditions that bring out the contradictions inherent in any regime, above all, capitalist regimes.[41] The study of internal wars focuses on the organizational and institutional conditions that facilitate the eruption of civil wars and that account for different possible outcomes—the suppression of challengers, the co-optation of challengers by incumbents, or the ultimate success of challengers.[42]

Analyses of regime crises and internal wars may overlap with the third direction of study of the preconditions of revolution: identification of conditions in the political sphere (and of their relations to broader social settings) that lead to revolution.

The works of Jean Baechler,[43] John R. Gillis,[44] Huntington,[45] Skocpol,[46] Trimberger,[47] Lawrence Stone,[48] and Charles Tilly[49] converge to some extent on this area of study. The most important of their themes are the political decay of regimes and their inability to cope with internal and/or external problems; the emergence of counterelites or new groups wanting to participate in the political regime or attempting to take it over; and the dislocation and change of broader strata, the emergence of new strata, and their impact on participants in the political process.

7. WEAK POINTS IN THE APPROACHES TO THE STUDY OF REVOLUTION

Let us briefly illustrate how the various approaches that take for granted the image of the pure revolution are unable to deal adequately with the great range of revolutionary and nonrevolutionary situations of change in general and those that developed in modern societies in particular. Almost all these approaches fail to distinguish between the conditions that lead to general dissatisfaction, to different types of violent collective action, to the overthrow of regimes, and/or to revolution and those that generate far-reaching social changes. In fact, the bulk of research on revolution has focused on the most easily identifiable aspect of this phenomenon—the political sphere—neglecting to examine systematically the relationship between transformation of the political sphere and transformation of other spheres of the social order.

Thus, studies that consider revolution to be but a form of collective behavior or violence do not carefully distinguish between social movements that become part of revolutions or lead to them and those that do not; nor do they inquire into the mechanisms and conditions in the broader social structure that may lead such social movements in revolutionary directions. In this way, these studies fail to appreciate the specificity of revolutionary phenomena. Although some students of peasant rebellions have distinguished between movements that evince reformatory and those that evince revolutionary orientations, they have generally not faced the analytical—as distinct from the ideological—problem of when such movements become revolutions.[50]

The study of the phenomenolgy of the revolutionary *Erlebnis* (with the partial exception of John Dunn's work) has become dissociated from the study of the structural causes and consequences of revolutions.[51] Likewise, students of the social-psychological preconditions of revolutions (e.g., James Davis and Ted Gurr) have failed not only to link these preconditions to structural aspects of the political and macrosocietal spheres— for example, interelite relations and relations between elites and the broader strata—but also to inquire into the conditions and mechanisms under which such linkages will lead to revolution rather than to other types of social change.

Similarly, the study of internal wars and of the crises and decay of regimes, whether by scholars such as Harry Eckstein, Huntington, Gillis, Baechler, and Karl Deutsch or by Marxist or Marxist-influenced thinkers like Martin Jänicke or Urs Jaeggi, while providing significant insights into the dynamics of social systems generally has been unable, to specify the concrete conditions that lead to crises of regimes, to different types of revolutions, or to structural changes.[52]

As W. C. Runciman has rightly pointed out,[53] Marxist-oriented analysts of political crises have tended to identify any emerging conflicts in capitalist societies as basic systemic contradictions.

The weaknesses of these various approaches are manifest even in the most promising expositions—the work of Tilly, Stone, Gillis, Huntington, and others who address themselves to the political and social conditions leading to revolution. Most of the conditions these scholars identify as leading to revolution have been advanced as the causes of both the decline of empires [54] and important internal changes within them.[55]

The other side of the picture is that most of the literature neglects the relationship between revolution and modernity. Truly enough the majority of scholars concerned with this problem acknowledge that revolutions are specific to modern civilization and recognize that the symbolism and imagery as well as the major organizational and institutional dimensions of revolutions are uniquely modern phenomena. However, they fail systematically to relate these dimensions to the basic characteristics or the dynamics of modernity.[56]

The study of the outcomes of revolution has been even less systematic, the work of Mardin, Trimberger, and Skocpol excepted. While most analysts of revolutionary situations recognize that revolutions result in economic (capitalist or socialist) development, in political modernization (especially centralization and some type of democratization), and in far-reaching social changes with potentially emancipatory results, they have yet rigorously to examine these features.

Insight into these problems can be gained, however, from works not directly concerned with revolution; for example, Moore's analysis of political routes to modernization;[57] Seymour Martin Lipset and Stein Rokkan's work;[58] and Huntington's study of revolutionary and reformatory experiences.[59]

8. IMPLICATIONS OF THE WEAKNESSES OF THE APPROACHES TO THE STUDY OF REVOLUTION

The tendency of all these approaches to take for granted the image of the pure revolution and to make this image the endpoint of a continuum has weakened scholarly appreciation of the historical and sociological uniqueness of that type of social change and transformation designated "pure revolution." Moreover, it has led to formalistic and schematic comparisons that fail to do justice to the sociological and historical specificity of different types of revolution.

Thus, widespread acceptance of the image of the pure revolution has given rise to disputes as to whether or not the Revolt of the Netherlands (ca. 1555–1585), the American Revolution, or the Turkish (ca. 1918–1923) and Mexican (ca. 1910–1920) revolutions are true revolutions. This tendency also has discouraged systematic analysis within the framework of the comparative study of revolutions of the Meiji Restoration of 1868—an event that certainly revolutionized a traditional society although it lacked some of the major components of a real revolution (above all, the requisite ideological and utopian elements).

The image of the pure revolution has likewise blocked attempts to explain the European revolutions of 1848 as well as the rise of fascism. (Moore [60] and Gino Germani,[61] among others, have to some degree circumvented this barrier.) It has also hampered analysis of the revival of revolutionary symbolism and activities in the student revolts and ethnic conflicts that disturbed the Western world in the sixties.[62] Finally, studies of revolution have largely ignored change and transformation in traditional societies.[63]

9. TOWARD A NEW APPROACH

In the following pages we indicate, if only in a preliminary way, an approach to the comparative study of revolutions and social transformations that addresses itself to the problems outlined above. This approach is based on certain assumptions, the most central of which is that the combination of components of social action that come under the umbrella of pure revolution constitutes a special process through which social change and transformation takes place.

It may of course be doubted whether even in the great revolutions—the English, French, and to some degree the American, Russian, and Chinese—these elements were combined in the way that the revolutionary image envisions. In subsequent chapters we address ourselves to this problem in greater detail. Still, there can be no doubt that the great revolutions combined these elements to a greater degree than did any other situations (traditional or modern) of social change and transformation. Even the fact that these revolutions became models and symbols of change does not mean that all later processes of social change also brought together the symbolic, organizational, and institutional components of change characteristic of the true revolution. In other words, while social conflict, heterodoxy, rebellion, change, and transformation are inherent in human societies, the specific constellation of elements subsumed in the image of the true revolution is not the only natural way of "real" change—in both traditional and modern settings—but rather just one of several possible ways.

The approach we advocate seeks (1) to identify those elements or characteristics of modern revolutions that distinguish them—both ideologically and organizationally—from other movements of protest and rebellion, political struggles, and processes of change; (2) to identify the specific sociohistorical conditions in which the tendency toward pure revolution may be given expression; and (3) to identify nonrevolutionary processes of social transformation in modern societies and the conditions that generate them.

NOTES

1. The development of sociological thought and analysis from the points of view presented here is analyzed in S. N. Eisenstadt and M. Curelaru, *The Form of Sociology: Paradigms and Crises* (New York: Wiley, 1976); see also R. Aron, *Main Currents in Sociological Thought*, 2 vols. (New York: Basic Books, 1966–1967); R. A. Nisbet, *Social Change and History: Aspects of the Western Theory of Development* (New York: Oxford University Press, 1964); and idem, *Tradition and Revolt: Historical and Sociological Essays* (New York: Random House, 1968).

2. See Aron, *Main Currents;* Nisbet, *Tradition and Revolt;* and idem, *The Sociological Tradition* (London: Heinemann, 1967).

3. These criticisms of the studies of modernization are analyzed in S. N. Eisenstadt, *Tradition, Change, and Modernity* (New York: Wiley, 1973), pt. 1; see also, for approaches that emphasize the differences between evolutionary and revolutionary approaches, W. L. Buhl, *Evolution und Revolution* (Munich: Wilhelm Goldmann, 1970); as well as W. F. Wertheim, *Revolution and Evolution: The Rising Waves of Emancipation* (Baltimore: Penguin, 1974).

4. On the image of revolution in modern social thought see M. Lasky, "The Birth of a Metaphor: On the Origins of Utopia and Revolution," *Encounter*, 34, no. 2 (1970), 35–45, and no. 3 (1970), 30–42; idem, *Utopia and Revolution* (Chicago: University of Chicago Press, 1976); K. Marx, *On Revolution*, ed. S. K. Padover (New York: McGraw-Hill, 1971); F. E. Manuel, "Toward a Psychological History of Utopias," in B. McLaughlin (ed.), *Studies in Social Movements* (New York: Free Press, 1969), pp. 370–400; G. Landauer, *Die Revolution* (Frankfurt am Main: Rutten, 1912); A. T. Hatto, "Revolution: An Enquiry into the Usefulness of an Historical Term," *Mind*, 58, no. 232 (1949): 495–517; idem, "The Semantics of 'Revolution,' " in P. J. Vatikiotis (ed.), *Revolution in the Middle East* (London: George Allen & Unwin, 1972); E. Rosenstock-Huessy,

Revolution als politischer Begriff in der Neuzeit (Breslau, 1931), Abhandlungen der Schlesischen Gesellschaft für Vaterländische Kultur, Geisteswissenschaftliche Reihe, vol. 5; and K. Griewank, *Der neuzeitliche Revolutionsbegriff* (Frankfurt am Main: Suhrkamp Paperback, 1973).

Analyses of the modern image and concept of revolution can be most easily found in the many anthologies and surveys of the literature on social movements and revolutions that have recently appeared and in which some of the most important studies of revolution—classical and modern alike—have been collected and analyzed and in which materials bearing on our discussion will be found. Among such works, of special interest are C. J. Friedrich (ed.), *Revolution: Yearbook of the American Society for Political and Legal Philosophy*, Nomos 8 (New York: Atherton, 1967); E. Kamenka (ed.), *A World in Revolution?* (Canberra: Australian National University Press, 1970); J. C. Davies (ed.), *When Men Revolt and Why* (New York: Free Press, 1971); R. S. Denisoff (ed.), *The Sociology of Dissent* (New York: Harcourt, Brace, Jovanovich, 1974); J. R. Gusfield (ed.), *Protest, Reform, and Revolt: A Reader in Social Movements* (New York: Wiley, 1970); McLaughlin, *Studies in Social Movements;* C. E. Black and T. P. Thornton (eds.), *Communism and Revolution* (Princeton: Princeton University Press, 1964); J. Gerassi (ed.), *Towards Revolution: The Revolution Reader—Writings from Contemporary Revolutionary Leaders throughout the World*, 2 vols. (London: Weidenfeld & Nicolson, 1971); K. Kumar (ed.), *Revolution* (London: Weidenfeld & Nicholson, 1971); B. Mazlish, D. Kaledin, and B. Ralston (eds.), *Revolution: A Reader* (New York: Macmillan, 1971); C. T. Paynton and R. Blackey (eds.), *Why Revolution? Theories and Analyses* (Cambridge: Schenkman, 1971); K. von Beyme, *Empirische Revolutionsforschung* (Opladen: Westdeutscher Verlag, 1973); U. Jaeggi and S. Papcke (eds.), *Revolution und Theorie*, vol. 1 (Frankfurt am Main: Athenäum, 1974); M. Jänicke (ed.), *Politische Systemkrisen* (Cologne: Kiepenheuer & Witsch, 1973); and T. Schieder (ed.), *Revolution und Gesellschaft* (Freiburg im Breisgau: Herder, 1973).

Among useful surveys of the literature on revolutions see H. Wassmund, "Revolutionsforschung," *Neue Politische Literatur*, 18, no. 4 (1973): 421–429; idem, "Revolutionsforschung," ibid., 20, no. 4 (1975): 425–433; C. Koepcke, *Revolution: Ursachen und Wirkungen* (Vienna: Günter Ozlog, 1971); T. Hartmut, *Die permanente Revolution: Ein Beitrag zur Soziologie der Revolution und zur Ideologiekritik*, (Opladen: Westdeutscher Verlag, 1973); K. Lenk, *Theorien der Revolution* (Munich: Wilhelm Fink, 1973); C. Lindner, *Theorien der Revolution* (Munich: Wilhelm Goldmann, 1972); G. P. Meyer, "Revolutionstheorien heute: Ein kritischer Überblick in historischer Absicht," in H. U. Wehler (ed.), *200 Jahre amerikanische Revolution und moderne Revolutionsforschung* (Göttingen: Vandenhoeck & Ruprecht, 1976), pp. 122–176; and E. J. Hobsbawm, "*Revolution*" (Paper submitted to the Fourteenth International Congress of Historical Sciences, San Francisco, September 1975).

The Marxist viewpoint is presented in M. Kossok (ed.), *Studien über die Revolution* (Berlin: Akademie, 1969); and idem (ed.), *Studien zur vergleichenden Revolutionsgeschichte,* 1500–1917 (Berlin: Akademie, 1974).

Among the more original recent works on revolution see, in addition to those cited in notes 33–38 below, J. Urry, *Reference Groups and the Theory of Revolution* (London: Routledge & Kegan Paul, 1973); B. Jessop, *Social Order, Reform, and Revolution* (New York: Macmillan, 1972); J. Dunn, *Modern Revolutions: An Introduction to the Analysis of a Political Phenomenon* (Cambridge: At the University Press, 1972); P. Calvert, *A Study of Revolution* (Oxford: Clarendon, 1970); A. Decouflé, *Sociologie des révolutions* (Paris: Presses universitaires de France, 1968); D. Willer and G. K. Zollschan, "Prolegomena to a Theory of Revolutions," in G. K. Zollschan and W. Hirsch (eds.), *Explorations in Social Change* (Boston: Houghton Mifflin, 1964), pp. 125–152; and L. Pellicani (ed.), *Sociologia delle rivoluzioni* (Naples: Guide, 1976).

5. On the ideological component of revolutions see H. Arendt, *On Revolution* (New York: Viking, 1963); J. L. Talmon, *The Origins of Totalitarian Democracy* (London: Secker & Warburg, 1952); J. Baechler, "Le funzioni dell'ideologia e l'azione rivoluzionaria," in Pellicani, *Sociologia delle rivoluzioni,* pp. 285–304; Black and Thornton, *Communism and Revolution;* A. C. Janos (ed.), "The Communist Theory of the State and Revolution," in ibid., pp. 27–42; R. Aron, *L'Opium des intellectuels* (Paris: Calmann-Levy, 1955), available in translation as *The Opium of the Intellectuals* (London: Secker & Warburg, 1957); E. Kamenka, "The Relevance —and Irrelevance—of Marxism," in Kamenka, *A World in Revolution ?,* pp. 53–71; Lasky, "Birth of a Metaphor"; A. MacIntyre, "Ideology, Social Science, and Revolution," *Comparative Politics,* 5, no. 3 (1973): 321–342; C. B. MacPherson, "Revolution and Ideology in the Late Twentieth Century," in Friedrich, *Revolution,* pp. 139–153; Manuel, "Toward a Psychological History of Utopias"; Marx, *On Revolution;* L. S. Feuer (ed.), *Marx and Engels: Basic Writings on Politics and Philosophy* (Garden City: Doubleday, 1959); R. A. Nisbet, "The Function of the Vision of the Future in Radical Movements" (Paper prepared for the Workshop on Radicalism, Columbia University Research Institute on International Change, 5 March 1975); Decouflé, *Sociologie des révolutions;* and R. C. Tucker, *The Marxian Revolutionary Idea* (New York: Norton, 1969).

6. The literature on the causes of revolutions is vast, and it will be cited at greater length in subsequent notes. A good overview of this literature can be found in the various readers cited in note 4 above and in L. Stone, "Theories of Revolution," *World Politics,* 18, no. 2 (1966): 159–176; L. Kramnick, "Reflections on Revolution: Definition and Explanation in Recent Scholarship," *History and Theory,* 11, No. 1 (1972): 26–63; and K. Kumar, Introduction to Kumar, *Revolution,* pp. 1–90.

7. On the outcomes of revolution see the various readers cited in note 5 above as well as T. Skocpol, "France, Russia, China: A Structural Analysis of Social Revolutions," *Comparative Studies in Society and History,* 18 (April 1976): 175–210; P. Zagorin, "Prolegomena to the Comparative History of Revolution in Early Modern Europe," ibid., pp. 151–174; idem,

"Theories of Revolution in Contemporary Historiography," *Political Science Quarterly*, 88, no. 1 (1973): 23–52; E. K. Trimberger, "A Theory of Elite Revolutions," *Studies in Comparative International Development*, 7, no. 3 (1972): 191–207; see also B. Moore, Jr., *Social Origins of Dictatorship and Democracy* (Boston: Beacon, 1966); E. V. Trapanese, "Rivoluzione e dispotismo burocratico," in Pellicani, *Sociologia delle rivoluzioni*, pp. 235–254; and F. Bencini, "Burocrazia e rivoluzione: La rivoluzione cubana, quindici anni dopo," in ibid., pp. 255–284.

8. See A. de Tocqueville, *The Old Regime and the French Revolution* (Garden City: Doubleday, 1955).

9. The bibliographical references on the major revolutions are given in chap. 6, notes 1–4; chap. 7, notes 3–14; and chap. 8, notes 19–54. At this stage it might be useful to look at such collections as L. Kaplan (ed.), *Revolutions: A Comparative Study from Cromwell to Castro* (New York: Random House, Vintage, 1973); H. Lubasz (ed.), *Revolutions in Modern European History* (New York: Macmillan, 1966); and Mazlish et al., *Revolution*.

10. On Tocqueville see A. Salomon, *In Praise of Enlightenment* (Cleveland: World Publishing, 1963), chap. 7; J. M. Zeitlin, *Liberty, Equality, and Revolution in Alexis de Tocqueville* (Boston: Little, Brown, 1961); I. Geiss, "Tocqueville und das Zeitalter der Revolution," *Neue Politische Literatur*, 19, no. 3 (1974): 395–396; and M. Richter, "Tocqueville's Contributions to the Theory of Revolution," in Friedrich, *Revolution*, pp. 75–121.

11. On Von Stein see S. Landshut, *Kritik der Soziologie* (Munich: Von Duncker & Humboldt, 1929), and L. von Stein, *Staat und Gesellschaft* (Zurich: Rascher, 1934).

12. Among the many writings by and about Marx bearing on revolution see Marx, *On Revolution;* Feuer, *Marx and Engels;* Kamenka, "Relevance—and Irrelevance—of Marxism"; S. K. Padover, "Karl Marx as a Revolutionist," in Marx, *On Revolution*, pp. ix-xxx; Tucker, *Marxian Revolutionary Idea;* and S. Avineri, *The Social and Political Thought of Karl Marx* (Cambridge: At the University Press, 1968).

13. E. Lederer, *Einige Gedanken zur Sociologie der Revolutionen* (Leipzig: Der Neue Geist, 1918); idem, "On Revolutions," *Social Research*, 3, no. 1 (1936): 1–18; Landauer, *Die Revolution;* T. Geiger, "Revolution," in A. Vierkandt (ed.), *Handwörterbuch der Soziologie* (Stuttgart: Ferdinand Enke, 1931), pp. 511–518; and W. Gombart, ""Formen des gewaltsamen sozialen Kampfes," *Kölner Vierteljahrschrift für Soziologie*, no. 5 (1925), reprinted in Jaeggi and Papcke, *Revolution und Theorie*, 1:24–134; Rosenstock-Huessy, *Revolution als politischer Begriff;* idem, *Die europäischen Revolutionen: Volkscharakter und Staatenbildung* (Stuttgart: Kohlhammer, 1951; originally published 1931); see also C. Brinkmann, *Soziologische Theorie der Revolution* (Göttingen: Vandenhoeck & Ruprecht, 1948); as well as the earlier work of P. A. Sorokin, *The Sociology of Revolution* (Philadelphia: Lippincott, 1925).

14. See, for instance, the discussion of the third meeting of the German So-

ciological Society: F. Tönnies, L. V. Wiese, and L. M. Hartmann, "Reden, Vorträge und Debatten über das Wesen der Revolution," *Verhandlungen des Dritten deutschen Soziologentages* (Tübingen: J. C. B. Mohr, 1923), pp. 1–40.

15. For materials on socialism and Marxism, from the point of view of our discussions, see the references cited in notes 2 and 5 above and also S. N. Eisenstadt and Y. Azmon (eds.), *Socialism and Tradition* (New York: Humanities, 1974).

16. C. J. Friedrich, "An Introductory Note on Revolution," in Friedrich, *Revolution*, pp. 3–9.

17. E. Kamenka, "The Concept of a Political Revolution," in ibid., pp. 122–138; see also idem, "Relevance—and Irrelevance—of Marxism"; for a similar definition see R. Dahrendorf, "Über einige Probleme der soziologischen Theorie der Revolution," *European Journal of Sociology*, 2, no. 1 (1961): 153–162.

18. S. P. Huntington, *Political Order in Changing Societies* (New Haven: Yale University Press, 1968), p. 264; see also the earlier formulation of Brinckman, "Soziologische Theorie der Revolution"; and R. M. MacIver, *The Web of Government* (New York: Macmillan, 1947), pp. 269–314.

19. C. Johnson, *Revolution and the Social System* (Stanford: Stanford University, Hoover Institution, 1964; idem, *Revolutionary Change* (Boston: Little, Brown, 1966). For the theoretical background of this approach I am greatly indebted to N. J. Smelser, *Theory of Collective Behavior* (New York: Free Press, 1963). See also, for a more schematic presentation of such a view of revolution, M. N. Hagopian, *The Phenomenon of Revolution* (New York: Dodd, Mead, 1975).

20. C. Tilly, "Does Modernization Breed Revolution?" *Comparative Politics*, 5, no. 3 (1973): 425–447; and idem, "Revolutions and Collective Violence," in F. I. Greenstein and N. Polsby (eds.), *Handbook for Political Science* (Reading: Addison-Wesley, 1975), 3:483–555.

21. V. Rittberger, "Über sozialwissenschaftliche Theorien der Revolution: Kritik und Versuch eines Neuansatzes," *Politische Vierteljahrschrift*, 12, no. 4 (1971): 492–529.

22. See the works by Kamenka that are cited in note 18 above.

23. On these concepts see Eisenstadt, *Tradition, Change, and Modernity*, p. 1; Nisbet, *Social Change and History*; and Buhl, *Evolution und Revolution*.

24. See V. I. Lenin, *State and Revolution* (New York: International Publishers, 1969); idem, "What Is to Be Done?" in Gusfield, *Protest, Reform, and Revolt*, pp. 458–472; and A. C. Janos, "The Communist Theory of the State and Revolution," in Black and Thornton, *Communism and Revolution*, pp. 27–41.

25. See on this point R. Bendix, *Max Weber: An Intellectual Protest* (Garden City: Doubleday, 1960); W. Mommsen, *Max Weber: Gesellschaft, Politik, und Geschichte* (Frankfurt am Main: Suhrkampf, 1972); and S. N. Eisenstadt (ed.), *Max Weber: On Charisma and Institution Building* (Chicago: University of Chicago Press, 1968), esp. pp. ix–lxi.

26. See, for instance; E. Luttwak, *Coup d'Etat* (New York: A. A. Knopf, 1969, Borzoi Books); D. C. Rapaport, "Coup d'Etat: The View of the Men Firing Pistols," in Friedrich, *Revolution*, pp. 53–74; on the distinction between revolution and coup d'état see Huntington, *Political Order in Changing Societies.*

27. For relevant material on social movements and peasant rebellions see Davies, *When Men Revolt and Why;* Gusfield, *Protest, Reform, and Revolt; Denisoff, Sociology of Dissent;* H. Landsberger (ed.), *Latin American Peasant Movements* (Ithaca: Cornell University Press, 1969); idem; *Rural Protest* (New York: Macmillan, 1974); McLaughlin, *Studies in Social Movements;* J. Paige, *Agrarian Revolution: Social Movements and Export Agriculture in the Underdeveloped World* (New York: Free Press, 1975); *Comparative Politics,* a special issue on "Peasants and Revolution," 8, no. 3 (1976); *Comparative Studies in Society and History,* 17 (October 1955); P. Zagorin, Protegomena to the Comparative History of Revolution in Early Modern Europe," *Comparative Studies in Society and History,* 18, no. 2 (1976), 151–174; T. Skocpol, "France, Russia, China: A Structural Analysis of Social Revolutions," *Comparative Studies in Society and History,* 18, no. 2 (1976), 175–210; E. Hermassi, "Toward a Comparative Study of Revolutions," *Comparative Studies in Society and History,* 18, no. 2 (1976), 211–235; E. R. Wolf, *Peasant Wars of the Twentieth Century* (New York: Harper & Row, 1973); and idem, "Peasant Rebellion and Revolution," in N. Miller and R. Aya (eds.), *National Liberation: Revolution in the Third World* (New York: Free Press, 1971), pp. 48–67.

28. For one of the few partial exceptions within the sociological literature see Jessop, *Social Order, Reform and Revolution;* see also A.D. Smith, *The Concept of Social Change* (London: Routledge & Kegan Paul, 1973), pp. 96–130.

29. S. Mardin, "Ideology and Religion in the Turkish Revolution," *International Journal of Middle East Studies,* 2 no. 3 (1971), 197–211; Trimberger, "Theory of Elite Revolutions," pp. 191–207; and idem, *Revolution from Above* (forthcoming).

31. For the literature on revolution see the references cited in note 4 above.

32. For illustrations of this approach see L. P. Edwards, *The Natural History of Revolution* (Chicago: University of Chicago Press, 1972); G. Pettee, *"The Process of Revolution,"* in Paynton and Blackey, *Why Revolution,* pp. 18–35; and C. Brinton, *The Anatomy of Revolution,* rev. and enl. ed. (New York: Random House, Vintage, 1965).

33. On crowd and mass behavior see Geiger, *Revolution;* L. V. Wiese, "Die Problematik einer Soziologie der Revolution," *Verhandlungen des Dritten Deutschen Soziologentages,* pp. 6–24; and L. M. Hartman, "Zur Soziologie der Revolution," *Verhandlungen des Dritten Deutschen Soziologentages,* pp. 24–40. For an earlier, classical exposition of the crowd see G. le Bon, *The Crowd* (New York: Macmillan, 1947; originally published 1895). Some of the best illustrations of this approach are I. K. Feierabend, R. L. Feierabend, and T. R. Gurr (eds.), *Anger, Violence, and Politics* (Englewood Cliffs: Prentice-Hall, 1972); T. R. Gurr, "A Causal Model of Civil

Strife: A Comparative Analysis Using New Indices," *American Political Science Review*, 62, no. 4 (1968): 1104–1124; and idem, "Psychological Factors in Civil Violence," *World Politics*, 20, no. 2 (1968): 245–278.

34. On social movements see McLaughlin, *Studies in Social Movements;* Davies, *When Men Revolt and Why;* A. S. Feldman, "Violence and Volatility: The Likelihood of Revolution," in H. Eckstein (ed.), *Internal War* (New York: Free Press, 1964); J. A. Geschwender, "Explorations in the Theory of Social Movements and Revolutions," *Social Forces*, 47, no. 2 (1968): 127–135; and T. R. Gurr, *Why Men Rebel* (Princeton: Princeton University Press, 1970).

35. For illustrations of psychological approaches to the study of revolutions see C. A. Ellwood, "Eine psychologische Theorie der Revolution (1905/06)," in Jaeggi and Papcke, *Revolution und Theorie I*, pp. 113–123; idem, "A Psychological Theory of Revolutions," in Paynton and Blackey, *Why Revolutions*, pp. 36–45; Gurr, *Why Men Rebel*; Le Bon, *The Crowd*; P. A. Lupsha, "Explanation of Political Violence: Some Psychological Theories versus Indignation," *Politics and Society*, 2, no. 1 (1971): 89–104; D. E. Morrison, "Some Notes towards a Theory of Relative Deprivation, Social Movements, and Social Change," *American Behavioral Scientist*, 14, no. 5 (1971): 675–690; E. N. Muller, "A Test of a Partial Theory of Potential for Political Violence," *American Political Science Review*, 66, no. 3 (1972): 928–959; and A. Oberschall, "Rising Expectations and Political Turmoil," *Journal of Development Studies*, 6, no. 1 (1969): 5–22.

36. W. Gamson, *Power and Discontent* (Homewood: Dorsey, 1968).

37. On peasant movements see the works cited in note 28 above; for material on the Third World see M. F. Lofchie, "Agrarian Socialism in the Third World: The Tanzanian Case, "*Comparative Politics*, 8, no. 3 (1976): 479–599; M. Selden, "Revolution and Third World Development: People's War and the Transformation of Peasant Society," in Miller and Aya, *National Liberation*, pp. 214–248; Wolf, *Peasant Wars;* idem, "Peasant Rebellion and Revolution"; Miller and Aya, *National Liberation;* and G. F. Hudson (ed.), *Reform and Revolution in Asia* (New York: St. Martin's, 1972).

38. See Dunn, *Modern Revolutions;* and Decouflé, *Sociologie des révolutions*.

39. As quoted by M. Skocpol, "Explaining Revolutions: In Quest of a Social-Structural Approach," in L. A. Coser and O. N. Larsen (eds.), *The Uses of Controversy in Sociology* (New York: Free Press, 1976), pp. 156–157.

40. See the references cited in notes 35 and 36 above.

41. The best collection of materials on this problem is Jänicke, *Politische Systemkrisen;* one of the few attempts to apply such an approach in comparative analysis can be found in G. A. Almond, S. C. Flanagan, and R. J. Mundt (eds.), *Crisis, Choice, and Change* (Boston: Little, Brown, 1973); see also J. Galtung, "Feudal Systems, Structural Violence, and the Structural Theory of Revolutions," in *International Peace Research Association, Studies in Peace Research* (The Hague: Van Gorcum, 1970), 1:110–188.

42. On internal wars see J. Baechler, "De la fragilité des systèmes politiques," *Archives, European Journal of Sociology*, 12, no. 1 (1971): 61–86; and S.

Neumann, "The International Civil War," *World Politics*, 1, no. 4 (1948–1949): 333–360.

43. Baechler, "De la fragilité des systèmes politiques"; and idem, *Les Phénomènes révolutionnaires*, available in translation as *Revolutions* (Oxford: Blackwell, 1976).

44. J. R. Gillis, "Political Decay and the European Revolutions, 1789–1848, *World Politics*, 22, no. 3 (1970), 344–370;

45. Huntington, *Political Order in Changing Societies;* H. Eckstein, "On the Etiology of Internal Wars," *History and Theory*, 4, no. 1 (1966): 133–163; idem, *"Internal War;* and B. C. Flanagan, "Das politische System und die systemische Krise," in Jänicke, *Politische Systemkrisen*, pp. 98–111.

46. Skocpol, *"France, Russia, and China";* and her forthcoming book on this subject to be published by Cambridge University Press.

47. Trimberger, *"Theory of Elite Revolutions";* and idem, *Revolution from Above.*

48. L. Stone, *The Causes of the English Revolution*, 1529–1642 (London: Routledge & Kegan Paul, 1972); idem, "The English Revolution," in R. Forster and J. P. Greene (ed.), *The Preconditions of Revolution in Early Modern Europe* (Baltimore: John Hopkins Press, 1970), pp. 55–108; and idem, "Theories of Revolution."

49. Tilly, *"Revolutions and Collective Violence."*

50. See the references cited in note 28 above.

51. Dunn, *Modern Revolutions;* and Decouflé, *Sociologie des révolutions.*

52. Almond et al., *Crises, Choice, and Change.*

53. W. G. Runciman, "Conventions and Contradictions, *"Times Literary Supplement*, 16 January 1976, pp. 46–48.

54. On the causes of the decline of empires and the causes of rebellion see S. N. Eisenstadt (ed.), *The Decline of Empires* (New York: Free Press, 1969). More recent research on the Mogul Empire is summarized in a series of articles in the *Journal of Asian Studies*: M. N. Pearson, "Shivaji and the Decline of the Mughal Empire," ibid., 35, no. 2 (1976): 221–236; J. F. Richards, "The Imperial Crisis in the Deccan," ibid., pp. 237–256; P. Hardy, "Commentary and Critique," ibid., pp. 257–264.

   In a discussion of the possible transformation of communist regimes, the reasons behind such transformation were not entirely distinct from the causes often given as those of revolutions. See S. Bridge, "Why Czechoslovakia? and Why 1968?" *Studies in Comparative Communism*, 8, no. 4 (1975): 413–429; and G. Golan, "Comment: Reform Movements and the Problem of Prediction," ibid., pp. 430–435.

55. See S. N. Eisenstadt, *The Political Systems of Empires* (New York: Free Press Paperback, 1969).

56. See, for instance, Griewank, *Der neuzeitliche Revolutionsbegriff;* and Hatto, "Revolution."

57. Moore, *Social Origins of Dictatorship and Democracy.*

58. S. M. Lipset and S. Rokkan, "Cleavage Structures, Party Systems, and

Voter Alignments," in S. M. Lipset and S. Rokkan (eds.), *Party Systems and Voter Alignments: Cross-National Perspectives* (New York: Free Press, 1967), pp. 1–64.

59. Huntington, *Political Order in Changing Societies.*

60. Moore, *Social Origins of Dictatorship and Democracy.*

61. G. Germani, *Autoritarismo, fascismo, eclassi sociali* (Bologna: Mulino, 1975, vol. 2; see also the general review of the literature on fascism by W. Schieder, "Faschismus und kein Ende?" *Neue politische Literatur,* 15, no. 1 (1970): 166–187.

62. See the literature cited in notes 3–4 to Chapter 10.

63. A. Fuks, "Patterns and Types of Social-Economic Revolution in Greece from the Fourth to the Second Century B.C.," *Ancient Society,* 5 (1974): 51–81; and A. Heuss, "Das Revolutionsproblem im Spiegel der Antiken Geschichte," *Historische Zeitschrift,* 216, no. 1 (1973): 1–72.

Chapter 2.   Protest, Rebellion, Heterodoxy, and Change in Human Societies

1. THE SOCIOLOGICAL APPROACH TO CHANGE

Given our assumption that modern, "real" revolutions are only one process of change, only one way in which social transformation occurs, it is best initially to put this phenomenon, in order to understand its specific characteristics, within the more general framework of analysis of social change.

One of the major premises of sociological analysis has been that the causes of social change are inherent in the construction of the social order. This premise reflects the specific sociological *Problemstellung*. This *Problemstellung*, which has been evolving very haltingly since the early nineteenth century (and which is distinct from those of the philosophical, ideological traditions and those of social reform) [1] does not inquire into the national conditions or characteristics of social order or the single best type of such order. Instead, its major focus is the analysis of the conditions and mechanisms of social order and its constituent components, of continuity and change in the social order in general as well as in different types of social orders. Thus, the fundamental problem of social order gradually became not how society emerges from a presocial base but how continuous interaction among human beings is possible. That is, how is the social order maintained given the essential social interdependence of human beings, on the one hand, and individual distinctiveness, on the other, and the fact that the human species is characterized by an open biological program [2] and by a consciousness of this openness and of the uncertainties it involves. Truly enough, sociologists long tended to formulate the problem of social order in purely Hobbesian terms, that is, in terms of the transition from a presocial, individual state into a social one. Nevertheless, sociological analysis increasingly shifted the locus of this problem to the institutional sphere itself, to the very construction of human society.

The crucial step in the development of sociological analysis has been the recognition of the distinction between two aspects of the problem of social order, of the existence of a continuous tension between them, and of the relations of this tension to the ubiquity of change in human societies.

One aspect of the problem of social order is organizational: at issue here is identification of the mechanisms, the institutional arrangements or processes, that make it possible to ensure some predictability in the interaction among people and the maintenance of the social division of labor. A large part of sociological analysis has been devoted to the identification of the mechanisms—roles, institutions, organizations, markets, contracts—that explain how the social division of labor is achieved in any society. Moreover, sociological analysis has tried to specify the principles or laws—class struggle, rules of cognition inherent in the human mind, the drives and motives of individuals—that underlie the social division of labor.

Still, however much organization served as the central focus of sociological analysis, it became clear that organizational frameworks and mechanisms of social interaction and the social division of labor do not in themselves make human behavior predictable, nor do they generate the acceptance of meaningful obligations without which there cannot be a social order. On the contrary, organization not only fails itself to solve the problems of potential social disorder but also in a sense exacerbates them by transposing these problems from organizational givens into foci of conscious concern that are formulated in symbolic terms and emphasizing even more the possibilities of disorder, arbitrariness, and randomness in social life and organization.

These disruptive possibilities of the organizational aspects of the social division of labor are rooted in the fact that in any given setting of social interaction, a combination of conflict and cooperation develops among different groups and actors over the production, distribution, and use of resources. The sustained functioning of any of the mechanisms of the social division of labor gives rise to attempts by different actors to monopolize access to positions and resources and to promulgate rules to support and perpetuate such arrangements. But while these rules produce stability in interaction, they are usually perceived as arbitrary, coercive, and unjust. They may generate a perception of ambiguity and disorder among actors. As a result, they cannot provide the basis of trust among participants in these relationships; instead, they build instability into the social relations they structure. The potential for instability and disorder and the likelihood that actors will perceive the social division of labor as arbitrary are increased by the fact that these fundamental indeterminacies are systematically related to the basic organizational features of social interaction—the structuring of collectivities, institutions, and macrosocietal orders.

In the construction of collectivities, institutions, and macrosocietal orders these indeterminacies become manifest above all because the goals and needs of any group and its members are never simply given. The specific content of such needs has to be defined concretely in each instance. Moreover, within any group there may arise differences of opinions on how to define concretely each such need. Similarly, the different needs of subgroups are never entirely compatible; therefore, tensions and contradictions exist within the collectivity. Such tensions center on the evaluation of the relative importance of different needs of a society and of different subgroups; on their congruence with the private goals of the individuals participating in any given subgroup, and on the distribution of, and access to, the resources necessary to meet individual as well as group needs. In other words, the organizational aspects of the social division of labor do not:

1. eliminate uncertainty and risks in institutional life;
2. guarantee that somebody will take care of the recognized organizational needs of the collectivity in general and of collective security in particular;
3. articulate or provide for the implementation of collective goals;
4. ensure the attainment of some measure of individual and collective pride and identity and the attainment or sustenance of the feeling of participation in some meaningful social or cultural order;
5. foster development and maintenance of feelings of mutual trust among members of the collectivity; and
6. guarantee that social actors will indeed fulfill their mutual obligations and perform the tasks and roles assigned to them.

Identification of tension between the organizational mechanisms of the social division of labor and acceptance of the social order constitutes one of the major achievements of sociological analysis. This recognition called for explanation, first, of how order could be attained in social life given both the multiplicity of goals of individuals and their interdependence and, second, of how the social order—what in more recent sociological analysis has been called the institutional framework—copes with the tension between these two basic problems of social life. Of central importance was recognition of the attempt to resolve this tension and the predicaments outlined above, to establish and maintain some meaningful order in the social realm and participation in it (which in any type of interaction constitutes an important goal). Accordingly, sociological analysis was mainly concerned with showing how this goal and the attempt to construct meaningful definitions of social life were built into the institutional framework of societies. Whatever differences separated sociological approaches and theories, they all agreed that reconciling the two aspects of the social order could be accomplished only through construction of a symbolic universe that delineates the boundaries of collectivities, the identity of persons, and provides the basis of such meaningful construction of social reality and of trust among individuals.

Thus, Marx focused on exploitation and the alienation which is inherent in the division of labor (and especially in a class division of labor), and on the ideological smokescreens developed by the ruling class in order to mask the feeling of alienation.[3] Similarly, Durkheim's emphasis on the inadequacy of purely contractual ties suggests that it is the process of the division of labor that creates the central problem of social order, and he underlined the importance of symbolic, precontractual elements. Weber's focus on the importance of the legitimation of material, power, or prestige interests accords with Durkheim's view.[4]

Because at the same time, however, sociological analysis recognized that the tension between the two aspects of social order is never fully resolved, a gradual reformulation of several central problems of social analysis occurred. Of special importance was the reformulation of problems of social disorder, disorganization, and transformation that can be found in philosophical speculation of all eras but most notably in modern sources. The sociological *Problemstellung* has developed by turning the analysis of these phenomena into a starting point for the understanding of the mechanisms of social order, the conditions of functioning and change of such order in general and its varying types in particular. This implies that social disorder is not prior to, and hence different from, social order but that it constitutes a special type of constellation of elements that in different combinations make up the core of continuity of social order itself; therefore, it implies that social disorganization may serve as a starting point for the analysis of both stability or continuity in the social order and social change or transformation. In this way sociological analysis focuses on the transformative propensities of social systems, perceiving such propensities not as external or random events but as major aspects of the social order.[5]

This approach to disorganization and change and their rootedness in the tension between the organizational and the legitimating aspects of social order was developed by some of the greatest figures of sociological analysis; around it crystallized some of the major breakthroughs in the development of social change analysis. The first such breakthrough in modern sociological analysis was Marx's work; his crucial analytical concept is that of alienation generated by the dynamics of man's self-created environment [6] so long as this environment is based on class revolutions; hence Marx's insistence on the ubiquity of alienation and conflict in class society. The weakness of Marx's analysis lies in its assumption of the temporariness of alienation and conflict in the class society, of their disappearance in the classless situation, and thus, in his concentration on those aspects of social conflict that could lead to conflict-free society. A second breakthrough came with Simmel's assertion of the perenniality of conflict in social life; however, Simmel's view is limited by his focus on the purely formal aspects of social interaction.[7]

Two further analytical contributions to this issue were made by Durkheim and Weber. Both used the analysis of disorganization as a central focus for a better understanding of the conditions and mechanisms by which the social order functions and for comparative analysis of various social orders. Durkheim's analysis of anomie is the counterpoint of his preoccupation with social integration, and he indicated how different types of anomie, criminality, and penal law are related to different types of division of labor and precontractual elements.[8] For Weber, the tension between the institution building and the institution destroying propensities of charisma constitutes a central concern of sociological analysis.[9] Like Marx, Durkheim and Weber pointed to the possibility that change and conflict originate in the constitutive aspects of the social order, but unlike Marx they left open the possibility of the permanence of such conflict. They were therefore more open to identifying the structural conditions under which conflict and change can emerge.

In the many classic sociological works, concern with the causes of change was, as we have briefly alluded to, closely connected with concern about the direction of change of human societies and with the comparative study of change in human societies. Later on we shall address ourselves to this problem at somewhat greater length. At this stage of our discussion we shall, however, briefly analyze the major approaches to the problem of social change in contemporary sociological theory.

2. ANALYSIS OF CHANGE IN CONTEMPORARY SOCIOLOGICAL THEORIES

The premise that change is inherent in the structure of social order has been most forcefully stressed in many of the principal theories of contemporary sociology and it has frequently been at the heart of theoretical controversies.

Many of these controversies in sociological theory were concerned with the structural-functional theory in general and with the limits of its applicability to the analysis of social and historical change in particular.[10]

The major controversies in sociology gave rise to a variety of new models or approaches, such as the conflict model espoused by Ralph Dahrendorf and John Rex, and in a different mode by Reinhard Bendix and Randall Colin, the exchange model espoused by George C. Homans and to some extent by Peter Blau, and the symbolic-structuralist one espoused by Claude Lévi-Strauss, or to the reaffirmation and further development of older models—the symbolic-interactionist one, out of which evolved ethnomethodology, and the Marxist one. The discussions around these various models and especially around the confrontation of these models with the structural-functional model were the main issues of the theoretical discussions and controversies in sociology, especially in macro-sociological analysis.

All these models claimed that the structural-functional model tended to minimize the autonomy of individuals and of subgroups, their interests and conflicts, and the cultural and symbolic dimensions of human activity, and that it subordinated all of them to the organizational needs or exigencies of the social system.

Each model emphasized an aspect or component of social life presumably neglected by the structural-functional school. Thus, the exchange and conflict models emphasized the motives, interests and conflicts arising in society between different social actors (individuals or groups); the symbolic-interactionist model emphasized that the normative definitions of situations in which people interact were not simply given by the values of society, but were continuously constructed by people who interact in these situations. The structuralists and to some degree the Marxists emphasized some "deeper" symbolic or symbolic-structural dimensions of human life or of the social order as the key to understanding the structures and dynamics of societies.

Closely related to this contention was the unwillingness of most of these approaches to accept the "natural" givenness of any single institutional arrangement in terms of its organizational or systemic needs of the social system to which it belonged. Any given institutional arrangements— be it the formal structure of a factory or a hospital, the division of labor in the family, the official definition of deviant behavior, or the place of a ritual in a given social setting or patterns of behavior that developed around it—were no longer examined only or mainly in terms of their contribution to maintenance of any given group or society. Instead, the very setting up of such institutional arrangements was transposed from a given into a problem to be explained, and these approaches asked what were the forces beyond the organizational needs of a society that could explain its major institutional arrangements.

The various models differed in their proposals as to how to cope with this problem, how to explain any concrete institutional order. One such approach, to be found especially in the individualistic and conflict models, as well as among the symbolic interactionist models, stressed that any such institutional order developed, maintained, and changed through a process of continuous interaction, negotiation and struggle between those who participated in it. In this approach it was stressed that the explanation of any institutional arrangement has to be attempted in terms of power relations, negotiations, power struggles, conflicts, and the coalitions which were formed during such processes. Concomitantly, strong emphasis was laid on the autonomy of any subsetting, subgroup or subsystem that found expression in the definitions of goals that differed from those of the broader organizational or institutional setting, as well as on the "environments" within which the social setting operated, above all the international system.

The second, seemingly contradictory approach was found especially among the structuralists and the Marxists. As indicated above, this approach tended to explain the nature of any given institutional order, especially its dynamics in terms of some principles of "deep" or "hidden" structure, akin to those which, according to linguists like Noam Chomsky, provide the deep structure of language. In attempting to identify the principles of such structures, the structuralists stressed the importance of the symbolic dimensions of human activity or some inherent rules of the human mind. In contrast to this, the Marxists stressed a combination of structural and symbolic dimensions, such as the relations among the forces of production and the relations among production, alienation, and class consciousness, as providing the principles of the deep structures of societies that explain their crucial institutional features and dynamics. In these attempts to explain the processes of continuation of institutional order all these approaches have also been concerned, in line with the classical sociological approach, with the analysis of social change.

The structural-functional approach, set forth in the works of Talcott Parsons and his disciples, emphasizes two major causes of change in social systems: first, the disequilibrating tendencies that exist in any relationship between a social system and its environment; second, the strain that exists between the normative and the structural elements of any social system. They have also emphasized that the generation of new resources, leading to potentially new levels of structural differentiation, may be an important source of change and that it is the development of new value orientations that may create the major control system through which such changes can become institutionalized. The conflict approach—both in its functionalist version as propounded by Louis Coser and in the writings of Ralf Dahrendorf, Reinhard Bendix, and, lately, of Randall Collins—has emphasized above all that the conflict of groups over their material or ideal interests is the principal source of change in societies.[11] The Marxists and most notably the neo-Marxists have identified the systemic contradictions (e.g., contradictions between the mode of production and the forces of production) that are inherent in any social (above all class) system as the leading cause of change.[12] The stress on inherent contradictions as generating the transformation of cultural and social models and orders has been a central thesis in the symbolic structuralist approach of Claude Lévi-Strauss.[13] But Lévi-Strauss's overriding concern has been the binary oppositions posed by the innate rules of the human mind. According to this approach, the symbolic transformations that occur through resolution of such contradictions as those between culture and nature account for the transformation of social orders (e.g., the development from totemic to caste society).

Whatever the differences among these approaches, many of them argue that any social system tends to change totally in the general direction of increasing complexity and differentiation. Indeed, a combined structural-functionalist–symbolic structuralist–neo-evolutionist–Marxist theory is one of the most interesting recent theoretical developments in sociology.[14]

Of late, proponents of the above approaches have charged that the other approaches cannot explain either the causes or the direction of change within any specific social system. Although it is not possible here to enter into a detailed analysis of this controversy, it might be worthwhile to point out some of the weak points of each of these approaches, as well as possible analytical convergences between them, emphasizing in particular those that bear upon the study of social change.[15]

The conflict approach, with its strong antisystemic bias, fails to explain the emergent systemic and boundary maintenance tendencies found in groups and collectivities. Neglecting the systemic qualities of social systems—often denying the existence of such qualities—this theory fails to indicate the relative importance of different conflicts for the generation of change and to evaluate the impact of conflicts upon the direction of change.

The weak point in the argument of the symbolic structuralists is the failure to specify the nature of the institutional foci and those mechanisms through which the symbolic dimensions of human activities impinge upon institutional life. Above all, this school fails to specify those institutional areas in which symbolic contradictions tend to concentrate or to designate the institutional mechanisms through which they may become activated.

Advocates of a social system approach claim that it is not possible to consider the emergence or institutionalization of social life apart from the usual routine of individual interaction. They assert that the latter has to be explained in terms of special mechanisms stemming from the needs of social organization. Yet they often fail to explain how these processes are related to individuals' goals, interactions, cultural orientations, and searches for meaning. Above all, they face the problems of identifying, first, the carriers of boundary maintaining mechanisms in various systems, second, the diverse roles of these carriers in processes of systemic continuity, and, third, the conditions undermining boundary maintaining mechanisms. These weaknesses of the social system approach become most evident in the study of social change.

The major weakness of the structural-functional approach is its seeming neglect of the power and conflict dimensions (most significantly, conflict over power) in the functioning of social systems and of the relation between such conflicts and social change in general. Similarly, it seems to neglect the inherent tendency of any social system to generate internal contradictions and the study of the relation of these contradictions to power conflicts. Consequently, the relationship between power conflicts and internal contradictions and the generation of new levels of resources through which systemic changes can take place has not always been systematically analyzed by the structural-functionalists.

Marxist and neo-Marxist approaches combine, paradoxically enough, some of the flaws of the symbolic structuralist position with those of the conflict approach. For instance, Marxists find it difficult to specify the institutional mechanisms or groups that embody the forces and relations of production. Hence, they fail also to specify which conflicts are most important for the transformation of actual systems. The result is that any new problem or conflict tends to be designated as a contradiction predictive of the transformation of any given system, particularly the capitalist.

3. THEORETICAL CONVERGENCES: SYMBOLIC AND INSTITUTIONAL DIMENSIONS OF SOCIAL ORGANIZATIONS—THE GROUND RULES OF SOCIAL INTERACTION

However great the controversies among the different analytical approaches, these very controversies hint at the possibility of some theoretical convergences. This convergence may be very helpful in the development of a mode of analysis of social change that seeks to avoid the weaknesses of the various approaches.

Indeed, from this spectrum of theoretical orientations emerges a more differentiated analysis of macrosocietal order and cultural traditions. This approach places great weight on the importance of bringing together the symbolic dimensions of cultural orientations with the organizational aspects of the social division of labor in the construction of a macrosocietal order; of identifying the multiple carriers of these dimensions; and of recognizing the existence in any macrosocietal order of a multiplicity of institutional and organizational levels. This new approach also systematically indicates how the combination of different levels of cultural and social organization generates tendencies toward change and conflict in any social system. It permits identification of some of the mechanisms through which any given process of social change may or may not be absorbed within a social system. Accordingly, this reorientation may also help in the analysis of problems of change in terms of understanding the process of change that unfolds within each specific society, as well as in comparative analysis.[16]

Acknowledgment of the importance of the interweaving of the symbolic and the organizational dimensions of social organization in the construction of macrosocietal orders has to a considerable degree come, significantly enough, from revision of the initial studies of modernization mentioned above. These revisions have shown that, contrary to assumptions of these earlier studies, within modernizing societies there emerge different untraditional responses to the relatively common problems of modernization such as growing structural differentiation and organization, and the general propensity toward demographic and structural change. This body of research indicates that there is a rather close connection between such broad principles of institutional organization and response and basic cultural orientation,[17] thus providing some of the first steps for the new theoretical approach presented here.

This new approach is able to specify in greater detail the institutional implication of the quest for social order that arises, as we have seen, from the tension between the organizational level of social division of labor and the problem of meaningful acceptance of the social order.

The quest is focused on the search for some ground rules, or parameters, of social order. Such ground rules,[18] structure the environment in a symbolic way that provides solutions to the potential arbitrariness inherent in social interaction; they provide some long-range predictability of social interaction and invest these solutions with meaning in terms of the various tensions of human existence in general and of social life in particular—even though, as will be analyzed in greater detail later on, these problems and uncertainties are not abolished but only transposed to a new, different level.

The most important of such ground rules of social interaction of parameters of social order are those which specify:

(a) the symbolic and institutional boundaries of collectivities—above all through the setting up of the basic attributes of social and cultural similarities that constitute the definition of the criteria of membership in different collectivities, i.e. of those who may participate in any given interaction. These attributes provide also the specification of the conditional and unconditional obligations connected with the participation of such communities, as well as the range of the goals or desiderata that are permitted to those participating in any interaction.

(b) the rules of distributive justice and equity, which are seen as appropriate and bounding with regard to the distribution of rights and obligations in the respective settings of interaction.

(c) criteria of regulation of access to power and of their use in different social settings and institutional spheres.

(d) the broader purpose of meaning and collective goals of any interaction or collective activity, and the closely related range of concrete needs and of their relative importance within it.

(e) legitimation of such institutional complexes in terms of the pre-valent rules of justice, equity, and broader societal goals.

These major types of ground rules of social interaction specify the nature and scope of the precontractual and legitimizing dimensions of social life through which the problems of social order are seemingly resolved.

This line of thought, which is congruent with the analytical emphasis that no institutional arrangement can be taken for granted, points also to the necessity to analyze the social processes through which such ground rules of social interaction are selected, institutionalized and maintained, and to explain the different contents of ground rules in different societies. It is through providing answers to these questions that the possible con-vergences of the different analytical approaches can be attained. At the same time, such new approaches might be able to overcome some of their weak points analyzed above.

4. THE SYMBOLIC DIMENSION OF HUMAN ACTIVITIES: CONTENTS OF THE GROUND RULES OF SOCIAL INTERACTION AND OF THE PARAMETERS OF SOCIAL ORDER

We shall start with the search for the roots or sources of the concrete contents of the different ground rules. This search brings us close to the attempts, most fully exemplified lately in the work of the symbolic struc-turalists inspired by Lévi-Strauss, to derive the criteria of such ground rules and of the deep or hidden structure of social organization from the symbolic (or cultural) sphere of human activity.

The close relationship between the ground rules of social interaction and the symbolic dimension of human activities is borne by the fact that even the most superficial look at the contents of these ground rules—as, for instance, the rules of membership of different collectivities, or of access to resources and of control over them, or the symbols of collective identity—indicates that they are very closely related to, or expressed in, various symbols that are related to some basic existential problems of human life, as well as to the tensions and problems inherent in organized social life, which were analyzed above.

But, contrary to what many structuralists have assumed, these symbolic orientations do not, by virtue of their presumably constituting the gen-eral rules or qualities of the human mind, influence the concrete crystal-lization of the ground rules of social interaction through some process of direct emanation.

Hence, it is important to specify, first, which aspects of the symbolic orientations are more relevant for the construction of the contents of the ground rules and, second, what is the nature of the concrete institutional mechanisms through which they become operative in social life.

Both classical and more recent sociological research does indeed provide some very important indications about these problems. They indicate, even if in a preliminary way, some of the most important symbolic problems which seem to be of special relevance from the point of view of the construction of a meaningful social order.* [19]

These problems can be divided into two broad sets—one concerned with what may be called existential problems of human cosmic existence, the other with the specific symbolic evaluation of the exigencies of social life. Within each of these sets several problem areas can be distinguished. Within the first set, the first problem areas are the evaluation of primordial givens of human life; and the definition of the relative importance of different dimensions of social existence—such as the religious, political, economic or ritual dimensions; of different dimensions of temporality, i.e., of the relative emphasis on past or future; and of the quest for salvation.

The second problem area within the set of cosmic problems focuses on the definition of the interrelations between the cosmic and social (including political and economic) orders, of their relative distinctiveness and autonomy, and of their mutual relevance; of the degree and nature of possible tension between such orders; of the ways of resolving such tension; of the relations of such a resolution to the predominant dimension of human existence and to the focus of human salvation; the nature of the access of different social actors to these orders and to their major contents and attributes, and above all the degree to which individuals and different groups are defined and perceived as having direct, autonomous access to the major attributes of these orders, as against such attributes being accessible only to some very specific groups or categories of actors who act as mediators for other groups.

Of great importance in this area is also to what extent individuals or groups perceive themselves either as passive recipients in relation to such orders or as active participators in their creation, and to what degree they perceive the possibility of changing them; the perception of man's control over his fate and over his social or natural environments; the degree to which he may influence any of these; and the degree of responsibility people have for the maintenance of such orders.

The second set of problems relates to the symbolic evaluation of the major organizational exigencies of interpersonal and social relations enum-

---

* It is not claimed here that these constitute an exhaustive list of the cultural orientations that are significant from the point of view of social relations. It is only a tentative list of some such orientations which were found to be of significance in some important aspects of institutional analysis.

erated above and above all those related to some of the basic dilemmas of social life—hierarchy versus equality; conflict versus harmony; individual versus community, as well as the relative emphasis on power, solidarity or instrumental inducements as major orientations to social order.

These broad themes or problems become related to the quest for social order on all levels of social interaction—ranging from the more informal interpersonal relations, through various formal or institutional settings, up to the construction of the macrosocietal order. On all such levels of social interaction it is the provision of some answers to these problems that provide the starting points for the symbolic construction of social reality, for the construction of the bases of a meaningful social and cultural order, and of participation in such order; of bringing people's discrete social activities into some patterns of meaningful experience which encompass the most crucial spheres of social and cultural life; and of developing and maintaining a meaningful personal life in some relation to these orders.

As in all other fields of human activities, such answers are constructed in three complementary ways: first, by providing symbolic models of the respective sphere of activities, i.e. in our case the social order; second, by providing the principles of structuring the basic framework of activities in any such field, in our case the structuring of the ground rules of social interaction and of the parameters of social order; and third, by providing some concrete symbolization of the relations between codes and models and their actualization in concrete situations. The aspect of these symbolic orientations most relevant for the construction of the bases or the criteria of the different ground rules of social interaction is the crystallization of such orientations into specific patterns of codes which connect the broad contours of institutional order with answers to the basic symbolic problems of human and social existence. Such codes are not just some general, broad, cultural value orientations. They are much closer to what Weber has called *Wirtschaftsethik*,[20] i.e., generalized modes of religious or ethical orientation to a specific institutional sphere and its problems; the evaluation of the sphere, and the provision of guidelines for its organization and for behavior within it in terms of the proper answers to some major problems of human existence.

5. THE INSTITUTIONALIZATION OF THE GROUND RULES OF SOCIAL INTERACTION

Whatever the exact relations between models of social and cultural systems and systems of codes on the one hand, and the ground rules of social interaction on the other, the contents of these ground rules do not emanate directly from the contents or dynamism of symbols. Hence we come to the problem of the nature of the processes of social interaction through which they are set up.

The answers to this question provided by those approaches that have stressed the negotiability of institutions, above all the exchange and the symbolic interactionist approaches, are deficient in that they have not distinguished between the different processes through which these ground rules—as distinct from others, more routine types of social interaction—are set up and maintained. This distinction involves several aspects.

The more routine or purely organizational exchange and interaction are undertaken mostly by individuals acting in their private capacity or as representatives of existing collectivities who engage in an ad hoc or continuous but relatively free exchange of simple, basic resources, whether they are wealth, services, power or esteem. In contrast, the interaction oriented to the setting up of the ground rules is based on potential long-range commitments and on the readiness to forego some of the benefits and risks inherent in the more direct exchange or interaction.

Moreover, the setting up of the ground rules of social interaction involves not only the exchange of simple, basic resources, but above all the interchange of these resources with symbolic orientations. Such interchange involves the combination of the structuring of control over relatively long-range distribution of the major types of resources with the construction of the meaning of the situations of social interchange.

The readiness to accept the definitions of the meaning of social situations implied in the setting up of the ground rules of social interaction has two complementary aspects. It entails the giving up, by the more powerful actors in any situation, of some of the immediate advantages which they may potentially or actually possess, in favor of lesser or less immediate advantages, such as the legitimation of their right to specify the broader goals of social order.

For those who have relatively small amounts or more dispersed resources, the readiness to accept such rules entails, first, giving up the possibilities of using freely their own resources and power or opting out of any given situation, and second, investing some actors with the rights of taking care of the basic predicaments of the organizational aspects of social life and hence of structuring the range and base of trust and solidarity.

Establishment of ground rules occurs through interaction between, on the one hand, elites (political, economic, educational) that engage in entrepreneurial-institutional activities [21] and that are ready (or appear to be ready) to use their resources for collective rather than private purposes, as well as elites that articulate models of social order and set up norms and/or organizational frameworks; and, on the other hand, those actor-individuals, social units, strata, groups, or their representatives that not only represent the direct interests of their respective groups but also attempt to articulate the potential solidarity of such collectivities, are willing to invest resources, and above all are ready to commit themselves to and support the frameworks of long-term interaction.

The articulators of models of social and cultural order and of solidarity create coalitions that differ from the most common subjects of coalition studies,[22] namely, coalitions composed of only one type of actor who acts *within* given frameworks of social interaction and who is related to other actors through symmetrical or asymmetrical relations of power. The former sort of coalition resembles those analyzed, for instance, by Seymour Martin Lipset and Stein Rokkan[23] in their study of the formation of European party systems. These coalitions differ also from interclass coalitions, which Barrington Moore analyzed in the *Social Origins of Dictatorship and Democracy*.[24] It is not that class positions or interests do not play an important role in any such coalitions—needless to say they constitute a very important component of them, as do simple political and economic interests. But the interests of seemingly similar classes are often, as we shall subsequently see in greater detail, structured in different ways by different elites.

One of the major challenges of sociological analysis is to identify exactly the nature of these coalitions and of their interaction in concrete situations. Yet even at this stage of our analysis we can postulate that it is through such coalitions acting in special institutional-ritual, legal, and communicative frameworks that the ground rules of social interaction become institutionalized.

Nevertheless, these ground rules are neither simply given nor guaranteed. Their continuity and that of their major institutional derivatives is predicated on the continuous control the various coalitions acting within their respective institutional frameworks exercise over those aspects of the flow of resources that are crucial from the point of view of access to different markets and positions. Of primary importance is control of the accumulation of information and its influence (as well as the influence of more diffuse reservoirs of power within the society) on the centers of constituent collectivities and on the way in which the construction and interpretation of the basic premises and symbols of the cultural and social order take place. Second is control of access to those positions that regulate production, the distribution of resources, and the conversion of economic resources into resources of power and prestige. Third is the control of access to those positions within the centers of society that regulate the setting up of reference orientations whereby individuals internalize social goals and values and that oversee the various processes of communication that influence the levels of demands as well as the evaluation of the social system by participants.

The institutional derivatives of the ground rules of social interaction can be maintained only insofar as the elites that are the active partners in such coalitions are able to retain control. But, as we shall see, such control is not, in any social interaction, given or assured. Indeed, the very institutionalization of the ground rules—particularly in macrosocietal settings—creates potential for conflict, tension, and change.

Given that the basic function of the ground rules of social interaction is to overcome, at least partially, the basic predicaments and uncertainties inherent in the social division of labor, it is but natural that the institutionalization of the ground rules of social interaction focuses above all on the setting up of nonmarket limitations to the free exchange of resources in social interaction.

The first and most important of these limitations is the structuring of the access of different groups and categories of people to the major types of markets which exist within any framework of interaction and of the possibilities of convertibility of resources that one exchanges in such markets.

Second, such limitation is effected through the setting up of public goods,[25] i.e., goods provided by the government of a country such as defense or health services which are set up in such a way that if one member of a collectivity is given these goods, they cannot be denied to other members; and of the respective prices taken—directly or above all indirectly (through taxation)—from different groups for the setting up of such public goods.

Third, such structuring of the flow of resources is manifest in the public distribution of private goods—i.e., the direct allocation of various services and rewards to different groups of the population according to criteria which differ greatly from those of pure exchange.

Closely related to the definition of public goods is the definition of the degree to which different groups, organizations, and institutional spheres enjoy institutional credit and credit autonomy, i.e., the degree to which resources provided to any such group or institution for its long-range functioning are not used in immediate exchange, but are given to a certain degree unconditionally. Lastly, the limitations on free exchange of resources is effected through additional and quite complicated mechanisms, involving specification of ascriptive titles and of limits of prestige, which have yet to be studied in greater detail.

6. THE INTERWEAVING OF THE SYMBOLIC AND THE ORGANIZATIONAL ASPECTS OF SOCIAL ACTION. SETTING UP GROUND RULES FOR THE MAJOR INSTITUTIONAL SPHERES

All these mechanisms combine the symbolic with the organizational aspects of social interaction and shape the basic ground rules of all major institutional spheres as well as of the macrosocietal order.

Thus, in the sphere of kinship and family relations [26] human sexuality is regulated not only in terms of species survival and social continuity. Sexual behavior, through symbolic transformation, also tends to become the focus of symbolic primordial similarities and affinities and to serve as the symbolic directive for such institutional arrangements as rules of descent, affinity, and preferential marriage, and prescriptions of exogamy and endogamy. In this process the mutual rights and obligations accruing from sexual and procreational activity are defined; for example, the relations between members of familial and of intermarrying groups serve as the basis of trust and the starting point for participation in the social order. Thus is formed, in Fortes's language, the moral fabric of kinship, the rules of amity that obtain in it, and the scope of these rules. [27]

In the economic sphere articulation of the symbolic dimensions with the organizational aspects of social activities is manifest first of all in the setting up of the broader goals or meanings of economic activities; for example, their contributing to the collectivity, to political ends, to the general welfare of the society or of subgroups within it, or to the welfare of individuals. Second, it is manifest in the specification of the rights to economic resources and values and to control over their use. Third, this articulation is manifest in the specification of the relative importance of different policies that are framed with respect to economic resources. Fourth, the interweaving of the symbolic with the organizational aspects of social activities takes place through the designation of certain economic tasks as vocations, as repositories of broader values, and through the creation of limitations on access to these vocations (such limitations are especially evident in occupations that touch on the vital, symbolic aspects of life—be the aspect death, law, or religion). [28]

In the sphere of social stratification, such combination is effected through the addition of the imagery of social hierarchy (the evaluative ordering of personal and cultural attributes) to the more organizational aspects of the social system; that is, the distribution of categories of people among institutional spheres or their control of different resources. Such evaluation, itself undertaken in terms of the fundamental symbolism of the cultural and social order, is manifest first of all in the principles of legitimation of differential access to positions of control over resources. It becomes a crucial component of the self-image of people as members of society and of the way in which they tend to see their own place in the social and cultural order. Thus, through addition of symbolic aspects to the organizational aspects of the differential distribution of rewards, the bases of strataformation—for instance, acquisition of rights to pursue certain goals or provision of access to positions—are established. [29]

Such a combination of the symbolic and organizational aspects of hierarchy provides specification of the types of attributes that constitute the basis of societal evaluation and hierarchy influences the status autonomy of different groups as manifested in their access to such attributes;

the composition of different status groups and the extent of status association as against status segregation of relatively narrow occupational and professional groups; and the political expression and organization of status and class interests and attributes.

In the political and the religious-cultural spheres, the institutional derivatives of the symbolic dimension of human existence are articulated initially in the definition of criteria for membership and the boundaries of political, ethnic, and cultural communities. In the political sphere they constitute the principal legitimation of the processes of the exercise of power, adjudication, and upholding law and order through reference to some idea of justice and to some broad conception of social and cultural order. Such legitimation specifies the scope of legal and political rights and procedures in terms of basic attributes of human and social identity. In turn, it influences, first, the nature of all the principles of distribution of political power and of access to it; second, the specification of the major orientations and goals of the polity; third, the basis of the control of resources by the rulers; and, fourth, the principal aspects of political struggle and organization that are prevalent in the society.[30] In the cultural sphere such specification sets up the symbols that define the boundaries of the cultural and social communities; the rights of access to knowledge and information and the allocation of these resources to different groups in the society; and the scope of the major types of knowledge in the society and especially the main types of problems into which inquiry is defined as legitimate.

The fundamental symbolic orientations also mold the contours of various types of collectivities, adding the symbolic to the organizational and ecological aspects of their structure. Through such symbolic transpositions ecological aggregates become primordial or local communities founded on symbolic attributes. This transformation takes place through specification of the rules of access to membership and of participation in such communities and of symbolic attachment to particular spatial aspects of the environment. Such rules influence the ways in which different resources are distributed within a spatial framework (city, region); the ways in which space is allocated among social groups and functional activities; and the ways in which space is used in order to represent the cosmic, social, or moral order.[31]

7. THE CONSTRUCTION OF SOCIETAL CENTERS AND OF THE MAJOR TYPES OF COLLECTIVITIES

The derivatives of codes as they influence the criteria of the ground rules of social interaction shape the macrosocietal order. It is indeed in the construction of the macrosocietal order that the interweaving of the symbolic and the organizational aspects of social life is most fully realized.

This symbolic articulation of the macrosocietal order is institutionally located in what Edward Shils has called centers of society.

> Membership in the society, in more than the ecological sense of being located in a bounded territory and of adapting to an environment affected or made up by other persons located in the same territory, is constituted by relationship to this central zone.

> The central zone is not, *as such,* a spatially located phenomenon. It almost has a more or less definite location within the bounded territory in which the society lives. Its centrality has, however, nothing to do with geometry and little with geography.

> The centre, or the central zone, is a phenomenon of the realm of values and beliefs. It is the centre of the order of symbols, of values and beliefs, which govern the society. It is the centre because it is the ultimate and irreducible; and it is felt to be such by many who cannot give explicit articulation to its irreducibility. The central zone partakes of the nature of the sacred. In this sense, every society has an "official" religion, even when that society or its exponents and interpreters conceive of it more or less correctly as a secular, pluralistic, and tolerant society. The principle of the Counter Reformation: *Cuius regio, ejus religio,* although its rigor has been lessened and its harshness mollified, retains a core of permanent truth.[32]

The construction of centers constitutes on the macrosocietal level the focus of the institutionalization of the symbolic and organizational aspects of social life, the meeting point between organizational givens and problems and broader patterns of meaning; that is, the translation of specific organizational problems into symbolic frameworks with normative programmatic specifications. These ordering and meaning providing functions are crystallized in the structure of the centers through the addition of the ground rules of social interaction and their fundamental institutional derivatives to the organizational activities related to the maintenance of the macrosocietal setting.[33] In other words, it is within the societal centers (or their equivalents in microsocietal settings) that final shape is given to the basic institutional frameworks—be they legal and political or ritual and communicative and their institutional derivatives—in which the ground rules of social interaction are upheld. It is also within these frameworks that the coalitions that set up such ground rules are brought closer together (we consider this question later).

Accordingly, the first such derivative of center formation is the institutionalization of certain societal places or areas or symbols as being most appropriate for the ordering of the quest for social and cultural order and for some participation in that order. This is effected mostly by specification of the conception of the society's origins, especially its view of its own origin and past, as well as its collective boundaries with regard to other collectivities or types of cultural order (both within and outside its own geopolitical location); by specification of the common societal and cultural collective identity (or identities) based on common attributes or on participation in common symbolic events that express this common identity; and by specification of the right to participation in distributive justice applicable to the members of the order.

It is in this aspect of the construction of macrosocietal centers that the symbolic and organizational emphasis on the various charismatic orientations to the nature of the cosmic, cultural (religious ideological, or scientific), social, and political orders and their interrelations finds its fullest societal expression. Indeed, designation of any unit or order as the locus of cosmic and/or societal order and its boundaries constitutes one of the principal attributes of a macrosocietal order.

Closely connected with the first aspect of center construction is the specification of the bases of legitimacy of the macrosocietal order. Another crucial component of centers is the variety of ways of combining the exercise of power with orientations to broader social and cultural order and of regulating power in such terms. Finally, there is the regulation, in terms of such orientations of intragroup and intergroup relations on the one hand and of internal and external force—or power—relations on the other.

The construction of these dimensions of societal centers is not intellectual or abstract: it rests on the addition of specific institutional derivatives that constitute, as it were, the distinctive institutional characteristics or aspects of the centers. All of these dimensions involve some combination of control over resources and access to positions, together with the elaboration of the symbolic aspects of social interactions and the specification of the differences between societal centers and peripheries.

The codes and ground rules in any group or society delimit with respect to its center or centers the range of the essential attributes of similarity and the boundaries of collectivities; indicate the parameters of the macrosocietal order or orders; and determine the degree to which orientations to centrality are important within the order. In other words, the different codes specify the relative importance, within any given center, of its components; the relative homogeneity of centers in a society; the relations between centers and collectivities; the degree of distinctiveness of the centers vis-à-vis the periphery; the relative penetration of centers into the periphery, the impingement of the periphery on the centers, and the relative autonomy of access of different groups to the centers; the self-image of the centers in terms of societal goals; and the types of broad policies undertaken by the centers. Similarly, the codes and ground rules influence the definition of the boundaries of the macrosocietal order and their relative openness and affect its relation to different societal, religious, and cultural orders. They specify also the ranges of combination of different types of collectivities that coalesce within any macrosocietal order; the relations between them, and the extent to which some of these collectivities extend beyond the boundaries of the given macrosocietal order.

Thus, the codes may be seen as constituting the hidden, or deep, structure of a social system. They set up its boundaries, influencing the organizational problems and needs of the society. Specification of the codes determines the range of the concrete needs of a society, and they set out the boundaries of the environment of constituent groups and the ranges of possible responses to the pressures of the environment. At the same time, by spelling out the manner in which some of the fundamental societal functions (allocation and integration, for example) are to be fulfilled, they ensure the continuity of these boundaries and define potential directions of change. The programmatic specifications of codes also influence the ways in which the general functions necessary for the working of social systems are performed within any concrete setting and hence also the range of their systemic sensitivities; the salience of potential conflicts over the continuity of the system; the types of conditions under which conflict may erupt, threatening the stability of the regime; and the ways in which the regime copes with problems of conflict. The ways of incorporating various types of political demands, including those for growing participation in the political order, are especially susceptible. In particular, the codes affect the intensity of conflicts and the perception of their acuteness; the flexibility or rigidity of response to them; and the relative importance of regressive—as against expansive—policies of coping with them.

8. THE INTERACTION OF EXISTENTIAL CODES, SOCIAL CODES, AND SYMBOLS OF COLLECTIVE IDENTITY. INSTITUTIONALIZATION OF CODES AND SOCIAL DIVISION OF LABOR AS SOURCE OF TENSIONS, CONFLICTS, AND CONTRADICTIONS

It would be wrong to assume that such rules of deep structure derived from the various codes are a sort of direct, even if institutional, emanation from the symbolic sphere.

Unlike the structuralist position that certain universal rules of the human mind are operative in all spheres of human activity, this theoretical perspective holds that the symbolic components that come together in a concrete historical situation have their own separate dynamic.[34] (Here the relative openness of the different systems of codes and their relation to the institutional order are of crucial importance.)

In any society there may be independent variations and combinations of religious, or existential, and social codes. Both sorts of code are extremely influential in shaping the ground rules of social organization, and different ground rules and their institutional derivatives, as well as the symbols of collective identity, are set up by conditions between different actors.

Thus, institutionalization of these codes involves a process of selection of various combinations and of different, although not unlimited, institutional possibilities. Moreover, this process of selection involves the choice, from among the given in any historical situation, of certain collective goals (e.g., industrialization, totalitarian versus democratic regimes). Finally, institutionalization of a model or pattern of codes entails specification of the appropriate here and now—the concrete setting, groups, or collectivity.

It is only through this process of selection that any model of cultural and social order, as well as patterns of codes, can become fully institutionalized and can impinge on the working of concrete social groups or collectivities. Each of these dimensions of selection has a structure and rules of its own. Each of these dimensions of selection is the domain of different social carriers: the setting up of the ground rules of social interaction is achieved through interaction among several types of social actors.

The institutionalization of the ground rules of social interaction within any social system provides the principles that structure the dynamic equilibrium of the system. Yet, at the same time, the very construction and institutionalization of the ground rules, especially as this process is bound up with the organizational structure of social activities and the social division of labor, creates the possibility of tensions, conflicts, and contradictions leading to change.[35]

Potential for tensions, conflicts, and contradictions is inherent in any social order (and particularly within the macrosocietal order) first of all because any such order involves a plurality of actors—individuals and groups—with differential and always contested control over natural and social resources.

Second, potential tensions and conflicts become more likely to erupt and tend to be diverted into systemic directions because of the interweaving of the plurality of actors with the basic characteristics of the institutionalization of any division of labor. Characteristics of this process conducive to social change are: the possible contradictory organizational implications of different prerequisites or needs of any institutional order; the differential distribution of groups among the principal institutional complexes; the heterogeneity and complexity of vertical and horizontal specialization, communication, and hierarchy among different social groups; as well as the variety and relatively autonomous organization of the media of exchange.

Third, tensions and contradictions are made more likely because of the multiplicity of structural principles that are generated from the symbolic codes that constitute the starting point for the structuring of the ground rules of social interaction. We have indicated that each ground rule may be carried by different social actors and coalitions, each of which may stress the centrality of any given code or of its institutionalization as distinct from that of others and each of which may seem to be promoting its own interests (at the possible expense of others).

Fourth, the potential for tensions and conflicts follows from the relative openness (analyzed above) of each such set of structural principles in their relations to each other in the process of institutionalization.

Fifth, probability of tensions and conflicts is heightened because the setting up of the ground rules of social interaction involves the selection of some as against other institutional possibilities and the ligitimation of certain inequalities.

Such legitimation of inequalities is the outcome of struggle, an outcome that is never accepted to the same degree or on the same terms by all parts of society despite strenuous efforts by institutional entrepreneurs to establish system maintaining norms. Groups differ in their attitudes toward these norms and in their willingness or ability to provide the resources demanded by the institutional system. Some groups may be greatly opposed to the premises of the institutionalization of a given system, may share its values and symbols only to a very small extent, and accept these norms as the least evil and as binding on them only in a most limited sense. Others may share the society's values and symbols and accept social norms to a greater degree, while regarding themselves as the more truthful upholders of these values. They may oppose the concrete levels at which their symbols are institutionalized by the elite in power and may attempt to interpret the symbols in different ways and, accordingly, to change the distribution of resources in the society. They may not accept fully the principles of distributive justice or reciprocity that the societal centers rely on to legitimize the existing distribution of powers and resources. Others, as we have seen, may develop new interpretations of prevailing symbols and norms. Thus, there is always in any social order considerable dissension over the distribution of power and scarce resources.

In other words, any institutional system is never entirely homogeneous in the sense of being unanimously accepted in its totality, and different degrees of acceptance may serve as foci of conflict and change. Even though for a very long period of time a great majority of the members of a society may identify to some degree with the prevailing values and norms and may be willing to provide the system with the resources it needs, the attitude of any given group toward the basic premises of the system may change greatly after its initial institutionalization. The fundamental processes through which the continuity of social systems and their essential institutional derivatives are maintained tend to generate continual shifts in the power and market positions of unequal groups and categories of people within the society and in their orientation to the premises of the social order.

Such shifts are generated by the internal momentum of the production and distribution of resources when combined with the attempts of the central elites to maintain, through continual attempts to mobilize resources from different groups and individuals, the boundaries of the system and to support the legitimacy of its values, symbols, and norms.

Thus, in greater detail, such shifts are generated, first of all, by the fact that over time the center has to devote more resources to the maintenance of the mechanisms of control, which may divert it from pursuing the charismatic societal goals. Second, there tend to occur shifts in the degree to which different elites are willing to forego some of the advantages that institutionalization of the ground rules of social interaction seems to demand that they relinquish. Third, such shifts may take place because the momentum of the internal development of resources generates changes in the distribution of power and positions in the society, as well as changes in people's access to them and in the terms of trade, i.e., in the prices of different commodities and resources that are exchanged between the center and the major groups of the society. Such shifts, in conjunction with the plurality of actors and collectivities within any social setting, may produce new types of positions and social categories as well as new types of social entrepreneurial elements.

Several changes follow these developments. First, changes occur in the degree and basis of acceptance of various aspects of the institutional structure. Second, struggles break out among various actors over institutional derivatives of the ground rules of social interaction. Third, the readiness of social groups to invest their resources in the institutional derivatives of the prevailing ground rules of social interaction, in the existing center, and in its mechanisms of control may increase or decrease.

The propensity toward conflicts, tensions, and contradictions is also enhanced by the crucial importance of international settings for the working of national social systems. Not only are international settings sources of external influence on societies but also they enable societal components to relate somewhat autonomously with groups in other societies. Such transnational relations may greatly vary among the components of a given social order in general and of a macrosocietal order in particular.

9. THEMES OF PROTEST GENERATED BY THE INSTITUTIONALIZATION OF CODES AND THE SOCIAL DIVISION OF LABOR

The preceding argument may be summarized thus: the potential for tensions, conflicts, and contradictions exists in human society first of all because the construction of any concrete social order is based on the selection of certain cultural orientations and the deemphasis or suppression of others and because members of the society are to some degree aware of this process and attempt to overcome certain aspects of it. Second, the process of selection and exclusion entailed by the institutionalization of the social and cultural order becomes most closely associated with (although not necessarily identical to) the exigencies of the social division of labor and with the maintenance of the distribution of power and wealth and resultant inequalities. Therefore, the process creates the potential for alienation and dissension in any society, and there tend to develop basic orientations and themes of protest as well as movements of protest, rebellion, and conflict.

One theme of protest is the tension between the complexity and fragmentation of human relations inherent in the institutional division of labor and the possibility of total, unconditional, unmediated participation in the social and cultural order. Hence, a widespread theme of protest is the elimination of the division of labor and its replacement with the ideal of community, of direct, unmediated participation.

A parallel theme is the tension inherent in the temporal dimension of the human and social condition—deferred versus immediate gratification. Hence, protest frequently focuses on patterns of gratification and allocation of rewards, attempting to reconcile spontaneity and discipline and to overcome tension between the inner self and the social persona. Themes of protest also tend to stress resolution of the tension between productivity and distribution and seek to merge these two aspects of economic life through a vision of plenty.

Other themes of protest are concerned with bringing the reality of institutional life closer to the model of the ideal society, with its principles of distributive justice; with reducing inequality in the distribution of power; and with making possible full expression of the internal self within the social and cultural order.

These themes of protest tend to converge and become most fully articulated around those aspects of institutional life that are the central foci of the ground rules of social interaction, that is, in the specification of attributes of similarity, of membership in collectivities, and of distribution of power in different spheres of society; in the definition of the meaning of social activities; and in the establishment of collective goals. Specifically, these foci are: one, authority (especially as vested in the various societal centers); two, the system of stratification in which the symbolic dimensions of hierarchy are combined with the structural aspects of the division of labor and the distribution of resources; and three, the family as the primary locus of authority and socialization.

It is around these symbolic and institutional foci that there develops within every society the image of its double,[36] of the "good," "true" society. This image is usually most fully elaborated in the symbolism of the just ruler, according to which the incumbent may be judged and evaluated (and in some extreme cases deposed) by the bearers of the true image. (In some movements of protest—above all in the millenarian, utopian ones that many cultures have witnessed [37]—there has arisen also an image of total change of the existing society, which is seemingly akin to the revolutionary image analyzed in Chapter 1.)

In most societies themes of protest become closely connected with symbols of personal identity that address physical attributes, bodily autonomy, and spontaneity of bodily expressions and postures: freedom of sexual relations, freedom of emotional expression, and freedom from restraints based on differences in age and sex.[38]

The themes of protest that develop within any society tend, above all, to challenge those codes or orientations that are most fully institutionalized. Thus, if a society is strongly rational, then protest will tend to favor mystic and sensate orientations.[39]

Alongside themes of protest a variety of processes of change develops in every society. Shifts in the relations among subgroups universally generate a range of social movements—rebellions, movements of heterodoxy, millenarian visions, and the like, as well as more central political conflict and struggle [40]—that give concrete expression to the different themes of protest. The various movements of heterodoxy, rebellion, and protest and political struggle may lead to countercoalitions among distinct social groups and types of institutional entrepreneurs seeking to revise the ground rules of social interaction and to institutionalize an alternative social order. Finally, in any society movements of protest may generate conflicts and contradictions and processes of change and transformation by becoming related to the basic organizational parameters of the social structure and to struggles for power within it.

Such conflicts, which may generate systemic changes, usually develop in an institutional order in which intergroup tension tends to undermine the frameworks and coalitions that sustain the ground rules of the system and their institutional derivatives. The undermining of the ground rules and their derivatives may place new demands on the centers of the system or order, perhaps demands for concrete benefits or for new principles of allocation of power and access to the centers, for new patterns of participation in the collectivity, or for a role in the definition of its boundaries and the criteria of its membership. Systemic changes also may occur when the flow of resources through which the institutional derivatives of the ground rules of social interaction are maintained becomes interrupted or when the positions of control and the institutional framework that structures these derivatives are called into question. In either case, systemic changes are caused by withdrawal from existing positions of control of resources, be they material or social resources, and/or by creation of new positions or new demands that cannot be regulated by prevailing mechanisms.

Moreover, systemic changes may be effected through direct confrontation between incumbent elites and advocates of alternative ground rules; for example, ideological or religious groups or other types of institutional entrepreneurs propounding different models of social order and carrying new codes. Insofar as different elites compete to perform and control major societal functions vested at any given moment in the centers and insofar as these elites undermine the coalitions that uphold the current ground rules, systemic changes will occur.

10. PROTEST, REBELLION, CHANGE, AND VIOLENCE

Protest, rebellion, and political conflict are always connected, in ways that have yet to be studied systematically, with outbreaks of violence.[41] Violence as such is ubiquitous in human relations. It is rooted in man's biological endowment, an endowment that is open: the genetic program does not provide for the details of the specific interactions among people and the details of social institutions and organizations, thus leaving many empty unregulated spaces. Hence, any ordered human relationship is based on the regulation and symbolic transformation of violence and aggression. Accordingly, the disruption of relatively stable social relations or organization may cause the eruption of unregulated, "open," "naked" aggression—that is, violence.[42]

But continual outbreaks of violence, as Charles Tilly and others have pointed out, are in any society a part of regular political struggle. Above all, violence is employed by relatively weak groups demanding a bigger piece of the cake.[43] In this situation violence is a sort of cybernetic noise;[44] that is, it signals the disruption of orderly relations between any actor or system and its environment. Accordingly, reconstructing a relatively stable social organization requires the reestablishment of control over aggression.

The close relation between violence and change is clearly evident in movements of protest. The control of violence, which is fundamental to any system of authority, is perceived by members of protest movements as the epitome of naked violence and as a mispresentation of the double image of society.

11. THE VARIABILITY OF CHANGE

While the potential for protest, conflict, and change is inherent in the very construction of the macrosocietal order, the nature, location, and orientation of these phenomena vary greatly. Yet just as the themes of protest in society are not randomly distributed but are systematically related to the parameters of the social order and its cultural traditions, so movements of protest within any society are systematically related to its basic organizational parameters.

The form protest movements take varies with the ways in which the major symbolic orientations and codes are combined in predominant and secondary cultural models and also with the internal dynamics of these codes; likewise, the form varies with the specific patterns of the institutionalization of the codes' derivatives within the ecological and organizational framework. Finally, protest movements are susceptible to change as they become institutionalized, gaining control of resources and access to power.

The symbolic and organizational dimensions of societies influence both their structure and the development of processes of change within them. Thus, as we have already seen, combinations of the symbolic and the organizational dimensions significantly affect the environments that they construct; their internal expansion; their adaptability to different historical settings; and their propensity to development. Moreover, by virtue of their influence on the construction of environments of societies, the particular constellations of symbolic and organizational aspects that characterize different societies also affect the intensity of conflicts within societies and the ways in which intergroup conflict may relate to systemic contradictions, as well as possible outcomes of change.

In the following chapters we shall analyze some basic patterns of societal conflict, contradiction, and change especially from the point of view of our interest in understanding the specificity of the types of social change subsumed under the rubric "modern revolution."

NOTES

1. The development of the specific sociological *Problemstellung* is analyzed in detail in S. N. Eisenstadt and M. Curelaru, *The Form of Sociology: Paradigms and Crises* (New York: Wiley, 1976), esp. chaps. 1, 3, 4.

2. E. Mayer, "Behavior Programs and Evolutionary Strategies," *American Scientist,* 62 (November–December 1974): pp. 650–659.

3. See K. Marx, *Early Writings,* ed. T. B. Bottomore (New York: McGraw-Hill, 1963), pp. 168–188, 189–194; and idem, *Selected Writings in Sociology and Social Philosophy,* ed. T. B. Bottomore and M. Rubel (Baltimore: Penguin, 1965), pp. 175–185.

4. The literature on these scholars is of course too extensive to cite in full. Some of the more important analyses are listed below. On Durkheim see R. Aron, *Main Currents in Sociological Thought* (Baltimore: Penguin,

1970), 2:21–107; on Weber see O. Stammer (ed.), *Max Weber and Sociology Today* (Oxford: Blackwell, 1971); R. Bendix, *Max Weber: An Intellectual Portrait* (Garden City: Doubleday, 1960), chap. 14; A. Giddens, *Politics and Sociology in the Thought of Max Weber* (New York: Macmillan, 1972); and W. Mommsen, *Max Weber: Gesellschaft, Politik, und Geschichte* (Frankfurt am Main: Suhrkamp, 1974); and on Simmel see D. N. Levine, introduction to D. N. Levine (ed.), *Georg Simmel on Individuality and Social Forms* (Chicago: University of Chicago Press, 1971), pp. ix–lxv.

5. This aspect of the development of sociological thought is analyzed in S. N. Eisenstadt, "The Development of Sociological Thought," in D. L. Sills (ed.), *The International Encyclopedia of the Social Sciences*, 17 vols. (New York: Macmillan and Free Press, 1968), 15:23–35; see also Eisenstadt and Curelaru, *Form of Sociology*, chap. 3.

6. See the reference cited in note 3 above.

7. See Levine, Introduction to Levine, *Georg Simmel.*

8. See the references cited in note 4 above; see also E. Durkheim, *The Division of Labor in Society* (New York: Free Press, 1964), vol. 1, pp. 200–232; vol. 3, pp. 353–373.

9. See the works cited in note 4 above and S. N. Eisenstadt (ed.), *Max Weber: On Charisma and Institution Building* (Chicago: University of Chicago Press, 1968), esp. pp. 11–12, 46–47, 54–61.

10. See especially, among the many works of the structural-functional school, T. Parsons and E. Shils (eds.), *Toward a General Theory of Action* (Cambridge: Harvard University Press, 1951); T. Parsons, *The Structure of Social Action* (New York: Free Press, 1968); idem, *The Social System* (New York: Free Press, 1951); T. Parsons and N. J. Smelser, *Economy and Society* (New York: Free Press, 1956); and N. J. Smelser, *Social Change in the Industrial Revolution* (Chicago: University of Chicago Press, 1959).

11. See, for instance, L. Coser, *Functions of Social Conflict* (London: Collier Macmillan, 1956); R. Dahrendorf, *Class and Class Conflict in Industrial Society* (Stanford: Stanford University Press, 1959); idem, *Essays in the Theory of Society* (London: Routledge & Kegan Paul, 1968); R. Bendix (ed.), *State and Society* (Boston: Little, Brown, 1968); R. Collins and M. Makowski, *The Discovery of Society* (New York: Random House, 1972); R. Collins, "A Comparative Approach to Political Sociology," in Bendix, *State and Society*, pp. 42–67; and idem, *Conflict Sociology: Toward an Exploratory Science* (New York: Academic Press, 1975).

12. On neo-Marxist analysis see J. Habermas, *Strukturwandel der Öffentlichkeit*, third ed. (Berlin: Luchterhand, 1968); idem, *Sozialphilophische Studien* (Berlin: Luchterhand, 1963); idem, *Technik und Wissenschaft als Ideology* (Frankfurt am Main: Suhrkamp, 1968); idem, *Knowledge and Human Interests* (Boston: Beacon, 1971); idem, *Legitimationsprobleme im Spätkapitalismus* (Frankfurt am Main: Suhrkamp, 1973); and A. Touraine, *Production de la société* (Paris: Seuil, 1975).

This approach has also, of course, been developed by many neo-Marxist scholars and structuralist-Marxists. For illustrations of such work see L. Sebag, *Structuralisme et marxisme* (Paris: Petite Bibliothèque Payot, 1964); M. Godelier, *Horizons, trajets marxistes en anthropologie* (Paris: Maspero, 1973); C. Meillassou, *L'Anthropologie économique des Guoro de la Côte d'Ivoire* (Paris: Mouton, 1974); many of the essays in the journal *Economy and Society;* and J. Habermas, *Zur Rekonstruktion des historischen Materialismus* (Frankfurt am Main: Suhrkamp, 1976).

13. C. Lévi-Strauss, *Structural Anthropology* (New York: Basic Books, 1963); idem, *Totemism* (Boston: Beacon, 1967); idem, *The Savage Mind* (London: Weidenfeld & Nicolson, 1966); idem, *The Elementary Structures of Kinship* (Boston: Beacon, 1969); idem, *Mythologiques: The Raw and the Cooked* (New York: Harper & Row, 1969); idem, *Mythologiques: Du miel aux centres* (Paris: Plon, 1967); idem, *Mythologiques: L'Origine des manières de table* (Paris: Pion, 1968); and idem, *Mythologiques: L'Homme nu* (Paris: Plon, 1971).

Of the many works that provide interpretations and criticisms of Lévi-Strauss, the following are very instructive: E. Leach, *Lévi-Strauss* (London: Fontana-Collins, 1970); M. Glucksman, *Structuralist Analysis in Contemporary Social Thought* (London: Routledge & Kegan Paul, 1974), chaps. 1–3; and I. Rossi (ed.), *The Unconscious in Culture: The Structuralism of Claude Lévi-Strauss in Perspective* (New York: Dutton, 1974).

14. These convergences are analyzed in greater detail in Eisenstadt and Curelaru, *Form of Sociology*, esp. pp. 261–264. The convergence between Marxist and neo-evolutionary approaches can be found in K. Eder (ed.), *Die Enstehung von Klassengesellschaft* (Frankfurt am Main: Suhrkamp, 1973); C. Seyfarth and W. M. Sprondel (eds.), *Religion und gesellschaftliche Entwicklung* (Frankfurt am Main: Suhrkamp, 1973); see also Habermas, *Zur Rekonstruktion des historischen Materialismus.*

15. For a fuller exposition of this approach, as bearing on the analysis of social change, see S. N. Eisenstadt, "Divergent and Convergent Theoretical Perspectives in the Analysis of Social Change," *Cornell Journal of Social Relations*, 2, no. 1 (1976): 87–95.

16. This approach has been presented in different stages of its development in Eisenstadt and Curelaru, *Form of Sociology*, chap. 13; S. N. Eisenstadt, *Tradition, Change, and Modernity* (New York: Wiley, 1973), esp. pt. 5; idem, "Some Observations on the Dynamics of Tradition," *Comparative Studies in Society and History*, 2 (October 1969): 451–475; and idem, "Anthropological Analysis of Complex Societies: The Confrontation of Symbolic-Structuralism and Institutional Approaches," in W. D. Sturtevant (ed.), *Anthropology: The United States*, special publication of the Anthropological Society of Washington, forthcoming.

17. These studies are analyzed in greater detail in Eisenstadt, *Tradition, Change, and Modernity*, esp. pt. 1; and in idem (ed.), *Post-Traditional Societies* (New York: Norton, 1972).

18. The concept of ground rules has been elaborated in greater detail in

S. N. Eisenstadt and M. Curelaru, *The Form of Sociology: Paradigms and Crises* (New York: John Wiley, 1976), Chapter 13.

19. See, for instance, O. E. Williamson, *Some Notes on the Economics of Atmosphere*, Fels Center Discussion Paper no. 29 (Philadelphia: University of Pennsylvania, 1973); idem, "Markets and Hierarchies: Some Elementary Considerations," *American Economic Review*, 63, no. 2 (1973): 316–325; and idem, *Markets and Hierarchies: Analyses and Antitrust Implications* (New York: Free Press, 1975).

20. J. R. Buchler and H. G. Nutini (eds.), *Game Theory in the Behavioral Sciences* (Pittsburgh: University of Pittsburgh Press, 1969), p. 8.

21. On the concept of institutional entrepreneurs see F. Barth, *The Role of Entrepreneur in Social Change in Northern Norway* (Bergen: Artok, 1963); S. N. Eisenstadt, *Essays on Comparative Institutions* (New York: Wiley, 1965), esp. chaps. 1, 12; and idem, "Societal Goals, Systemic Needs, Social Interaction, and Individual Behavior: Some Tentative Explorations," in H. Turk and R. R. Simpson (eds.), *Institution and Social Exchange: The Sociologies of Talcott Parsons and George C. Homans* (Indianapolis: Bobbs-Merrill, 1971), pp. 36–56.

22. On the study of coalitions see, for instance, S. Groennings, E. W. Kelly, and M. Leirserson (eds.), *The Study of Coalition Behavior* (New York: Holt, Rinehart & Winston, 1970); J. S. Coleman, "Foundations for a Theory of Collective Decisions," *American Journal of Sociology*, 71, no. 6 (1966): 615–627; and W. Gamson, "Experimental Studies of Coalition Formation," in L. Berkowitz (ed.), *Advances in Experimental Social Psychology* (New York: Academic Press, 1964), 1:81–110.

23. See S. M. Lipset and S. Rokkan, "Cleavage Structures, Party Systems, and Voter Alignments," in S. M. Lipset and S. Rokkan (eds.), *Party Systems and Voter Alignments: Cross-National Perspectives* (New York: New York University Press, 1967), pp. 61–65.

24. B. Moore, *The Social Origins of Dictatorship and Democracy* (Boston: Beacon, 1960).

25. On the concept of public goods in relation to societal analysis see A. Kuhn, *The Study of Society: A Unified Approach* (Homewood: Dorsey, 1963); and M. Olson, Jr., *The Logic of Collective Action* (New York: Schocken, 1968).

26. R. Needham, "A Structural Analysis of Aimol Society," *Antropologica, Bijdragen tot de Taal, Land- en Volkenkunde*, no. 116, (1960): 81–109; idem, *Rethinking Kinship and Marriage* (London: Tavistock, 1971); M. Bloch, "The Long Term and the Short Term: The Economic and Political Significance of the Morality of Kinship," in J. Goody (ed.), *The Character of Kinship* (Cambridge: At the University Press, 1973), pp. 75–89; D. M. Schneider, *American Kinship: A Cultural Account* (Englewood Cliffs: Prentice-Hall, 1968); idem, "What Is Kinship All About?" in P. Reining (ed.), *Kinship Studies in the Morgan Centennial Year* (Washington, D.C.: Anthropological Society of Washington, 1962), pp. 32–64; M. Fortes, *Kinship and the Social Order* (Chicago: Aldine, 1969); J. Pitt-Rivers, "The Kith and the Kin," in Goody, *Character of Kinship*, pp. 89–105; and

M. J. Meggitt, "Understanding Australian Aboriginal Society: Kinship Systems or Cultural Categories," in Reining, *Kinship Studies*, pp. 64–88.

27. Fortes, *Kinship and the Social Order*.

28. K. Polanyi, *Trade and Market in Early Empires* (New York: Free Press, 1957); and the works cited in note 18 above.

29. In the field of stratification see Weber, *From Max Weber*, pts. 3, 4; idem, *Religion of India;* idem, *Religion of China;* idem, *Economy and Society;* S. N. Eisenstadt, General introduction to S. N. Eisenstadt (ed.), *Political Sociology* (New York: Basic Books, 1971), pp. 3–24; and idem, *Social Differentiation and Stratification* (Glenview: Scott, Foresman, 1971).

30. These points are elaborated upon in Eisenstadt, General introduction to Eisenstadt, *Political Sociology*.

31. P. Wheatley, *The Pivot of the Four Quarters: A Preliminary Enquiry into the Origins and Character of the Ancient Chinese City* (Edinburgh: University of Edinburgh Press, 1971); R. M. Morse, "The Claims of Tradition in Urban Latin America," in D. B. Keath (ed.), *Contemporary Cultures and Societies of Latin America* (New York: Random House, 1974), pp. 480–495; and P. Sicca, *L'immagine della citte da Sparta a Las Vegas* (Bari: Laterze, 1970).

32. E. Shils, *Center and Periphery: Essays in Macrosociology* (Chicago: University of Chicago Press, 1975), pp. 3–61.

33. These points were first worked out in detail in Eisenstadt, General introduction to Eisenstadt, *Political Sociology*.

34. This discussion follows and elaborates upon S. N. Eisenstadt, "Post-Traditional Societies and the Continuity and Reconstruction of Tradition," in Eisenstadt, *Post-Traditional Societies*, pp. 1–29; the other essays in *Post-Traditional Societies* provide very important illustrations and elaborations of the points made in this section; see also idem, "Anthropological Analysis of Complex Societies," op. cit.

35. This discussion elaborates upon the preliminary statements in Eisenstadt, *Tradition, Change, and Modernity*, pt. 3; and in Eisenstadt and Curelaru, *Form of Sociology*, chap. 13.

36. On the concept of the double of a society see A. Decouflé, *Sociologie des révolutions* (Paris: Presses universitaires de France, 1968); and also P. Mus, "La Sociologie de Georges Gurvitch et l'Asie," *Cahiers internationaux de sociologie*, 43 (1967): 1–21.

37. On millenarian movements see Y. Talmon, "Millenarism," in Sills, *International Encyclopedia of the Social Sciences*, 10:349–363. On the relations between religious and social movements see G. Lewy, *Religion and Revolution* (New York: Oxford University Press, 1974).

38. These points have been most fully elaborated in the work of Mary Douglas. See M. Douglas, *Natural Symbols* (Baltimore: Penguin, 1973); idem (ed.), *Rules and Meanings* (Baltimore: Penguin, 1973); and idem, *Implicit Meanings* (London: Routledge & Kegan, Paul, 1976).

See also R. Needham (ed.), *Right and Left: Essays on Dual Symbolic Classification* (Chicago: University of Chicago Press, 1973); Needham's work follows Hertz's and Mauss's classical analyses. For earlier expositions of these views see R. Hertz, *Mélanges de sociologie religieuse et de folklore* (Paris: F. Alcan, 1928); idem, *Death and the Right Hand* (London: Cohen & West, 1960; originally published 1907); M. Mauss, "Les Variations saisonnières dans les sociétés Eskimo," *L'Année sociologique,* 9 (1904–1905): 39–132; idem, *The Gift* (New York: Free Press, 1954); and idem, "Une Catégorie de l'esprit humain: La Notion de personne et celle de 'moi'." *Journal of the Royal Anthropological Institute,* 68 (July–December 1938), pp. 263–281.

39. Very instructive illustrations of these points can be found in S. N. Eisenstadt and R. S. Graubard (eds.), *Intellectuals and Tradition* (New York: Humanities, 1973), esp. chaps. 3, 4, and 5.

40. On social movements see the literature cited in notes 4 and 28 to Chapter 1.

41. The problem of violence and aggression has been analyzed from many points of view. For a balanced view of the biological aspects see R. H. Hinde, *Biological Bases of Human Social Behavior* (New York: McGraw-Hill, 1974). The sociological aspects are discussed in H. Bienen, *Violence and Social Change: A Review of Current Literature* (Chicago: University of Chicago Press, 1968); and earlier on, and in a rather simplistic way, in relation to revolution in P. A. Sorokin, *The Sociology of Revolution* (Philadelphia: Lippincott, 1925). Some of the applications to modern society and movements are presented in C. Leiden and K. M. Schmidt, *The Politics of Violence: Revolution in the Modern World* (Englewood Cliffs: Prentice-Hall, 1968).

42. This point is discussed at length by Douglas in the works cited in note 38 above and by the symposium on the "Ritualization of Behaviour in Animals and Man," reported on in *Philosophical Transactions of the Royal Society of London* (series B, biological sciences), 251, no. 772 (1966): 247–526, in which the biological aspects of ritual and aggression are considered as well.

43. See C. Tilly, L. Tilly, and R. Tilly, *The Rebellious Century, 1830–1930* (Cambridge: Harvard University Press, 1975), esp. chaps. 1, 6.

44. The concept of cybernetics, as applied to violence in social systems is pursued in A. Wilden, *System and Structure: Essays in Communication and Exchange* (London: Tavistock, 1972).

Chapter 3.   Change in Traditional Societies—
A Brief Overview

1. CHANGE IN PRIMITIVE SOCIETIES

That human societies are continually making internal adjustments and that entire civilizations become transformed testify to a universal societal predisposition to change. Although the anthropological literature of the thirties, forties, and fifties depicts primitive societies as tending but little toward change in general and transformative change in particular (change of the existing institutional symbolic premises),[1] it recognizes that even these societies experienced conflicts and contradictions— conflicts among social categories and contradictions among the principles of social organizations, especially those of kinship, territorial attachment, and power. The classical anthropological literature also assumed, however, that given the relatively low level of technology, the absence of a written transmission of culture, the low level of structural differentiation, and most important the embedment of the central symbolic and organizational activities in the basic (principally, kinship and territorial) units of the society, conflicts, rebellions, and protests in these societies were not articulated in organizationally and symbolically specific and distinctive ways. It was usually assumed that such phenomena were rooted in the existing structural and interpersonal units; they did not transcend the prevailing symbolic and institutional premises.[2] This embedment was said to be manifest above all in characteristic *rituals of rebellion*[3] in which social relations are turned upside down; in which the exalted becomes the lowly and vice versa without, however, generating a new conception of order or authority.

Accordingly, the processes of change within primitive societies seemed but rarely to give rise to new cultural symbols and conceptions of social order and new institutional complexes. Instead, three major types of change were seen as most typical of these societies. First, there are changes in the relative position of the different units within any given society, be it a segmentary system (composed of acephalous social segments such as lineages or clans), a tribal federation, or a primitive monarchy. Second, there is segmentation; that is, the establishment of structurally similar units beyond the territorial scope of the mother unit.[4] Third, there are changes that herald the transition from a relatively segmentary and egalitarian society to a more centralized though still "primitive" society with some hierarchical arrangements and structures. This latter type of society could take different forms.[5] For example, through alliances among various units a clan or tribal federation could arise. Or. the society might become more complex in that associational structures such as age-sets or voluntary associations came to predominate. Finally, the existing overall unit might be obliterated (as in the case of the Kingdom of the Zulu) [6] and a new, more centralized, and broader social unit established.

Anthropologists have attributed the sorts of changes outlined above mostly to external causes—population pressures, warfare, and conquest.[7] Yet such causes cannot themselves explain the transition from primitive societies to archaic and historical civilization. There must have existed, at least within those primitive societies from which more complex primitive societies and especially the first civilizations developed the potential for far-reaching changes that led to higher levels of technology, writing, and the new, more differentiated conceptions characteristic of literate societies.

Recent archeological and anthropological research is providing a more dynamic picture, indicating how this transformation might have taken place. The evidence suggests that there existed within the most primitive societies potentialities for transformative change. Such potentialities developed in primitive societies insofar as there existed within them tensions among different cultural models or codes and tensions among such codes and various structural principles (e.g., achievement versus ascription) and insofar as these different principles became interwoven with such structural categories as age, kinship, or territoriality and with distinct groups and interests. These tensions often gave rise to discrepancies and conflicts between political and social status and to differentiation and competition between those groups that specialized in the articulation of models of cultural order and those that accumulated wealth or political power.[8]

These discrepancies and tensions provided the potentialities for change that could become activated by demographic and ecological fluctuations or external factors. In a recent treatment of this problem Elmer Service, one of the earlier proponents of a critical reappraisal of the simple evolutionary approach, pointed out that it is the internal dynamics of the political system, the motives of the political leaders, and their emergence as a differentiated social category that provides the important push toward change in primitive societies in general and to breakthroughs to civilization in particular. Service's argument can be extended to other types of institutional entrepreneurs, religious as well as economic. Recent research has also stressed that intersocietal economic activities constitute an important agent of change in primitive and archaic societies.[9] Thus, while we need more systematic knowledge about change in primitive societies, the great importance of certain combinations of internal and external developments in generating change is recognized. Moreover, it is agreed that the processes of change that have been unfolding in different human societies manifest similarity as well as great variability.

The relative importance of these internal and external factors and the conditions that have shaped within them different patterns of change and transformation can be studied in somewhat greater detail in the cradles of civilization—the Mediterranean, the Near East, Mesoamerica, India, and China,[10] for which historical records, and not only archeological evidence, exist.

2. MAJOR CHARACTERISTICS OF ARCHAIC AND HISTORICAL CIVILIZATIONS. THE DIMENSIONS OF SOCIETAL DIFFERENTIATION

I

Whatever the limitations of our data about the concrete historical processes through which archaic and historical civilizations emerged, some common characteristics can be identified. The development of these civilizations was connected with (1) technological innovations that made possible the production and accumulation of surplus; (2) ecological and demographic trends resulting in the development of denser population clusters and centers—be they economic (urban), ritual (temples) or political; (3) the invention of writing; and (4) increasing international contact. These four factors gave rise to the features that distinguish early civilizations from primitive societies:

1. growing internal structural differentiation;
2. growing differentiation and rationalization within the symbolic sphere;
3. intensification of interrelationships between societies and of intersocietal differentiation;
4. distinctiveness of centers vis-à-vis the periphery.

The tendency toward structural differentiation,[11] which has been amply recognized in the literature, is manifest in the relatively greater degree of disembedment of the performance of specific institutional functions from the basic ascriptive—kinship and territorial—communities and their organization into distinct activities and roles; that is, the disembedment of the political role of the subject from membership in a local community and the growth of autonomous units—political, economic, religious, educational—that perform functionally more specialized tasks.

A second crucial dimension of structural differentiation is the increasing specialization of the major types of institutional entrepreneurs—political and economic elites and articulators of models of cultural and social order and of the solidarity of different collectivities (some of which become disembedded from ascriptive groups such as communities, tribes, or even social strata).

A third important aspect of growing differentiation is connected with the development of social hierarchies as autonomous features of social organization; that is, the development of what often has been designated class society.[12] This tendency is evident above all in the crystallization of different social positions and roles into relatively closed strata; the regulation, through customary and/or legal injunctions, of access to at least some of these positions; and the regulation of the symbolic and real uses of resources by different groups.[13]

Closely related to these three aspects of increasing differentiation is the tendency to delimit carefully the boundaries of collectivities—ethnic, regional, tribal, religious, cultural—and the scope and boundaries of institutional complexes—political, economic, cultural. This tendency is of course bound up with the growing importance of intersocial differentiation and relationships. Differentiation in intersocietal relations is manifest primarily in the growth of relatively continuous, semistable international frameworks composed of structurally distinct types of societies; for example, great patrimonial or semi-imperial units together with tribal federations, temple-cities, and/or city-states as in the Near and Middle-East or Southeast Asia.

Such international relations were important in the origins of archaic and historical societies as well as in their development. Throughout their history these civilizations were vulnerable to their international setting, from which influences could impinge differentially on various societal components. Of special importance in this regard was the relative autonomy of cultural models and their carriers and of economic systems, each of which could provide a unique impetus for change.

II

In close association with (but not necessarily in the same direction or of the same intensity as) increasing structural differentiation and increasing distinctiveness of the center (discussed subsequently), changes in the symbolic sphere occurred in both archaic and historical societies. Most important were: (1) disembedment of prevailing symbols from their primordial dimensions; (2) development and differentiation of autonomous symbolic systems (e.g., religious or philosophical) and their organization according to their symbolic contents and their methods of formulating problems and framing answers; and (3) growing doubt about the premises of these problems and answers alike.[14]

III

Beyond the aspects of differentiation discussed above there arose in all these societies another crucial distinction; namely, the growing symbolic and institutional—and not only ecological—differentiation between the center (or centers) and the periphery.[15]

This trend is manifest in the development of various types of centers (political, religious, or societal) that were to some extent structurally and symbolically differentiated from the major local groups on the periphery. The latter continued at least in the less developed societies to be organized along the pattern of more primitive societies (however, they did have links with the new centers). As against this, the more specialized organizational and symbolic political activities, as well as the components of center formation, came to be crystallized in specific institutional frameworks. The growing distinctiveness of the center also involved a transformation of relations between the center and the periphery. Among the most important activities of the center (or centers) were direction of the accumulation and distribution of the economic surplus; lawmaking and codification of laws; and representation of the major symbols of identity of the collectivity and the cultural order. A closely related development was the emergence of what may be called a political class, or political elite, structurally differentiated not only from the lower classes of the periphery but also, at least in embryonic form, from the upper strata—be they tribal chiefs and aristocrats or leaders of local territorial or family units. It is the combination of these developments that usually has been identified with the emergence of the State.

In these centers there took place the fullest institutional articulation of the relations between the organizational and symbolic dimensions of human activity. As we shall see in greater detail later on, the way in which this function was performed resulted in crucial institutional differences in societies at similar levels of differentiation.

3. TRADITIONAL LEGITIMATION. INSTITUTIONALIZATION, TENSIONS, AND CONTRADICTIONS

Whatever the differences across archaic and historical societies, they shared a pattern of legitimation akin to, but transcending, that of primitive societies: traditional legitimation. Traditional legitimation rests on the acceptance of some past figure, event, or order (whether real or symbolic) as the focus of the collective identity, as the delineator of the scope and nature of the social and cultural order, as the ultimate legitimizer of change, and as the delineator of the limits of innovation. Granted, in historical societies, the central symbol might have been a great innovative creation that destroyed what till then had been perceived as the major symbol of the legitimate past.[16]

This type of legitimation had several structural derivatives in primitive and historical societies alike. Most important was that certain segments of the social structure were—or attempted to be—designated the legitimate upholder, guardian, and symbolizer of the collective symbols, their legitimate carriers and interpreters, and hence the legitimizers of any innovation or change.

In archaic and historical societies, traditional legitimation was symbolically and structurally more fully articulated than in primitive societies, and this very articulation tended to create new foci of tensions and contradictions and new potentials for change.

This new potential for change was rooted in the specific articulation of traditional legitimation that developed in these societies in conjunction with the processes of differentiation analyzed previously and above all in conjunction with the growth of the distinction between center and periphery. The incumbents of the centers, if designated the legitimate carriers and upholders of the premises and symbols of traditional legitimation, attempted to limit access to these positions. Their monopoly of the symbols and the resources of the center frequently gave rise to questioning especially by other elite groups and therefore to sharpened tensions or conflicts, and concomitant processes of change and transformation.

Developments in the symbolic field tended to result in the challenging of the bases of legitimation of the social and political order. This tendency was encouraged by the relative elaboration and differentiation of the symbolic system; that is, the very basis of traditional legitimation (grace, revelation, myth), could become a focus of dissension. Moreover, as we have seen above, in many of these societies the central symbol of tradition was a great innovative creation that destroyed the earlier symbol of the legitimate past; therefore, in such a society the cenral symbol itself suggested the possibility of fundamental change.[17]

In sum, processes of differentiation analyzed above tended to intensify questioning of the legitimacy of the social or political order through the accumulation of technological and communicative resources and through the emergence of relatively autonomous institutional subsystems and components. The potentialities for change created by the processes of differentiation were intensified by the emergence of different types of institutional entrepreneurs; that is, articulators of models of social and cultural order as well as of the solidarity of these collectivities; by the problematic place of these cultural specialists—the forerunners of modern intellectuals; and by the tensions within this group and between it and the political powers.

Accordingly, all these societies experienced far-reaching and sharply articulated conflicts and contradictions among the components of the social order. The most important contradictions existed between cultural models and their carriers and the political system; among various kinship units and among broader collectivities; among these collectivities and their carriers; and among the major institutional complexes.

The problematics and variety of these contradictions and conflicts can perhaps be seen most clearly in the symbolism of political power and authority that developed in the civilizations we are considering. Without exception this symbolism constituted the most important single, continuous theme of social and political protest and focus of the image of the double of society. In both archaic and historical societies these themes and symbols combined the reversal of roles found in rituals of rebellion and orientations that transcended the premises of the existing system.[18]

These potentialities to change were enhanced by the growing importance to all these societies of international relations and systems, by the consequent crosscutting of the boundaries of such systems, and by the continual impingement of population shifts, international trade, and cultural movements on them, as well as by the development of longer term and better organized, violent, intersocietal political relations, that is, organized warfare.

4. REBELLION, HETERODOXY, AND POLITICAL STRUGGLE IN TRADITIONAL SOCIETIES

The heightened predisposition to change and the heightened potential of the transformative capacities of the societies we are discussing were most evident in the development of well-defined movements of rebellion, heterodoxy, and protest, as well as in a higher level of articulation of political struggle than that which presumably existed in primitive societies. Even if the picture of change in primitive societies as moving between rituals of rebellion, on the one hand, and secession or amalgamation of tribal units, on the other, is simplistic, it is indeed in archaic and historical societies that more fully articulated movements of change and protest orientations can first be fully identified.

There tended to develop in these societies relatively autonomous and long-term rebellions and movements of protest. Any of these movements could be organized by carriers of the models of cultural order or articulators of the solidarity of various collectivities—the former upheld a particular cultural orientation, the latter, a social code (hierarchy versus equality, coercion versus solidarity or instrumental inducements, and the like). Similarly, heterodox movements arose that were aimed not infrequently at some of the essential features of the predominant cultural models and traditions. And, various entrepreneurs engaged in institution building above all in the economic and educational spheres.

The attempt to reformulate symbolic parameters and institutional premises could move either in the direction of extending the scope of critical orientations and substantive rationality or in the direction of restrictive antirationalism. Such antirational tendencies in the social and cultural order may be given expression in several ways. They may be expressed in relatively simple, populistic antirationalism and anti-intellectualism. In more differentiated societies, they may develop into more elaborated antinomian sects and ideologies grounded in the negation by intellectuals of the rational or critical premises of their own traditions. These antinomian tendencies often are connected with upholding the dimensions of human existence (for example, mystic or ritual aspects) that a given tradition denies; they can be connected with extreme expressions of subjectivism and privatization; and they may emphasize, even if in intellectual terms, symbols of primordial attachment. Similarly, the issues of political struggle and conflict tended symbolically, ideologically, and organizationally to become much more articulated than those in primitive societies.

Moreover, connections between the different types of movements—rebellion, heterodoxy, protest, and political struggle—often took place: these connections generated new tensions and orientations to change. In all these societies there developed contrary tendencies with respect to the relations between the symbolically and organizationally better articulated movements of protest and the processes of political struggle. On the one hand, increased structural differentiation, combined with greater articulation of the symbols of collective and cultural identity of the societies, encouraged organizational and symbolic linkages among the various themes, orientations, and movements and between them and the processes or acts of invention, institutional innovation, and political struggle.

At the same time, there was a tendency toward relative segregation of the different manifestations of protest, political struggle, and innovation. This tendency reflected the traditionalism of these societies and the fact that technological development and structural differentiation were at a low level compared to that of modern societies. Moreover, these movements threatened rulers and elites, which sought to reinforce the segregative tendency by a variety of measures ranging from outright suppression to sophisticated co-optation. (None of these measures was, of course, permanently successful.)

The patterns of change archaic and historical societies actually exhibited reflected the influences of the different combinations of ten-

dencies we have just outlined (organizational and symbolic distinctiveness of movements of protest, political struggle, and institution building;
linkages among them versus segregation), along with the influences of
external factors—war, trade, and demographic change—and the impetus
toward change that accompanies structural differentiation.

5. THE VARIABILITY OF TRADITIONAL SOCIETIES. THE EVOLUTIONARY PERSPECTIVE

The processes of change we have been examining were present in
all archaic and historical societies. Yet these societies exhibited a
great variety of social, political, and cultural organizations. And, as we
have already indicated, from the dawn of civilization no social, political,
economic, or religious structure developed in isolation. Different political
systems—city-states, tribal federations, patrimonial chiefdoms, and kingdoms (and in later stages feudal and Imperial systems)—tended not only
to coexist but also to impinge on one another. Often, they merged, and
change in these systems often meant system transformation. There developed also in these societies a multitude of economic systems: hunting-
gathering societies, sedentary agricultural societies based on simple or
advanced cultivating technologies, and maritime societies. Patterns of
stratification likewise varied considerably. Finally, there arose numerous
cultural models of cosmic social orders as well as of cultural-institutional
systems, and these models often crystallized into central—great—and
peripheral—little—traditions.

Sociological theory has always been interested in explaining both the
great variability of social systems as well as their similarities. Proffered
explanations of course are very closely related to the analysis of processes
of change. Indeed, most analyses and explanations of social change in
classical and contemporary sociological theory have grappled with two
problems: (1) the causes of change and (2) the possible directions of
change in actual societies. Most of the classical sociological theories
(which reflect the evolutionary perspective of Marx and, to a lesser
degree, of Durkheim and Weber) attempt simultaneously to confront
these two foci of analysis. The causes of social change within any single
society—differentiation, rationalization, or the elimination of alienation
through class warfare—have often been seen as closely related to, if not
identical with, the overall direction of development of human societies.
This approach has been followed by classical evolutionists, including
Marx and the Marxists, and neo-evolutionists alike, all of whom seek to
order the development of human societies and the processes of change
within them according to stages.

The many attempts to classify societies according to stages generally have viewed technological development and structural differentiation or similar concepts as the fundamental question of comparative analysis. Among the more recent exponents of the evolutionary approach, Gerhard Lenski and Jean Lenski have defined evolution in terms of technological advance and its consequences.[19] They classify societies according to the basic mode of subsistence. Each stage is characterized by a key technological development:

1. spear-thrower, bow and arrow
2. plant cultivation
3. metallurgy
4. plow
5. iron tools and weapons
6. new energy sources

These innovations tend to create, or facilitate the creation of, seven principal types of societies.

	1 Simple hunting- gathering societies	
	2 Advanced hunting- gathering societies	
Fishing societies	3 Simple horticultural societies	Simple herding societies
	4 Advanced horticultural societies	
Maritime societies	5 Simple agrarian societies	Advanced herding societies
	6 Advanced agrarian societies	
	7 Industrial societies	

The major dependent variables of these societal types have been designated by Lenski and Lenski as follows: population size—in terms of density (larger communities) and overall societal size; permanence of settlement; division of labor; religious beliefs—basic belief structures; and social inequality—change in the nature of stratification.

Talcott Parsons and Robert N. Bellah have proposed differentiation as the essential criterion of evolution.[20] According to Bellah,

Evolution will be defined as a process of increasing differentiation and complexity of organization which endows the organism, social system or whatever the unit in question may be, with greater capacity to adapt to its environment so that it is in some sense more autonomous relative to its environment than were its less complex ancestors. . . . this does not imply inevitability of evolution or that simpler forms must necessarily become extinct.[21]

Usually, such differentiation has been conceived in rather broad evolutionary terms as continuous development from the ideal-typical primitive society or band, in which roles are allocated on an ascriptive basis and in which the division of labor is based primarily on family and kinship units. Development proceeds through various stages of specialization and differentiation.

According to this view,[22] specialization is manifest first in the degree to which central social and cultural activities as well as basic resources—manpower, economic resources, political and cultural loyalties—are disembedded or freed from kinship, territorial, and other ascriptive units.

Second, structural differentiation is manifest when all the major institutional spheres develop (through the activities of people filling strategic positions in each major sphere) their own organizational units and complexes and specific criteria of action and in this way facilitate the actualization of their potentialities: technological innovation, cultural or religious creativity, or expansion of political power or participation.

The major stages that Parsons and Bellah have proposed are: primitive societies, archaic societies, the historic intermediate empires, the seedbed societies (Israel and Greece), and early and later modern societies. These stages are most fully elaborated by Bellah with respect to the religious sphere. Bellah assumes a series of five ideal stages that "may be regarded as relatively stable crystallizations of roughly the same order of complexity along a number of different dimensions." These dimensions are: religious symbol systems, religious action, religious organization, and social implications.[23]

> *Primitive religion:* The vital development is the introduction of a symbol system, which as a mediator presupposes some differentiation between man and nature. Symbolization is central because it is the means by which man can transcend a simple, passive endurance of the environment and can gain control and find meaning through his knowledge. Thus, he becomes free and truly human. There is an extremely detailed congruency between the mythic world and the actual world.
>
> *Archaic religion:* The characteristic feature is "the emergence of a true cult with the complex of gods, priests, worship, sacrifice, and in some cases divine or priestly kingship." There is more of a sense of individual roles and willfulness.

Historic religion: Religions in this category are in some sense transcendental, establishing a religious realm separate from and above the secular world.

Early modern religion: The defining characteristic is "the collapse of the hierarchical structuring of both this and the other world." In a sense, the dualism moves to the level of the individual, and so religious action becomes "identical with the whole of life."

Modern religion: "[It is] characterized by a deepening analysis of the very nature of symbolization itself." The dualistic world is replaced by an infinitely multiplex one that centers on the autonomous individual.[24]

The Marxist and neo-Marxist schools have combined in different ways the stress on technological cause and structural complexity or differentiation to explain social transformation and to define the stages of human evolution.[25]

Of special interest is the recent attempt by Jürgen Habermas to add to the purely structural or technological criteria of stages of social evolution the evolution of the learning capacity.[26] Habermas, following the work of Piaget and Kohlberg, argues in terms of stages of cognitive and moral development.

Most of the evolutionary approaches share several basic assumptions about the dynamics of change. They all assume that the most crucial aspect of societal change is the freeing of activities and resources from existing institutional frameworks, the creation of potentially new—free-floating—resources or forces of production. The more differentiated and specialized institutional spheres become, the more interdependent and potentially complementary is their functioning within a given institutionalized system. But this very complementarity creates complex problems of integration. The growing autonomy of each sphere of social activity and the concomitant increase in interdependence and interpenetration among them make it difficult for each sphere to maintain its integrity and to regulate its normative and organizational relations with other spheres. And at each higher level or stage of differentiation, the increased autonomy of the spheres of social activity creates problems of integrating specialized activities in an overall institutional framework.

Moreover, the growing autonomy of institutional spheres, and the extension of their organizational scope, not only increases the range and depth of social and human problems but also opens up new possibilities for development and creativity—for technological innovation; expansion of political power or rights; cultural, religious, philosophical, and personal creativity. Growing differentiation also makes the system more sensitive to the physical-technical environment.

Hence, these free-floating resources pose new problems of integration, and they may become the basis for a more differentiated social order that will be better adapted to deal with an expanded environment.

The evolutionary approaches rest on several other basic theoretical assumptions. The most important of these is that societies are best conceived as systems coping with various internal and external problems. These problems are usually defined by reference to the four phases or needs of Parsonian analysis or, somewhat more concretely, by specification of the major crises of modern political systems, as proposed by Gabriel Almond, Lucian Pye, and others.[27]

A second assumption is that alongside internal and external problems there develop institutional capacities to cope with them. Most important in this regard are the specialized institutional and organizational mechanisms that are characteristic of each stage and whose development assures adequate coping with these problems. (It is also often assumed that there exists only one good institutional way of coping).

In our analysis of the theory of revolutions we encountered an assumption closely related to the preceding; namely the processes of evolution in the economic, political, institutional, and cultural spheres tend to coalesce in each stage in relative similar patterns and the breakthrough from one stage to another takes place in the same direction in all institutional spheres. This co-variance is frequently formulated in terms of systemic needs and/or prerequisites of the economic, political, or cultural systems; in this view the output from each system tends to be conceived as necessary to the emergence and functioning of every other system (that is, as a prerequisite).

The transition from one stage to another is seen as involving novelty and discontinuity. Insofar as the mechanisms of transition have been analyzed at all (for instance, in theories of modernization and of the convergence of industrial societies) they are defined in terms of the crystallization of new institutional kernels that ultimately will have similar, irreversible structural and organizational outcomes in all the major institutional spheres and dimensions of the macrosocietal order. These institutional kernels are seen as ensuring the breakthrough from one stage to another.[28] Analysts have at least implicitly assumed that transition from one stage to another is connected with or affected by a variety of social activities, movements, rebellions, and more central political struggles—that is, by the combination of elements that, as we saw in Chapter 1, are found in the image of the true revolution.

The approaches we are considering do not assume that every society necessarily goes through all developmental stages. They recognize that many societies stagnate at a given stage. Yet, if they do not stagnate, if new institutional kernels that mandate breakthrough to the next stage develop, the society's transformative capacities will manifest themselves in the emergence of a new social system, in total systematic change.

Thus, these approaches acknowledge the close, almost unvarying connection among developments in different institutional spheres and the similarity of stages of development across societies; they explain intersocietal differences by reference to stages of development; and the universality of the scheme of development. Above all, these approaches stress that the tendencies toward the evolution of new social and cultural forms that will be more adaptive in terms of the relations between these societies and their environments lead ultimately to greater mastery of the environment and that the enhancement of these adaptive capacities can be attributed to a combination of technological innovation and structural differentiation.[29]

6. A PRELIMINARY CRITICAL ANALYSIS OF THE EVOLUTIONARY PERSPECTIVE

It would be out of place here to analyze critically at length all the assumptions of the evolutionary perspective. Later on, after having examined the patterns of change in selected historical societies we shall return to this task. But even a superficial look at the history of human societies as presented by the evolutionists indicates that their approach is simplistic, that far-reaching changes that historical and even primitive societies have experienced cannot be accounted for by their assumptions.

A major fact to be considered in this regard is that at seemingly similar levels of technological development or structural differentiation we find among primitive, archaic, and historical societies social structures very diverse in form: the dimensions of differentiation are not equally elaborated in them. Thus, as we have already seen with respect to primitive, segmentary societies, their social structure may be based on simple kinship units or on more complex associations; both types of societies may differ from more centralized kingdoms.[30] With respect to archaic civilizations, Service (challenging the earlier evolutionist position) has shown that China, Mesoamerica, India, and the Middle East exhibited a great variety of combinations of elements such as urbanism, hydraulic works, and political and religious centralization. The findings he summarized [31] indicate that the societies that emerged at the dawn of civilization varied broadly with respect to the general characteristics enumerated above—distinction between center and periphery, structural differentiation, boundaries among components of the macrosocietal order, as well as symbolic elaboration.

Of special interest from the point of view of our analysis is the fact

that such differences obtained not only in the organizational and ecological aspects of primitive societies and early civilizations but also in
their symbolic configurations, above all, in the constellations of cultural
orientations and codes that corresponded to various levels of structural
differentiation.

One society in which, as we shall subsequently see in greater detail,
the dimensions of differentiation did not develop to the same degree
was Japan.[32] There, structural differentiation increased while differentiation between center and periphery remained relatively constant. More
important, structural differentiation was not paralleled by symbolic
elaboration. Japan did not distinguish sharply the transcendental from
the mundane, or what in Western parlance we classify as religion,
philosophy, and magic. Nevertheless, there existed the strong commitment to the cultural and social orders that is characteristics of high
civilizations which do emphasize this tension. Thus, the Japanese case
illustrates a crucial point closely connected with the preceding: across
societies, different cultural codes and orientations may be associated
with similar levels of differentiation; conversely, the same codes may
be associated with different levels of structural differentiation.

Given that constellations of cultural codes influence essential aspects
of the institutional makeup of a society, then societies at similar levels
of structural differentiation may generate different ground rules of
social interaction and their institutional derivatives. These ground rules
and their institutional derivatives in turn influence the development of
movements of protest—rebellions and heterodoxies, for instance—in a
society or in sectors thereof, the degree to which these movements
form interconnections as well as connections with the more central
political struggle, on the one hand, and the processes of institution
building in the economic and cultural spheres, on the other.

Similarly, movements of protest affect the coalescence and rates
and directions of change of the components of the macrosocietal order;
the degree to which forces of change within the existing order are
controlled; the degree and directions of transformability of the society—
that is, the degree to which processes of change give rise to cultural
models and social orders that transcend the original institutional premises of the society; and the degree to which systems move toward
growing and/or symbolic differentiation.

Closely related to the preceding points is the fact, revealed by a glance
at the historical evidence, that forces of change do not impinge equally,
in any given society on all the ground rules of interaction (attributes of
membership, specification of social goals, rules of distributive justice and
equity, or principles of distribution of power). Rather, in any situation
of change the many dimensions of social life are not uniformly altered:
the specific characteristics of the institutional makeup of the society in

no small degree determine this lack of uniform effect. For example, the criteria of membership and the boundaries of collectivities may change while the rules regarding distribution of power or of access to power or the rules of distributive justice remain intact. That is, change may occur in but one social collectivity (say, the political regime).

The relative openness of the institutionalization of social and cultural models also relates to the variability of patterns of change. Given this openness, aspects of the social system may in seemingly similar situations become combined in different ways; in apparently similar situations of change there may emerge different patterns of winning coalitions, each leading, as Weber showed throughout his work, to distinct constellations of the principal components of the macrosociological order. In short, the major features of a society's institutional framework may greatly vary both individually and collectively across societies (for example, the structure of the centers, the relations between center and periphery, the patterns of strata formation, and the modes of production).

The sociological and anthropological literature in the sixties began to question evolutionist assumptions along the lines indicated above. These disciplines necessarily have been seeking to account for different predispositions to change and the constellations of change in various societies. In relating structural variability to cultural and goal orientations, the classifications of primitive societies presented in the late fifties (discussed above) implicitly recognized this problem. More recently, Henderson has underlined the importance of the multiplicity of cultural models or orientations in explaining evolutionary or change potentials in them.[33]

Suggestive attempts to summarize the research on these problems were made more than a decade ago in a conference devoted to this problem—suggestions that are of great importance both in the analysis of primitive societies as well as for our more general analytical concerns.[34]

It was proposed that societal transformations require three kinds of elements: elite groups (groups instrumental in creating or maintaining new patterns of relationships); resources; and patterns of social relationships or institutions that foster transformation. The conditions permitting the emergence of elite groups, the mobilization of resources by elites, and their effective role in institutionalization are seen to correspond to two broad types of society: *pluralistic,* or *disembedded,* versus *monistic,* or *coalescent.* Monistic societies are either social systems in which the boundaries of the various sectors—economic, religious, political, and soon—are coterminous or social systems in which one sector dominates all others.

A number of hypotheses were developed and offered for discussion: (1) Internal development is less likely in monistic societies than in pluralistic societies. Monistic societies may, however, produce new elites under conditions of breakdown, especially induced by outside conquest. (2) Monistic societies tend to commit a large share of available resources to validating the existing system, thus reducing resources available for development. (3) Monistic societies experience greater difficulty than pluralistic ones in coping with new kinds of groups such as traders. It is likely that in monistic societies such groups will be segregated or encapsulated, which will limit their ability to mobilize resources. (4) Monistic societies are most likely to consolidate and freeze their boundaries, thus reducing the flow of innovations from the outside. (5) Monistic societies are more likely to witness the cyclical replacement of unspecialized cliques than the emergence of new specialized elites.

The probability that elites will arise in pluralistic societies, on the other hand, is enhanced if (1) there is competition among ruling groups and alienation between rulers and ruled; (2) the new elite stands for the autonomy of sectors, without at the same time destroying their symbiotic relationships; (3) there exists a multiplicity of cultural models; and (4) the new elite develops an ideology that is itself pluralistic and open, offering the possibility of choice, and that operates within a concept of time as nonrepetitive rather than cyclical.

7. THE PROBLEM OF REVOLUTION IN A COMPARATIVE ANALYSIS OF SOCIAL CHANGE

In the following pages we shall attempt to develop these suggestions in a more systematic way. Without denying some of the valid points in the evolutionary perspectives and especially the importance of the expansive tendencies of human societies, as well as the similarities in the stages of differentiation across societies, we advocate revision of many of the evolutionists' assumptions.

The preceding considerations do not, of course, deny or belittle two basic features of sociological analysis in general and analysis of revolutions in particular. First, obviously we do not take issue with the simple point that social change, especially far-reaching change—revolution, for example—is the result of the combined action of numerous social forces—demographic, ecological, and institutional—and that change in one part of a system affects all other parts. Second, we accept the distinction between routine personnel or group changes and far-reaching structural changes in institutional spheres (the political sphere in particular).

On the contrary, these features support the major points of our approach, outlined in Chapter 1. The combination of social activities and processes that come under the umbrella of pure revolution and that are implicit and explicit in its action stages constitutes a special type of process through which social change and transformation take place. As we said earlier, while social conflict, heterodoxy, rebellion, structural change, and transformation are inherent in human societies, the specific constellation of these elements subsumed in the image of the true revolution or in the classical evolutionary or neo-evolutionary perspective is but one of several routes to change.

Hence, the caveats raised in this chapter demand a broader approach to the study of social change. Developing such an approach constitutes one of the major challenges in sociological analysis. In the following pages we sketch tentatively such a broadened approach.

Given our initial interest in the problematics of revolutions, which by definition are primarily political phenomena, we shall concentrate on the problem of the degree to which far-reaching changes in political regimes are connected with changes in other spheres of the macrosocietal order. Following the general theoretical considerations presented above we shall attempt to analyze how different constellations of cultural orientations, ecological settings, and institutional contours influence patterns of change.

In Chapter 4 we analyze the basic patterns of change in historical, or traditional, society.

NOTES

1. Some of the classical presentations of primitive societies in this period are M. Fortes and E. E. Evans-Pritchard (eds.), *African Political Systems* (New York: Oxford University Press, 1940); M. Gluckman, "The Kingdom of the Zulu in South Africa," in ibid., pp. 25–55; idem, *Order and Rebellion in Tribal Africa* (New York: Free Press, 1963); idem, *Politics, Law, and Ritual in Tribal Society* (Chicago: Aldine, 1965); R. Firth, *We, The Tikopia* (New York: American Book, 1936); E. E. Evans-Pritchard, *The Divine Kingship of the Shilluk of the Nilotic Sudan* (Cambridge: At the University Press, 1948); idem, *The Political System of the Annuak of the Anglo-Egyptian Sudan* (London: London School of Economics, 1940); and D. Forde, "Word Organization among the Yako," *Africa*, 20, 4 (1950): 267–289. A representative collection of articles on primitive political systems is R. Cohen and J. Middleton (eds.), *Comparative Political Systems: Studies in the Politics of Pre-Industrial Societies* (New York: Natural History Press, 1957).

2. This argument is more fully elaborated in S. N. Eisenstadt, *Essays in Comparative Institutions* (New York: Wiley, 1965), pp. 77–107.

3. Gluckman, *Order and Rebellion in Tribal Africa*, pp. 110–137.

4. Fortes and Evans-Pritchard, *African Political Systems*.

5. For further analysis of these types see S. N. Eisenstadt, "Primitive Political Systems: A Preliminary Comparative Analysis," *American Anthropologist*, 61, no. 2 (1959): 205–220; and a more recent elaboration in R. N. Henderson, *The King in Every Man* (New Haven: Yale University Press, 1972), pp. 12–27; see also P. C. Lloyd, "Conflict Theory and Yoruba Kingdoms," in J. M. Lewis (ed.), *History and Social Anthropology* (London: Tavistock, 1968), pp. 25–62.

6. M. Gluckman, "The Rise of a Zulu Empire," *Scientific American*, no. 4 (1960): 157–168.

7. See Fortes and Evans-Pritchard, *African Political Systems;* for illustrations of more recent expositions see M. Harner, "Population Pressure and the Social Evolution of Agriculturalists," *Southwestern Journal of Anthropology*, 26, no. 1 (1970): 67–86.

8. Among the most interesting of such recent approaches are I. Goldman, *Ancient Polynesian Society* (Chicago: University of Chicago Press, 1970); M. D. Sahlins, *Social Stratification in Polynesia* (Seattle: University of Washington Press, 1958); idem, "Poor Man, Rich Man, Big-Man, Chief: Political Types in Melanesia and Polynesia," *Comparative Studies in Society and History*, 5, 3 (April 1963): 285–303; idem, *Tribesmen* (Englewood Cliffs: Prentice-Hall, 1968); M. H. Fried, *The Evolution of Political Society* (New York: Random House, 1967); idem, "State: The Institution", in D. L. Sills (ed.), *The International Encyclopedia of the Social Sciences*, 17 vols. (New York: Macmillan and Free Press, 1968), 15:143–150; E. R. Service, *Primitive Social Organization: An Evolutionary Perspective*, 2d ed. (New York: Random House, 1971); and idem, *The Hunters* (Englewood Cliffs: Prentice-Hall, 1966).

9. E. R. Service, *Origins of the State and Civilization: The Process of Cultural Evolution* (New York: Norton, 1975), esp. chap. 17. For some of the somewhat earlier environmental approaches see also J. H. Steward (ed.), *Theory of Cultural Change* (Urbana: University of Illinois Press, 1955); and R. M. Adams, "Anthropological Perspectives on Ancient Trade," *Current Anthropology*, 15, no. 3 (1974): 239–249.

10. For some basic materials on these civilizations see R. M. Adams, *The Evolution of Urban Society* (Chicago: Aldine, 1966); F. Katz, "Die sozialökonomischen Verhältnisse bei den Azteken im 15. und 16. Jahrhundert," in *Ethnographische Forschungen* (Berlin: VEB Deutscher, 1956), 3: pt. 2; idem, "The Evolution of Aztec Society," *Past and Present*, no. 13 (1958): 14–25; R. M. Adams, "Early Civilizations, Subsistence, and Environment," in C. H. Kraeling and R. M. Adams (eds.), *City Invincible: A Symposium on Urbanization and Cultural Development in the Ancient Near East* (Chicago: University of Chicago Press, 1960), pp. 269–297; idem, *The Evolution of Urban Society: Early Mesopotamia and Prehistoric Mexico* (Chicago: Aldine, 1966); Gordon V. Childe, *Man Makes Himself* (New York: New American Library, Mentor, 1936); idem, *What Happened in History* (New York: Penguin, 1946); idem, "The Birth of Civilization," *Past and Present*, no. 2 (1952): 1–10; H. Frankfort, *Kingship and the Gods* (Chicago: University of Chicago Press, 1948); idem, *The Birth of Civilization in the Near East* (London: Williams & Norgate, 1951); O. Lattimore, *Inner Asian Frontiers of China* (Boston: Beacon Paperback, 1962); idem, *Studies in Frontier History: Collected Papers, 1928–1958* (New York: Oxford University Press, 1962), pp. 469–491; S. C. Malik, *Indian Civilization: The Formative Period* (Simla: Indian Institute of Advanced Study, 1968); A. L. Oppenheim, *Ancient Mesopotamia: Portrait of a Dead Civilization* (Chicago: University of Chicago

Press, 1964); F. Oppenheimer, *The State: Its History and Development Viewed Sociologically* (1914; reprint ed., New York: Vanguard, 1926); A. Palerm, *Irrigation Civilizations: A Comparative Study* (Washington, D.C.: Pan American Union, 1955), pp. 10–25; Ping-ti-Ho, *The Cradle of the East* (Chicago: University of Chicago Press, 1975); R. L. Raikes, "The End of the Ancient Cities of the Indus," *American Anthropologist*, 66, no. 1 (1964): 284–289; W. T. Sanders and J. Price, *Mesoamerica: The Evolution of a Civilization* (New York: Random House, 1968); F. Katz, *The Ancient American Civilizations* (New York: Praeger, 1972); and P. Wheatley, *The Pivot of the Four Quarters: A Preliminary Inquiry into the Origins and Character of the Ancient Chinese City* (Edinburgh: University of Edinburgh, 1971).

11. The concept of structural differentiation as applied to the comparative study of civilization is most fully elaborated in T. Parsons, *Societies: Evolutionary and Comparative Perspectives* (Englewood Cliffs: Prentice-Hall, 1966); R. N. Bellah, "Religious Evolution," *American Sociological Review*, 29 (June 1964): 358–374; and G. A. Almond and G. B. Powell, *Comparative Politics: A Developmental Approach* (Boston: Little, Brown, 1966).

12. See on this K. Eder (ed.), *Die Entstehung der Klassengesellschaft* (Frankfurt am Main: Suhrkamp, 1973).

13. S. N. Eisenstadt, *Social Differentiation and Stratification* (Glenview: Scott, Foresman, 1971).

14. For the various aspects of differentiation in the symbolic field see Bellah, "Religious Evolution"; C. Geertz, "Ideology as a Cultural System," in D. Apter (ed.), *Ideology and Discontent* (New York: Free Press, 1964), pp. 47–77; and N. Elias, *Über den Prozess der Zivilisation*, 2 vols. (Bern: Francke, 1969). For historical analyses of these processes see E. Voegelin, *Order and History*, 4 vols. (Baton Rouge: Louisiana State University Press, 1954–1974); and *Daedalus*, issue on "Wisdom, Revelation, and Doubt," Spring 1975.

15. The process of development of different centers is analyzed in E. Shils, *Center and Periphery: Essays in Macro-Sociology* (Chicago: University of Chicago, 1975), chap. 3; Eisenstadt, *Social Differentiation and Stratification*, chaps. 4, 5; and idem (ed.), *Political Sociology* (New York: Basic Books, 1971), esp. pp. 112–116.

16. Of relevance in this context and especially in the study of traditional societies are the concepts of great and little traditions as developed by Redfield and Singer. See R. Redfield, *Peasant Society and Culture* (Chicago: University of Chicago Press, 1956); idem, "The Social Organization of Tradition," *Far Eastern Quarterly*, 15, no. 1 (1965): 13–21; R. Redfield and M. Singer, "The Cultural Role of Cities," *Economic Development and Cultural Change*, 3 (1954): 53–73, reprinted in R. Redfield (ed.), *Human Nature and the Study of Society* (Chicago: University of Chicago Press, 1962), 1:143–414; S. N. Eisenstadt, *Tradition, Change, and Modernity* (New York: Wiley, 1973), pt. 3; idem (ed.), *Post-Traditional Societies* (New York: Norton, 1974); and Shils, *Center and Periphery*, chap. 11.

17. These tendencies are analyzed in Voegelin, *Order and History*, esp. vols.

1–3; in *Daedalus,* Spring 1975; in S. N. Eisenstadt and R. Graubard (eds.), *Intellectuals and Tradition* (New York: Humanities, 1973), pt. 1; and, of course, in Max Weber, *The Religion of India: The Sociology of Hinduism and Buddhism,* trans. H. H. Gerth and D. Martindale (New York: Free Press, 1958); and in idem, *The Religion of China: Confucianism and Taoism* (New York: Macmillan, 1964).

18. See on this in greater detail Eisenstadt, *Political Sociology,* pt. 2; and idem, *Tradition, Change, and Modernity,* pt. 2.

19. G. Lenski and J. Lenski, *Human Societies: An Introduction to Macro-Sociology,* 2d ed. (New York: McGraw-Hill, 1974), esp. chap. 5.

20. See Parsons, *Societies: Evolutionary and Comparative Perspectives;* and Bellah, "Religious Evolution."

21. Bellah, *"Religious Evolution,"* pp. 358–374.

22. For an exposition and some initial criticism of this view see S. N. Eisenstadt, "Social Change, Differentiation, and Evolution," *American Sociological Review,* 29 (June 1964): 375–385.

23. Bellah, "Religious Evolution," 358–374.

24. Ibid.

25. Eder, *Die Entstehung der Klassengesellschaft.*

26. J. Habermas, *Zur Rekonstruktion des historischen Materialismus* (Frankfurt am Main: Suhrkamp, 1976), p. 144; see especially part 3 and the discussion between Luhman and Habermas. See also H. U. Wehler (ed.), *Evolution und Geschichte,* Geschichte und Gesellschaft, no. 1 (Göttingen: Vandenhoeck & Ruprecht, 1976).

27. T. Parsons, E. Shils, and F. Bales, *Working Papers in the Theory of Action* (New York: Free Press, 1953); and L. Binder et al. *Crises and Sequences in Political Development: Studies in Political Development,* 7 (Princeton: Princeton University Press, 1971).

28. Some of these problems, especially as applied to theories of modernization, are discussed in Eisenstadt, *Tradition, Change, and Modernity,* pts. 1, 2.

29. The adaptive aspect of evolution is analyzed in Service, *Origins of the State;* and Parsons, *Societies: Evolutionary and Comparative Perspectives.*

30. See Eisenstadt, "Primitive Political Systems"; for a fuller exposition see Henderson, *King in Every Man.*

31. Service, *Origins of the State,* esp. chap. 16.

32. This aspect of Japanese society is brought out in R. N. Bellah, *Intellectuals and Society in Japan,* op. cit.; in Eisenstadt and Graubard, *Intellectuals and Tradition,* pp. 89–117; and in H. Nakumura, *The Ways of Thinking of Eastern People* (Honolulu: East-West Center Press, 1964), esp. pt. 4.

33. See Eisenstadt, "Primitive Political Systems"; and Henderson, *King in Every Man,* esp. pp. 23–27 and 503–528.

34. E. Wolf, "Report on a Conference: The Evolutionist Interpretation of Culture," *Current Anthropology,* 8, no. 1–2 (1967): 127–129.

Chapter 4.   Patterns of Change in Traditional Societies

PART 1   PATTERNS OF CHANGE

1. INTRODUCTION

In this chapter we analyze some of the major patterns of change that can be identified in traditional societies. We do not present a detailed analysis of all the processes of change in these societies, nor do we analyze the conditions under which different types of traditional societies emerged. Instead, we concentrate first on the analysis of selected patterns of change in order to identify coalescence in directions of change and restructuring of the macrosocietal order; and second on the degrees and types of societal transformability (that is, the degree to which processes of change generated in any society give rise to cultural models and social orders that transcend the original institutional premises, as well as the degree to which such systems move toward growing structural and/or symbolic differentiation.) Third, we examine the conditions that gave rise to these patterns.

During the first part of our analysis we distinguish three ideal types of patterns of change in traditional societies. Subsequently we analyze important variations within each of these types.

The first broad pattern of change in traditional societies is characterized by relatively little coalescence or convergence among changes in the basic ground rules of social interaction—especially between changes in the criteria of access to power and those in the other ground rules—and by a small degree of coalescence in the directions of change among tendencies toward restructuring the major components of the macrosocietal order. It is characterized also by a low level of convergence among protest movements and between them and the more central political struggle. Finally, the political system remains relatively intact and there is but little ideological articulation of political struggle.

This *pattern of segregative change* is typical of patrimonial regimes:

the ancient Egyptian kingdoms (ca. 2600-332 B.C.), the Assyrian (ca. 1300–612 B.C.) and Babylonian (ca. 1900–641 B.C.) kingdoms, and such smaller kingdoms as ancient Akkad [1] (third century B.C.); the nomadic kingdoms or empires—those of the Hyksos (1720–1567 B.C.), the Hittites (ca. 1600–1500 B.C.), the Mongols (second century A.D.), and the first Germanic and Slavic tribes to settle in Europe (first century A.D.), which were rather loosely organized;[2] and the more centralized kingdoms of India and Southeast Asia (first century B.C. and A.D.), and to some extent the Mesoamerican kingdoms of the second century A.D.[3] It can also be found in other traditional political regimes such as the city-states and semitribal or tribal federations of the ancient Mediterranean, the ancient Near and Middle East, the Indian subcontinent, Southeast Asia, and Mesoamerica.[4]

Each of these types of political systems reached different levels of technological development, as proposed by Gerhard Lenski and Jean Lenski. The segregative pattern could also be associated with different stages of structural, economic, or societal differentiation, as Talcott Parsons and Robert N. Bellah have pointed out. Patrimonial regimes in particular tended toward a low level of differentiation in the political sphere.

The pattern of segregative change is furthest from the assumptions about the nature and process of transition from one stage of social development to another adhered to both by the various evolutionary schools and by theories of revolution. The two other patterns of change that can be identified in traditional societies better approximate these assumptions. The *coalescent pattern of change* is characterized by relatively high coalescence among directions of change in the different ground rules of social interaction and among tendencies toward restructuring the collectivities and institutional spheres of the macrosocietal order; by a strong tendency toward the internal restructuring of the political system itself; as well as by marked convergence and integration of the various movements of protest and political struggle. This pattern of change is also connected with a much higher level of articulation of the issues and of autonomy of the organization of political struggle.

Coalescent change developed above all in the Imperial systems [5]— the Roman (31 B.C.–A.D. 527) and the Hellenistic (323–30 B.C.),[6] the Chinese (ca. first century B.C. to A.D. 1911),[7] the Byzantine (A.D. 324–1653),[8] the Russian (A.D. 1721–1917),[9] the Abbasside (A.D. 720–1258),[10] and the Ottoman empires (A.D. 1451–1788) [11]—in the Absolutist regimes of early modern Europe,[12] as well as in combinations of Imperial-feudal elements—the major examples of which were to be found in medieval Western and Central Europe [13] and to some extent in Japan.[14]

The third pattern of change developed in the exceptional city-states, most significantly, ancient Greece and Rome,[15] and in the exceptional tribal federations such as ancient Israel [16] and certain early Islamic states.[17] The *pattern of exceptional change* is characterized by a very high degree of coalescence among movements of protest and political struggle and above all by a high degree of symbolization and articulation of the ideologies of political struggle. In this regard, this pattern is similar to the coalescent pattern prevalent in the Imperial and Imperial-feudal regimes. At the same time, however, the pattern of change in these exceptional societies did not result in parallel changes in the major institutional spheres.

We shall now proceed to a detailed analysis of these three patterns of change. Our starting point in each section will be the relationship between far-reaching changes in the political sphere and in political regimes, on the one hand, with changes in other institutional spheres, on the other.

2. THE PATTERN OF SEGREGATIVE CHANGE. PATRIMONIAL, TRIBAL, AND CITY-STATE REGIMES

The relatively far-reaching changes in patrimonial, tribal, and city-state [18] regimes were in most instances caused by a combination of internal and external forces. In the extreme case, conquest, external forces were of course decisive. Yet even here external pressure usually intensified internal interelite and intergroup conflicts—thus, the decline of the regime cannot be attributed solely to one sort of factor.

Far-reaching changes in these political regimes usually meant that incumbents or dynasties changed along with the hierarchical standing of different families, ethnic groups, or regions; the boundaries of polities; the concrete contents of the symbols of legitimation; and the policy orientations of the rulers (coercive, manipulative, or solidary). Whereas new economic or religious groups often emerged under these conditions, new types of religious institutions and orientations rarely did. Nor did newly constituted social strata come to impinge directly on the center. Furthermore, these groups tended not to become well-articulated entities but rather were co-opted by the rulers into existing or emerging political frameworks. Above all, the principles of access to political power did not necessarily change. Where they did, it was the policies of the rulers that were altered.

Thus, in most examples of segregative change the ground rules that structured the boundaries of the political collectivity changed; sometimes these changed together with the principles of distributive justice and, more rarely, with changes in the meaning of institutional spheres, as well as with changes in the concrete institutional derivatives of the ground rules.

To repeat, these societies exhibited a relatively high degree of dissociation between changes in, and restructuring of, the political regimes and collectivities and changes in the major boundaries or symbols of other types of collectivities—national, ethnic, religious—as well as in the other institutional spheres.

The relative lack of connection among the components of the macro-societal order can be seen even when changes in the political sphere had rather far-reaching results: the destruction of a particular regime; its submergence or incorporation into another regime (either as an integral part thereof or as an enclave); the segregation of the existing polity because of immigration or colonization; or even the transformation of the polity (into Imperial or feudal systems or into subunits or enclaves of such systems). Such extreme changes in political regimes or boundaries were not always accompanied by changes in the boundaries or symbols of either ethnic or religious collectivities or in the boundaries or structural principles of economic and cultural institutions.[19]

Needless to say, in any concrete situation these areas of potential change impinged on one another. But each collectivity tended to have distinct boundaries, and its continuity was carried by a unique coalition; hence, the demise or change of one collectivity did not necessarily involve the others.

Truly enough, in an undifferentiated patrimonial, tribal, or city-state regime such as existed in the ancient Near East or in ancient India, the demise of a political regime might mean the disappearance of a whole people as well as their specific religion.[20] But in more complex settings the potential existed for greater autonomy and distinctiveness of economic frameworks; ethnic, national, cultural, and religious collectivities and institutions; and frameworks of social stratification. This possibility was especially great wherever close connections were maintained with a high civilization like Hinduism or Buddhism or, to a much smaller degree, Islam.[21] At the same time, local—familial, ethnic, religious, or cultural complexes—could become incorporated into new political regimes without necessarily losing their own identity.

However, these undifferentiated patrimonial, tribal, and city-state regimes were conducive to the development of relatively widespread economic systems based on interstate commerce and even agricultural markets that cut across political boundaries and survived the demise of political regimes.[22] Of course, many economic activities (especially in the smaller patrimonial regimes) were confined to relatively limited markets (limited in the sense of being narrower than the political regime) or, as in the case of the city-states, to markets lying outside the political boundaries). But at the same time, the dynamics of change of these political systems, in particular, the more structurally differentiated, were highly conducive to the functioning of relatively broad frameworks of economic activities and institutions; the functioning of international markets with boundaries of their own; and the existence of economically differentiated and specialized enclaves. Conversely, far-reaching changes in technological or economic activities and in institution building, although often contributing indirectly to specifically political crises, were not always connected with the restructuring of the political sphere.

Only those regimes that developed into feudal or Imperial systems manifested marked convergence between changes in the political regimes and changes in other components of the macrosocietal order; most notably personnel, dynastic, and territorial changes corresponded with the development of new structural principles or cultural orientations. But such development took place, as we shall see later, through a rather special constellation of forces.

3. COALESCENCE OF PROTEST MOVEMENTS AND IDEOLOGICAL ARTICULATION OF POLITICAL STRUGGLE IN SEGREGATIVE CHANGE

I

This pattern of change is very closely associated with a relatively low level of coalescence, or high level of segregation, among movements of protest and conflict. Concomitantly, this pattern is correlated with a low level of ideological articulation of political issues and political activities.[23]

Needless to say, these characteristics could reinforce each other. Widespread rebellion often weakened incumbents, and ad hoc coalitions did develop between the leaders of rebellions and central elites. Coalitions also were formed by various religious groups, sects, and heterodoxies and leaders of rebellions, on the one hand, and members of the central elites, on the other. However, patrimonial, tribal, and city-state regimes exhibited only weak tendencies toward organizational or symbolic merger of these different types of activities or collectivities and toward generation of common, long-term programs or new types of institutional activities (especially those leading to the restructuring of the principles of access to power).

On the whole, movements of protest, political struggle, and religious sects, as well as patterns of institutional innovation, went their own way. Some rebellions simply petered out; some movements gave rise to new secondary or marginal groups within the society. The stronger of these newly formed groups did alter the relative strength of central groups and some, as we shall see later, developed into important structural enclaves. But, to repeat, they rarely produced new conceptions of social order or reorganized institutional structures; only rarely did they directly affect the restructuring of the political centers. At most, such movements of protest helped effect policy changes on the part of rulers.

The close connection between segregative tendencies and a relatively low level of ideological articulation of political issues manifested itself above all in the nature of the organs and mechanisms of political struggle predominant in these societies. The most important mechanism was direct bargaining among various groups. Indeed, the leading participants in the political struggles of these societies were the direct representatives of the basic groups in the center and in the periphery (for example, kinship, territorial, and religious groups); they tended to be organized in cliques, competing for access to the center (usually, the royal household), creating continuously shifting and crosscutting allegiances and coalitions among themselves. The principal mechanisms of political struggle on the part of aristocratic as well as peripheral groups were petitioning and pressuring the political center to co-opt new elements and/or to change their composition: to alter the details of the distribution by the center of various resources to the major groups, as well as to extend the lines of clientele and patronage.

Paralleling the segregation of movements of protest, rebellion, and political struggle, as well as the low level of articulation of political issues, was the low level of ideological articulation of the themes of protest and of the more central political struggle. However numerous rebellions might have been, they rarely articulated social or political goals that went beyond direct socioeconomic demands. Rarely did movements of protest display strong utopian or transcendental elements oriented to the *political* scene. Whatever utopian orientations they might have developed tended to look toward the millennium or to stress the solidarity of existing primordial communities. New political orientations generally were not articulated nor did innovative religious or political leaders participate in such rebellions.[24]

The pattern of political struggle characteristic of these patrimonial, tribal, and city-state regimes was closely related to the nature of the coalitions that implemented the major changes in the political sphere. These coalitions were composed of members of the central ruling family and of representatives of territorial groups and established religious groups. The leaders of broader solidarities participated only passively in them. It was most unusual for religious innovators, economic entrepreneurs, or leaders of socially active groups to participate.

Similarly, central political activities in the societies we are examining infrequently were concerned with far-reaching transformation or change in the symbolic sphere or in the ideological bases of the legitimation of the sociopolitical order. Truly enough, they often altered the concrete contents of the symbols of legitimation. New regimes adapted or appropriated these symbols but such political changes were not envisaged in terms of a new symbolic conception of the political order or of its legitimation.[25]

Insofar as important symbolic innovations took place, as occurred in most of the high civilizations (witness the examples of Hindusim and Buddhism), they were otherworldly. To reiterate, such innovations rarely focused on the transformation of the sociopolitical order, and they tended to be restricted to relatively segregated social enclaves.

The internal restructuring of the economic and religious spheres tended likewise to occur within relatively segregated enclaves. Some of the most important changes in patrimonial, tribal, and city-state regimes were indeed in the nature and scope of these enclaves. However, such changes did not significantly alter relations between them and the political centers.[26]

II

The patrimonial, city-state and tribal regimes characterized by the pattern of segregative change revealed many differences—in technological level or structural differentiation, in the relative strength of the major participants in the political struggle (the king, with his potentially wider political group; the traditional aristocratic groups; other, more flexible religious or urban groups, and in the impingement of external forces on the centers and their sensitivity to such forces. While these differences could greatly influence the intensity of political struggle and the tempo of changes within political regimes, on the whole, the overall pattern of segregative change remained intact. At the same time, however, there existed significant and far-reaching variations in the actual course of change.

The most important of these variations divided those political systems embedded in relatively archaic, local frameworks and cultures and those connected with high civilizations (above all, with otherworldly religions such as Hinduism, Buddhism, and to a degree Zoroastrianism. In the ancient Near East, certain aspects of institution building and of the structuring of collectivities were linked to changes in the religious or cultural spheres but not to restructuring of the political sphere. We turn to the analysis of these variations in Chapter 5.

4. CONFLICTS AND CONTRADICTIONS IN SEGREGATIVE CHANGE

The preceding analysis can be reformulated in terms of the ways in which contradictions and conflicts were structured in patrimonial, tribal, and city-state regimes. Different intergroup conflicts did not necessarily focus on the same ground rules and systemic contradictions. Likewise, intensification of conflicts and contradictions with respect to individual ground rules or dimensions of the macrosocietal order might affect other spheres but did not directly threaten their existence—above all, the continuance of the political center. Hence, the transformative capacities of these societies were not evident in the development of new structural principles binding on all institutional spheres: rather, they operated in individual spheres or influenced the mode of incorporation of segregated units within society, their multiplication, and possibly their orientations.

5. THE PATTERN OF COALESCENT CHANGE. IMPERIAL AND IMPERIAL-FEUDAL SOCIETIES

I

We now turn to the second major pattern of change that can be identified in traditional societies and that was to be found, as indicated above, in Imperial and Imperial-feudal societies.[27] This pattern is characterized by a much higher degree of coalescence of the dimensions of change and restructuring of the basic ground rules of social interaction and principal collectivities and institutional spheres (especially by convergence between changes in the political sphere, on the one hand, and changes in other institutional spheres, on the other).

Its most common form was dynastic change, which is not greatly dissimilar from the typical type of change in patrimonial regimes and which often was connected with alteration of the boundaries of the polity. Sometimes such changes (for instance, in the case of the Byzantine Empire)[28] led to the disappearance of the political system without similarly eliminating ethnic, religious, or regional collectivities or religious, cultural, or economic institutional complexes. Yet there also developed in Imperial and Imperial-feudal societies a pattern of change in which the macrosocietal order was affected in its totality.

As indicated above, the political processes within these civilizations were connected with the internal restructuring of the political system itself, particularly, the principles of access to power. Thus, dynastic changes were often associated with changes in the composition of political elites and with changes in the political organization and articulation of broader strata and in their impact on the central political framework and its structural principles.[29]

In more detail, changes of ruler or dynasty in Imperial and Imperial-feudal systems often went hand in hand with changes in administrative, political, and ministerial personnel and changes in the relative predominance of groups in the political arena—in many cases, even with usurpation of political power and decisionmaking by military groups, for example. Moreover (and of special importance from the point of view of our discussion), such changes frequently were accompanied by changes in intergroup relations (specifically, between the central elites and broader social groups and strata); in the principles of hierarchization; and in the distribution of power in the society. They were also often connected with the emergence of new groups and strata that were neither familial nor regional and with far-reaching changes in the principles of structural organization of these groups.

Thus, the pattern of coalescent change meant the rise or fall of professional, cultural, and religious elites and institutions; shifts in the strength of the monarch vis-à-vis the aristocracy and of the aristocracy vis-à-vis urban groups and the free peasantry; and shifts in the relative strength and independence of the bureaucracy. It also meant changes in the principles of political articulation and access to the center, leading to the broadening or narrowing of the autonomous access of different groups to the center and to each other.[30] Religious and ideological changes were connected not only within the relative standing of various religious elites in the center but also with the restructuring of the symbols of political power and legitimation and with certain changes in social group structure and access to power mentioned above.[31] Finally, political changes along this pattern tended to be associated with, and facilitated by, changes in the scope of markets and in the frameworks of economic activity and changes in the scope and modes of economic production and distribution— above all, shifts in the mode of agricultural production and its orientation to different markets.[32]

II

Imperial and Imperial-feudal societies thus manifested a closer connection in the rates of change and in the restructuring of the components of the macrosocietal order than the patrimonial, city-state and tribal systems discussed earlier.

Truly enough, in the Imperial systems the actual boundaries of ethnic, religious, cultural, and political collectivities, and to some degree different institutional systems, tended not to coincide. Indeed, many of their great traditions survived—predominantly in the churches; for example, the Greek Orthodox church after the decline of the Byzantine Empire. But, with the partial exception of Islam (which we discuss later), these great traditions tended to lose their vitality under such conditions. (Buddhist and above all Hindu societies stand in sharp contrast to this situation.)

On the other hand, the ethnic, regional, and national collectivities or religious sects that survived the demise of the empire to which they belonged were more resilient. However, their articulation and organization tended to become much weaker as compared with that of groups similarly situated vis-à-vis the patrimonial, tribal, and city-state regimes discussed above.

A similar picture emerges with respect to the relation between the economic frameworks and the political boundaries of the empires.[33] Of course, economic entrepreneurs, most notably, commercial and industrial ones, had many outside connections and served foreign markets. Yet, unlike entrepreneurs in the patrimonial, city-state, and tribal regimes, they tended to orient a much larger portion of their activities around the Imperial boundaries.

Finally, the articulation of social hierarchies as well as status consciousness was largely dependent upon the boundaries of the empires.

Hence, changes in the scope and structural principles of the economic systems or of strata formation tended to impinge more directly on the political centers while far-reaching changes in political regimes affected the functioning of economic institutions and the structuring of social hierarchies.

6. COALESCENCE OF PROTEST MOVEMENTS AND IDEOLOGICAL ARTICULATION OF POLITICAL STRUGGLE IN IMPERIAL AND IMPERIAL-FEUDAL SOCIETIES

The Imperial and Imperial-feudal systems tended toward a high level of ideological articulation of political struggle, as well as a much closer connection between such struggle and movements of rebellion and protest.[34]

The relatively high level of ideological articulation and organization of the political process was manifest in the emergence of political leaders or entrepreneurs who attempted to promote the value or interests of one group or stratum. Frequently, the rulers themselves, their representatives, or members of the ruling elite filled such leadership roles.

Leaders in these societies sought to generate support among different groups and strata, to cooperate with different elites and functional groups, to tap various free-floating resources, and to organize and channel them to augment their own power. To this end they tried to (1) develop social and political organizations of different degrees of articulation; (2) obtain political influence and power in the political institutions; (3) win support from cultural, professional, and religious groups and elites; (4) forge new symbols of social and political identification; (5) become themselves the representatives of certain values; (6) redefine the relations between the society's great and little traditions; and (7) establish, through cooperation with, or coercion of, different groups and elites, regulatory and integrative organizations and institutions to which different groups and strata would have recourse in order to regulate their conflicts.

Most Imperial and Imperial-feudal regimes displayed autonomous political organizations (such as loosely organized political parties) that were more differentiated than the cliques that predominated in patrimonial, tribal, and city-state regimes.

The high level of articulation of political activities encouraged coalescence among the major types of protest—between rebellions and heresies between these movements and institution building by secondary elites, above all in the economic and cultural spheres; and between all such movements and the political processes of the centers.[35] And, such ad hoc coalitions *could* develop into permanent structures.

These ad hoc arrangements aside, there tended to develop an organizational and symbolic merging of the different movements of protest that in turn generated new symbolic and institutional patterns. The focus in such cases was the orientations and activities of these movements in attempting to change the ground rules of social interaction—that is, the criteria of membership in collectivities; the principles of distributive justice and of access to power; the definition of the meaning of social activities; and, most important, the relations between these desired changes and the rules of access to power prevalent in the society.

This last tendency was closely related to the high level of symbolic and ideological articulation of political struggle. This articulation was manifest in the fact that in these societies political struggle exhibited several dimensions specifically connected with restructuring the various ground rules of social interaction. One such dimension focused upon the redistribution of economic resources (especially land and debts) among different social groups within the society. This dimension could merge into the struggle over the basic socioeconomic makeup of the whole community and over the contents and patterns of participation in its center and in the political life of the community of what in modern political parlance is called the scope of political equality.[36]

7. CONFLICTS AND CONTRADICTIONS IN IMPERIAL AND IMPERIAL-FEUDAL SOCIETIES

We may here, as we did with respect to patrimonial, tribal, and city-state regimes, reformulate our analysis in terms of the nature of the conflicts and contradictions in Imperial and Imperial-feudal societies.

Unlike conflicts in the former group, intergroup and interelite conflicts in societies characterized by the pattern of coalescent change tended to converge on several ground rules of social interaction.

Nevertheless, as in any traditional society, tendencies toward coalescence among movements of protest were vigorously resisted by the ruling elite. The attempt to weaken these tendencies and to separate movements of protest and especially to divorce these from institution building and the political process was largely successful. As a result, coalescence among all such movements was indeed rare. It could, however, develop and would necessarily lead, in contrast to the first pattern of change, either to partial transformation of the regime or to its demise.

A final point is in order here. The extent of coalescence was by no means uniform in all Imperial and Imperial-feudal societies. The Chinese Empire was characterized by comparatively little convergence between changes in the political and economic spheres; likewise, political changes were not paralleled by changes in the structuring of different strata. In contrast, the Byzantine Empire was characterized by a relatively high degree of ideological articulation of political struggle and coalescence of movements of protest. The Roman and the Ottoman empires were able to control and segregate movements of protest for long periods of time. Still different patterns of change developed in the Islamic world and in Europe. We analyze these variations in Chapter 5.

8. THE PATTERN OF CHANGE IN EXCEPTIONAL CITY-STATES AND TRIBAL FEDERATIONS

The exceptional city-states were those of ancient Greece and Rome;[37] the most important exceptional tribal federations existed in the ancient Near East—most notably, Israel—and later in the Islamic world.[38] We use the term "exceptional" because these societies exhibited a very high degree of coalescence of movements of protest and political struggle and a high degree of symbolization and ideological articulation of political struggle. In both these aspects, this pattern of change sometimes exceeded the pattern of coalescent change.

In some of these exceptional cases there developed not only the special dimensions of political struggle that we identified for the Imperial and Imperial-feudal systems (for instance, demand for wide-scale redistribution of economic resources), as well as conflict over the fundamental socioeconomic makeup of the community. In addition, these societies experienced struggle over the overall patterns and principles of participation in the center and the scope of participation of different social groups in the political life of the community.[39]

Very often, these struggles were connected with deep-rooted social conflicts and movements—movements that sought to reconstruct crucial aspects of the social order, thus often displaying characteristics akin to those of avowedly revolutionary struggles.[40]

The exceptional tribal-federations produced a new definition of political responsibility and participation. This definition tended to stress greatly the place of political power vis-à-vis the religious and cosmic orders; the ultimate primacy of the latter; and consequently the accountability of the rulers to the representatives of the true, cosmic order.

The exceptional city-states produced a new type of political symbolism, the fullest expression of which was the idea of citizenship. The crux of this concept was the full and equal participation of individuals qua individuals, freed of particularistic-primordial ties, in the body politic and individual political or legal responsibility. This concept implied responsibility of the rulers to the ruled.

The conception of wide participation in the political and/or cultural order and of citizenship developed in different directions in Greece and Rome. Rome focused on law and legal institutions and on the possibility of extending the idea of citizenship beyond the original confines of the city-state: this focus was the starting point for transformation of the system. The Greek conception did not prove capable of transcending in legal and institutional terms the confines of the city-state.

In marked contrast to the Imperial and Imperial-feudal systems, the exceptional city-states and tribal federations did not reveal a strong predisposition for institution building or for transformation of the political system or for combining changes in political regimes with those in other dimensions of the macrosocietal order.

The process of political struggle that unfolded in these societies gave rise but rarely to long-term, successful institutional restructuring. The intensification of political struggles often led to the demise of the city-state or tribal federation, or (as in the case of Rome and the early Solomonic Kingdom) to its transformation into a more centralized, semi-Imperial or Imperial regime, or (as in the case of the Greek city-states) to its incorporation into another political regime.

(It should be noted that the demise of the political regime did not necessarily signal either the eradication of the boundaries and symbols of the cultural and social orders or the end of other basic institutional complexes, above all, the economic.)

PART 2   DEVELOPMENT OF PATTERNS OF CHANGE

1. INTRODUCTION

We saw in the first part of this chapter, in very general terms, that the closer the connection among different types of movements of protest and the central political struggle, the higher the degree of coalescence on the whole among changes in, and tendencies toward restructuring, the components of the macrosocietal order and the closer the connection between these movements and processes and institutional innovation. We noted, too, some variations of, as well as some exceptions to, these general patterns. How do we explain these broad patterns of change, their variations, and their exceptions?

The common sociological emphasis on the organizational aspects of social life—the social division of labor, structural differentiation, class relations—seems inadequate to this task. Rather, we shall attempt to construct an explanation based on certain combinations of cultural orientations and structural characteristics that cut across similar levels of technology and of structural differentiation or class composition; and on those aspects of the institutional structure of societies that are most closely related to the institutionalization of the ground rules of social interaction—namely, centers and center-periphery relations and the structuring of social hierarchies and principal collectivities.

2. STRUCTURE OF CENTERS. CENTER-PERIPHERY RELATIONS AND STRATA FORMATION IN IMPERIAL AND IMPERIAL-FEUDAL REGIMES. STRUCTURING OF COLLECTIVITIES

I

In the Imperial societies (and to a considerable degree in Imperial-feudal systems center-periphery relations were characterized by a high level of distinctiveness of the center, the perception of the center as a distinct symbolic and organizational unit. In these societies the centers typically attempted not only to extract resources from the periphery but also to permeate it, to reconstruct it symbolically, and structurally to mobilize it. At the same time the potential existed for impingement of at least part of the periphery on the center (or centers).[41]

The political and to some extent the cultural-religious centers in all these empires were conceived as autonomous, self-contained foci of the charismatic elements of the sociopolitical and often also of the cosmic cultural order; the centers most embodied the charismatic qualities of the cosmic order as the latter became reflected in the social order or related to it. Indeed, the political, religious, and cultural centers constituted the foci and loci of the great traditions that developed in these societies, and within these centers the great traditions tended to be most fully elaborated as symbolically and organizationally distinct from local traditions.

The differentiation, specification, and crystallization of the centers, political centers in particular, as independent, structurally and symbolically distinct entities could best be discerned within these empires in external manifestations such as temples and palaces (granted, similar monuments of centrality could probably be found within patrimonial regimes). The distinctiveness and autonomy of the Imperial centers was evident mainly in their unique symbolic and institutional crystallization. In structural terms, the autonomy and distinctiveness of the centers was evident in their separation from the social units of the periphery, in their ability to develop and maintain their own unique symbols and criteria of recruitment and organization.

The structural and symbolic autonomy of the centers was closely associated with the relations between center and periphery, above all, with the permeation of the periphery by the center and with the weaker impingement of the periphery on the center.

In most of these empires there developed the conception that the sociopolitical and the cultural order that was represented in the centers and that encompassed the periphery differed from local traditions. The very distinctiveness of the center was articulated so that broader groups and strata—the periphery—could become more directly related to it. Unlike patrimonial regimes, the Imperial systems were based on the assumption that the periphery could have at least symbolic access to the center; such access was largely contingent upon weakening the social and cultural closure and self-sufficiency of the periphery and upon its developing active orientations to the social and cultural order upheld by the center.

The center permeated the periphery by developing channels of communication and by attempting to disrupt the ascriptive ties of the groups on the periphery. These channels of communication emphasized the symbolic and structural separateness of the center.

Concomitantly, the centers of Imperial (and Imperial-feudal) societies tended to pursue a variety of activities closely related to the implementation of the basic ground rules of social interaction. They upheld the symbols of collective identity; they articulated collective goals and rules of distributive justice; they regulated intergroup conflicts; and they related all of the preceding to the criteria of access to power prevalent in the society.

This tendency toward regulation of intergroup relations was closely associated with the structure of the major markets within Imperial societies. These markets were characterized by a relatively wide scope—and the possibility existed for wide access to them; and by a relatively free flow of resources—primarily economic but also political (support or influence)—within them. At the same time, however, the centers attempted to control access to these markets as well as the flow of resources among them, thereby emphasizing the unique position of the centers (or center) as sole guardian of the traditions, particularly of legitimation, of these societies. Hence, impingement of the periphery on the center was necessarily weaker than permeation of the periphery by the center. Still, this tendency was reinforced (albeit to varying degrees across these empires) by the multiplicity of centers and collectivities, of ethnic, religious, and political communities, as well as by the very wide scope of the Imperial markets.

II

The structuring of social hierarchies and strata formation in the Imperial and Imperial-feudal societies corresponded to center-periphery relations.[42] The growing distinction between center and periphery, on the one hand, and the plurality of autonomous centers, on the other, promoted the emergence of a new ruling class and special occupational groups that could constitute the bases of the hierarchical ordering of the society. More important than such differences in the group basis of social hierarchies were certain symbolic and organizational features. Foremost was the tendency, within Imperial as well as Imperial-feudal systems, for the boundaries of social strata to correspond to those of the political framework (and in the Imperial-feudal to those of the broad cultural—Christian European, for example—framework). And in contrast to the pattern in patrimonial societies the central political frameworks and their symbols upheld the status of the most active and powerful strata.

Finally, Imperial societies generally evidenced relatively autonomous articulation of strata and relatively widespread status or class identity as distinct from, but related to, the political and to some degree the cultural sphere.

These broad characteristics found concrete expression (1) in the existence of strata with autonomous access to the social and cultural attributes that served as bases for the criteria of status and with autonomous access to the centers of society; (2) in the development of tendencies (most notably in the more autonomous or central strata) toward status association among relatively diversified, even if smaller, occupational groups; (3) in the relatively high degree (again, most notably in the more autonomous or central strata) of countrywide strata consciousness and devaluation of ethnic, religious, or regional elements; and (4) in the movement toward political expression of strata consciousness.

The combination of the political premises and characteristics of the Imperial systems and the cultural orientations predominant in the traditions to which they were connected influenced powerfully the relations among the different collectivities and institutional complexes of these societies.[43] First, there evolved a relatively high degree of ideological symbolization of the principal, religious, political, and even ethnic or national collectivities. Second, although in fact each collectivity tended to develop a relatively high degree of autonomy and its own boundaries, all subscribed to an ideal of coalescence among them. At the same time, each collectivity (except in the Islamic world, which we consider in Chapter 5) served as a referent for every other collectivity: being a good Hellenist was identified with citizenship in the Byzantine Empire and vice versa. These mutual orientations converged primarily around the centers. Third, the ideal of coalescence encouraged attempts to arrange the various collectivities in a hierarchical order, which proved a focus of struggle among their carriers or representatives.

Articulation of, and linkages among, the principal collectivities was the task of political and economic elites, as well as articulators of models of cultural order and representatives of the solidarity of the collectivities. It was these elites that impinged on the centers and the periphery alike and shaped the protest movements and political activities and struggle within the Imperial societies. And any of these elites—articulators of collective solidarity and of cultural models, political entrepreneurs—could launch a movement of change.

3. CULTURAL ORIENTATIONS OF IMPERIAL AND IMPERIAL-FEUDAL SOCIETIES

The Imperial and Imperial-feudal societies were also characterized by certain prevalent cultural orientations or codes. Most of these empires, with the partial exception of the Roman and Hellenistic, developed in close relation to a great civilization or tradition; for example, the Chinese blend of Confucianism, Taoism, and Buddhism;[44] the Christian tradition in its variety;[45] and the Islamic one.[46] Most of these great traditions emerged around the first millennium before Christ (in the so-called Axial Age)—the age of the Hebrew prophets, the Greek philosophers, Jesus and the Apostles, Confucius, the codifiers of the Brahmanic tradition, and the Buddha.[47]

These traditions or civilizations were carried by distinct groups and were represented in special cultural artifacts. They all made universal claims, which in principal (but often—above all, in the Chinese case—in principle only) transcended ethnic, regional, and political boundaries. And they shared several fundamental culture orientations. First, the cosmic (religious) and the mundane order were sharply distinguished although their mutual relevance and impingement were recognized. Second, a strong emphasis was placed on the transcendence of the cosmic order and on the necessity of bringing together, or bridging the gap between, the transcendental sphere and the mundane order. (This point applies also to the Chinese conception of cosmic order despite the fact that the Confucian system identified no transcendental God.) Third, a high level of commitment to both the cosmic and the social order was demanded. Fourth, emphasis was placed on the autonomous access of social strata to the cultural and social orders. Fifth, and of crucial importance to our discussion, some kind of this-worldly activity was identified in the political, military, cultural (especially in the European case), and economic spheres as a means to bring together the transcendental-cosmic and the mundane world, or, to use Weber's nomenclature, to achieve salvation.

Thus, the Imperial and Imperial-feudal societies emphasized the tension between the cosmic and the mundane world, as did the Hindu, Buddhist, and Islamic traditions, and they as much as the latter stressed this-worldly activity. However, the Christian and Chinese traditions focused on a greater variety of institutional spheres than did the Islamic.

Needless to say there were differences in the cultural orientations of the Imperial societies. Later on we analyze these differences in greater detail and relate them to differences in the patterns of change that we examined earlier.

4. STRUCTURE OF CENTERS. CENTER-PERIPHERY RELATIONS AND STRATA FORMATION IN PATRIMONIAL REGIMES. STRUCTURING OF COLLECTIVITIES

I

The patrimonial regimes,[48] unlike the Imperial and Imperial-feudal societies, displayed few symbolic or organizational differences between the center and the periphery. Such distinctions as existed reflected ecological and demographic peculiarities; for instance, greater population density in the center. The relatively low level of center-periphery differentiation was manifest most clearly in the nature of the links between the center and the periphery: these links led to few fundamental structural changes within either the periphery or the center.

The center impinged on local (rural, urban, or tribal) communities mainly to administer the law, preserve peace, collect taxes, and maintain cultural and/or religious links to itself. With very few exceptions, most of these tasks were performed through existing local units and subcenters (familial, territorial, and/or ritual). In these societies no attempt was made to create structural channels that would undermine, as was the case in the Imperial systems, the prevailing social and cultural patterns of either the center or the periphery. This can perhaps be most clearly seen in the legal activities: patrimonial rulers concerned themselves with criminal and administrative law and special religious laws but disregarded the development of civil and contractual law. In the latter areas, the centers tended to uphold local arrangements not to impose societywide legal and political frameworks and orientations.[49]

The conception of the center held in most patrimonial societies stressed its role as keeper of a static social and cosmic order, entrusted with this order and the well-being and integrity of the society. The activities and policies pursued by the central elites flowed from this conception.[50]

Thus, considerable emphasis was placed on regulating intergroup relations according to the prevailing criteria of justice, on maintaining adaptive relations with the external and internal environment, and on symbolizing the existing order. This emphasis found its fullest expression in the types of policies promulgated by patrimonial rulers. The central elites attempted first to secure a monopoly on symbolizing the direct relation between the cosmic and the social order, especially insofar as the symbols of these orders were related to political organization. Second, they attempted directly to control external relations or at least to control the external relations of the subunits of the society. Last, these elites focused on providing the component groups and strata of their societies with various internal adaptive facilities—especially for the mediation of conflicts and peacekeeping, on the one hand, and for the accumulation, provision, and distribution of economic resources, on the other.

Among these prescriptive and regulative policies of special importance were those aimed at the accumulation, in the centers, of available resources and the monopolization by the center of the distribution of surplus throughout the society. Insofar as the rulers of patrimonial regimes engaged in more active economic policies, these were predominantly, to use Bert F. Hoselitz's nomenclature, of an *expansive* nature—that is, directed at extending control over large territories—rather than *intrinsic*—characterized by intensive exploitation of a fixed resource basis. In addition, in Karl Polanyi's terms, these policies were redistributive.[51]

Thus, the central elites attempted to control the land either by outright ownership, in which case peasant families became tenants, and/or by supervising and controlling the transfer of land owned by kinship or other local units. In sharp contrast, the rules of centralized Imperial systems often attempted to weaken the position of the aristocracy by promoting a relatively free peasantry.

Activities of secondary importance to patrimonial elites were the development of symbols of a new common political and cultural identity, the crystallization of autonomous collective political goals, and the development of new types of intergroup relations and of frameworks regulating such relations. In the Imperial and Imperial-feudal societies and in the exceptional city-states, however, such concerns were vitally important.

The characteristic relations between center and periphery in patrimonial regimes greatly influenced the conception of the relation between political boundaries and cultural, social, or ethnic ones. With the partial exception (as we shall see) of certain Buddhist societies, there did not develop a strong emphasis on the ideological dimension of membership in different communities or on the necessity of convergence of these boundaries in one territorial framework around one territorial focus or center. Hence, there existed a relatively weak symbolic attachment to frontiers and to territory. However strong the attempts of the rulers to maintain the frontiers of their domain, these boundaries were but rarely perceived in terms of the cultural identity of the collectivity.

Both the center and the periphery in patrimonial societies could identify themselves with numerous points of reference, with manifold cultural and ethnic symbols, with several different great traditions, each having a unique territorial boundary. Regional, family, or other groups had diverse foci of territorial identity, often dividing their allegiance between, or shifting it to, different cultural or religious centers; hence, allegiance could quite easily be transferred from one territorial focus, or center, to another.

II

Closely related to these characteristics of center-periphery relations in patrimonial systems were those of the system of hierarchies and stratification that developed within them.[52] In general, the pattern was the relative weakness of independent strata—especially those of intermediate status—and the preponderance, within these strata, of bureaucratic elements. (The higher strata consisted primarily of oligarchic groups.)

The centers attempted to control the macrosocietal criteria and symbols of evaluation although they allowed, and even encouraged, component groups and strata to maintain—so long as they did not impinge on the macrosocietal level—autonomous though segregated status arrangements. The centers also encouraged or forced these collectivities not to attempt to convert their resources, especially prestige, into media that might have allowed participation in the broader societal settings.

Given the emphasis on such segregated status units as well as the center's desire to control access to the macrosocietal criteria and symbols of status (especially those that could facilitate access to the center), there tended to develop, on the one hand, numerous highly elaborated hierarchies of rank and position, which often were related to the differential access of various groups to the center. On the other hand, despite or perhaps because of the elaborate system of rank-hierarchy in the center or subcenter, strata with countrywide strata consciousness did not evolve. Instead, smaller groups—territorial, occupational, or local—became the major status units, tending strongly toward status segregation but little toward autonomous political orientations.

In short, the pattern of stratification and strata formation in the patrimonial societies was characterized by narrow status consciousness and weak societywide strata organization or consciousness; a very strong tendency toward separation of small family, territorial, ethnic, and political groups; the centrality of the family within the system of stratification; and emphasis on relatively specific styles of life restricted to certain sectors.[53]

Status segregation could be based on the self-conception of a given group as endowed with a special social standing, as upholding distinctive, local family or occupational traditions or life-styles that could be ascriptively defined and whose status orbit was often exclusively local. Or, it could be based on the ownership of particular resources.

Finally, the combination of a lack of structural distinction between center and periphery, of a high degree of status segregation, and of a relatively low level of symbolic articulation of societal components was connected with the lack of distinctiveness and autonomy on the part of secondary elites. The latter tended to be embedded in ascriptive groups; they were largely without symbolic and organizational autonomy, autonomous access to the center, and links among themselves.

5. PATTERNS OF INCORPORATION OF SOCIAL UNITS IN PATRIMONIAL REGIMES

The rulers of patrimonial societies also developed specific patterns of absorption of social units that were structurally different from those most prevalent in these societies.[54] We have noted the great importance of structural enclaves—economic or religious—in these societies. The ruling elites were indeed concerned with co-opting such enclaves, be they highly active, differentiated economic groups that could contribute to the extraction and accumulation of resources or differentiated religious orders, with more transcendental orientations, that could add to the luster of the centers.

However, co-optation was attractive only so long as an enclave was to a degree external to the structural core of the society, so long as these units did not impinge on the society's internal structural arrangements and especially on the relations between the center and the periphery. This fact explains the strong predisposition among patrimonial regimes to permit ethnically alien group, which could be segregated to a greater degree than indigenous elements, to engage in structurally more differentiated activities in the economic or religious spheres.

Such attempts at segregation differed greatly from those that were made in the more coercive Imperial systems. In the latter, the center attempted to control the access of component groups to broadly shared institutional frameworks and markets. The rulers of patrimonial systems sought above all to maintain an ecological segregation of these sectors, encouraging the tendency toward relatively closed, narrow markets.

6. CULTURAL ORIENTATIONS PREVALENT
IN PATRIMONIAL REGIMES

Most patrimonial regimes revealed some specific cultural orientations distinct from those characteristic of the Imperial and Imperial-feudal societies.

First, they generally did not recognize a tension between a higher, transcendental order and the social order. If this tension constituted an important element in the religious sphere proper, there was no concept of overcoming the tension through mundane activity (political, economic, or scientific) oriented toward reshaping or transforming the social and political order, i.e. through this-worldly activity.

Second, there was a strong emphasis on the *giveness* of the participation of all social groups in delineating the contours of the sociopolitical order—to the extent that such shaping was possible in traditional systems. The component groups and elites of these societies rarely regarded themselves as actively responsible for the shaping of these contours. On the contrary, they turned to magic and ritual to sustain existing social arrangements.

Third, patrimonial societies lacked commitment to a broader social or cultural order; this order was perceived as something to be mastered or adapted to but not as commanding a high level of commitment among those who participated in it or who were encompassed by it.

Fourth, and closely related to the preceding orientation, there was relatively little emphasis on the autonomous access of the constituent groups or strata to the principal attributes of the sociopolitical order. Usually, such access was seen as being mediated by actors (ascriptive groups or ritual experts) appointed by the center or subcenters and representing the given order.

Like the Imperial systems the patrimonial regimes—particularly those associated with high civilizations such as Buddhism and Hinduism—manifested variant patterns of change. Later we examine these differences at some length.

7. STRUCTURE OF CENTERS. CENTER-PERIPHERY
RELATIONS AND PATTERNS OF CONFLICTS,
CONTRADICTIONS, AND TRANSFORMABILITY
IN IMPERIAL AND PATRIMONIAL SYSTEMS

The preceding analysis explains in greater detail the different ways in which conflicts and contradictions developed in patrimonial and Imperial regimes. As we saw above, intergroup conflicts in patrimonial societies did not necessarily converge on the same ground rules and systemic contradictions, and the conflicts and contradictions concerning each type of ground rule or dimension of the macrosocietal order, while touching on others, did not necessarily impinge directly on them and above all did not impinge directly on the criteria of access to power and on the political center. In Imperial regimes, however, intergroup and interelite conflict tended to converge on different ground rules of social interaction, and the institutional contradictions related to one could profoundly affect those related to other ground rules or dimensions of the macrosocietal order. These differences in the structuring of conflicts and contradictions can be explained in terms of center-periphery relations in these two types of societies.

The continuity of patrimonial, tribal, and city-state regimes, given their characteristic center-periphery relations, was to no small degree predicated on balancing the structural and territorial groups of which they were composed.[55] A sharp increase in the power of any of these groups—a possibility dictated by the very nature of both the external environment and the internal process of political struggle—could easily disturb this balance.

Such disturbance could take place through intensification of the contradictions inherent in these regimes, which in their turn gave rise to new patterns of change. These cleavages were generated by regional and religious allegiances; by conflicts among strata within the periphery (especially between urban and rural sectors); or, (and most important) by conflicts and dissensions within the elite groups closest to the center or most active within it.

The concrete form of these cleavages differed greatly across patrimonial regimes; their salience in a given system was dependent on the degree to which they converged on the concrete links among segregated sectors.

Insofar as the links among societal sectors or the level of their political articulation did not change, the basic contours of the patrimonial regime did not change. Only where there developed powerful groups organized according to orientations and structural principles markedly different from those of the patrimonial regime and only where these groups generated new types of linkages among themselves did the changes that these contradictions produced give rise to new, nonpatrimonial systems.

This chain of events was most likely in regimes that manifested great heterogeneity of constituent units—especially where there were relatively strong, independent political or religious groups and elites to serve as foci for new charismatic orientations and centers, on the one hand, and/or commercial or manufacturing groups or free peasant communities to serve as a basis for more differentiated resources, on the other. Such forces fostered the transformation of patrimonial systems into Imperial or Imperial-feudal regimes.

Hence, the transformative capacities of most of these systems were evident not in the development of new structural principles bearing on all institutional spheres but rather in the direction of changes in different segregated units; in the multiplication of such units; and possibly in changes in their orientations (though not in the basic segregative principles of the society).

In the Imperial systems conflicts converged on the central nerve of the structuring of center-periphery relations; namely, the availability of free resources for the relatively wide markets of these societies and the ability of the rulers to control access to these markets.[56] The availability of resources and the ability of the rulers to control them could be easily undermined by the society's processes of change. The main factors generating processes of change in the empires were (1) the constant need of the rulers for different types of resources and especially their dependence on certain convertible resources; (2) the rulers' attempts to maintain their own positions of power in terms of both traditional legitimation and effective political control over the relatively free forces in the society (i.e., those not bound entirely by ascriptive ties); (3) the great sensitivity of the internal structure of these societies to external pressures and to political and economic developments in the international field; (4) the consequent needs of the rulers to step up the mobilization of certain resources in order to deal with problems arising out of changes in international military, diplomatic, and economic situations; and (5) the development of autonomous orientations and goals among the major strata and their demands on the rulers.

However, there developed strong contradictions among these five factors, especially insofar as the rulers sought very expensive goals that exhausted economic and human resources: eventually they found themselves facing several fundamental dilemmas. In such situations, the special sensitivities of the political system were brought out, and forces were generated that could upset the delicate balance between political participation and apathy, on which continuity of the system depended. This meant that the rulers' tendency toward maintenance of active control over different strata could become predominant, effectively checking the power of the relatively free strata and increasing the strength of traditional forces. This pattern could take a number of forms: the reluctance to have children, or *demographic apathy*, as it is sometimes called; the weakening of the more independent economic elements and their subordination to conservative, aristocratic-patrimonial (or feudal) elements; and the depletion or the withdrawal of capital.

Insofar as such policies and conflicts were not extreme, they could result in accommodable changes within the existing institutional patterns— that is, changes of dynasty connected with changes in administrative, political, and ministerial personnel. Where they were extreme, they could give rise to the transformation of the major principles of the regime—to sweeping changes in the social structure, for instance. Such changes manifested themselves in the emergence of new groups, in shifts in the relative strength and predominance of established groups, in alterations of the internal structure, composition, strength, and alignments of the principal groups and strata, in the restructuring of the symbols of the political regime, or in new levels of political articulation and access of these groups and elites. Where intensification of conflict was greatest, the system could become transformed into a modern or a patrimonial regime or become extinct.

Of course, Imperial and patrimonial regimes varied greatly in respect to both the degree to which the processes of change developed within them and the direction change took. In Chapter 5 we attempt to analyze some of these differences in a systematic way.

8. STRUCTURE OF CENTERS. CENTER-PERIPHERY RELATIONS AND STRATA FORMATION IN EXCEPTIONAL CITY-STATES AND TRIBAL FEDERATIONS

Center-periphery relations and the structure of social hierarchies within most city-states and tribal federations paralleled the patrimonial model. These societies also evinced little symbolic and structural difference between center and periphery; little mutual permeation and impingement; a high degree of status segregation with relatively weak strata consciousness; and the concomitant cultural orientations. But the pattern in the Greek city-states, in Rome, and in some of the Near Eastern—above all the Israeli and Islamic—tribal federations was markedly different. In these exceptional societies, center-periphery relations were characterized by a growing symbolic and structural (but not organizational) differentiation between the center and the periphery and by their mutual impingement, being in this way rather similar to the Imperial regimes.

But the structural differentiation between the center and the periphery was not, in both these types of exceptional society, fully institutionalized in special, continuous frameworks. This peculiarity was related, above all, as we shall see in greater detail later, to the size of the society and of its internal markets.

Lack of full institutionalization of the centers could be seen in the exceptional city-states [57] in the fact that while the society's central symbols and the offices concerned with the internal and external problems of the community were distinguished from the periphery, most members (citizens) of the community could participate in the center. Even when many groups enjoyed only limited participation, such limitations were not dissimilar from the social distinctions made within the periphery.

The most important structural outcomes or derivatives of this combination of structurally and symbolically distinct centers and overlapping memberships in the centers and the periphery were the relatively small degree of development of a special ruling class and specialized secondary elites as an autonomous social formation distinct from the leadership of different social groups and divisions.

In the exceptional tribal federations, religious, tribal, or changing political foci served as centers, but these centers were only rarely fully institutionalized.[58] Full institutionalization very often resulted in the transformation of exceptional tribal federations into patrimonial, feudal, or embryonic Imperial regimes. Most of these centers were structural enclaves within the tribal framework, enclaves that often were short-lived but nevertheless sometimes served as the nuclei of new, more differentiated social and cultural orientations and organizations.

Unlike the city-states, these exceptional tribal federations did not evolve into relatively unified though highly diversified communities with an elaborate division of labor. Unlike the patrimonial systems, these regimes did not develop a unified administrative and political framework to perform common tasks for a variety of structural units. Hence, the degree of dependence of these units on the common center was much smaller. The centers tended to emphasize (though haphazardly) the shared symbolic and external relations of these units and/or only to a lesser extent to regulate relations among the major groups in the society.

Whatever variations they exhibited, these centers were always composed of two structural elements that rarely coexisted peacefully or merged into more or less homogeneous social formations. The first such element consisted of the representatives of the various tribal or kinship units. The second such element consisted of special groups of elites. These special groups basically may have been, like the Levites of Israel or some of the semicastes of traders and ironmongers in Arabia, kinship or territorial units.

Out of these various elements of the center there developed only in embryonic form a specific, cohesive ruling class or other specialized elites having a clear conception of center-periphery relations. Among these groups continuous tensions and conflicts existed that together with other characteristics of the tribal frameworks weakened the institutionalization of the centers.

Indeed, among the different elements of which the centers were comprised there usually developed distinct conceptions of the nature and function of the centers in relation to other groups in the society. On the one hand, there was the conception of the center as performing certain given, mostly ritual, or at best intermittent political functions for the constituent parts of the federation and as governed entirely by the interests of these components. In this view the centers were merely an extension of the conceptions of centrality held by these units and of their ritual and political activities. On the other hand, the centers sometimes developed a conception of the sociopolitical and cosmic order that transcended the constituent units. Finally, within the more heterogeneous centers, there often arose new types of charismatic orientations that usually resulted from redefinition of the nature of the cosmic and social orders and of the relation between the two and that typically were developed by ritual, religious, or political elites.

9. CULTURAL ORIENTATIONS OF EXCEPTIONAL CITY-STATES AND TRIBAL FEDERATIONS

However weak the institutionalization of the distinctiveness of the center in the exceptional city-states and tribal federations, this distinctiveness was, as in the Imperial and Imperial-feudal societies, related to specific types of cultural orientations and political symbols.

Political symbolism in the exceptional city-states was based on several important assumptions.[59] The first, and perhaps most significant, was recognition of the autonomy of the moral order as distinct from the tribal or social order. This perception was coupled with a quest for the integration of these orders through the autonomy of the individual. It also brought with it recognition of the possibility of tension and conflict between the moral and social orders, as in the moral protest of the autonomous individual that is depicted in Greek tragedy. At the same time, this quest for integration was based on the conception of complete identity of the social and political order and on the assumption of totalistic participation of citizens in the body politic. This conception was usually extended to include the capacity of all citizens to represent the essence and center of the community.

It was in the more socially and culturally diversified city-states that these orientations ushered in the breakdown of some of the structural and symbolic limitations of traditionalism. This can be seen in the fact that the periphery was able to participate in the formation of the center and that the very contents of the sociocultural order were no longer regarded as given but as susceptible to conscious change.

While the beginnings of the breakdown of tradition took place in only a few of the city-states, they marked changes similar to those associated with modernity. But unlike the case of Imperial or Imperial-feudal societies and because of the institutional limitations of city-states (with which we deal later), in most cases the cultural orientations prevalent in the exceptional city-states and tribal societies did not generate institutional orders positively oriented toward change.

In the exceptional tribal federations parallel developments in the symbolic realm took place.[60] First was the perception of dissociation between the mundane and cosmic orders; growing rationalization of the conception of the cosmic order; and increasing emphasis on its transcendence. Accordingly, the mythical time dimension gave way to a more historical time sense. Second, the nature of the relations between this new type of cosmic order and the social-political order was redefined. The reformulated definition emphasized the need for the social order to be judged in terms of a transcendental model—which meant that political authorities became accountable to the representatives of the transcendental order.

These developments generated two different tendencies. The newly emerging political elite might attempt to control or monopolize the symbolization of the new cosmic order and of its representation. This tendency had the effect of moving the regime in an Imperial or Imperial-feudal direction. The second, and much stronger, tendency was transfer of the older tribal pattern of wide political participation to the new cosmic order—largely against the claims of the political elite. Here the symbols of political participation were translated into a more universalistic scheme. In this case, representatives of the older, true tribal order (tribal elders or heads of tribal subunits, for example) or the carriers of the new symbolic order (priests and especially prophets) conceived of themselves—not the political elite—as the carriers of the new cosmic order in its political-social implications. Each of these groups claimed a sort of symbolic, even structural, political primacy over the other and especially over whatever new political elite had developed within the new centers, thus generating new tensions that could not (for reasons we explain in Chapter 5) be institutionalized within the existing framework of these federations.

PART 3   ANALYTICAL CONCLUSIONS

1. CULTURAL ORIENTATIONS. SYMBOLIC ARTICULATION. INSTITUTIONAL STRUCTURE AND PATTERNS OF CHANGE

The analysis presented in the preceding sections pointed up the very close relation between, on the one hand, the degree of distinctiveness of the center, center-periphery relations, the principles of hierarchization, and the types of cultural orientation and, on the other hand, the degree of connection between institution building and manifestations of protest, the level of articulation and ideologization of central political struggle, and the coalescence of changes in the components of the macrosocietal order.

We saw that the tendency toward connection, articulation, and coalescence tended to be greater in those societies characterized by symbolic and institutional distinctiveness between the center and the periphery; a relatively wide, autonomous strata orientation and a multiplicity of autonomous secondary elites; and a cultural order that recognized a high level of tension between the transcendental and the mundane order, a relatively strong this-worldly orientation for resolution of this tension, and/or a high level of commitment to these orders, which were not taken as given.

Conversely, the tendencies toward relative segregation of movements of rebellion, heterodoxy, institution building, and political protest and struggle and toward nonuniformity in the rate and direction of change and restructuring of the components of the macrosocietal order were most pronounced in societies that manifested relatively little symbolic and institutional distinction between center and periphery; a strong tendency toward narrow status association and a small degree of autonomy of secondary elites; either a low level of distinction and tension between the transcendental and the mundane order or a high level of distinction combined with otherworldly resolution of tension between the orders; and a low level of commitment to the sociopolitical and even the cultural order and a tendency to accept them as given.

Thus, a closer look at the materials presented above reveals a close relation between certain aspects or types of cultural orientation and crucial features both of the structuring of institutions and of the patterning of organization and conflict—most notably, those features that are not given in the organizational division of labor but that are intimately associated with the ground rules of social interaction and their major institutional foci and derivatives (that is, center-periphery relations, the formation of social hierarchies and stratification systems, and the relatively wide institutional—as distinct from technological or ecological—scope of markets). How do we account for this correlation? A good starting point for explaining the relationship among cultural orientations, center-periphery relations, structures of social hierarchies, and movements and processes of change is the fact that, as our earlier discussion made clear, symbolic articulation of the fundamental problems of human existence goes hand in hand with symbolic and institutional distinctiveness of the major aspects of the social order.

A high degree of symbolic articulation of the data of human existence, of nature, of social life, means that these data are not regarded as given but are subject to questioning in any formulation of them.

This definition is akin to Clifford Geertz's definition of rationalization, which we quote: "the tendency to pose the basic problems of the major symbolic spheres in terms of growing abstraction of their formulation, of growing logical abstraction of their formulation, of growing logical coherence and general phrasing." [61]

Presentation of the data of human existence as problematic need not be couched in rational terms; it may, for instance, be mystic or esthetic.

Cultural orientations or codes differ in the extent to which they identify the data of human existence as given and accordingly accept or question them. Such problematic articulation is greatest where there is a perception of tension between the transcendental and the mundane order; a high degree of commitment to the sociopolitical order; when it is not accepted as given; and emphasis on this-worldly rather than other-worldly resolution of the tension between the transcendental and the mundane.

The materials presented in this chapter indicate that the higher the degree of symbolic articulation of the problematics of human existence, the greater also the symbolic articulation of the major aspects of social order (that is, of those aspects of the institutional structure that are not given in the organizational division of labor mentioned above). In societies in which these cultural orientations prevail, there tend to develop a higher level of distinction of the center and of its symbolic articulation of center-periphery relations; complex social hierarchies and systems of stratification; and relatively wide institutional markets. These societies likewise exhibit a high level of symbolic articulation of collective activities in general, of rebellions in particular; as well as a strong ideological component to political struggle. That is, such activities and organizations are formulated in broad symbolic terms, and they evince a high degree of linkages among themselves and of impingement on the centers of society.

Finally, and of special importance from the point of view of our analysis, these materials indicate that the greater the symbolic articulation of the problematics of human existence and of the components of the social structure, the stronger will be—other conditions being equal—the tendencies toward coalescence of the different types of rebellion, heterodoxy, and political struggle, as well as toward convergence among the rate and direction of change in all institutional spheres.

2. ORGANIZATION AND AUTONOMY OF INSTITUTIONAL ENTREPRENEURS AND ELITES. CULTURAL ORIENTATIONS. INSTITUTIONAL STRUCTURE. PATTERNS AND DIRECTIONS OF CHANGE

We have yet to explain the relationship between symbolic articulation of the data of human existence and patterns of change. To this end it is necessary to specify the actual social mechanisms and actors that carry change orientations into the institutional spheres. These actors are, first of all, institutional entrepreneurs and elites.[62] Most important among them are the manifold functional, political, economic, religious, and cultural entrepreneurs so often mentioned in the sociological literature; in addition, there are the articulators of models of cultural order and of the solidarity of the principal ascriptive solidarities (which may or may not develop with the different types of elites). Equally significant are the major institutional frameworks—regulative, legal, and communicative—in which these groups exercise their specific entrepreneurial or articulating activities. These entrepreneurs are, on the one hand, the most active carriers of the prevailing cultural orientations; on the other, as we noted in Chapter 2, various coalitions of these enterpreneurs or elites constitute the actors most active in crystallizing and upholding the ground rules of social interaction and their principal institutional derivatives. They do so above all by controlling the goals sought by different groups and categories of people; by controlling the access of different groups to the major markets; by converting their resources in various markets; and by constructing public goods and publicly distributing private goods.

These activities shape the institutional (as distinguished from the ecological or technological) scope of the major markets in the society; the access of these elites and other collectivities to each other and to the center; the institutional and symbolic articulation of the essential aspects of the institutional structure, different collective actions in general, and movements of rebellion, protest, and political struggle in particular; and the relationships among these collective activities. Societies at the same level of technology or organizational differentiation differ in these concrete contours. At work here are the unique characteristics of the elites, especially their multiplicity and their symbolic and institutional differentiation and autonomy, and the corresponding autonomy of the institutional, professional, legal, and communicative frameworks within which these elites uphold the cultural and social order and the principal ground rules of social interaction.

Such institutional autonomy is not concomitant with specialization and differentiation in terms of the social division of labor but rather with the autonomous symbolic definition and institutional bases of their respective spheres and activities. The opposite of this autonomy is not necessarily the nonexistence of specialized elite tasks but rather their embedment in broader ascriptive collectivities or networks or other institutional spheres and their subsumption under the symbols of these other collectivities and institutions.

It is the structure and autonomy of entrepreneurial activities that provide the crucial link between cultural orientations and institutional structure. On the one hand, this autonomy is greatly dependent on the types of symbolic orientation generated by the cultural codes and carried by these elites. On the other hand, the degree (and, as we shall see in Chapter 5, the specific institutional location too) of symbolic and institutional autonomy of these elites greatly influences both the way in which they perform their major regulative activities and the organization of collective activities and fundamental aspects of the institutional structure.

The crucial link between the degree of the autonomy of the institutional entrepreneurs, the main aspects of the institutional structure, and the processes of change is the scope of resources and activities not embedded in ascriptive collectivities and, hence, the scope of institutional markets (i.e., markets of money, prestige, and power) that cut across the major ascriptive communities, as well as the freedom of flow of such resources among the most important institutional markets of the society.

In sum, where the cultural codes generate a high degree of symbolic articulation of the problems of human existence, there will be a strong tendency toward autonomous elites and frameworks. And, the greater the autonomy of the institutional entrepreneurs, the wider the institutional scope of markets and of free resources within them and the freer the flow of such resources among markets.

Under such conditions, the greater is the autonomous control elites exercise over the process of conversion of the resources of major groups in the various markets; over their autonomous access to the markets; over their tendency to organize collective action, in general, and rebellions and political struggle, in particular, in relatively articulated and autonomous ways; over the autonomous access of such elites and collectivities to each other; over the linkages among them; and over their common convergence on the centers.

Conversely, the smaller the degree of symbolic articulation of institutional spheres, the narrower the scope of markets and free resources; the greater their embedment within ascriptive communities; the more limited the flow of free resources among them; and the smaller the degree to which these elites organize collective action in autonomous ways.

The autonomy of institutional entrepreneurs and of the linkages among them affect the structuring of the systemic contradictions that develop in a society and, accordingly, the degree of coalescence of changes and continuities in the components of the macrosocietal order. The greater their autonomy and the more developed the linkages among them—particularly important is that these linkages converge around common foci—the greater the coalescence in the direction of change and the restructuring of different components or dimensions of the macrosocietal order. Conversely, the weaker the linkages, the more dispersed the institutional loci of the ground rules of social interaction and systemic contradictions and the less the coalescence among the changes in the manifold dimensions of the macrosocietal order.

The relationship among cultural orientations, the structures of markets and of institutional entrepreneurs, and processes of change is threefold. First, questioning the data of human existence and the features of social organization generates potentialities for the development of alternative concepts of social, political, or cultural orders that may reverse, even transcend, existing arrangements. Second, the symbolic articulation of the essential aspects of the social organization tends to generate potentially free-floating resources; that is, sources or activities that are not entirely embedded, either organizationally or symbolically, in existing—above all, ascriptive—units and therefore are susceptible to redirection. Third, the more autonomous entrepreneurs can both activate the alternative conceptions of social order and serve as the organizers or mobilizers of newly freed resources, bringing together resources and activities from different spheres and crystallizing them in new directions.

Thus, it is the structure of these elites—specifically, their autonomy and the autonomy of the frameworks within which they act—that constitutes the key institutional link between symbolic articulation of the problems of human existence and symbolic articulation of the major institutional spheres and explains discrepancies among corresponding features of these spheres across societies, as well as the dynamics of change of different societies. Accordingly, the very activities and mechanisms that construct the central institutional framework of any given society may become the most important forces for change within it and to a very large degree shape its pattern and direction of change.

It is indeed a moot question (which at this stage of research we cannot answer) whether the emergence of different types of cultural orientations gives rise to these aspects of the structure of elites and collectivities or whether elites and collectivities with particular attributes or latent tendencies toward the development of certain attributes create or select the corresponding orientations. Probably, there is feedback through which groups or persons with a given structural tendency select consonant orientations; the institutionalization of these orientations reinforces the structural tendency.

The systematic study of these processes of selection and feedback is one of the most important tasks for comparative sociobiological research. But even at this stage of knowledge our materials attest to the close relationship between the structure of institutional entrepreneurs and the pattern of change that develops in a society.

Thus, we find in our examples, other conditions being equal, that the higher degree of symbolic distinction of the center and of strata formation and coalescent patterns of change in the Imperial, Imperial-feudal, and exceptional city-states and tribal federations were carried primarily by a multiplicity of autonomous elites—functional ones as well as representatives of the solidarity of different collectivities with relatively autonomous bases and potentially autonomous access to the center and to each other. This multiplicity of elites and their impingement on center and periphery alike greatly influenced the various movements of protest and the political activities and struggle within these societies.

Given the high level of institutional distinctiveness of the centers and of structural differentiation in general, there developed within these societies a much greater number of movements of protest, whether peasant rebellions, cliques, or broad social movements. Similarly, the great traditions to which most of these systems were connected provided an important breeding ground for religious sects, heterodoxies, and general intellectual movements. Furthermore, any of the numerous secondary elites (articulators of collective solidarity and articulators of cultural models and traditions) and secondary political entrepreneurs with some orientation to both the periphery and the center could become a starting point for a movement of protest or for political struggle.

In contrast, patrimonial, city-state, and tribal regimes lacked structural distinction between center and periphery and manifested a high degree of status segregation, little organizational and symbolic articulation of movements of rebellion, and weak linkages among themselves and with the center. This combination of features was associated with a relatively low level of symbolic articulation of different collectivities and secondary elites; a high degree of embedment of institutional entrepreneurs in ascriptive groups with little symbolic and organizational autonomy or autonomous access to the center or linkages among themselves; and hence noncoalescent patterns of change.

Truly enough, these broad patterns exhibited considerable variation—very closely related to differences in cultural orientation, structure of elites, and environment. In Chapter 5 we undertake the analysis of these differences.

NOTES

1. On these societies and civilizations see R. H. Hall, "The Keftians, Philistines, and other Peoples of the Levant," in *The Cambridge Ancient History*, vol. 2, eds. J. B. Bury, S. A. Cook, and F. E. Adcock (Cambridge: At the University Press, 1940), 275–295; C. J. Gadd, "The Cities of Babylonia," in ibid., vol. 1, eds. I E. S. Edwards, C. J. Gadd, and N. G. L. Hammond, third ed., 1971, pp. 93–144; G. Contenau and R. Grousset, *Les Premières Civilisations*, 3d ed. (Paris: Payot, 1935); G. Contenau, *La Vie quotidienne à Babylone et en Assyrie* (Paris: Hachette, 1950); idem, *La Civilisation d'Assur et de Babylone* (Paris: Payot, 1937); S. Moscati, *The Face of the Ancient Orient* (Garden City: Doubleday, 1962), esp. chaps. 2, 3, 5; L. J. Wiseman (ed.), *People of the Old Testament* (Oxford: Clarendon, 1973); H. Kees, *Ägypten: Kulturgeschichte des alten Orients* (Munich: C. H. Back, 1933), pp. 201 ff.; L. Delaporte and C. Huart, *L'Iran antique* (Paris: Albin Michel, 1943); M. Ehtecham, *L'Iran sous les Achéménides* (Fribourg, 1946); and M. and J. J. M. Roberts (eds.), *Unity*

and Diversity: Essays in the History, Religion, and Literature of the Near
East* (Baltimore: Johns Hopkins Press, 1975).

2. A. Christensen, *L'Iran sous les Sassanides* (Copenhagen: Levin and
Munksgaard, 1936); idem, "Sassanid Persia," in *Cambridge Ancient History*, 12:109–137; R. P. de Menasce, "L'Eglise mazdéenne dans l'Empire
sassanide," *Journal of World History*, 2 (1955): 554–565; F. Altheim,
Reich gegen Mitternacht (Hamburg: Rowohlt, 1955); F. Altheim and R.
Stiehl, *Ein asiatischer Staat: Feudalismus unter den Sassaniden und ihren
Nachbarn* (Wiesbaden: Franz Steiner, 1954); A. Christensen, *Le Règne
du roi Khawadh et le communisme mazdakite* (Copenhagen: Munskgaard,
1925); also *The Cambridge Medieval History*, 9 vols. (Cambridge: At
the University Press, 1933–1936, and L. Halpern, *Charlemagne et l'Empire
Carolingien* (Paris: Albin Michel, 1949).

3. G. J. Resink, *Indonesia's History between the Myths: Essays in Legal History and Historical Theory* (The Hague: W. van Hoeve, 1968); L. P.
Briggs, "The Ancient Khmer Empire," *Transactions of the American Philosophical Society*, 41, pt. 1 (1951): 1–75; P. Pelliot, *Mémoire sur les
coutumes du Cambodge de Tcheon Takouan* (Paris: Librairie d'Amérique
et d'Orient, 1951); S. G. Morley, *The Ancient Maya*, 3d ed., rev. G. W.
Brainerd (Stanford: Stanford University Press, 1956); G. W. Brainerd,
"Changing Living Patterns of the Yucatan Maya," *American Antiquity*,
22, no. 2 (1956): 162–164; W. R. Bullard, "Maya Settlement Pattern in
Northeastern Peten, Guatemala," ibid., 25, no. 3 (1960): 355–372; D. H.
C. Dobby, *Southeast Asia* (London: University of London Press, 1956);
G. Groslier, *Recherches sur les Cambodgiens* (Paris: A. Challamel, 1921),
pp. 21–23; F. W. Riggs, *Thailand: The Modernization of a Bureaucratic
Polity* (Honolulu: East-West Center Press, 1966); and L. P. Briggs,
"The Hinduized States of Southern Asia: A Review," *Far Eastern Quarterly*, 7, no. 4 (1948): 376–393.

4. Moscati, *Face of the Ancient Orient*, esp. chaps. 2, 3, 5; and the materials
cited in note 3 above.

5. On the general characteristics of traditional Imperial systems see S. N.
Eisenstadt, *The Political Systems of Empires* (New York: Free Press
Paperback, 1969).

6. See A. E. R. Boak, *History of Rome to 565 A.D.* (New York: Macmillan,
1955); R. Syme, *The Roman Revolution* (Oxford: Blackwell, 1939); and
W. W. Tarn and G. T. Griffith, *Hellenistic Civilization* (London: Methuen,
1953).

7. On the Chinese Empire see E. O. Reischauer and J. K. Fairbank, *A History of East Asian Civilization*, vol. 1, *East Asia, the Great Tradition* (Boston: Houghton Mifflin, 1960), chaps. 2–10; W. Eberhard, *A History of
China* (London: Routledge & Kegan Paul, 1950); E. Balazs, *Chinese
Civilization and Bureaucracy: Variations on a Theme* (New Haven: Yale
University Press, 1964); D. Bodde, "Feudalism in China," in R. Coulborn
(ed.), *Feudalism in History* (Princeton: Princeton University Press, 1956),
pp. 49–92; W. Eberhard, *Conquerors and Rulers: Social Forces in Medieval China* (Leiden: E. J. Brill, 1952); Ping-ti Ho and Tang Tsou (eds.),

China's Heritage and the Communist Political System: China in Crisis (Chicago: University of Chicago Press, 1968), 1:1–448. O. Lattimore, *The Inner Asian Frontiers of China* (New York: Capitol, 1951); M. Elvin, *The Pattern of the Chinese Past* (London: Eyre & Methuen, 1973); and W. E. Willmott (ed.), *Economic Organization in Chinese Society* (Stanford: Stanford University Press, 1972).

8. On the Byzantine Empire see L. Brehier, *Les Institutions de l'Empire byzantin* (Paris: Albin Michel, 1949); idem, *La Civilisation byzantine* (Paris: Albin Michel, 1950); J. M. Hussey, *Church and Learning in the Byzantine Empire, 867–1185* (New York: Oxford University Press, 1937); idem; "The Byzantine Empire in the Eleventh Century: Some Different Interpretations," *Transactions of the Royal Historical Society*, 32 (1950): 71–85; G. Ostrogorsky, *History of the Byzantine State* (Oxford: Blackwell, 1956); C. Diehl, "The Government and Administration of the Byzantine Empire," *Cambridge Medieval History*, 5:726–744; and E. Stein, "Introduction à l'histoire et aux institutions byzantines," *Traditio*, 3 (1949–1951): 113–138.

9. B. H. Summer, *A Short History of Russia* (New York: Harcourt, Brace, 1949); and R. Pipes, *Russia under the Old Regime* (London: Weidenfeld & Nicolson, 1975).

10. On the Islamic states and civilizations see P. M. Holt, A. K. S. Lambton, and B. Lewis (eds.), *The Cambridge History of Islam*, 2 vols. (Cambridge: At the University Press, 1970); M. G. S. Hodgson, *The Venture of Islam: Conscience and History in a World Civilization*, 3 vols. (Chicago: University of Chicago Press, 1974); B. Lewis, *The Arabs in History* (London: Hutchinson, 1950), pp. 64–115; W. Muir, *The Caliphate: Its Rise, Decline, and Fall* (London: Religious Tract Society, 1924); A. Metz, *The Renaissance of Islam* (London: Luzac, 1937); H. Laoust, *Les Schismes dans l'Islam: Introduction à une étude de la religion musulmane* (Paris: Payot, 1965); B. S. Turner, *Weber and Islam: A Critical Study* (London: Routledge & Kegan Paul, 1974); M. A. Shaban, *The Abbasid Revolution* (Cambridge: At the University Press, 1970); and H. A. R. Gibb, *Studies on the Civilization of Islam* (Boston: Beacon, 1962), pp. 3–46, 141–150.

11. H. Inalcik, *The Ottoman Empire: The Classical Age, 1300–1680* (London: Weidenfeld & Nicolson, 1973); P. Wittek, *The Rise of the Ottoman Empire* (London: Royal Asiatic Society, 1938); A Lybner, *The Government of the Ottoman Empire* (Cambridge: Harvard University Press, 1913); and W. L. Wright (ed. and trans.), *Ottoman Statecraft* (Princeton: Princeton University Press, 1935).

12. M. Beloff, *The Age of Absolutism* (London: Hutchinson, 1954); J. O. Lindsay (ed.), *The New Cambridge Modern History* (Cambridge: At the University Press, 1957), vol. 7; G. Pagès, *La Monarchie d'Ancien Régime en France* (Paris: Armand Colin, 1946); G. Zeller, *Les Institutions de la France aux XVIᵉ siècle* (Paris: Presses universitaires de France, 1948); P. Sagnac, *La Formation de la société française moderne* (Paris: Presses universitaires de France, 1945), 1:50–147; F. L. Ford, *Robe and Sword:*

The Regrouping of the French Aristocracy after Louis XIV (Cambridge: Harvard University Press, 1953), esp. vol. 2, pp. 79–104; M. Ashley, *England in the Seventeenth Century* (Baltimore: Penguin, 1952); F. L. Carsten, *The Origins of Modern Prussia* (New York: Oxford University Press, 1954); H. Rosenberg, *Bureaucracy, Aristocracy, and Autocracy: The Prussian Experience, 1600–1815* (Cambridge: Harvard University Press, 1958), pp. 46–88; G. Clark, *The Seventeenth Century* (Oxford: Clarendon Press, 1950); idem, *Early Modern Europe, 1450–1720* (New York: Oxford University Press, 1957); and B. Barber and E. G. Barber (eds.), *European Social Class: Stability and Change* (New York: Macmillan, 1965).

13. D. Bodde, "Feudalism in China," in R. Coulborn (ed.), *Feudalism in History*, pp. 49–92; M. Bloch, *Feudal Society*, trans. L. A. Manyon (Chicago: University of Chicago Press, 1961); J. Prawer and S. N. Eisenstadt, "Feudalism," in D. L. Sills (ed.), *The International Encyclopedia of the Social Sciences*, 17 vols. (New York: Macmillan and Free Press, 1968), 5:393–403; D. Hintze, *Wesen und Erbreitung des Feudalismus: Sitzungsberichte der Preussischen Akademie der Wissenschaften* (Berlin: Philologische-Historische Klasse, 1929), pp. 321–347; and O. Brunner, *Neue Wege der Verfassungs- und Sozialgeschichte*, rev. ed. (Göttingen: Vandenhoeck & Ruprecht, 1968), pp. 128–159.

14. C. Nakane, *Japanese Society* (London: Weidenfeld & Nicolson, 1970); D. M. Earl, *Emperor and Nation in Japan: Political Thinkers of the Tokugawa Period* (Seattle: University of Washington Press, 1964); J. W. Hall, *Japan from Prehistory to Modern Times* (London: Weidenfeld & Nicolson, 1970); J. W. Hall and M. B. Jansen (eds.), *Studies in the Institutional History of Early Modern Japan* (Princeton: Princeton University Press, 1968); and J. W. Hall and P. J. Mass (eds.), *Medieval Japan: Essays in Institutional History* (New Haven: Yale University Press, 1974).

15. See on these societies Syme, *Roman Revolution;* L. Homo, *Roman Political Institutions* (London: Routledge & Kegan Paul, 1962); A. W. Gomme, *Essays in Greek History and Literature* (New York: Oxford University Press, 1939); M. T. Finley, *The Ancient Greeks* (New York: Viking, 1963); A. W. Gomme, "The Working of the Athenian Democracy," *History*, 36 (1951): 12–28; and V. Ehrenberg, *The Greek City-State* (Oxford: Blackwell, 1960).

16. See Moscati, *Face of the Ancient Orient*, esp. chaps. 2, 3, 5.

17. On ancient Israel see T. J. Meek, "Moses and the Levites," *American Journal of Semitic Languages and Literature*, 56, 2 (1939): 113–120; M. Greenberg, "A New Approach to the History of the Israelite Priesthood," *Journal of the American Oriental Society*, 70, 1 (1950): 41–46; R. de Vaux, *Ancient Israel* (London: Downton, Longman & Todd, 1961); A. Alt, *Essays in Old Testament History and Religion* (Oxford: Blackwell, 1966); V. Nikiprowetzky, "Ethical Monotheism," *Daedalus*, a special issue on "Wisdom, Revelation, and Uncertainty," Spring 1975, pp. 69–90: H. H.

Ben-Sasson (ed.), *A History of the Jewish People* (Cambridge: Harvard University Press, 1976), pt. 1; and Roberts, *Unity and Diversity*, pp. 169–191.

For some comparative data see H. Rosenfeld, "The Social Composition of the Military in the Process of State Development in the Arabian Desert," *Journal of the Royal Anthropological Institute*, 95 (January-June 1965): 75–86.

18. On the concept of patrimonialism as developed here, which stresses not only the organization of power and administration, in the Weberian tradition, but also the overall institutional structure of society, see S. N. Eisenstadt, *Traditional Patrimonialism and Modern Neo-Patrimonialism*, Sage Research Papers in the Social Sciences, Studies in Comparative Modernization, no. 90–003 (Beverly Hills, 1973). A somewhat more narrow definition can be found in G. Roth, "Personal Rulership, Patrimonialism, and Empire Building in the New States," in S. N. Eisenstadt (ed.), *Political Sociology* (New York: Basic Books, 1971), pp. 575–582.

19. These patterns and trends of change are fully illustrated in the literature presented in note 18 above. See also J. C. van der Leur, *Essays in Asian Social and Economic History: Indonesian Trade and Society* (The Hague: Van Hoeve, 1955); B. Schrieke, *Ruler and Realm in Early Java: Selected Writings of B. Schrieke*, in Indonesian Sociological Studies (The Hague, 1957); O. W. Wolters, *Early Indonesian Commerce: A Study of the Origins of Srivijaya* (Ithaca: Cornell University Press, 1967); M. A. P. Meilink-Roelofsz, *Asian Trade and European Influence in the Indonesian Archipelago between 1500 and about 1630* (The Hague: M. Nijhoff, 1962); D. J. Steinberg (ed.), *In Search of Southeast Asia* (New York: Praeger, 1971); and E. R. Leach, "The Frontiers of Burma," *Comparative Studies in Society and History*, 3 (October, 1960): 49–68.

20. See for instance Moscati, *Face of the Ancient Orient;* as well as the references cited in notes 1–2 above.

21. On general trends see the works cited in notes 3–4 above; see also Steinberg, *In Search of Southeast Asia;* more detailed data are presented in Chapter 5. (See pages 134–39).

22. See, on this, Schrieke, *Ruler and Realm;* Van der Leur, *Indonesian Trade and Society;* Moscati, *Face of the Ancient Orient;* and notes 1, 3, and 5–18 to Chapter 5.

23. For general information on political struggle and rebellions in these societies see the references cited in notes 1–4 above.

24. B. R. O. Anderson, "The Idea of Power in Javanese Culture," in C. Holt (ed.), *Culture and Politics in Indonesia* (Ithaca: Cornell University Press, 1972), pp. 1–70; S. Kartodirdjo, "Agrarian Radicalism in Java: Its Setting and Development," in ibid., pp. 71–125; T. Stern, "Ariya and the Golden Book: A Millenarian Buddhist Sect among the Karen," *Journal of Asian Studies*, 27, no. 2 (1968): 297–327; G. J. Resink, *Indonesia's History between the Myths: Essays in Legal History and Historical Theory* (The Hague: Van Hoeve, 1968); H. J. Benda, "Peasant Movements in Colonial Southeast Asia," *Asian Studies*, 3, no. 3 (1965): 420–434; idem, "The

Structure of Southeast Asian History: Some Preliminary Observations," *Journal of Southeast Asian History*, 3, no. 1 (1962): 106–138; and F. Hills, "Millenarian Machines in South Vietnam," *Comparative Studies in Society and History*, 13 (July 1971): 325–350. See also M. Osborne, *Region of Revolt: Focus on Southeast Asia* (New York: Pergamon, 1970); J. van der Kroef, "Javanese Messianic Expectations: Their Origin and Cultural Context," *Comparative Studies in Society and History*, 1 (June 1959): 299–323; and W. H. Rassers, *Panji, the Culture Hero: A Structural Study of Religion in Java* (The Hague: M. Nijhoff, 1959).

25. See the data in the works cited in notes 1–4 and 24 above; see also R. Heine-Geldern, *Conception of State and Kinship in Southeast Asia*, Cornell University, Asian Program Data Paper no. 18 (Ithaca, April 1956), pp. 1–13; P. Wheatley, *City as Symbol* (London: Lewis, 1969); and idem, *The Pivot of Four Quarters: A Preliminary Inquiry into the Origins and Character of the Ancient Chinese City* (Chicago: Aldine, 1971).

26. On such changes see Van der Leur, *Indonesian Trade and Society;* Schrieke, *Ruler and Realm;* Wolters, *Early Indonesian Commerce;* Meilink-Roelofsz, *Asian Trade and European Influence;* and P. Wheatley, "Satyānrta in Suvarnadvīpa: From Reciprocity to Redistribution in Ancient Southeast Asia," in J. A. Sabloff and C. C. Lamberg-Karlovsky, eds., *Ancient Civilization and Trade* (Albuquerque: University of New Mexico Press, 1975), pp. 227–283.

27. On the concept of Imperial systems see Eisenstadt, *Political Systems of Empires*, esp. pp. vii–xxii.

28. See Ostrogorsky, *History of the Byzantine State.*

29. These aspects of the political systems and of processes of change in them are analyzed in detail in Eisenstadt, *Political Systems of Empires*, esp. chap. 12, in which fuller bibliographical references are given.

30. These processes are fully documented in ibid., esp. chaps. 11 and 12.

31. On the relations between political and religious organizations in the Imperial systems see S. N. Eisenstadt, *Tradition, Change, and Modernity* (New York: Wiley, 1973), chap. 8; and idem, *Political Systems of Empires*, chap. 4.

32. On the economic conditions and processes of Imperial systems see Eisenstadt, *Political Systems of Empires*, chap. 3.

33. Ibid.; and see the materials cited in notes 5–13 above.

34. See in detail ibid., chaps. 7–11.

35. For illustrations of all these processes see ibid., chaps. 10, 12; as well as the literature cited in notes 5–13 above; and in notes 19–70 to Chapter 5.

36. This is analyzed in detail in ibid., chaps. 11 and 12, and illustrated in the materials cited in note 35 above.

37. See the literature cited in note 15 above.

38. See the literature cited in note 15 above; and in notes 46–56 to Chapter 5; see also E. Gellner and C. Micaud (eds.), *Arabs and Berbers: From Tribe to Nation in North Africa* (London: Duckworth, 1973).

39. See A. Fuks, "Patterns and Types of Social-Economic Revolution in Greece from the Fourth to the Second Century B.C.," *Ancient Society,* 5 (1974): 51–81; A. Heuss, "Das Revolutionsproblem im Spiegel der antiken Geschichte," *Historische Zeitschrift,* 216, 1 (1973): 1–72; see also S. N. Eisenstadt, Introduction to chapter 6 of S. N. Eisenstadt (ed.), *Political Sociology* (New York: Basic Books, 1970), pp. 178–185, and the readings cited therein.

40. See Fuks, "Patterns and Types of Social-Economic Revolution"; and Heuss, "Das Revolutionsproblem."

41. The center-periphery relations in Imperial systems were first discussed in Eisenstadt, *Political Systems of Empires,* pp. vii–xxii.

42. The analysis of the structuring of hierarchies in these societies was first presented in S. N. Eisenstadt, *Social Differentiation and Stratification* (Glencoe: Scott, Foresman, 1971), chap. 6.

43. The symbolic structuring of the collectivities in the empires is fully illustrated in, for instance, Ostrogorsky, *History of the Byzantine State;* Balazs, *Chinese Civilization;* and the other historical works cited in notes 5–14 above.

44. On Chinese civilization see Reischauer and Fairbank, *East Asia;* Balazs, *Chinese Civilization;* Ho and Tsou, *China's Heritage;* D. S. Nivison and A. F. Wright (eds.), *Confucianism in Action* (Stanford: Stanford University Press, 1959); A. F. Wright (ed.), *Studies in Chinese Thought* (Chicago: University of Chicago Press, 1953); and J. K. Fairbank (ed.), *Chinese Thought and Institutions* (Chicago: University of Chicago Press, 1957).

45. On the varieties of Christian tradition see, at this stage of our discussion, F. Heer, *The Intellectual History of Europe* (Garden City: Doubleday, 1968); and the various articles on "Christentum" in *Die Religion in Geschichte und Gegenwart,* 3d ed. (Tübingen: J. C. B. Mohr, 1961), 1:1685–1721.

46. On Islamic civilization see the works cited in note 10 above; see also G. E. von Grünebaum, *Medieval Islam: A Study in Cultural Orientation* (Chicago: University of Chicago Press, 1946); idem (ed.), *Studies in Islamic Cultural History, American Anthropological Association,* 86, 2 (1954); and C. J. Adams, "The Islamic Religious Tradition," in J. O'Dea, T. O'Dea, and C. J. Adams, *Religion and Man: Judaism, Christianity, and Islam* (New York: Harper & Row, 1972), pp. 159–221.

47. On general developments in this realm see E. Voegelin, *Order and History,* 4 vols. (Baton Rouge: Louisiana State University Press, 1954–1974); and *Daedalus,* Spring 1975.

48. On patrimonial regimes see Eisenstadt, *Traditional Patrimonialism.*

49. On legal policies of patrimonial systems see ibid., pp. 34–35. For a good illustration see G. Vernadsky, "The Scope and Contents of Chingis Kahn's Yasa," *Harvard Journal of Asiatic Studies,* 3 (1938): 337–380.

50. On the conceptions of the centers and of social and religious order in patrimonial societies see H. D. Evers, *Kulturwandel in Ceylon* (Baden-Baden: Lutzeyer, August 1964); E. Sarkisyanz, *Buddhist Backgrounds of*

the Burmese Revolution (The Hague: M. Nijhoff, 1965); C. F. Callagher, "Contemporary Islam: A Frontier of Communalism, Aspects of Islam in Malaysia," *American University Field Staff Reports,* Southeast Asia Series, vol. 14, no. 10 (Washington, D.C., 1966); J. Peacock, *Rites of Modernization: Symbols and Social Aspects of Indonesian Proletarian Drama* (Chicago: University of Chicago Press, 1968); R. N. Milton, "The Basic Malay House," *Journal of the Royal Asiatic Society* (Malay branch), 29, no. 3 (1965): 145–155; J. M. Pluvier, *Confrontations: A Study in Indonesian Politics* (New York: Oxford University Press, 1965); and B. Anderson, "The Language of Indonesian Politics," *Indonesia,* no. 1 (1966): 89–116.

51. B. F. Hoselitz, *Sociological Aspects of Economic Growth* (New York: Free Press, 1960); K. Polanyi, C. M. Arensberg, and H. W. Pearson, *Trade and Market in Early Empires* (New York: Free Press, 1957).

52. For patterns of hierarchies in patrimonial societies see especially H. D. Evers (ed.), *Loosely Structured Social Systems: Thailand in Comparative Perspective,* Yale University, Southeast Asia Studies Cultural Report Series, no. 17 (New Haven, 1969). See also L. H. Palmier, *Social Status and Power in Java,* London School of Economics Monographs on Social Anthropology, no. 20 (London, 1969). For the technical meaning of the term "prestige" as it shall be employed here and in subsequent analyses see Eisenstadt, *Social Differentiation,* pp. 29–34.

53. See Eisenstadt, *Traditional Patrimonialism,* pp. 40–50; F. W. Riggs, *Administration in Developed Countries* (Boston: Houghton Mifflin, 1964); and idem, *Thailand.*

54. On the pattern of incorporation of enclaves in patrimonial regimes see the references cited in note 26 above.

55. These segregative tendencies are analyzed in somewhat greater detail in Eisenstadt, *Traditional Patrimonialism,* pp. 75–77.

56. The crucial importance of free-floating resources in the Imperial systems is analyzed in Eisenstadt, *Political Systems of Empires,* esp. chaps. 2, 6, and 12.

57. See the materials cited in note 15 above.

58. See, in addition to the materials cited in notes 38–39 above, C. Meier, *Entstehung des Begriffs Demokratie: Vier Prolegomena zu einer historischen Theorie* (Frankfurt am Main: Suhrkamp, 1970); and idem, *Res Publica Amissa: Eine Studie zur Verfassung und Geschichte der späten römischen Republik* (Wiesbaden: Franz Steiner, 1966).

59. On the political symbolism of ancient city-states see the works cited in note 58 above; Fuks, "Patterns and Types of Social-Economic Revolution; and Voegelin, *Order and History,* vols. 1–3.

60. On political symbolism in tribal federations see Voegelin, *Order and History,* vol. 1, and the reference cited in note 40 above.

61. C. Geertz, *The Interpretation of Cultures* (New York: Basic Books, 1973), pp. 171–172.

62. On the concept of institutional entrepreneurs see the discussion in Chapter 2 (page 32–33).

Chapter 5.   The Variability of Patterns of Change and Transformation in Traditional Societies—Some Selected Cases

PART 1   PATTERNS OF CHANGE IN PATRIMONIAL REGIMES

1. VARIABILITY OF CULTURAL ORIENTATIONS. TYPES OF ENTREPRENEURS AND PATTERNS OF CHANGE

In Chapter 4 we demonstrated through comparison of Imperial systems, patrimonial regimes, exceptional city-states and tribal federations how different formulations of the problems of human existence, generated by the perception of tension between the transcendental and the mundane order and by commitment to these orders, influence the structure of secondary elites and thereby the major institutional derivatives of the ground rules of social interaction (especially the structure of centers, center-periphery relations, strata formation, and patterns of change).

In this chapter we explore more systematically the relationship between cultural orientations, on the one hand, and institutional structure and patterns of change, on the other. The cultural orientations we examine are the locus of the resolution of tensions between the transcendental and the mundane order—above all, the interweaving of this-worldly and otherworldly orientations in the delineation of this locus; and the perception of autonomy of access among broader strata to the major attributes of the cosmic and the social order, or conversely the degree to which access is mediated or monopolized by some group or by the center. We also analyze the impact of the more specifically social codes such as the strength of power orientations in the political realm and the relative emphasis on instrumental or solidary orientations in social life.

2. CHANGE IN PATRIMONIAL REGIMES.
BUDDHIST SOCIETIES

Let us look at how cultural orientations influence the location of the activities of the principal institutional entrepreneurs and through this the construction of different institutional constellations and patterns of change.

The first variation we analyze was common among the patrimonial, city-state, and tribal regimes related to religions or traditions that did not stress the tension between the cosmic and mundane orders and those regimes connected to the great traditions that emphasized this tension, particularly religious systems having a strong otherworldly orientation such as Buddhism [1] and Hinduism. These great traditions, and their local variants, were carried by relatively autonomous, often international elites such as the Buddhist Sangha—and to a smaller degree the Zoroastrian clergy [2]—the like of which could not be found among the little traditions.

These elites created centers that in the religious sphere were distinct from their own periphery, as well as special interlinking networks between these centers and the periphery, and between great and little traditions. In this way, they provided a new dimension in the definition of the local political community, adding a higher level of symbolic articulation, a broader orientation to broader cultural dimensions. This new dimension served as basis and framework for the crystallization of specific symbols and boundaries of collective identity, of national communities. Accordingly, these national collectivities often evinced, as did the religious traditions, a much greater continuity than the political regimes.

But, given the strong otherworldly emphasis of these great traditions, above all Buddhism, these cultural orientations did not generate distinctiveness in the political centers and in the relations between these centers and their periphery, nor did they tend to produce far-reaching restructuring of other institutional spheres. Truly enough, these autonomous religious groups, especially the Sangha in Buddhist societies, participated in political life. [3] The basis of this participation was their organizational dependence on the rulers' quest for legitimation. But such participation was set mostly within the frameworks of the various patrimonial regimes, in which these elites often became politically very powerful.

These religious elites did sometimes enter into coalitions with the articulators of the solidarity of local or supralocal communities—coalitions with the king himself or leaders of ethnic collectivities, adding to the latter, as we already have seen, a new, broader dimension.

These orientations and their institutional impacts also explain some of the characteristic differences between patterns of change in these societies and patterns of change in other patrimonial regimes, tribal federations, city-states, and Imperial systems. [4] To wit, rebellions tended to have relatively well articulated millenarian orientations, and there developed broad heterodox movements that sometimes became connected with political groups (these political groups did not manifest a high level of articulation of their goals). Similarly, there arose within these societies large-scale religious heterodoxies, the symbols of which sometimes became connected with the symbols of broader solidarities; this process resulted often in the construction of new symbols of political-religious membership and political community. Nevertheless, these symbols, which usually served as legitimators of change, were only rarely actively involved in the restructuring of political regimes, nor were they connected over the long run with popular rebellions. In a few popular uprisings against alien or "bad" rulers political rebellions and religious heterodoxies did join forces temporarily.

3. CHANGE IN OTHERWORLDLY CIVILIZATIONS. INDIA

I. Cultural Orientations. Ecology and Structure of Centers.
Social Hierarchies and Institutional Entrepreneurs

The situation in the Hindu civilization of India was rather different. Like Buddhism, which started as a heterodox sect within Hinduism, the latter was an otherworldly great civilization; yet its negation of the mundane world was not as total as that of Buddhism.[5]

Hinduism, as most fully articulated in the Brahmanic ideology and symbolism, is based on recognition of tension between the transcendental and the mundane order—tension that derives from a perception that the mundane order is polluted in cosmic terms. This pollution can be overcome through ascriptive ritual activities that identify social purity with cosmic purity and through adherence to the arrangement of social ritual activity in a hierarchical order that reflects an individual's standing in the cosmic order.

Accordingly, Hinduism emphasizes the differential ritual standing of social units called castes and of the occupations or tasks tied to these units; this religion arranges mundane activities in a hierarchy based on their otherworldly significance vis-à-vis eliminating the pollution of the mundane order and ensures the transmission of such differential ritual standing through the basic, primordial, kinship units. In all these ways it has a much more direct relation to worldly activities than Buddhism.[6]

Given this strong articulation of the tension between the cosmic and the mundane order, there did develop, within the Hindu civilization, a distinctive center, the ideological core of which was the Brahmanic ideology and symbolism. But because of its otherwordly emphasis, its wide ecological spread, and its strong embedment in ascriptive primordial units, this center was not organized as a homogeneous, unified setting or organization. Rather, it consisted of a series of networks and organizational-ritual subcents—pilgrimages, temples, sects, schools—throughout the subcontinent, often cutting across political boundaries.[7]

The religious center or centers became very closely associated with the broad, ethnic Hindu identity (even more closely associated than the religious symbols and symbols of political community in Buddhist societies). The vague, general, yet resilient boundaries of Hindu ethnic identity constituted the broadest ascriptive framework within which the Brahmanic ideology could be worked out.

At the same time, however, as in the other otherworldly religions, the major center of Hinduism was not political. Accordingly, center-periphery relations in most Indian principalities and kingdoms did not in themselves greatly differ from such relations in other patrimonial regimes, city-states, or tribal federations. The various political centers although organizationally more compact than the ritual centers were not permanent—regimes rose and fell—nor did they serve as major foci of Indian cultural identity. The political units and centers that developed in India were relatively weak in terms of the major orientations of the cultural system and the commitments they could command thereby. Hindu India's essential religious and cultural orientations, then, were not necessarily tied to any particular political framework. This was true not only in the last centuries of Moslem and later English rule but also earlier.

Although there arose in India small and large states and semi-Imperial centers, there did not develop any single state with which the cultural tradition was identified. Classical Indian religious thought did of course have a lot to say about the problem of policy, about the behavior of princes, and the duties and rights of subjects. But, to a much higher degree than that in many other historical civilizations, politics was viewed in secular terms, which emphasized its distance from the ideological center of the civilization, its traditions, and identity.[8] This fact gave Indian civilization its internal strength and explained its capacity to survive under alien rule.

The relative independence of the cultural traditions, centers, and symbols of identity from the political center was paralled by the relative autonomy of the social structure—the complex of castes and villages and the networks of cultural communication.[9] These kinship and caste groups were the major socializing agents, the major foci of status and collective identity, and the major channel for transmission of ascriptive access to fundamental institutional positions. They were also the carriers of a type of linkage among occupational position, political power, and ritual status characteristic (as we see below) of the structuring of social hierarchies in the Indian caste system. Finally, these kinship and caste groups were composed of numerous, often crosscutting units organized in multiple networks of various caste and subcaste groups. These groups and networks were to a very high degree autonomous and self-regulating in terms of their own cultural and social identity, as well as in terms of their economic, social, and religious interrelations, having but limited recourse to the political center or centers.

All these factors affected the process of strata formation in Indian society. First, because of the emphasis on the link between family units and ritualistic-cosmic standing, differences in life-style among the many status groups, or castes, were normative and rigid. The rules of caste specified the proper symbolic consumption of resources and rights of access to the major institutional positions.

Second, because of the emphasis (reinforced by ritual) on ascription and heredity, there was a very strong connection between kinship groups, on the one hand, and status identity and organization, on the other. As we have seen, kinship group was simultaneously a major socializing agent, focus of collective identity, and channel for transmission of ascriptive access to fundamental institutional positions. Intercaste mobility was almost totally precluded by the rules that governed marriage.

Third, occupational positions were inextricably linked to ritual status. Every occupation—agricultural laborer, landowner, artisan, or merchant— was clearly assigned to one of the four major status (caste) categories: the Brahmans, the Rejanya or Kshatrya (warrior-rulers), Vaishya (merchants), and the Sudras (servants). This practice was closely connected with a strong tendency to place the lowest groups (the Untouchables) beyond the pale of the system.

It was within these groupings and networks that there developed the major types of institutional entrepreneurs and elites: political and economic entrepreneurs and articulators of models of cultural order and of ascriptive solidarity. Their entrepreneurial activities were structured by the two fundamental aspects of Indian social life. On the one hand, these activities were rooted in and defined by the combination of ascriptive, primordial, and ritual characteristics; on the other hand, such definitions strongly emphasized the appropriate performance of mundane activities. Hence, entrepreneurial activities were bound up with (but not entirely identical to) the articulation of the solidarity of the major ascriptive groups and to a smaller degree the principal cultural models. These two aspects of Indian society generated a powerful motivation for innovative entrepreneurial activities in the appropriate institutional sphere.[10]

These organizations and activities were based on a combination (within each caste group) of ownership of different resources and control over their use and conversion. Thus, full control was achieved only through intercaste relations.

II. The Institutional Framework

Out of the multiplicity of centers and networks throughout the subcontinent, the distinction between the religious or ethnic (Indian) and the political centers, on the one hand, and the structure of entrepreneurial activities, on the other, there developed one of the most complex institutional frameworks in the history of mankind.

The first specific characteristic of this institutional framework was the discrepancy between the Brahmanic ideology of cultural and social order and the concrete patterns of social organization that evolved in connection with this ideal—and the implications of this discrepancy for the institutional contours of Indian society.

In theory, the castes were defined as countrywide, and, therefore, in principle they engendered a countrywide caste consciousness and organization. In practice, however, there was no such uniformity, just as no identity among functions, positions, ritual standing, and use of resources was assumed in the official ideology. (Interestingly, it was the British who, by incorporating caste classification into their census, gave the sharpest push to the establishment of a unified hierarchy.)

Of course, the Brahmanic ideology and system of worship was in a sense India-wide and served, as we indicated above, as a focus for the overall cultural identity of the society. Moreover, among many Brahman groups (as well as among other, especially higher castes) there evolved to a limited degree very wide, if not countrywide, social contacts and networks. But on the whole the basis of caste organization and interrelation was local or regional.

The ideal of the caste division of labor, focused on a countrywide ritual order, could not be applied on the regional or local level amid the diversity of ecological and political settings. With regard to the use of both political power and money, there developed, on this level, a great variety of activities that could not be entirely bound by the official ritual caste prescriptions. First of all, there was no perfect correspondence between occupational positions and caste. The number of occupations was vast, and diversification of job categories tended to create independent local or regional hierarchies of status that could undermine the standing of local groups of Brahmans. These anomalies could serve as starting points for the crystallization of new caste groups, often changing the interrelations and mutual obligations among different castes although usually upholding the major symbols of the caste order.[11]

The limits of the pure ideological pattern, in which the political order was subservient to the ritual, were most evident in the relation between the Brahmans and the political powers. While the subservience of the rulers to the Brahmans remained true on the ideological level, the actual dependence of any given group of Brahmans on the political rulers for upholding their status was very great. In many cases, if not most, it was up to the rulers to define the relative ritual standing of the caste groups. Hence, they were able both to gain concessions from the Brahmans and to change the conditions of access to the higher ritual and nonritual positions, thereby weakening the closed styles of life and the segregation of different status (caste) groups.[12]

III. Patterns of Mobility

Out of the combination of characteristics of Indian civilization previously enumerated and the discrepancy between the Brahman's ideology, and its concrete application, there evolved a multitude of channels of mobility as well as special motivational aspects to mobility. Given the fundamental premises of Indian civilization, such mobility was mostly group—caste—mobility, and as M. S. Srinivas and many others have shown there were at least two types of mobility.[13] In the case of *simple* mobility, various caste groups attempted to improve their relative (mostly local) position in the economic and political spheres. In the case of *Sanskritization,* caste groups tried to improve their standing according to the central value system by attempting to assimilate into their life-styles certain aspects of Brahmanic ideology and culture, thus hoping to attain higher legitimate standing in the ritual field.

Common to both these types of mobility were two mechanisms or bases. The first mechanism was the multiplicity of reference orientations and structural channels of advancement that evolved in Indian society and the relative devaluation, in terms of the central components of Indian cultural identity, mundane—economic and political—activities. The second mechanism was the development of different levels of motivation; that is, the partial ideological dissociation between ultimate commitment to the religious sphere on the one hand, and commitment to the mundane sphere, on the other hand, together with a steady, secondary ideological stress on the importance of mundane activities.

These mechanisms created the possibility of directing motivation into secondary institutional channels without undermining the parameters of the sociocultural order. They generated a very strong tendency toward structural change, toward this-worldly—economic, political—activities (which were at the same time devalued), but they lessened the likelihood of new types of linkages between the mundane and the religious sphere that would transcend the premises of the Brahmanic ideology.

IV. Patterns of Change

It was within this institutional and ideological framework that there developed the movements of change and the relation between rebellion and heterodoxy, on the one hand, and broader institutional changes, on the other, specific to Indian civilization. Given the religious orientation of this civilization and its complexity, India frequently produced religious movements or sects with either universalistic-transcendental tendencies (like the Bhakti movement) or more traditionalistic–ritually militant ones. Both types of religious movement tended to take up and reformulate basic elements of Indian culture, especially the Brahmanic ideal and the ideal of renunciation, or Sannyasa.[14]

One of the distinctive characteristics of these movements, as compared with religious heterodoxies that developed elsewhere in otherworldly civilizations—above all, Buddhism—was the creation of specific though limited links between them and the processes of institutional change and institution building.

Many of India's movements of change were rooted in specific castes: political movements especially in the Kshatriyas; economic ones especially in the Vaishyas. These movements generated important changes in the institutional spheres in which these castes were especially active. Moreover, these putative religious movements often became closely connected with major structural components of the processes of change in Indian society, particularly, with the processes of village, region, and caste change and caste mobility, with the crystallization of new caste groups, and with the continual restructuring of caste activities and boundaries.

Significantly, there was a constant crosscutting of structural and ideological tendencies; that is, conservative ideological movements might join forces with structural, innovative ones. For example, new princes or merchant groups might ally themselves with orthodox religious sects. Conversely, reformist religious movements sometimes coalesced with forces favoring Sanskritization.[15]

V. The Interweaving of Change and Continuity

Throughout Indian history the specific characteristics of the processes of change encouraged a strong propensity for piecemeal innovation within different institutional spheres. Such innovation was closely connected with developments in the religious sphere but the latter always preserved its central symbols of identity. Thus, India witnessed the rise of new organizational settings, the redefinition of political units, changes in technology and in levels of social differentiation, some restructuring of the economic sphere, and changes in social and economic policies as well as changes in the religious sphere itself (manifest above all in the development of new movements and sects of which the Bhakti of the sixteenth century was probably the most important).[16]

Throughout the traditional period in Indian history (i.e., up to about the nineteenth century) this high level of generation of change and adaptability to it remained consonant with the basic premises and symbols of Indian tradition. The continuity of the central symbols of cultural identity and the relation between the collective identity and these symbols was always maintained. The processes of change never went beyond either the dominant evaluation of the dimensions of human existence (cosmic, ritual, political, economic) or the basic relations between the ritual-religious sphere, on the one hand, and the economic and political sphere, on the other.[17] Hence, these processes were in but very few cases connected with restructuring either the political sphere or relations between the political and economic spheres and the religious sphere.

The ideal of renunciation, a major aspect of Brahmanism, while setting up a new focus of commitment, did not lead to upgrading the secondary institutions or linking them to the ultimate level of sociocultural reality and identity.[18] This ideal did not generate new types of motivations or orientations that could tie activities in the nonreligious spheres to the fundamental parameters of Indian cultural identity. None of India's movements or activities of change produced new linkages between the mundane and the religious sphere.

To sum up, traditional Indian civilization exhibited great heterogeneity in the structural-organizational aspects of its institutional spheres together with continuity in its parameters and identity. All these processes explain the very high level of general change in Indian civilization and its adaptability to change—as well as the limits of this adaptability.

PART 2   PATTERNS OF CHANGE IN IMPERIAL AND IMPERIAL-FEUDAL SYSTEMS

1. INTRODUCTION

Imperial and Imperial-feudal systems developed fully only in those high civilizations or great traditions that stressed the tension between the transcendental and the mundane order and identified this-worldly activities as a means of overcoming this tension (granted, embryonic Imperial systems developed in ancient Persia and in the Empire of Ashoka).

But beyond this common core there developed various Imperial systems which differed with respect to the institutional working out of these cultural orientations, and especially in the interweaving of this-worldly and otherworldly orientations; in the delineation of the institutional foci of each of these orientations; as well as with respect to their combination with other cultural orientations, and especially with the degree of autonomy of access of broader strata to the major attributes of the economic and the social order (conversely, the degree to which such access was mediated or monopolized by some group or by the center); and, in the more specifically social codes or cultural orientations, the relative strength of power as against solidary or instrumental orientations.

These systems varied also in terms of certain crucial aspects of the processes of change within them. Above all, they differed in the extent to which tendencies toward the merging of the many types of movements of protest, institution building, and political struggle were given expression. Indeed, it was but rarely that there developed in the traditional Imperial systems a full merging of these movements and of the restructuring of the dimensions of the macrosocietal order. As in all other traditional societies, in the Imperial systems these tendencies toward coalescence were countered by fundamental traditional orientations, by limited levels of structural resources, as well as by attempts of the ruling elite to weaken them and to segregate these different types of activities.

But unlike patrimonial rulers, Imperial rulers were not always successful, and the tendencies toward coalescence resulted either in the partial transformation of the empires or in their demise. Several factors operated here. At this stage of our analysis we shall concentrate on one such factor; namely, the different constellations of the cultural orientations mentioned above. First we shall analyze how variations in these constellations influenced the major orientations of central elites and entrepreneurial groups, the foci of their institutional activities, the extent to which different entrepreneurial activities were combined in the same roles or organizations, the scope of their autonomy, the nature of their solidary relations with the center and with broader strata, the extent to which the ownership of resources overlapped with control over their use and conversion in the macrosocietal setting, and thereby the processes of center and strata formation as well as the movements and processes of change that characterized the Imperial and Imperial-feudal systems. Second, we shall consider how ecological settings interacted with these orientations, their institutional derivatives, and the processes of change.

2. THE RUSSIAN EMPIRE

I. Cultural Orientations. Structure of Centers and of Institutional Entrepreneurs

Within the late (post-Mongol) Muscovite variant of Christian civilization [19] the center succeeded in attaining a relatively high degree of subordination of the cultural to the political order and a relatively low degree of autonomous access of the major strata to the principal attributes of the social and political orders. The political sphere became the monopoly of the rulers; the economic sphere became less central, and economic activities were left to proceed autonomously as long as they did not impinge directly on the center.

In this context the center tried to monopolize activities that were of central importance from the point of view of the maintenance of the cosmic and social orders—above all, political activities; however, the broader strata were granted autonomy in other mundane—primarily economic—activities without being permitted significantly to imbue them with wider meanings in terms of the basic parameters of the cultural-political spheres.[20]

To this end, the center rigorously segregated access to the attributes of the cosmic order (salvation), which was given to all groups of the society with comparatively weak mediation by the Church, from access to the attributes of the political and social orders, which were after the post-Mongol period almost totally monopolized by the political center. Furthermore, the center kept separate the loci of this-worldly resolution of the tension between the transcendental and the mundane order.

Religious heterodoxies became otherworldly oriented and/or dissociated from the political sphere. However, sometimes, as in the case of the True Believers, they focused to a degree on the economic sphere.[21]

In order to maintain its monopoly, the center had to wage war against those strata (above all, the aristocracy and the free city-states) that were, especially in the earlier Kievan period, the carriers of a more autonomous access to the attributes of the social and cosmic orders. This struggle gave rise to a very strong power orientation and coercive policies on the part of the center. The major mechanism through which the center attained its goals was forced segregation between the political power elites, which were also the articulators of the cultural order especially in its political dimensions, the various institutional elites, and the articulators of the models of the nonpolitical cultural order, on the one hand, and the economic and educational elites and the articulators of the solidarity of the major ascriptive collectivities, on the other. Specifically, access of these elites to each other and especially to the center was limited by the central political elite—although not entirely successfully. Hence, the ownership of resources, vested in various social groups, was sharply separated from control over their use and conversion, which was vested in the center—a control that minimized the importance of the existence of multiple centers of potential power.

II. Strata Formation

A parallel trend can be discerned in the process of strata formation in Russia.[22] The center also attempted to control the goals and identities of the main groups and strata in the society. Establishing and maintaining the attributes and conditions that referred to participation in the center remained perquisites of the center. So did the sanction and regulation of most other attributes, even those that referred mainly to peripheral spheres of action. But in general the elite tended to be relatively permissive about the use of such resources for different segregated desiderata and goals as long as the latter did not impinge on access to the central power positions, did not appear ostentatious, and did not tend to create too great a demand for new skills. (Such a demand could have resulted in the formation of numerous new and independent positions that in turn could have become foci of independent central markets or of new collective identities.)

The center did not encourage these groups to develop the rigid styles of life sanctioned by its own norms and symbols. On the contrary, it minimized the legitimation of such styles of life and instead encouraged a rather indiscriminate dispersal of these groups' resources. If a member of a peripheral group succeeded in getting into the symbolic and power structure, he had to give up his convertible resources, which left him in a relatively weak bargaining position vis-à-vis the major holders of power (the Imperial court and ultimately the Tsar).

The various mechanisms that upheld the predominance of the center until the end of the nineteenth century affected the process of strata formation in several ways. The most general effect was the relative lack, throughout Russian society in this period, of class consciousness and class organization, a lack most evident among the lowest group, the peasantry. There was almost no way of expanding the peasants' local collectivities into a wider framework despite some tradition of informal association for various purposes among peasants of neighboring villages and regions.

Nor were urban groups very different in this respect. One important indicator of their weakness was their ineffective organization, even among the so-called middle-class occupations. Every occupational group and guild was completely dependent, for the development of its organization, on the official sanction of the center. Thus, the self-identity of most of these groups had a narrow occupational and geographical basis. They seem to have been concerned with the wider society only to the extent that the legislation of the center compelled them to be.

To a somewhat lesser degree, lack of class consciousness and weak class organization characterized the aristocracy. This was true even though the aristocracy had a much higher social standing and a much greater control of resources than any other group. Moreover, by virtue of its proximity to the center, as well as the survival of its semifeudal traditions, the aristocracy enjoyed more countrywide links than the urban middle classes or the peasantry. Whatever autonomy this group managed to retain from the pre-Absolutist period was shattered by the Tsars, who succeeded in transforming it into a service aristocracy. Such autonomy as the Russian aristocracy later developed represented essentially a voluntary concession by the Tsars. Only at the end of the eighteenth and the beginning of the nineteenth century did this situation begin to change.[23]

A related feature of the Russian system was that a closed, normatively prescribed style of life did not develop within most of these status groups although customary patterns of course developed, especially among the aristocracy and certain urban groups. Similarly, the peasantry, living in village communities, tended to follow traditional patterns of life. But these patterns were on the whole neither wholly regulated by internal or external normative sanctions nor upheld as models and symbols by those who participated in them. Among the aristocracy living in the capital, normative prescriptions tended to develop as by-products of state service and participation in court life, but this was far less true of aristocrats who lived on their own domains. Thus, there were few, if any, normative restrictions on aristocrats' engagement in business (like those, for instance, in prerevolutionary France).[24]

The relative lack of a normatively prescribed style of life could be seen in the patterns of intergroup marriage: the available evidence (meager though it is) indicates that the crossing of class boundaries was not uncommon. The preceding analysis seems to be borne out by what little we know of movement from one social stratum to another. Given the relatively free use of resources (which we have already noted), the main impediment to social mobility was not a lack of ability or willingness to use resources to acquire higher positions but the legal status of certain groups, especially the serfs. Insofar as there was mobility, it usually gave rise to new patterns of local and occupational group life that were just as segregated as the old ones. Thus, the overall pattern remained largely intact.

Of special importance in this context was the Orthodox church, the major channel of mobility from the lower strata. But it seems that the basic pattern of mobility was repeated here, too. Entrance into the Church's orders entailed breaking family ties and renouncing one's style of life, but it did not offer compensatory opportunities for forming links with other strata. In theory, the Church provided access to the center and therefore to political power; however, in practice it was not permitted to become an independent entity either politically or socially.[25]

The same constraints applied to mobility into the aristocracy and the bureaucracy although unique characteristics distinguished such movement. Specifically, since the rulers had almost total control of initial access to the bureaucracy, upward mobility in this sphere had to be sponsored by the ruler or by somebody acting on his behalf. Accordingly, at this level there was an obvious dissociation between the family as a primary agent of socialization, on the one hand, and as a provider of ascriptive access to high positions, on the other. Although in principle most scions of the aristocracy were expected to enter some sort of government service (civilian or military), the decisions as to who should enter was not theirs but the Tsar's.

All these characteristics converged in the structure of center-periphery relations. Among Imperial societies the Russian regime was characterized by one of the lowest levels of autonomous access and impingement of the periphery on the center. At the same time the center permeated the periphery to a relatively high degree in order to mobilize resources, assure its commitment to and identification with the center, and to control broader, societywide activities. Consequently, the policies developed by the Russian center were mainly regulative and coercive; there was little autonomous expression of the goals of broader groups.

III. Patterns of Change

These combinations and implementations of the basic cultural orientations, as well as the nature of the major elites and their interrelations greatly influenced the processes of change in Tsarist Russia.[26]

The center itself, strongly oriented from at least the period of Peter the Great to modernization, generated far-reaching processes of economic and social change. Faced with these changes, the center continually shifted among three orientations: (1) promotion of modernization culminating in the liberation of the peasants under Alexander II; (2) encouragement of relatively autonomous developments in the economic sphere; and (3) control of all these developments, especially their political expressions or repercussions. Here again the major mechanisms of control were regulation of autonomous access of the various groups to the center; conversion of economic into political resources; and maintenance of segregration of the major strata and institutional entrepreneurs.

While the center could not, given the strong emphasis on the tension between the transcendental and the mundane order, eliminate among different potential institutional entrepreneurs and collectivities certain autonomous orientations to the essential attributes of the cosmic and social order, it attempted to curb the autonomous political expression of such orientations and above all the possibility of linkages among various types of social protest and between them and potential institutional elites.

For a very long time the Russian center was very successful in these attempts. Accordingly, it minimized the transformative potentialities of Russian society. But, as we shall see later, this success had far-reaching consequences in terms of the nature of the Russian revolutionary elites and the outcome of the revolution.[27]

3. THE BYZANTINE EMPIRE

The Russian Empire may be very briefly compared within the earlier Byzantine Empire,[28] with which it shared some of the basic cultural pressures and orientations of Eastern Christianity. The Byzantine Empire did not experience anything so dramatic as the Mongolian conquest, which created in Russia the preconditions for weakening the autonomous orientations and structures of the major strata. Unlike the Russian, the Byzantine center was unable entirely to eliminate the autonomous access of the major strata to the attributes of the cosmic and social order and to divert the more active orientations of these strata either into otherworldly activities or into activities with no political implications. Nor was the Byzantine center able to segregate this-worldly and otherworldly orientations of different groups, strata, and elites to the same extent as the Russian center although this attempt was often made, and the religious supremacy of the Emperor over the Patriarch was the official doctrine of the Byzantine Empire and church.[29]

Cultural-religious orientations did not become as totally subjugated to the political sphere as happened in Russia, and the Church, oriented as it was toward otherworldly activities, never became politically as fully controlled as the Russian one. Similarly, strata such as the aristocracy and the peasantry enjoyed relatively more autonomous access to the center and combined ownership of resources with some control over their use, thereby generating multiple bases of political power. Byzantine society was also characterized by greater autonomy of secondary elites and stronger linkages among them and the broader strata.[30]

The Byzantine Empire consequently displayed a higher degree of coalescence among the various movements of protest and political struggle than Russia exhibited, and the Byzantine system evinced a relatively high degree of internal transformability, of internal restructuring especially with respect to changes in the strength of Imperial and aristocratic rulers and the free peasantry. Indeed, the very intensity of this struggle led to the ultimate demise of this Empire.

4. THE CHINESE EMPIRE

I. Cultural Orientations and Structure of Centers
A different constellation of cultural orientations, center-periphery relations, structures of entrepreneurs, and patterns of change developed in the traditional Chinese Empire.

China's Confucian-Taoist-Buddhist-Legalist tradition as compared to monothestic religion was characterized by a somewhat weaker stress on the tension between the transcendental and the mundane order; a very weak conception of a historical-transcendental time dimension; a strong this-worldly focus of overcoming the tension between the mundane and the transcendental; and a relative openness or flexibility in its formulation as well as in its accessibility to broader strata.[31]

The contents of this tradition were conceived as fixed in a static pattern of basic precepts and orientations. Yet in several aspects the Confucian system was among the most open ever to occur in a traditional society. First of all, it was not a system of revealed religion and had no fixed theological dogma or image of an all-demanding deity. Second, under Confucianism the cultural order was conceived ideally as encompassing all strata and parts of the population, almost all mankind, and it was open to everyone through to different degrees. In actuality, this ideology was very closely tied to the political framework of the Chinese Empire. The Empire was legitimized by the Confucian symbols, and the Confucian symbols and the Confucian ethical orientation found their natural place and framework, their major referent, within the Empire. Thus, in sharp contrast for instance to the Indian social and cultural order, China, of all the great Imperial civilizations, manifested the closest interweaving, almost identity, of cultural and political centers.

The Chinese tradition was probably the most this-worldly of all the great traditions. Connected with the Imperial system, the official Confucian-Legalist framework tolerated otherworldly orientations of folk religious sectarianism or private speculation, but its thrust was the cultivation of the sociopolitical and cultural orders as the major focus of cosmic harmony.[32] It emphasized this-worldly duties and activities within the existing social framework—the family, broader kin groups, and Imperial service—and the connection between proper performance of these duties and the ultimate criteria of individual responsibility. Of course, the tradition also emphasized individual responsibility, along with a strongly transcendental orientation, but this responsibility was couched largely in terms of the importance of the political and familial dimensions of human existence.[33]

Moreover, the Chinese tradition, as enunciated in the official ideology of the center, did not distinguish between the societal order represented by the center and that represented by the various types of peripheral collectivities. There existed also a basic affinity between the symbols of the center and the status identities of the peripheral groups. Orientation (not entirely passive) to the center and to participation in it constituted an essential component of the collective identity of many local and occupational groups. The Chinese tradition also was characterized by somewhat more flexible access, on the part of the more active groups, to the center even if the center itself was relatively monolithic.

All these orientations greatly influenced the structure of the Chinese center and of the major elites and strata in Chinese society. The Chinese center was an absolutist one in terms of both political and cultural orientations, each of which constituted an independent basis of access to the center and each of which had certain solidary ties to the periphery but attempted to control the channels of this solidarity. This control was manifest above all in the fact that the macrosocietal system of stratification was focused entirely on the political-cultural center. The Imperial center, with its strong Confucian orientation and legitimation, was the sole distributor of macrosocietal prestige and honor. Various social groups or strata did not develop autonomous status orientations except on a purely local level; the major, almost the only, wider orientations were bound to this political-religious center.[34]

II. Strata Formation

The process of strata formation in China was characterized by three features. First, there developed a strong emphasis on the general affinity between the central and the peripheral groups as members of one cultural order. Second, this emphasis on participation in the cultural order tended to limit the number of ascriptive positions vis-à-vis central positions. Third, the central elites attempted to regulate not only the collective goals and identities of various strata and groups but also their use of the resources at their disposal. To this end, the central elites prohibited such use for direct access to the center, directing the resources toward channels that they monopolized. For instance, the many peripheral collectivities were officially encouraged to have some of their members participate more actively in the center by taking examinations and graduating as literati.[35] Thus, in China as in Russia, the ownership of resources was dissociated from control over their use.

These institutional arrangements had four important consequences for the process of strata formation in Chinese society.

1. A relatively clear ideological evaluation of different occupational positions developed; this evaluation was based on their ideological proximity to the basic tenets of the Confucian order. The literati, and to some extent the gentry, had the highest prestige, followed by the peasants. The merchants and the military had less prestige; vagabonds, beggars, entertainers, and so on, the least.

2. The official picture of society enshrined in the Confucian ideology was complemented by a strong normative definition of the styles of life and collective identities of different social strata. Part of this style of life, in each case, was a strong orientation toward the center and toward participation in it.

3. Family groups not only served as the chief agents of socialization but also cultivated distinctive styles of life that related to the social strata or localities to which they belonged (in contrast to the role of family groups in Russia). Although there was a strong correlation between family status and rights of access to the center, this was never fully legitimized and—as in Russian society—was not automatic. At the same time, because of the importance of kinship in Chinese society, the fact that kinship units were oriented toward the center was a major incentive behind participation in it.[36]

4. The uppermost groups (the literati and the bureaucracy) developed a high degree of countrywide class consciousness and solidarity. This consciousness was rooted in the common cultural tradition, the sharing of avenues of access, and the fact that these avenues—the schools and the academies—were to some extent independent of the center although very strongly oriented to it. (This common consciousness resulted in a measure of autonomous organization on the part of the various schools and academies.)

Because of their distance from the center and their lack of direct access to it, the merchants and the other urban groups could not evolve a broad class consciousness. In China as in Russia, these groups never coalesced into a common stratum although there were of course many ties among localities. The same absence of class consciousness characterized the Chinese peasantry, which lacked adequate channels of communication and access to the center. (Such access although officially encouraged was not granted to the peasantry as a corporate entity but only to individuals who were nonrepresentative members.)

Closely related to the development of class consciousness was the process of mobility in China. As is well known, China did not have a hereditary aristocracy of the European type; its highest group was the bureaucracy, which anyone could enter by passing examinations in the literary classics. China's was a sponsored type of mobility, directed at the attainment of positions within a rigid institutional framework. The same situation existed to some extent in Russia, but in China the effects of sponsored mobility on interstrata relations were quite different. At least from the peasants' point of view, and no doubt from that of other groups as well, there was greater continuity between the life-styles of the groups from which mobile persons originated and those that they later joined.[37] Thus, social mobility in Imperial China was probably one of the major mechanisms underlying the stability of the Confucian system.

III. Major Institutional Entrepreneurs. The Literati

Of crucial importance in the linkage between the center and the periphery in general and in the process of strata formation in particular was the structure of the major group connecting the Imperial center to the broader society: the literati,[38] that is, all those who took the Confucian examinations or studied for them. This elite was a relatively cohesive collection of groups and quasi-groups that shared a cultural background enhanced by the examination system and by adherence to Confucian teaching and rituals. This elite, which was relatively widespread, was in principle recruited from all strata, even the peasantry. In fact, most literati were members of the gentry. Its organizational framework was almost identical with that of the state bureaucracy (which encompassed ten to twenty percent of all the literati), and except for some schools and academies it had no organization of its own. Moreover, political activity within the Imperial-bureaucratic frameworks was a basic referrent of the Confucian ethical orientation.

As indicated above, the literati exercised a virtual monopoly over access to the macrosocietal order and over control of the conversion of resources in the macrosocietal setting. But this control was based not only on coercive orientations and measures (as in Russia) but also on solidary ties. The linkages between the solidarity of the broader groups and those of the center were controlled by the literati, which resulted in broader groups having little autonomy of access to the center and in the interweaving of the solidarity of the periphery with that of the center.

The literati constituted a source of recruitment to the bureaucracy that maintained firm ties to the strata and combined within itself the activities of political elites and of articulators of models of cultural order besides enjoying close relations with the articulators of the solidarity of collectivities (the heads of family and of wider kinship groups). Its special position and orientation to both the center and the broader strata permitted it to fulfill certain crucial integrative functions in the Imperial system, enabling the literati to influence the political activities of the rulers as well as those of the leading strata of the population. The literati exerted this influence by upholding the ideal of a hierarchical social-cultural order binding on rulers and ruled alike.

IV. Movements of Protest. Rebellions, Heterodoxies, and Political Struggle

All these characteristics of the literati, and the fact that their existence as an elite group was contingent on preservation of the ideal and reality of a unified Chinese Empire, were among the most important stabilizing mechanisms in the Imperial system, helping it to regulate and absorb changes throughout its long history. But these same characteristics also severely inhibited development of a reformative or transformative capacity in China's culturally and politically most articulate groups and greatly influenced the patterns of change in this Empire.

It was the monopolization by this stratum of linkages among broader social groups and elites and between these and the center that assured the relatively low level of coalescence among the different types of protest and political struggle and the relatively low level of ideological articulation, broader political activity, and political struggle that characterized the Chinese system.[39]

The only close relation between ideological struggles and changes in the central elite groups and actual policies of the center developed in some of the orthodox Confucian controversies among the central elites. However, these changes were usually limited to the center and to the literati.[40]

The major types of protest and political conflict that China experienced—rebellions and the transformation of provincial governors into relatively autonomous warlords; conquests by foreign dynasties—did not usually exhibit a distinctly new level of political articulation.[41] Their specific symbols included strong apolitical, ahistorical, and semimythical or utopian elements that generally were bound to the existing value structure and orientations. Most rebellions provided only secondary interpretations of the prevailing value structure and did not create any radically new orientations. The political orientations of the military governors and warlords were likewise set within the existing value and political frameworks. Although they strove for greater independence from, or seizure of, the central government, they envisaged but rarely the establishment of a new type of political system.

Similarly, the major heterodoxies—Taoism, Buddhism, and especially the various secondary Confucian schools—worked within the actual social framework or tended toward withdrawal from it. These movements were but little directed against the concrete structure of social relations and the basic facets of the sociopolitical order. The secondary religions like Buddhism and Taoism, with some important exceptions which were crushed by the bureaucracy, also did not have any far-reaching transformative effects on the Chinese social and political order.[42]

V. Low Level of Coalescence Among Changes

The monopolization by the literati of the linkages among broader social groups and elites and between these and the center also resulted in a relatively low level of coalescence between restructuring the political regime, on the one hand, and restructuring the economic sphere or various strata on the other.[43] In this regard, China was different from other Imperial systems.

The closest relation between changes in political regime (or political policy) and in strata formation that existed in the Chinese Empire was one common to all Imperial societies: we are speaking of those political changes that were connected with changes in the relative strength and standing of free peasants vis-à-vis would-be aristocratic elements.[44] But even this connection manifested itself in China (in contrast to the Byzantine Empire, for instance) more on the level of rulers' policies than of political articulation of these strata. Similarly, the great urban and commercial development under the Sung, while associated with changes in government policies, was not correlated with changes in the mode of impingement of these groups on the center.

Moreover, China displayed less connection between changes in political boundaries or dynasties and changes in economic (agrarian or commercial) institutions than did most other Imperial systems. Only in the cultural sphere, above all, in the ideology of Confucianism, were changes closely related to changes in the political sphere. This led to political struggle and to alteration of the composition of elites and policies. But, as indicated above, these changes were confined to the center—to the literati, the bureaucracy, and the Emperor. In contrast to the Roman or Byzantine empires, the Chinese witnessed little participation of broader strata or secondary elites in these changes.

As we saw in regard to monopolization of access to the macrosocietal order, the literati appealed to common orientations as well as to force to segregate different types of change. Segregation was achieved by the literati in general and the bureaucracy in particular, which combined the role of functional elites with that of articulators of models of cultural order; monopolized through these combined roles the linkages between the center and the periphery; and structured these linkages in terms of the Confucian ideology within the framework of the Imperial institutions.

These characteristics and activities of the literati ensured that most of the ideological innovations or transformative tendencies that this ideology spawned were oriented toward perfecting the scope of individual responsibility, which discouraged institutional linkages among different types of movements of protest and political conflict.[45] For similar reasons, on the institutional level there developed few points of internal strength, cohesion, and self-identity for various groups on which new institutional frameworks could be founded, or which could support institutional changes. Hence, the reform movements that arose in the Empire and later, during the modernization of China, were characterized by a certain closure, either being confined to the center and/or exhibiting a ritual emphasis on certain specific and very limited types of local status. Those movements that were not confined to the central elites were composed mostly of noncohesive groups alienated from them and from the broader strata of society. As a result, these movements remained very weak in terms of institution building and restructuring of the center.

5. THE ISLAMIC CIVILIZATION

I. Cultural Orientations. Structure of Centers and of Institutional Entrepreneurs

Two rather special patterns of relations among cultural orientations, center-periphery relations, institutional entrepreneurs, and patterns of change developed in the Islamic world [46] and in medieval and early modern Europe.

The most important cultural orientations that crystallized in the Islamic realm were the distinction between the cosmic, transcendental realm and the mundane order and the possibility of overcoming the tension inherent in this distinction by total submission to God and by this-worldly—above all, political and military—activity; the strong universalistic element in the definition of the Islamic community; the principled autonomous access of all members of the community to the attributes of the transcendental order, to salvation, through submission to God; the ideal of the *ummah,* the political-religious community of all believers distinct from any ascriptive, primordial collectivity; and the image of the ruler as the upholder of the ideal of Islam, of the purity of the *ummah,* and of the life of the community.[47]

These cultural orientations about the nature of man, the relation of man to God, and the relationship among the political, social, and cosmic (or religious) spheres influenced identification of the rights and obligations of rulers and subjects and the principles of lawmaking and codification of laws, stratification, and institution building.

Of special importance from the point of view of our analysis is the fact that in the Islamic realm the original vision of the *ummah* specified complete convergence between the sociopolitical and the religious community. The Islamic state developed through conquest motivated by a new universal religion and borne by conquering tribes; therefore, the identity between polity and religion was very great initially. Similarly, many of the later caliphs (such as the Abbasides and Fatimites) came to power on the crest of religious movements, legitimized themselves in religious terms, and sought to retain popular support by stressing the religious aspect of their authority and by courting the religious leaders and religious sentiments of the community. Political problems (e.g., determination of proper succession and the scope of the political community) originally constituted the main theological problems of Islam. But owing to widespread Moslem conquest, to the tensions between tribal conquerors and conquered peoples, to the emphasis on total submission to God, as well as to the strong ideological dissociation between the universal Islamic community and primordial, local, or ethnic communities, after the initial attempts of the first caliphs and the beginning of the Abbaside Caliphate, the ideal of a common political and religious community was never realized. Accordingly, there developed in Islamic polities a growing dissociation among the political, religious, and local communities and institutional spheres, albeit with a strong latent religious-ideological orientation toward the unification of these spheres.[48]

The identity of the religious community was forged out, upheld (mainly by the Holy Law—*Sharia*) enunciated, and developed by the religious leaders, the *ulemas,* and enforced by the rulers. Between these two groups there developed a very peculiar relation in which the *ulemas* became politically passive or subjugated to the rulers even though they remained relatively autonomous in the performance of their legal-religious functions.[49]

Hence, although the basic cultural orientations of Islam seemed to generate conditions conducive to the establishment of Imperial or exceptional tribal systems, these systems were not after the first Caliphates the most common ones in the Islamic realm, and they themselves tended to move in the direction of patrimonial society.[50] This tendency was reinforced by the structure of the elites and institutional entrepreneurs that developed in Islam in conjunction with the cultural and ecological parameters of Islam.

The strong ideological dissociation of the universal Islamic community and the different primordial communities generated a weak solidarity between its carriers and the political and/or religious articulators of the cultural model of Islam. This combination gave rise to the very high degree of symbolic and organizational autonomy of the political elites. It gave rise also to the relatively high symbolic but minimal organizational autonomy of the religious elite and to increasing separation of the two. The religious leadership was greatly dependent on the rulers and did not develop into a broad, independent, and cohesive organization. Religious groups and functionaries were not organized as a separate entity; nor did they constitute a tightly organized body except when, as in the Ottoman Empire, organized by the state.[51]

The combination of religious orientations, structure of elites, and relations between elites and local ascriptive communities produced in Imperial and patrimonial Islamic systems alike some unique types of ruling groups. Most important were the military-religious rulers who emerged from tribal and sectarian elements. These rulers (e.g., the Mamelukes) tended to fuse universalistic religious and political power orientations, emphasizing very strongly the dissociation of the rulers from the population and creating special channels of mobility such as the *gulan* system in general and the Ottoman *devshism* in particular, through which the ruling group could be recruited from alien elements.[52]

Except in the case of so-called missionary orders that established new regimes, there developed but few structural linkages between the political elites and the articulators of cultural models and economic entrepreneurs (though often there were close family relations among them).

The characteristics of the relationship between political and religious leaders and the broader ascriptive solidarities naturally limited the autonomous political participation of the latter. Usually, political elites were dissociated from religious ones and although the two were the major carriers of the expansion of Islam in the classical realm, their cooperation in this did not usually give rise to common structural transformation.

Because the religious leadership was not organized as a separate church and did not constitute a closely organized body independent of the rulers and because the broader strata had no autonomous access to the center, there developed either relatively narrow political participation, confined mostly to the court and to the bureaucracy, or extreme sectarian-political activities. Indeed, religious sects and popular movements frequently arose in these states, but in a stable regime the religious check on political authority was ineffective since there was no machinery other than revolt for enforcement. Either such sects and movements were aimed at the destruction of the existing regime and the establishment of a new, religiously pure, and true one or they were politically passive.[53]

At the same time there developed in the Islamic world a fairly weak connection between heterodoxy and rebellion, on the one hand, and institution building (above all, in the economic sphere), on the other. In the geographical heart of Islam, only in the early expansive phase did there arise a close connection between religious movements and urban economic developments.[54] In the later period the heavy hand of military patrimonial sultanates weakened such possibilities, tending more and more, as in the case of the Ottoman Empire, to allocate these activities to segregated enclaves of foreigners. However, Moslem traders and sometimes trade-oriented religious orders were of crucial importance in the spread of Islam only eastward into India and Southeast Asia and westward into Africa.[55]

II. Structuring of Social Hierarchies. Patterns of Change and Rebellion. Shifts Among Tribal, Patrimonial, and Imperial Patterns

Given these characteristics of the political process of Islam there developed in most Islamic regimes, despite the strong ideological emphasis on the coalescence of the political and the religious realm, a pattern of change similar to the pattern of segregative change. (Indeed, most Islamic polities developed from patrimonial, city-state, and tribal regimes.)[56] It was only in Shii Islam in general and in Iran in particular that a much closer relation among the components of the macrosocietal order—and hence among the changes in them—crystallized.[57]

But even in Sunni Islam the pattern differed significantly from that of segregative change because of a latent tendency toward coalescence, closely associated with the ideological emphasis on the unity of the *ummah*. Despite the strength of patrimonial features in most Islamic polities (especially during periods of stabilization or decline), the very momentum of the basic cultural orientations of Islam generated, at least in the geographical heart of Islam, a dynamic of change that went beyond the typical patrimonial or Imperial pattern. This dynamic affected the specific dimensions of the symbolic hierarchization of status that Islam generated and that cannot be found at least in the same form in other patrimonial or Imperial settings.[58]

The first such dimension was the development of a relatively autonomous religious sphere based, in principle, on the total equality of all believers. This dimension, which was not easily integrated with the other dimensions or bases of status, gave rise to new, comparatively segregated patterns of mobility into the religious establishment.

Across the Islamic world, this dimension influenced in different ways the patterns of stratification. In the Imperial societies it either reinforced the commitment of the various groups of the society to the center and the center's control over the attributes of status or it created a relatively segregated—even if wide—social stratum that might serve as a focus of political activism and discord. In the patrimonial regimes this dimension tended even more to give rise to a separate stratum that here, too, might become a focus of political rebellion. In these regimes, however, this separate stratum was even less integrated into the system of strata formation than in the Imperial regimes.

Another dimension of stratification generated by the impact of Islam in different types of regimes was related primarily to the group basis of stratification. Islam brought together under one religious (and often also political) canopy diverse tribal, urban, rural, and regional groups that originally had had but little in common. In this way, new channels of mobility and interconnections among different groups and sectors—beyond the religious sphere—were created. The effect of this was either to reinforce the segregation of various status segments, or to intensify conflicts among them. It also created the tendency for status hierarchies to cut across political boundaries.

The unique features of Islam combined to produce a special dimension of the process of change. First of all, Islam generated some of the basic parameters of the shifts between the different political forms of Islamic societies. The strong universalistic orientations and the activism of Islam created general conditions conducive to the development of Imperial or exceptional tribal systems and coalescent patterns of change. This tendency became activated in periods of establishment of new political regimes, either of Imperial systems (the last and most enduring of which was the Ottoman Empire) or of semitribal ones (like those in the Maghreb or even lately among the Swat).[59] At the same time, the relative weakness of autonomous and organized political expression on the part of the major social and religious groups tended to undermine the bases of the Imperial or tribal framework, often moving the regime toward the patrimonial model. This tendency subsided after the establishment of a new regime. In this context it encouraged the crystallization of relatively autonomous boundaries of religious, legal, political, and economic collectivities and institutions. The Islamic world exhibited perhaps the highest degree of such separateness of any Imperial system.

Thus, the cultural identity of Islam was in practice upheld by the framework of law and prayer carried by the *ulemas* and protected by the rulers always aspiring to reunify the *ummah*. Within this framework, we witness in Islamic history—above all, in the heartland of Islam—a constant

shift between the upsurge of almost totalistic political-religious movements that aimed at complete transformation of the political regime
through such illegitimate means as assassination and rebellion and the
strong otherworldly attitude and political passivity that helped to maintain the despotic character of existing regimes.[60]

6. WESTERN EUROPEAN CIVILIZATION

I. Cultural Orientations. Structural Pluralism

A still different set of relations among cultural orientations, center-
periphery relations, structure of secondary elites, and patterns of change
developed in the Imperial and Imperial-feudal structures of medieval
and early modern (Western and Central) Europe.[61]

European civilization was characterized by a very high number of
crosscutting cultural orientations and structural settings. The symbolic
pluralism, or heterogeneity, of European society was evident in the multiplicity of traditions— the Judeo-Christian, the Greek, the Roman, and the
various tribal ones—out of which its own cultural tradition crystallized.[62]

Most important among Europe's cultural orientations were an emphasis
on the autonomy of the cosmic, cultural, and social orders and their inter-
relatedness, which was defined in terms of the tension between the transcendental and the mundane order; along with a variety of ways to resolve
this tension, including this-worldly (political and economic) and otherworldly activities. A second important cultural orientation was a high
level of activism and commitment on the part of broader groups and
strata to the mundane and transcendental orders. A third was the conception of a high degree of relatively autonomous access of different groups
and strata to these orders; this orientation was to some extent countered
by, and in constant tension with, the strong emphasis on the mediation of
this access by the Church or the political powers. Finally, European
civilization possessed a definition of the individual as an autonomous and
responsible entity with respect to access to these orders.

This complex of symbolic orientations became connected with a very
special type of structural-organizational pluralism.[63] The type of pluralism
Europe exhibited differed greatly from the Byzantine type although that
Empire shared many aspects of its cultural models with Western Europe.
In the Byzantine Empire pluralism was manifest in a relatively high degree of structural differentiation within a fairly unified sociopolitical
framework in which different social functions were apportioned to different
social categories. The structural pluralism that developed in Europe was
characterized, above all, by a combination of lower but steadily increasing levels of structural differentiation, on the one hand, and constantly
changing boundaries of collectivities, units, and frameworks, on the other.

Among these collectivities and units there did not exist a clear-cut division of labor. Rather, they were in constant competition over their standing with respect to the attributes of the social and cultural orders; over performance of the major societal functions—economic, political, cultural; as well as over the very definition of the boundaries of ascriptive communities.

The combination of these cultural orientations and structural conditions generated several basic institutional characteristics. Particularly of interest to us are the structure of centers and center-periphery relations, which showed great variations in medieval and early modern times in Western and Central Europe.[64] Europe displayed an interesting mixture of the Imperial pattern and pure feudal (as distinct from simple decentralization or disintegration of large patrimonial or tribal units) institutions. These institutions shared several crucial characteristics with Imperial societies probably because, as Otto Hinze demonstrated long ago, they emerged within a civilization that had an Imperial past and Imperial aspirations. The most important of these aspirations was the symbolic and to some degree the organizational distinctiveness of the center. But unlike pure Imperial societies, feudal systems were distinguished by a multiplicity of centers and subcenters, all of which had multiple orientations (political, cultural, and economic). These centers and subcenters tended to be arranged in a complicated but never unified, rigid hierarchy in which none of the centers was clearly predominant. Naturally enough, the activities of the more central higher centers were wider in scope than those of the local subcenters, but the former did not enjoy a monopoly of any one of the components of central activities. Each of the local subcenters exercised some control over certain of its resources, over certain central activities, as well as over its access to the higher centers.

Moreover, the various centers were not completely separate from one another. They were structurally interrelated to a degree and shared political and cultural orientations. Of course, any group that had control over resources necessary to the development of the political or cultural orientations of the centers enjoyed some legitimate and autonomous, even if differentiated, access to the centers. Not only the Church but also many local or status groups were partially autonomous in terms of being able to convert their resources from one institutional sphere to another and from the periphery to the centers.[65]

Finally, the societies of Western Europe were always characterized by a high degree of commitment by center and periphery alike to common ideals or goals, the center permeating the periphery in attempts to mobilize support for its policies and the periphery impinging on the center in order to influence the shaping of its contours. Both traditional rulers (monarchical as well as feudal) and (as we see later on) leaders of modern nation-states or class societies emphasized the development of common symbols of cultural and political identity, collective political goals, and regulation of the relations among different, relatively independent groups.

II. Strata Formation, Center Formation, and Institution Building

There developed in Europe six specific characteristics of strata formation.

First, the multiplicity of centers in European societies prevented the development of a castelike occupational system despite strong tendencies in this direction. Every major autonomous social unit—the Church, the court, the various social strata and the collectivities within these strata— produced a different scale of evaluation, each with a logical claim of general validity. As a result, a complex system of status hierarchies developed. Persons who ranked high in one hierarchy might rank low in another and vice versa (sociologists call this phenomenon *status incongruency*). Thus, another result was gradual blurring of the distinction between free and unfree groups.

Second, there was a strong tendency toward unified class consciousness and class organization, a tendency especially evident among the higher strata. The fullest expression of this was found in the system of representation that culminated in the Assemblies of Estate, which realized the possibility (available to most groups simply by virtue of their identity as corporate or semicorporate bodies) of political participation in the center. In sharp contrast to China, Europe manifested countrywide class consciousness and organization not only among the higher status groups but also among the middle and even the lowest free groups and strata.

Third, unlike Russia and China but not entirely unlike India, Western and Central Europe developed a close relationship between family and broader kinship identity, on the one hand, and class identity, on the other. Family and wider kin groups were very important agencies both for orienting their members toward the attainment of high positions and for transmitting these positions by ascription. In Europe, however, there was a good deal of open conflict over the degree to which each stratum should participate in the center. Theoretically at least such conflict could not have occurred in India, where the levels of differential participation were fixed by ritualistic ascription (although there were exceptions to the rule).[66]

Fourth, each social stratum, especially the middle strata, encompassed a great variety of occupational and entrepreneurial positions and organizations and linked them in a common way of life with a common avenue of access to the center. Thus, Europe again resembled India more than either Russia or China.[67] These strata combined ownership of resources with attempts to control the use and conversion of these resources either directly or through their participation in the center.

Fifth, a possibility closely related to the four preceding characteristics was that of differential yet common participation in various cultural orders and centers on the part of different groups and strata. This feature, in turn, made the life-styles of distinct strata overlap. Thus, the availability of several channels of access to the same center—channels that could be used by many social strata—made contact among strata much easier.[68]

Sixth, we find a high degree of mobility among strata at all levels of society. This characteristic had its roots, as Marc Bloch indicadated in *Feudal Society,* in the feudal period, and it seems to have existed up to the end (or at least the middle) of the Absolutist era. Thus, the fact that Europe's social strata had a collective consciousness and organization that embraced the whole society facilitated changes in the family and ethnic composition of various groups. On the whole, this mobility was more of the contested (i.e., open, competitive) than the sponsored (contended by the rulers) type although the latter variety was present, too. In sharp contrast to China but in some ways paralleling India (with its pattern of subcaste formation), European society developed not only a process of mobility within a relatively fixed system of positions but also a process that in itself created new positions and status systems. The most obvious illustration of this phenomenon was the development of cities, which occurred, of course, long before the Age of Absolutism. Especially in the late medieval city, new points of contact arose among different groups and strata and served as foci for the celebration of new forms of political and social consciousness.[69]

The preceding analysis indicates that crystallization of the structural tendencies of European societies, combined with the specific cultural orientations prevalent in Europe, gave rise to (1) a multiplicity of centers; (2) a high degree of permeation of the periphery by the centers and of impingement of the periphery on the centers; (3) a relatively small degree of overlap of the boundaries and restructuring of class, ethnic, religious, and political entities; (4) a comparatively high degree of autonomy of groups and strata and of their access to the centers of society and a strong tendency among the former to combine ownership of resources with control over their use and conversion in the macrosocietal settings; (5) a high degree of overlap among various status units, together with a high level of countrywide status (class) consciousness and political activity; (6) a multiplicity of cultural and functional (economic or professional) elites enjoying a relatively high degree of autonomy, a high degree of crosscutting, and a close relationship with the broader, more ascriptive strata; (7) a relative high level of autonomy of the legal system with regard to other integrative systems—above all, the political and the religious species; and (8) a high degree of autonomy of cities as centers of social and structural creativity and identity formation.

III. Patterns of Protest and Change

In close relation to these institutional features of traditional European civilization there developed a special pattern of change. This pattern was characterized by a comparatively high degree of articulation of political struggle and of symbolic and ideological structuring of movements of protest and political struggle alike; as well as by a high degree of coalescence of change and restructuring of political regimes and other components of the macrosocietal order.

Thus, changes within any component of the macrosocietal order impinged on other components and most significantly, on the political sphere. These changes gave rise to the continual mutual restructuring of these spheres, which did not necessarily coalesce into a unified political or cultural framework.

As compared with the pure Imperial systems, Western European societies were characterized by much less stability of regimes, by constant changes in regime and collectivity boundaries and by continual restructuring of centers. At the same time, however, they evinced a much greater capacity for institutional innovation cutting across political and national boundaries and centers.

The patterns of change characteristic of European society were activated by a strong predisposition on the part of secondary elites relatively close to the center to be the major carriers of religious heterodoxies and political innovations; a relatively close relationship among these autonomous secondary elites within broader social strata and hence also among movements of rebellion; and a concomitant tendency on the part of these elites and the broader social strata to pursue activities oriented to center formation and to combine activities with institution building in the economic, cultural, and educational spheres. These factors ensured confrontation between the construction of centers and the process of institution building. Institution building in most spheres was seen as highly relevant to the construction of centers and judged according to its contribution to the basic premises of these centers; at the same time, centers were judged according to their capacity to promote just and meaningful institutions. These factors likewise ensured competition among different groups or strata and elites over access to the construction of the centers.[70]

7. A COMPARATIVE NOTE. JAPAN

Let us briefly compare the European pattern to the Japanese, which we subsequently analyze in more detail. Suffice it to say here that Japan also experienced continual coalescence of changes in the political and socioeconomic spheres. Moreover, institution building was closely connected with center formation in Japan, but the articulation of political struggles as well as the role of religious sects and movements within them were much weaker than in Europe.

Traditional Japanese society shared certain structural characteristics with Imperial-feudal systems:[71] distinctiveness of the center; very strong mutual impingement of center periphery; a relatively high degree of articulation of strata formation in terms of status and of political orientation; as well as a tendency toward fairly wide strata identity, which could not be entirely suppressed by the Tokugawa regime and which served as one of the bases of the overthrow of this regime.

Prior to and surviving the Tokugawa regime, there developed in Japan a tendency toward crosscutting structural and organizational pluralism not unlike the European pattern. Still, in Japan pluralism developed within the framework of a continuous national identity.

In Japan, of course, center-periphery relations and class formation were associated with sociopolitical and cultural orientations that largely differed from the European ones. While Japan, like Europe, stressed commitment to the maintenance of the cultural and social orders and centers, this commitment was not connected with a conception of strong tension between the transcendental and the mundane order and of the necessity of overcoming this tension. The Japanese cultural tradition accepted the transcendental and mundane orders as given and as closely interwoven; any transcendental tendencies were mainly, as Robert N. Bellah has put it, subterranean.[72]

The Emperor system and symbolism constituted the pivot of this order, a pivot that rested on the commitment of all members and units of the community to the center. The symbolism of the Emperor was couched largely in primordial terms but not based on religious precepts or on autonomous access to it. Such access was in principle mediated for all groups by the Emperor or by his representatives.[73]

It was the element of commitment that provided the basis for center-periphery relations and strata formation in Japan, dimensions organizationally but not symbolically similar to those of Europe. Accordingly, early Japanese feudalism did not rest on contract or on the autonomous political expression of the warrior strata; there was almost no conception of political rights or of the distinctiveness or autonomy of the legal system. Hence, while Japanese class or hierarchical symbolism was indeed related to collective commitment to the center, it lacked that articulation and autonomy characteristic of the European system. Japan therefore exhibited relatively weak horizontal strata. Its hierarchy was based on vertical crosscutting of different collectivities with a strong sense of hierarchical arrangements and almost no conception or equality of access that characterized the Japanese status system.[74]

The characteristics of strata formation were also closely related to the structure of secondary elites in Japan—above all, to the very weak development of specialized (i.e., economic, political, administrative, or cultural) elite groups. Most such elites were almost totally embedded in the strong solidary units based on kinship and/or in the political frameworks of the center. Secondary elites that did emerge had little autonomy, as the examples of both religious and legal elites indicate.[75]

This crucial difference between the European and the Japanese experience manifested itself in the nature of the coalitions that implemented modernizing changes in these societies. It was most evident in the almost total lack of participation in the processes of restructuring in Japan by religious sects or heterodoxies. These groups were allowed to lead a segregated existence in the intellectual and esthetic sphere as long as they did not impinge on the basic premises and ground rules of the system.[76] Somewhat later, with the onset of modernization, this pattern showed up in the weakness of autonomous religious groups, which either developed as marginal oppositionary groups or became absorbed in the Emperor system.

PART 3   ANALYTICAL AND COMPARATIVE CONCLUSIONS

1. SYMBOLIC ARTICULATION. STRUCTURE OF ELITES. PATTERNS OF CHANGE

At the end of Chapter 4 we indicated that the relations between, on the one hand, cultural orientations and, on the other, the structuring of institutions in general and of patterns of social change in particular are mediated by three major variables: first, the degree of problematization of the facts of human existence and the symbolic articulation of the principal dimensions of the institutional order; second, the structure—and especially the degree of autonomy—of the institutional entrepreneurs or elites that are the major carriers of such orientations; and, third, the scope of institutional markets and the flow of free resources.

We saw that the greater the problematization of the data of human existence, the greater the potential for autonomy among such entrepreneurs; the higher also (other—especially technological and ecological—conditions being equal) the level of free-floating resources and activities and the wider the scope of institutional markets (i.e., of markets of money, prestige, and power) that cut across the major ascriptive communities; the greater the free flow of resources among them; as well as the higher the level of symbolic articulation and autonomy of the principal collectivities and institutional spheres.

Conversely, the smaller the degree of problematization of the data of human existence, of the symbolic articulation of institutional spheres, the smaller the autonomy of institutional entrepreneurs and elites and the narrower the scope of institutional markets; the greater their embedment within ascriptive communities, the more limited the flow of free resources among them, and the smaller the degree of institutional distinctiveness of the major spheres of social organization.

We also explored at the end of the Chapter 4 the relationship between these aspects of cultural orientations and social organization, on the one hand, and the processes of change, on the other. We noted first that questioning the dimensions of human existence and social organization generates potentialities for a social order different from the existing one in the sense not only of reversal of existing arrangements but also of possible transcendence of them. Second, we suggested that because the symbolic articulation of the major aspects of social organization and the wide scope of markets produce potentially free-floating resources, important possibilities for crystallizing these resources in new directions are created. Third, we indicated that the more autonomous entrepreneurs can serve as activators of alternative conceptions of social order as well as organizers of newly freed resources. They can actualize the new potentialities for crystallizing these resources in new directions and, by linking together such resources and activities from different spheres, generate coalescent change.

We illustrated these assertions in a comparative analysis of patrimonial regimes, Imperial (and Imperial-feudal) symptoms, and exceptional city-states and tribal federations. We noted that the concrete patterns of such potentials of change varied greatly not only across the major types of systems we examined but also within them. In this chapter we have analyzed some of these differences in greater detail and have shown how differences in cultural orientation and in the structure of elites, along with combinations of these differences with distinct ecological settings, influenced variations in the structuring of institutions in general and in particular processes of change in selected patrimonial, Imperial, and Imperial-feudal societies. In the next section we attempt to draw together, in a very tentative way, some of the lines of this analysis.

To repeat, the actualization of various potentialities of change depends on two sets of conditions and on the interrelations between them: the first set is the complex of cultural orientations and their institutional implications; the second is the ecological setting, which provides the organizational framework for the realization of these potentialities.

Let us start with the analysis of the institutional implications of different cultural orientations.

Yet the various cultural orientations produce diverse alternative conceptions of social order; different degrees of wideness of markets, of availability of free resources; and different foci for their institutionalization and for possible directions of change. These differences are greatly influenced by the nature of the entrepreneurs and the coalitions of entrepreneurs likely to be the carriers of these orientations.

2. CULTURAL ORIENTATIONS INFLUENCING PATTERNS OF CHANGE. COMMITMENT TO THE COSMIC AND SOCIAL ORDERS

Perception of a high level of commitment to social and cultural order if not accompanied by perception of considerable tension between the transcendental and the mundane order does not encourage the autonomous articulation of models of social order or political elites. That is, as was the case in Japan, this perception tends to be carried by elites embedded within ascriptive groups but strongly oriented toward the performance of obligations beyond these groups, especially toward the centers that represent the social and cultural orders. It tends further to give rise to coalitions between institutional elites and articulators of the solidarity of the different collectivities. This situation results in a relatively high level of potentially free resources but not a wide scope of markets. Either markets are embedded in ascriptive collectivities or they cut across them and are controlled by the center.

Because of the lack of perception of tension between the cosmic and the mundane order and because of emphasis on the givenness of these orders, there rarely developed within such societies utopian orientations and conceptions of alternative social orders. Accordingly, the free resources generated were usually directed toward organizational expansion and change; little symbolic redefinition of institutional complexes, of the collectivity, and of center-periphery relations occurred. Given heterogeneous ecological settings and weak centralization, such tendencies frequently gave rise to structural differentiation without fostering symbolic elaboration.

3. CULTURAL ORIENTATIONS INFLUENCING PATTERNS OF CHANGE. PERCEPTION OF TENSION BETWEEN COSMIC AND MUNDANE ORDERS. OTHERWORLDLY FOCI OF SALVATION

Perception of a high degree of tension between the transcendental and the mundane order, a high level of commitment to these orders, and depiction of these orders as nongiven tend to generate a relatively high degree of problematization of the facts of human existence. Hence, they tend also to generate tendencies toward a relatively high level of free-floating resources, toward a wide scope of markets, and toward a high level of symbolic articulation of the major institutional spheres as well as of the alternative conceptions of social order.

A higher level of generation of free resources, a wider scope of markets, greater symbolic articulation of the major institutional spheres and alternative conceptions of social and political order, and hence stronger tendencies toward coalescent transformative change result from (as we saw in our analysis of Imperial and Imperial-feudal societies) the perception of a high level of tension between the cosmic and the mundane order. These transformative potentialities are carried by elites (articulators of the models of cultural order, political elites, and even articulators of the solidarity of ascriptive collectivities) enjoying a high level of autonomy. Different conceptions of this tension and, above all, of ways to overcome it tend, as the materials presented in this chapter indicate, to reinforce or create different constellations of such entrepreneurs and diverse patterns of change.

Our preceding analysis stressed two variables of special importance in this context. One is the distinction between—and relative emphasis of—this-worldly and otherworldly resolution of the tension between the orders. The second, cutting across the first, is the relation between the attributes or foci of the resolution of this tension, the attributes of salvation, and the attributes of the major primordial and other ascriptive collectivities.

The concrete foci of the resolution of the tension between the cosmic and the mundane order influence the level of generalization of resources, the scope of markets, and the symbolization of institutional spheres, as well as the nature of alternative conceptions of social order. Generalization of resources, broadening of markets, symbolization of institutional spheres, and creation of alternative conceptions are fostered in institutional spheres most closely related to the foci of tension resolution (salvation) and inhibited in those spheres not related to such foci. Hence, these processes are least active when the focus of salvation is on otherworldly activities rather than a combination of otherworldly and this-worldly activity.

The possibility of linking the free resources generated either by such conceptions or by the appropriate technological and structural conditions and directing them into new institutional channels is greater insofar as there exists a close relation among the attributes of salvation, that is, resolution of the tension between the transcendental and the mundane order and the attributes of the major primordial collectivities. Such linkage is effected by appropriate combinations of different types of entrepreneurial activities with varying degrees of autonomy and distinct institutional foci for their activities.

Thus, other conditions being equal, emphasis on otherworldly resolution of the tension between the orders tends to generate broad markets and distinctive centers in the religious sphere but not to alter other institutional spheres. The internal dynamics of the latter is determined by the combination between the levels of technological development and social differentiation of the society, on the one hand, and the relatively low level of symbolic articulation of these spheres, on the other. Such societies experience little generation of free resources or markets beyond the religious sphere and very little connection between such free resources as exist in other spheres and in the religious sphere. The segregation of the internal dynamics of these spheres from the workings of the cultural and religious centers is greater insofar as the foci of the otherworldly resolution of the tension between the cosmic and the mundane order is dissociated, as in Buddhism, from the major ascriptive, primordial communities.

Here the articulators of the models of cultural order, while autonomous in their religious activities, are from the point of view of institutional activities, embedded in broader ascriptive collectivities (as are the political and economic elites, too). Hence, they do not develop autonomous activities or orientations or the ability to create new types of institutional complexes.

In such cases, the attributes of otherworldly resolution of this tension may combine with the main attributes and symbols of the collectivities but not with the principles of restructuring of the major institutional spheres and of center-periphery relations. The restructuring of institutional spheres that takes place in such societies usually is effected by internal or external elites not associated directly with religious activities.

Insofar as otherworldly resolution of the tension between the transcendental and the mundane order is based, as in Hinduism, on a close relation between the (otherworldly) attributes of salvation and the major attributes of the basic ascriptive groups, there tend to develop free resources and wide markets that go beyond the purely religious sphere. These free resources may be directed into various secondary channels although ultimate control of their conversion is also vested in the religious sphere.

Such orientations will likely generate, reinforce, and be carried by elites that combine, on the one hand, a degree of autonomy in their specific functions (political, economic, etc.) and some internal differentiation of these functions with, on the other hand, strong embedment in solidary groups and with a predominance of articulators of the models of cultural order who are the carriers and examples of otherworldly salvation.

While here the conception of alternative orders is, as in Buddhism, very limited and on the whole otherworldly, it may become connected to concrete activities in different institutional spheres; but in any case, it will not give rise to extensive restructuring of these spheres. Hence, the processes of institutional change will be limited to the organizational level, giving rise to many new organizational complexes but to few changes in the fundamental meanings and structures of institutions.

4. CULTURAL ORIENTATIONS INFLUENCING PATTERNS OF CHANGE. THIS-WORLDLY FOCI OF SALVATION

The conception of a high level of tension between the transcendental and the mundane order, along with emphasis on this-worldly activities, tends to generate the highest level of free resources, the widest scope of markets, the greatest articulation of symbolic activities and of their institutional derivatives, and the largest variety of alternative conceptions of social and political order.

The perception of this tension gives rise to, or at least is associated with or carried by, such entrepreneurs as articulators of the models of cultural order, political elites, and articulators of the solidarity of different collectivities, all with a fairly high level of autonomy. Accordingly, societies in which these orientations are prevalent tend to develop multiple coalitions of such entrepreneurs, which may be able both to mobilize free resources as well as to channel them in new directions. Given the potentially mutual orientations of such institutional entrepreneurs, the directions of change may coalesce.

Nevertheless, this pattern varies according to the specific contents of these orientations. At work here are (1) the degree of interweaving or segregation of this-worldly and otherworldly foci of salvation (a problem that is inherent in most high civilizations and religions); (2) the degree of institutional spread of the foci of this-worldly resolution of the tension between the transcendental and the mundane order; and (3) the relations between the major attributes or foci of the resolution of this tension and the basic attributes of the principal ascriptive collectivities.

The weaker the emphasis on the otherworldly realm (as in China), the more the focus of salvation is this-worldly; the more this-worldly salvation is focused on a single institutional area (as in both China and Islam), the stronger the tendency for the multiplicity of potentially autonomous elites—especially articulators of models of cultural and social order and political elites—to be brought together within a single social framework or category exhibiting little internal differentiation and the greater also the tendency for the dissociation between the ownership of resources and the control over their use and conversion in the macrosocietal setting.

Such a structure will generate only a limited scope of free resources and markets even if symbolization of the dominant institutional spheres is relatively strong. The flow of resources among markets will be relatively small: most of the free resources will be directed toward the main institutional spheres. Concomitantly, in such situations the different elite activities will find very weak independent bases for the autonomous mobilization of resources; hence, the potential for internal transformability will be relatively small.

The stress on a single institutional focus of this-worldly salvation was common to China and Islam (in Islam the focus was the political-military sphere). In both cases this stress gave rise to a similar structure of entrepreneurs and similarly weakened the society's transformative capacities. But in Islam there existed also a very strong otherworldly emphasis (related to the this-worldly one) that produced a conception of an alternative social and political order and the special type of sectarian political dynamics characteristic of that tradition.

The more institutionally segregated the relations between symbolically tightly interwoven this-worldly and otherworldly foci of salvation (as in Russia), the more there tends to arise a situation in which the different elites instead of merging become increasingly separated. They retain, however, powerful mutual orientations as well as powerful orientations to the center. Hence, such situations are characterized by a dissociation between ownership of resources and control over their use and conversion, connected with wider markets and freer flow of resources albeit under stricter control from the center; and stronger tendencies toward institution building as well as impingement on the center, which can be checked only by coercive measures. At the same time, the close symbolic interweaving of the foci of salvation creates a potent and potentially articulate conception of alternative social orders.

In contrast to all the foregoing cases, Western Europe manifested the greatest potentialities of transformability. Europe displayed both a tight interweaving of this-worldly and otherworldly foci of salvation and a relative multiplicity of this-worldly arenas that served as such foci. These foci generated a rich variety of conceptions of alternative social orders and of their concretization, as well as different autonomous entrepreneurs (articulators of models of social order, functional elites, even articulators of the solidarity of ascriptive collectivities), and encouraged coalitions among these entrepreneurs along with the tendency for them to combine ownership resources with control over their use and conversion. However, in India, this combination was not based on ascriptive criteria. Hence, there developed a multiplicity of directions of crystallization of free resources and of linkages among them.

The comparison between Europe and Islam brings out the importance of the third dimension mentioned above; namely, the degree of association between the attributes of salvation and the attributes of the basic ascriptive collectivities, an association that was very weak in Islam and very strong in Europe.

The greater such association, the more channels of flow of resources; the stronger the bases of solidarity of various entrepreneurs; and the greater their ability to mobilize resources and to manipulate resources from different spheres. Conversely such linkage is weaker to the extent that there is dissociation between the foci of salvation and the attributes of ascriptive collectivities and the latter fail to provide autonomous bases of solidarity for these entrepreneurs, and the greater the dissociation between ownership of resources and control over their use.

5. CULTURAL ORIENTATIONS, ECOLOGICAL CONDITIONS, AND PATTERNS OF CHANGE. COMPACT AND CROSSCUTTING MARKETS

The structural or institutional implications of different cultural orientations and constellations that we identified above can be discerned in distinct types of societies, and in all of them they are connected with, or carried by, relatively similar types of institutional entrepreneurs. But seemingly similar institutional implications and especially the processes of institution building and of change may in fact diverge in different concrete settings. We now examine the influence of ecological-political settings on these processes.

Ecological and ecological-political setting influences above all the availability of resources for institutional restructuring and the capacity to institutionalize the potential for change that may develop in any society or situation. Obviously, this capacity is dependent not only on the cultural orientations of various elites and strata but also on a combination of these orientations with available resources and with the ability of the elites to organize these resources. In the preceding analysis we encountered a central aspect of the availability of resources; namely, the scope of the markets within a society. (We noted that the smaller the scope of institutional markets and the concomitant availability of free resources, the more limited are the capacities to institutionalize change.) Ecological settings influence the availability of resources for different markets mostly by determining the nature of crosscutting among markets and the relative importance of a society's internal and external markets.

These differences are most clearly seen in comparisons of Imperial and patrimonial systems with city-states and most tribal federations; and of all the former Imperial-feudal regimes. City-states (and some tribal federations) manifested the greatest dependence on external markets. The Imperial and patrimonial systems differed from the Imperial-feudal and some of the tribal federations and city-state regimes in the degree of unification (within relatively common frameworks) of their mostly internal markets. Such differences in the structuring of markets had far-reaching consequences for the institutionalization of processes of change in the various types of societies.

We may now attempt to draw, on the basis of the materials presented earlier, some conclusions about how the interaction among cultural orientations, elites, and ecological settings affects the capacity to institutionalize the potential for change that may develop in any society.

Comparison beween the Byzantine and the Russian empires, on the one hand, and the Western European Imperial-feudal patterns and the Islamic and Hindu civilizations, on the other, shows that Imperial systems evolved fairly unified frameworks for their major (relatively compact) markets; Western Europe and Islamic world (as well as India) developed crosscutting markets.

The relative predominance of internal markets, whether compact or crosscutting, generated in all these cases great reservoirs of resources that could be mobilized in new directions. Hence, the predominance of internal markets enhanced the society's institution building and transformative capacities although the degree and direction of these processes greatly depended on the orientations and structure of the elites—in all these societies access to markets and their contours were structured by the activities of the dominant elites. In Imperial societies these activities were ultimately controlled by political elites. In the Imperial-feudal systems and in the tribal federations, the structure of the crosscutting markets and the linkages between them were heavily influenced by the multiplicity of elites, which often cut across political boundaries. In both Imperial and Imperial-feudal societies the nature of such linkages greatly depended on certain characteristics of these elites that we analyzed above.

Thus, in the Islamic world, these linkages were provided mostly by the *ulemas* and the various orders, and given the official disregard in Islamic tradition of the principal local ascriptive collectivities, these elites usually did not develop very strong solidary connections with such collectivities. The lack of solidary linkages among the *ulemas*, the political rulers, and the broader ascriptive collectivities minimized their effectiveness in structuring broad markets, in mobilizing resources, and in directing resources into new coalescent channels. Still, the basic orientations of this tradition fostered tendencies, at least in extreme situations, toward coalescence between political and religious change. In Europe, the existence of such solidary linkages maximized the tendency toward mobilization of resources in multiple directions and coalescence of changes.

From the point of view of ecological setting, the Western European and Islamic civilizations seem close to the Hindu. But because in the latter case ritual ascriptive networks and caste organization provided the sole or principal social linkages and because little this-worldly emphasis was placed on political or economic activities, the connection between religious movements and transformation of political and economic systems was much weaker than that either in Islam or in Europe.

In sum, the nature of the institutionalization of potentialities of change varies with the cultural orientations and solidary relations of elites as well as across societies in which compact as opposed to crosscutting markets predominate. In societies with highly compact markets, the central controlling mechanisms are an easy target for the processes of change, which often creates a situation of all-or-nothing struggle; the possibility of breakdown within such regimes inevitably increases. Crosscutting markets generate a multiplicity of centers of autonomous forces and create opportunities for finding manifold ways to restructure the various institutional spheres. We shall again see the importance of these variables in Chapter 7 when we analyze the differences between the first and later revolutions and in Chapter 8 when we analyze their outcomes.

6. DEPENDENCE ON EXTERNAL MARKETS AND PATTERNS OF CHANGE. CITY-STATES AND TRIBAL FEDERATIONS

Analysis of the exceptional city-states and tribal federations reveals that great dependency on external markets minimizes the possibility of institutionalization of change. This contrasts with the effects of both compact and crosscutting internal markets. Like the Imperial and Imperial-feudal systems, these exceptional regimes manifested a relatively high degree of coalescence of rebellions, heterodoxies, and central political struggle and strong transformative tendencies; however, these tendencies were but rarely fully realized and institutionalized within the framework of these systems.

Indeed, the intensification of political struggle more commonly led to the demise of the exceptional regimes or their incorporation into other societies. Thus, these changes resulted in lack of coalescence among the rates of change of the different components of the macrosocietal order.

The explanation of this special pattern of change lies in the fact that the exceptional societies attempted to maintain in their international systems standards of institutional activities that were more appropriate to bigger societies with wide internal markets.[77] Hence, they tended to specialize in serving external markets while keeping the level of internal specialization low.

This type of ecological specialization produced a relatively low level of free internal resources that could become mobilized to serve the transformative capacities implicit in these societies' patterns of protest and political struggle, as well as a fairly low level of organizing and linking activities among their embryonic elites. Such capacities and activities developed in the Roman case alone—owing in no small degree to the relatively autonomous structure of the Roman ruling class. In all other cases the lack of these resources and capacities, combined with the internal pattern of political struggle, generated tendencies that culminated in the demise of the existing macrosocietal order.

7. MULTIPLICITY OF PATTERNS OF CHANGE IN TRADITIONAL SOCIETIES. REVISION OF THE EVOLUTIONARY PERSPECTIVE

Thus we see that institutional variants of relatively similar cultural orientations are the result of struggles among different types of seeming similar elites and collectivities and of the relationships among them within ever changing ecological settings.

The Russian case (as well as the Spanish, which we analyze subsequently) shows how the crystallization of different combinations of apparently similar cultural orientations and the concomitant transformation of an Imperial-feudal system into a more patrimonial regime were influenced by struggles and coalitions among various elites in distinct ecological settings. Still, we know very little about how struggles among diverse types of elites and collectivities in interaction with distinct ecological settings give rise to different types of ecological-political systems.

As we asked at the end of Chapter 4, is it the emergence of different types of cultural orientations that produces these aspects of the structure of elites and collectivities or is it elites and collectivities with particular attributes or with latent tendencies toward the development of certain attributes that create, generate, or select consonant orientations? We suggested that through a process of continuous feedback groups or persons with certain structural tendencies select specific orientations and that the institutionalization of these orientations reinforces the structural tendencies. This problem should provoke further research, for which our analysis may serve as a starting point.

At present the data indicate that mutual selection and feedback is a relatively open process. The importance of this openness was underlined at the end of Chapter 3, when we pointed out some of the weaknesses of the classical evolutionary perspective. We shall now, on the basis of the materials presented in this chapter, present a more detailed criticism of that approach. The following analysis elaborates a criticism leveled earlier; namely, the evolutionary perspective which focuses on stages and systemic needs and problems is at most only partially valid.

At the end of Chapter 3 we indicated in a general way that across societies diverse cultural codes and orientations may be combined in various ways among themselves. They may also be connected with similar levels of structural differentiation. Conversely, the same codes may be combined with different levels of structural differentiation. Thus, the preceding analysis stressed the relative openness of both the institutionalization of social and cultural models and processes of change. Given this openness, different aspects of social systems may in apparently similar situations be combined in different ways; in apparently similar situations of change there may emerge different patterns of winning coalitions, each leading to unique constellations of the major components of the macrosociological order. Hence, the central aspects of the institutional frameworks of these societies (the structure of their centers, center-periphery relations, patterns of strata formation, modes of production) may vary greatly among seemingly similar societies.

Because constellations of codes influence crucial aspects of the institutional features of a society, societies with similar levels of differentiation may develop different ground rules of social interaction and their institutional derivatives. These differences may in turn influence the degree to which various movements of protest—rebellions, heterodoxies, and so on—develop in a society or sectors thereof and the degree to which these become connected among themselves, as well as with the more central political struggle, on the one hand, and the processes of institution building in the economic and cultural spheres, on the other. Movements of protest influence in their turn the degree of coalescence of rates and directions of change of different components of the macrosocietal order; the degree to which forces of change are contained within the existing order; the degree and direction of transformability of the society (that is, the degree to which processes of change give rise to cultural models and social orders that transcend the society's original institutional premises); and the degree to which the social system moves in the direction of growing structural and/or symbolic differentiation.

These general considerations were tentatively elaborated in the preceding section in the analysis of the different possible combinations of elites, collectivities, and ecological settings. Our discussion suggested that at any level of development, in any situation of change, the responses to the problems created by social change of any sort may be crystallized or integrated in distinct ways.

Whereas the range of choices in any specific situation is not entirely random, even structurally similar situations manifest a variety of alternatives. In every situation of change there exists some degree of freedom, of possible innovation, and hence a multiplicity of possible institutional responses. Thus, in most situations of change different codes and models and their institutional derivatives continually interact with resources potentially available for new institutionalizations. Different models and constellations of existential codes and symbolic evaluations of the social order, and the institutional derivatives thereof, compete as it were to be selected and institutionalized in one of the many concrete ways that are possible in a given situation. In any situation of change, crystallization of different institutional patterns greatly depends on the actual constellations of relations among collectivities, elites, ecological settings, and structures of movements.

Within each situation of change, the problems that arise present various elites and groups of the society with a series of choices between different cultural and institutional possibilities. The way in which such choices are made or institutionalized is not fully determined by the conditions preexisting in any given society or situation.

Resolution of such choices takes place and becomes institutionalized through struggle among the members—actual and potential—of the different coalitions through which the ground rules of social interaction are set up. It is through the activation of such coalitions that the choices among the alternatives that exist in any situation of change are made and the new structures and new insitutional complexes constructed.

Such choices and alternatives are usually highly visible when they are perceived as a deliberate act by an elite in revolutionary, religious, political, or ideological struggles. But the process of selection and choice also takes place in less extreme situations and may manifest itself through the accumulation of more dispersed pressures and responses of elites and through the less dramatic but constant interaction among different groups and entrepreneurs.

Such responses vary greatly. Thus, increasing systemic sensitivity to a broader and more complex environment, to new problems and exigencies, does not necessarily imply the development of the ability to deal with these problems, nor does it indicate the ways in which they may be solved.

In any situation of change, at any level of differentiation, an adequate degree of institutional response may or may not be achieved, and the potentialities released through the process of differentiation, for example, may be wasted (that is, fail to become crystallized into a stable institutional pattern).

In relatively similar situations of change, there may arise diverse types of institutional structures. These structures may differ greatly from many points of view. Of special interest from the point of view of our analysis, they may vary with respect to the degree to which they involve total change—the coalescence of rates and directions of change in the major dimensions of the macrosocietal order. In some situations of change, change may occur in all these dimensions; in other situations, only one dimension will be affected.

To repeat, in any given situation of change (for example, in increasing differentiat:on) transition to a new social system does not necessarily take place in all aspects of differentiation or in all components of the macro-societal order.

Similarly, not every change in a society will increase differentiation. On the contrary, the evidence shows that many social changes do not give rise to overall changes in the scope of differentiation. It is not only that differentiation may in fact decrease within societal components but also that the most important changes may develop in different directions. For example, on the organizational-institutional level, the scope of mechanical solidarity may be extended as against the development of new levels of structural differentiation and/or organic solidarity and different combinations of ascriptive (political, religious, national) communities and of cultural traditions may form. Moreover, at similar levels of structural differentiation, different combinations of ecological settings, collectivities, and elites, may produce either patrimonial, Imperial, or tribal regimes based mostly on internal markets or city-states or tribal federations based on external markets. The former group includes societies based on both compact and crosscutting markets.

Societies also greatly differ in regard to the degree to which they are isolated from, or closely associated with, structurally similar or different societies. Here again, certain types of tribal federations, like those of the ancient Near and Middle East and city-state federations and feudal systems stand out as examples of complex interaction as compared to large, self-contained patrimonial or Imperial systems.

Given the variety of possible developments it may well be that within the same broad international situation, different aspects or dimensions of social and cultural activity will become more concentrated in some social settings—whether total societies or special enclaves—than in others. Furthermore, it may be that such enclaves constitute a unique type of reference point within international subsystems and serve as models that may become available beyond the given internal level of differentiation of a given society and even provide certain resources that may guide the changes in these societies in new directions.

The preceding analysis recognizes far more possibilities and directions of social changes than does the evolutionary perspective, and it poses a series of new and challenging problems to sociological and historical analysis.

Specification of these problems entails far-reaching revision of many assumptions of sociological analysis. Above all, this approach stresses the relative openness and specificity of different historical situations. At the same time, it stresses the possibility of meaningful comparative analysis of historical situations that goes beyond the assumptions of most comparative studies—particularly those with an evolutionary orientation.

8. SYMBOLIC AND STRUCTURAL PREMISES OF TRADITIONAL SOCIETIES. THEIR EFFECTS ON PATTERNS OF CHANGE

In the preceding section of this chapter we attempted to identify certain conditions that may account for some of the variations in patterns of change within traditional societies. Needless to say, this is only a beginning. There are many aspects of processes and outcomes of change that we did not examine: the causes of more or less intensive processes of change in different types of regimes; the shifts in policy orientation within regimes; and the degrees and types of discontinuities attendant upon such changes. We pursue these questions in our analysis of modern revolutions and their outcomes.

Many of these conditions seem to be common to all societies. Yet at the same time our analysis indicated, if only in a preliminary way, certain characteristics of processes of change in traditional societies that distinguish them from modern processes of change.

The most important common aspects of the processes of change in the societies we analyzed was the development of limitations on the various movements of change, on linkages between them, and on the conception of alternative social orders; consequently, their transformative capacities were relatively limited.

These common characteristics of the process of change were rooted in the combination of the uniquely traditional features of these societies and the levels of their technology and organizational differentiation. Given their traditionalism, there generally developed a rather weak conception of the possibility of the conscious reshaping of the social order and cultural models through the autonomous activity of individuals. This conception was emphasized in the speculations of some intellectuals and in the more intellectual or esoteric heterodoxies (and it was incorporated into the cultural orientations and symbols of rulers, wider groups, or rebels only in exceptional circumstances).

Truly enough, in traditional societies great acts of cultural creativity were performed by individuals or small groups—the best examples of which are the Hebrew prophets, Jesus, the Greek philosophers, Confucius, the Brahmanic ancestors, and the Buddha. But the creation and institutionalization of these innovations was not seen as an autonomous act by human beings; rather, it was perceived as a rediscovery through revelation of the true, traditional model based on traditional legitimation and bound by its own traditional premises.

Only in ancient Greece (above all, Athens) and to a smaller extent Rome were such limitations challenged by radical tendencies closely related to the incipient undermining of certain (different in each case) premises of traditionalism. But as these societies did not have the resources for the institutionalization of such tendencies, they served as (in Parsons's terminology) "seed societies," which later societies emulated.[78] The limited transformative capacities of Greece and Rome were also reinforced by the autonomy of various components of the macrosociological order as well as of diverse organizational—local, occupational, religious—units.

These capacities were also reinforced by the relatively low level of structural differentiation in these societies. Given these limited levels, such units were able, in most situations of change within traditional societies to maintain a degree of self-sufficiency and continuity.

The continuity of these organizational units was fostered by the interlinking mechanisms characteristic of situations of change in traditional societies. Continual emphasis on traditional premises also had structural implications of great importance for our analysis. Most important were limitations on the linkages among different strata, institutional entrepreneurs, and centers. Such limitations were evident even in those societies—the Imperial and Imperial-feudal systems—in which such linkages were strongest, and they were reinforced by the policies of rulers (the more coercive the rulers, the stronger were these limitations). Still, even in the relatively less coercive systems (e.g., the Chinese and Byzantine empires as compared with the Russian), traditionalism itself tended to generate such limitations.

Interlinking mechanisms such as ritual features and media of communication that connected the great with the little traditions and the intermediary elites like religious specialists and bureaucratic groups tended to maintain traditional cultural orientations. Hence, they reinforced the comparative closure of the new centers and limited the possibility of access or participation in these centers by broader groups and of the mutual claims of the centers and the groups on one another.

The fundamental characteristics of traditionalism in these societies also constrained innovative groups and reduced their impact upon the centers of society. The different acts or processes of creativity and innovation in the cultural and the institutional field usually were not *directly* connected with each other. Rather, each innovation created conditions conducive to the development of others; they could reinforce each other and generate new levels of resources but did not necessarily converge upon the restructuring of the centers.

Thus, a vital aspect of the patterns of change in these societies was the significance of innovations carried by relatively segregated, autonomous groups that often did not develop within the societies in which they originated but within other societies or special cultural-ecological enclaves in changing international systems. Hence, in the spread of innovations, groups of warriors, cultural specialists, and traders, along with processes like conquest or missionary activitity, were of crucial importance. This was true even of those processes that led to the establishment of Imperial systems that later manifested a greater degree of coalescence among the major dimensions of the macrosocietal order. Once such new traditional complexes of great traditions, high civilizations or Imperial systems were established, there arose within them, significantly enough, the limitations inherent in traditionalism. These limitations gave, however, in these societies rise to tensions between the tendencies to, on the one hand, segregation between different types of protest and innovation and, on the other hand, to linkages between them that were greater than in other "archaic" or "patrimonial" societies. But even in these societies these tensions did not burst beyond the limits of traditionality specified above.

NOTES

1. On Buddhism, from the point of view of this discussion, see P. A. Pardue, *Buddhism: An Historic Introduction* (New York: Macmillan, 1958); W. T. de Bary (ed.), *The Buddhist Tradition in India, China, and Japan* (New York: Random House, Vintage, 1972); P. Lévy, *Buddhism: A "Mystery Religion"?* (New York: Schocken, 1968); H. Bechert, *Buddhismus: Staat und Gesellschaft in den Ländern des Theravada-Buddhismus,* 4 vols. (Frankfurt am Main: Alfred Metzner, 1966–1968); S. J. Tambiah, *World Conqueror and World Renouncer* (Cambridge: At the University Press, 1976); E. M. Mendelson, *Sangha and State in Burma: A Study of Monastic Sectarianism,* (ed.), J. P. Ferguson (Ithaca: Cornell University Press, 1975); R. F. Gombrich, *Precept and Practice: Traditional Buddhism in the Rural Highlands of Ceylon* (Oxford: Clarendon, 1971); M. Nash, G. Obeyesekere, H. M. Ames, J. Ingersoll, D. E. Pfanner, J. C. Nash, M. Moerman, M. Ebihara, and N. Yalman, *Anthropological Studies in Theravada Buddhism,* Yale University, Southeast Asia Studies Cultural Report Series, no. 13 (New Haven, 1966); and E. B. Harper (ed.), *Religion in South Asia* (Seattle: University of Washington Press, 1964).
2. See A. Christensen, *Le Règne du roi Khawadh et le communisme mazdakite* (Copenhagen: Munskgaard, 1925); idem, *L'Iran sous les Sassanides* (Copenhagen: Munskgaard, 1936); idem, "Sassanid Persia," in *The Cambridge Ancient History,* 15 vols. (Cambridge: At the University Press, 1965), 12:109–137; and R. P. de Menasce, "L'Église mazdéenne dans l'Empire sassanide," *Journal of World History,* 2, no. 3 (1955): 554–565.
3. On the participation of the Sangha in the political life, rebellions, and change in Buddhist societies see Tambiah, *World Conqueror;* Bechert, *Buddhismus;* Mendelson, *Sangha and State in Burma;* G. Obeyesekere, F. Reynolds, and B. L. Smith (eds.), *The Two Wheels of Dhamma: Essays on the Theravada Tradition in India and Ceylon,* American Academy of Religion Studies in Religion, no. 3 (1972), esp. chaps. 1, 2, and

3; J. Bunnag, *Buddhist Monk, Buddhist Layman: A Study of Urban Monastic Organization in Central Thailand,* Cambridge Studies in Social Anthropology, No. 6 (Cambridge: At the University Press, 1973); Gombrich, *Precept and Practice;* Nash et al., *Theravada Buddhism;* Harper, *Religion in South Asia;* P. Mus, "Traditions asiennes et bouddhisme moderne," *Eranos Jahrbuch,* 32 (1968): 161–275; and idem, "La Sociologie de Georges Gurvitch et l'Asie," *Cahiers internationaux de sociologie,* 43 (December 1967): 1–21; and R. L. Winzeler, "Ecology, Culture, Social Organization, and State Formation in Southeast Asia," *Current Anthropology,* 1, no. 4 (1976): 623–641.

4. Tambiah, *World Conqueror;* Bechert, *Buddhismus;* E. Sarkisyanz, *The Buddhist Background of the Burmese Revolution* (The Hague: M. Nijhoff, 1965); idem, *Russland und der Messianismus des Orients* (Tübingen: J. C. B. Mohr, 1955), pp. 327–368; F. E. Reynolds, "Civic Religion and National Community in Thailand," *Journal of Asian Studies,* 36, no. 4 (1977): 267–282; C. F. Keyes, "Millenialism, Theravada Buddhism and Thai Society," *Journal of Asian Studies,* 36, no. 4 (1977): 283–303; T. Stern, "Ariya and the Golden Book: A Millenarian Buddhist Sect among the Karen," *Journal of Asian Studies,* 27, no. 2 (1968): 297–327; and W. H. Rassers, *Pañji, the Culture Hero: A Structural Study of Religion in Java* (The Hague: M. Nijhoff, 1959).

5. On the basic tenets of Hinduism see M. Biardeau, *Clefs pour la pensée hindoue* (Paris: Seghers, 1972); M. Weber, *The Religion of India: The Sociology of Hinduism and Buddhism,* trans. H. H. Gerth, and D. Martindale (New York: Free Press, 1958); C. Bouglé, *Essais sur le régime des castes* (Paris: Presses universitaires de France, 1969); L. Dumont, *Homo Hierarchicus: Essai sur le système des castes* (Paris: Gallimard, 1966); L. Dumont and D. Pockok, *Contributions to Indian Sociology,* 9 vols. (Paris: Mouton, 1957–1966); L. Dumont, *Religion, Politics, and History in India: Collected Papers in Indian Sociology* (Paris: Mouton, 1970); and the following discussion of *Homo Hierarchicus* in the *Journal of Asian Studies,* 35, no. 4 (1976): J. F. Richards and R. W. Nichols, Introduction, pp. 579–580; P. Kolenda, "Seven Kinds of Hierarchy in *Homo Hierarchicus,*" pp. 581–596; M. Derret and J. Duncan, "Rajadharma," pp. 597–610; J. Masson Moussaieff, "The Psychology of the Ascetic," pp. 611–626; and S. Barnet, L. Fruzzetti, and A. Ostor, "Hierarchy Purified: Notes on Dumont and His Critics," pp. 627–646.

See also H. Stern, "Religion et société en Inde selon Max Weber: Analyse critique de hindouisme et bouddhisme," *Information sur les sciences sociales,* 10, no. 6 (1971): 69–113; N. W. Brown, *Man in the Universe: Some Cultural Continuities in India* (Berkeley: University of California Press, 1966); and R. Thapar, *A History of India* (Baltimore: Penguin, 1966); Mus, *Traditions asiennes;* and idem, "*Georges Gurvitch.*"

6. The interweaving of otherworldly orientations and secular activities in Hinduism is discussed in Biardeau, *Clefs pour la pensée hindoue;* Dumont, *Homo Hierarchicus;* J. C. Heesterman, "Priesthood and the Brahmin," mimeographed (Leiden, 1975); and D. G. Mandelbaum, *Society in India,* 2 vols. (Berkeley: University of California Press, 1970).

7. On Indian centers see Mandelbaum, *Society in India;* B. S. Cohn, *India: The Social Anthropology of a Civilization* (Englewood Cliffs: Prentice-Hall, 1971); B. M. Morrison, *Political Centers and Cultural Regions in Early Bengal* (Tucson: University of Arizona Press, 1970); M. Singer and B. S. Cohn (eds.), *Structure and Change in Indian Society* (Chicago: Aldine, 1968); R. Fox, *Kin, Clan, Raja, and Rule: State–Hinterland Relations in Pre-Industrial India* (Berkeley: University of California Press, 1971); H. van Gerrit, *The Mahabharata: An Ethnological Study* (Amsterdam: Uitgeversmaatschappij Holland, 1936); B. Stein (ed.), *Essays on South India,* Asian Studies at Hawaii, no. 15 (Honolulu: University Press of Hawaii, 1976); Heesterman, "Priesthood and the Brahmin"; M. Singer, "The Social Organization of Indian Civilization," *Diogenes,* 45 (Winter 1964): 84–119; M. Singer (ed.), *Traditional India: Structure and Change* (Philadelphia: American Folklore Society, 1959); J. H. Hutton, *Caste in India* (Cambridge: At the University Press, 1946); J. C. Heesterman, "Brahmin, Ritual, and Renouncer," in *Wiener Zeitschrift fur die Kunde Süd- und Ostasiens,* special reprint from vol. 8, 1964; and idem, "The Conundrum of the King's Authority," mimeographed (Leiden, 1976).

8. On secular elements of Indian politics see Dumont, *Religion, Politics, and History in India;* J. C. Heesterman, *The Ancient Indian Royal Consecration: The Rajasuya Described According to the Yajus Texts and Annotated* by J. C. Heesterman (Paris: Mouton 1957); D. H. H. Ingalls, "Authority and Law in Ancient India," *Journal of the American Oriental Society* (supp.), 74 (1954): 34–45; H. N. Sinha, *Sovereignty in Ancient Indian Polity* (London: Luzac, 1938); J. C. Heesterman, "Kautalya and the Ancient Indian State," in *Wiener Zeitschrift fur de Kunde Süd- und Ostasiens,* special reprint from vol. 15:5–22; and idem, "Conundrum of the King's Authority."

9. On the caste system and networks see Singer and Cohn, *Indian Society;* Mandelbaum, *Society in India;* Fox, *Kin, Clan, Raja, and Rule;* K. Ishwaran (ed.), *Change and Continuity in India's Villages* (New York: Columbia University Press, 1970); M. N. Srinivas, *Social Change in Modern India* (Berkeley: University of California Press, 1966); and A. Beteille, *Caste, Class, and Power: Changing Patterns of Stratification in a Tanjore Village* (Berkeley: University of California Press, 1965). The specific aspects of the caste system as a system of social hierarchy are analyzed in S. N. Eisenstadt, *Social Differentiation and Stratification* (Glenview: Scott, Foresman, 1971), pp. 106–109; and R. B. Inden, *Marriage and Rank in Bengali Culture: A History of Caste and Clan in Middle Period Bengal* (Berkeley: University of California Press, 1976).

10. On the entrepreneurial element in caste organization see the references cited in notes 7 and 9 above, as well as Singer and Cohn, *Indian Society,* pts. 3, 4; S. H. Rudolph and L. I. Rudolph, "Rajput Adulthood: Reflections on the Amar Sing's Diary," *Daedalus,* Spring 1976, pp. 145–169; and M. Singer, *When a Great Tradition Modernizes* (New York: Praeger, 1972), esp. pt. 4.

11. On the patterns of change in Indian society and their limits see Singer

and Cohn, *Indian Society;* Singer, *Traditional India;* Stein, "South India"; J. F. Staal, "Sanskrit and Sanskritization," *Journal of Asian Studies,* 22, no. 3 1963): 261–275; and Fox, *Kin, Clan, Raja, and Rule;* and Ishwaran, *India's Villages.*

12. On the relations among the political, the religious, and the economic orders in Indian history see Mandelbaum, *Society in India;* Stein, "South India"; Heesterman, "Priesthood and the Brahmin"; B. M. Morrison, *Early Bengal;* S. Sinha, *State Formation and Rajput Myth in Tribal Central India,* Duke University Comparative Studies on Southern Asia, Man in India, vol. 42, no. 1 (Durham, 1962): 35–80; R. E. Frykenberg (ed.), *Land Control and Social Structure in Indian History* (Madison: University of Wisconsin Press), esp. pp. 53–122, 175–216; Stern, "Religion et société en Inde"; and S. M. Rudolph and L. I. Rudolph, with M. Singh, "A Bureaucratic Lineage in Princely India: Elite Formation and Conflict in a Patrimonial System," *Journal of Asian Studies,* 34, no. 3 (1975): 717–754.

13. Srinivas, *Social Change;* idem, "A Note on Sanskritization and Westernization," *Far Eastern Quarterly,* 15, no. 4 (1956): 481–496; and Staal, "Sanskrit and Sanskritization."

14. On the Brahman versus the Sannyasa see Heesterman, "Brahmin, Ritual, and Renouncer"; and the discussion of Dumont's *Home Hierarchicus* cited in note 5 above.

15. Some of these trends are analyzed in Srinivas, *Social Change;* Singer and Cohn, *Indian Society;* Srinivas, "Note on Sanskritization"; Staal, "Sanskrit and Sanskritization"; D. H. A. Kolff "Sannyasi Trader-Soldiers," *Indian Economic and Social History Review,* 8, no. 2 (1971): 214–220; and S. N. Gordon, "Scarf and Sword: Thugs, Marauders, and State-Formation in Eighteenth Century Malwa," ibid., 6; no. 4 (1969): 403–429.

16. On these movements of change see Mandelbaum, *Society in India,* esp. vol. 2; Weber, *Religion of India;* Dumont, *Homo Hierarchicus;* Singer and Cohn, *Indian Society;* and Singer, *When a Great Tradition Modernizes.*

17. This point has been stressed by Dumont throughout his work; see also Weber, *Religion of India;* and H. Stern, "Religion et sociéte en Inde."

18. Heesterman, "Brahmin, Ritual, and Renouncer"; idem, "India and the Inner Conflict of Tradition," in S. N. Eisenstadt (ed.), *Post-Traditional Societies* (New York: Norton, 1972), pp. 97–115; and Kolff, "Sannyasi Trader-Soldiers."

19. On the Russian traditional regime see R. Pipes, *Russia under the Old Regime* (London: Weidenfeld & Nicolson, 1974); I. Young, "Russia," in J. O. Lindsay (ed.), *The New Cambridge Modern History* (Cambridge: At the University Press, 1957), 7:318–388; M. Raeff, *Origins of the Russian Intelligentsia: The Eighteenth Century Nobility* (New York: Harcourt Brace Jovanovich, 1966); B. H. Summer, "Peter the Great," *History,* 32, no. 115 (1947): 39–50; idem, *A Short History of Russia* (New York: Harcourt, Brace, 1949); M. Beloff, *The Age of Absolutism* (London: Hutchinson, 1954), chap. 6; idem, "Russia," in A. Goodwin (ed.), *The*

European Nobility in the Eighteenth Century (London: Black, 1953);
J. Blum, *Lord and Peasant in Russia* (Princeton: Princeton University
Press, 1961); H. Seton-Watson, *The Russian Empire, 1801–1917* (New
York: Oxford University Press, 1967); and S. Tushkarev, *The Emergence
of Modern Russia, 1801–1917* (New York: Holt, Rinehart & Winston,
1963).

20. See Pipes, *Russia under the Old Regime.*

21. On the true believers see A. Gerschenkorn, *Europe in the Russian Mirror:
Four Lectures in Economic History* (Cambridge: At the University Press,
1970).

22. This is analyzed in Eisenstadt, *Social Differentiation,* chap. 6, based mostly
on materials cited in notes 19 and 21 above; see also Pipes, *Russia under
the Old Regime,* chaps. 6–8.

23. On some of the processes of change see Pipes, *Russia under the Old Regime,* chaps. 5, 10, 11; H. Seton-Watson, *The Decline of Imperial Russia, 1855–1914* (London: Methuen, 1952); idem, *Russian Empire;* and
Tushkarev, *Emergence of Modern Russia.*

24. See on this Raeff, *Origins of the Russian Intelligentsia;* and Pipes, *Russia under the Old Regime,* chaps. 7, 10.

25. On the place of the Church in Russia see Pipes, *Russia under the Old
Regime,* chap. 9.

26. Seton-Watson, *Decline of Imperial Russia.*

27. Pipes, *Russia under the Old Regime,* chaps. 10, 11; idem (ed.), *Revolutionary Russia* (Cambridge: Harvard University Press, 1968); E. J. Simmons (ed.), *Continuity and Change in Russian Soviet Thought* (Cambridge: Harvard University Press, 1965); and C. E. Black (ed.), *The
Transformation of Russian Society: Aspects of Social Change since 1861*
(Cambridge: Harvard University Press, 1960).

28. See the literature cited in note 8 to Chapter 4, especially G. Ostrogorsky,
History of the Byzantine State (Oxford: Blackwell, 1956); L. Brehier,
Les Institutions de l'Empire byzantin (Paris: Albin Michel, 1949); and
idem, *La Civilisation byzantine* (Paris: Albin Michel, 1950).

29. On the relations between Church and Emperor in the Byzantine Empire
see L. Bréhier, *Le Schisme oriental du XIe siècle* (New York: B. Franklin,
1969, reprint of 1899 ed.); J. M. Hussey, *Church and Learning in the
Byzantine Empire, 867–1185* (New York: Oxford University Press, 1937);
and idem, "The Byzantine Empire in the Eleventh Century: Some Different Interpretations," *Transactions of the Royal Historical Society,* 32
(1950): 71–85.

30. On the social structure of the Byzantine Empire and of its elites see, in
addition to the works cited in notes 28–29 above, G. Ostrogorsky, "Die
Perioden der byzantinischen Geschichte," *Historische Zeitschrift,* 163,
no. 2 (1941): 238–254; P. Charanis, "On the Social Structure and Economic Organization of the Byzantine Empire in the Thirteenth Century,"
Byzantinoslavica, 12 (1951): 94–153; idem, "Internal Strife at Byzantium
in the Fourteenth Century," *Byzantion,* 15 (1940–1941): 208–230; idem,

"The Aristocracy of Byzantion in the Thirteenth Century," in *Studies in Roman Economic and Social History in Honor of Allan Chester Johnson*, P. R. Coleman-Norton, ed. (Princeton: Princeton University Press, 1951), pp. 336–356; and idem, "Economic Factors in the Decline of the Byzantine Empire," *Journal of Economic History*, 13, no. 4 (1953): 412–425. On the overall pattern of change in the Byzantine Empire see F. G. Maier, "Tradition und Wandel: Über die Gründe der Widerstandskraft von Byzanz," *Historische Zeitschrift*, 218, no. 2 (1974): 265–282.

31. On the Chinese tradition see E. O. Reischauer and J. K. Fairbank, *A History of East Asian Civilization*, vol. 1, *East Asia: the Great Tradition* (Boston: Houghton Mifflin, 1960); M. Weber, *The Religion of China: Confucianism and Taoism*, transl. by H. Gerth (New York: Free Press, 1964); C. K. Yang, "The Functional Relationship between Confucian Thought and Chinese Religion," in J. K. Fairbank (ed.), *Chinese Thought and Institutions* (Chicago: University of Chicago Press, 1957), pp. 269–291; A. F. Wright (ed.), *The Confucian Persuasion* (Stanford: Stanford University Press, 1960); D. S. Nivison and A. F. Wright (eds.), *Confucianism in Action* (Stanford: Stanford University Press, 1959); and A. F. Wright (ed.), *Studies in Chinese Thought* (Chicago: University of Chicago Press, 1953).

32. On the place of the secondary religions see Weber, *Religion of China;* Reischauer and Fairbank, *East Asia;* the analysis in S. N. Eisenstadt, *The Political Systems of Empires* (New York: Free Press Paperback, 1969), esp. chap. 4; and the references cited in note 42 below.

33. Some of these problems of individual responsibility are discussed in Nivison and Wright, *Confucianism in Action*, chaps. 3, 8, 9, 10; and in Wright, *Studies in Chinese Thought*, chaps. 4 and 5; and in idem, *The Confucian Persuasion*, chaps. 4, 7, 8. The problem of transcendence in ancient China is discussed in B. I. Schwartz, "Transcendence in Ancient China," *Daedalus*, Spring 1975, pp. 57–68.

34. On the Chinese status system and its relation to the political system see E. Balazs, *Chinese Civilization and Bureaucracy: Variations on a Theme* (New Haven: Yale University Press, 1964); and F. Michael, "State and Society in Nineteenth Century China," *World Politics*, 7, no. 3 (1955): 419–433.

35. This analysis is based on Eisenstadt, *Social Differentiation*, pp. 101–106; and idem, *Political Systems of Empires*, esp. chap. 12; see also I. M. Lapidus, "Hierarchies and Networks: A Comparison of Chinese and Islamic Societies," in F. Wakeman (ed.), *Conflict and Control in Late Imperial China* (Berkeley: University of California Press, 1975), pp. 26–42.

36. On the place of kinship in the Chinese system of stratification see Ping-ti Ho, *The Ladder of Success in Imperial China: Aspects of Social Mobility, 1368–1911* (New York: Columbia University Press, 1962); M. Friedman (ed.), *Family and Kinship in Chinese Society* (Stanford: Stanford University Press, 1970); and E. A. Kracke, "Religion, Family, and Individual in the Chinese Examination System," in Fairbank, *Chinese Thought and Institutions*, pp. 251–268.

37. The pattern of mobility in Chinese society is analyzed in Ho, *Ladder of Success;* R. Marsh, *The Mandarins: Circulations of Elites in China, 1600–1900* (New York: Free Press, 1961); and W. Eberhard, "Social Mobility and Stratification in China," in R. Bendix and S. M. Lipset (eds.), *Class, Status and Power* (London: Routledge & Kegan Paul, 1967), pp. 171–182.

38. On the literati see Balazs, *Chinese Civilization and Bureaucracy;* Chang Chung-li, *The Chinese Gentry: Studies on Their Role in Nineteenth Century Chinese Society* (Seattle: University of Washington Press, 1955); B. O. van der Sprenkel, *The Chinese Civil Service: the Nineteenth Century* (Canberra: Australian National University Press, 1958); M. Weber, "The Chinese Literati," in H. H. Gerth and C. W. Mills (eds.), *Essays in Sociology* (New York: Oxford University Press, 1958), pp. 416–444; C. K. Yang, "Some Characteristics of Chinese Bureaucratic Behavior," in Nivison and Wright, *Confucianism in Action,* pp. 134–165; E. A. Kracke, *Civil Service in Early Sung China, 960–1067* (Cambridge: Harvard University Press, 1953); and idem, "Sung Society: Change within Tradition," *Far Eastern Quarterly,* 14, no. 4 (1955): 479–489.

39. On the political struggle in China see the historical analysis in Reischauer and Fairbank, *East Asia.* Some of the aspects presented here are analyzed in C. O. Hucker (ed.), *Chinese Government in Ming Times: Seven Studies* (New York: Columbia University Press, 1969); B. E. McKnight, *Village and Bureaucracy in Southern Sung China* (Chicago: University of Chicago Press, 1971); J. T. C. Liu, "An Administrative Cycle in Chinese History," in J. A. Harrison (ed.), *China: Enduring Scholarship* (Tucson: University of Arizona Press, 1972, 1:75–90; Eisenstadt, *Political Systems of Empires,* esp. chaps. 10, 11; and the references cited in notes 40–41 below.

40. On some of the ideological aspects of political struggle in China see Nivison and Wright, *Confucianism in Action;* H. R. Williamson, *Wang An-shih: A Chinese Statesman and Educationalist of the Sung Dynasty* (London: A. Probsthain, 1937); F. H. Michael, "From the Fall of T'ang to the Fall of Ch'ing," in H. F. McNair (ed.), *China* (Berkeley: University of California Press, 1946), pp. 89–110; O. Franke, "Der Bericht Wang An-shih's von 1058 über Reform des Beamtentums," *Sitzungsberichte der preussischen Akademie der Wissenschaften* (Berlin: 1931–1933), pp. 264–312; J. T. C. Liu, "An Early Sung Reformer: Fan Chung-yen," in Fairbank, *Chinese Thought and Institutions,* pp. 105–132; idem, *Reform in Sung China: Wang An-shih, 1021–1086, and His New Policies* (Cambridge: Harvard University Press, 1959); P. A. Cohen and J. E. Schrecker (eds.), *Reform in Nineteenth Century China* (Cambridge: Harvard University Press, 1976); J. T. C. Liu, "Eleventh Century Chinese Bureaucrats: Some Historical Classifications and Behavioral Types," *Administrative Science Quarterly,* 4, no. 2 (1959): 207–226; A. F. Wright, "The Formation of Sui Ideology, 581–604," in J. K. Fairbank (ed.), *Chinese Thought and Institutions,* pp. 71–106; L. C. Goodrich, *The Literary Inquisition of Ch'ien-Lung* (Baltimore: Johns Hopkins Press, 1953); W. de Bary, "Some Common Tendencies in Neo-Confucianism," in Nivison and Wright, *Confucianism in Action,* pp. 25–49; and H. H. Dubs, "Wang Mang and His Economic Reforms," *T'oung pao,* 35, no. 4 (Leiden, 1939): 263–265.

41. The patterns of rebellions and warlords in China are discussed in Eisenstadt, *Political Systems of Empires*, chaps. 10, 11; for illustrative analyses of case studies see F. Wakeman, Jr., "Rebellion and Revolution: The Study of Popular Movements in Chinese History," *Journal of Asian Studies*, 36, no. 4 (1977): 201–238; J. B. Parsons, "The Culmination of a Chinese Peasant Rebellion," *Journal of Asian Studies*, 16, no. 3 (1957): 387–401; E. Pulleyblank, *The Background of the Rebellion of An Lu-shan* (New York: Oxford University Press, 1955), chaps. 3, 5; A. Feuerwerker, *Rebellion in Nineteenth-Century China* (Ann Arbor: University of Michigan, Center for Chinese Studies, 1975); H. S. Levy, "Yellow Turban Religion and Rebellion at the End of Han," *Journal of the American Oriental Society*, 76, no. 4 (1956): 214–227; idem, "How a Prince Became Emperor: The Accession of Hsuan Tsung, 713–755," *Sinologica*, 6, no. 2 (1959): 101–119; C. O. Hucker, "The Tung-Lin Movement of the Late Ming Period," in Fairbank, *Chinese Thought and Institutions*, pp. 132–167; Liu, "Fan Chung-yen"; idem, *Reform in Sung China*; and idem, "Eleventh Century Chinese Bureaucrats." On foreign conquerors see W. Eberhard, *Conquerors and Rulers* (Leiden: E. J. Brill, 1952); F. H. Michael, *Frontier and Bureaucracy: The Origin of Manchu Rule in China* (Baltimore: John Hopkins Press, 1952); and J. W. Dardess, *Conquerors and Confucians: Aspects of Political Change in Late Yuan China* (New York: Columbia University Press, 1973).

42. On the impact of Buddhism and Taoism on Chinese society see Reischauer and Fairbank, *East Asia*; M. Kaltenmark, *Lao Tzu and Taoism* (Stanford: Stanford University Press, 1969); A. F. Wright, *Buddhism in Chinese History* (Stanford: Stanford University Press, 1959); C. Y. Chia, "The Church-State Conflict in the T'ang Dynasty," in E. T. Zen and J. de Francis (eds.), *Chinese Social History* (Washington, D.C.: American Council of Learned Societies, 1956), pp. 197–207; and for a more general discussion see A. P. Wolf (ed.), *Religion and Ritual in Chinese Society* (Stanford: Stanford University Press, 1974).

43. See, for instance, Kracke, "Sung Society"; as well as Reischauer and Fairbank, *East Asia*. On the economic organization of China and some of its relations to the political setting see W. E. Willmott (ed.), *Economic Organization in Chinese Society* (Stanford: Stanford University Press, 1972; M. Elvin, *The Pattern of the Chinese Past* (London: Eyre Methuen, 1973); K. Wang, "The System of Equal Land Allotments in Medieval Times," in Zen and De Francis, *Chinese Social History*, pp. 57–185; Y. C. Wang, "The Rise of Land Tax and the Fall of Dynasties in Chinese History," *Pacific Affairs*, 9, no. 3 (1936): 201–220; and Wright, "Formation of Sui Ideology."

44. See Eisenstadt, *Political Systems of Empires*, chaps. 4–6; and the references dealing with reformers in note 41 above; see also Parsons, "Culmination of a Chinese Peasant Rebellion"; Elvin, *Pattern of the Chinese Past*; and Wilmott, *Chinese Society*.

45. See the references cited in notes 33, 40, and 41 above.

46. On Islamic civilization in general see P. M. Holt, A. K. S. Lambton, and

B. Lewis (eds.), *The Cambridge History of Islam,* 2 vols. (Cambridge: At the University Press, 1970); H. A. R. Gibb, *Studies on the Civilization of Islam* (Boston: Beacon, 1962), esp. chap. 1; and C. Cahen, *Leçons d'histoire musulmane,* 3 vols. (Paris: Centre de documentation universitaire, 1957), esp. vol. 2.

47. On the basic tenets of Islam see, in addition to the general works cited in note 46 above, G. E. Von Grünebaum, *Medieval Islam: A Study in Cultural Orientation* (Chicago: University of Chicago Press, 1946); idem (ed.), *Studies in Islamic Cultural History,* American Anthropologist Memoir No. 76 (Menaska, Wisc., 1954); B. Lewis, *The Arabs in History* (London: Hutchinson, 1950), pp. 64–115; A. Metz, *The Renaissance of Islam* (London: Luzac, 1937); M. G. S. Hodgson, *The Venture of Islam: Conscience and History in a World Civilization,* 3 vols. (Chicago: University of Chicago Press, 1974); B. Lewis, "The Concept of an Islamic Republic," *Die Welt des Islams,* 4, no. 1 (1955): 1–10; idem, *Islam in History: Ideas, Men, and Events in the Middle East* (London: Alcove, 1973); G. E. von Grünebaum, "The Sources of Islamic Civilization," in Holt et al., *Cambridge History of Islam,* 2:469–510; and C. J. Adams, "The Islamic Religious Tradition in J. O'Dea, T. O'Dea, and C. J. Adams, *Religion and Man: Judaism, Christianity, and Islam* (New York: Harper & Row, 1972), pp. 159–221.

48. Gibb, *Studies in the Civilization of Islam,* pp. 3–46, 141–150; I. M. Lapidus, "The Separation of State and Religion in the Development of Early Islamic Society," *International Journal of Middle East Studies,* 6, no. 4 (1975): 363–385; and H. K. Sherwani, "The Genesis and Progress of Muslim Socio-Political Thought," *Islamic Culture,* 27, no. 3 (1953): 135–148.

49. On the place of law see J. Schacht, "Law and Justice," in Holt et al., *Cambridge History of Islam,* 2:539–568.

50. On these tendencies in sultanic direction in Islamic societies see B. S. Turner, *Weber and Islam: A Critical Study* (London: Routledge & Kegan Paul, 1974).

51. On the ulema under the Ottomans see, in addition to the works cited in note 46 above, H. A. R. Gibb and H. Bowen, *Islamic Society and the West* (New York: Oxford University Press, 1957), 2: chaps. 8–12.

52. D. Ayalon, *L'Esclavage du Mamelouk* (Jerusalem: Israel Oriental Society, 1951); N. Itzkowitz, *Ottoman Empire and Islamic Tradition* (New York: Knopf, 1972); P. Wittek, *The Rise of the Ottoman Empire* (London: Royal Asiatic Society, 1938); and B. Miller, *The Palace School of Muhammad the Conqueror* (Cambridge: Harvard University Press, 1941).

53. On sectarian tendencies in Islam see H. Laoust, *Les Schismes dans l'Islam: Introduction à une étude de la religion musulmane* (Paris: Payot, 1965); Lewis, *Islam in History,* pp. 217–266; C. Cahen, "La Changeante portée sociale de quelques doctrines religieuses," in *L'Elaboration de l'Islam,* Colloque de Strasbourg, 12–14 June, 1959 (Paris: Presses universitaires de France, 1961), pp. 5–22; and M. S. Stern, *Isma'ilis and Qarmantians,* in ibid., pp. 99–108.

54. On these developments see C. Cahen, "Economy, Society, and Institutions" in Holt et al., *Cambridge History of Islam*, 2:511–538; idem, *Leçons d'histoire musulmane*, esp. vol. 2; idem, "Les Facteurs économiques et sociaux dans l'ankylose culturelle de l'Islam," in R. Brunschwig and G. E. von Grünebaum (eds.), *Classicisme et déclin culturel dans l'histoire de l'Islam* (Paris: Besson & Chante Merle, 1957), pp. 195–217; idem, "Zur Geschichte der städtischen Gesellschaft im Orient des Mittelalters," *Saeculum*, 9, no. 1 (1958): 59–76; idem, "La Changeante portée sociale de quelques doctrines religieuses"; S. D. Goitein, *Studies in Islamic History and Institutions* (Leiden: E. J. Brill, 1966), esp. pp. 217–241; and E. Ashtor, Républiques urbaines dans le Proche-Orient à l'époque des croisades," *Cahiers de civilisation médiévale*, 18, no. 2 (1975): 117–131.

55. On the spread of Islam see Holt et al., *Cambridge History of Islam*, vol. 2; and N. Levtzion (ed.), *Conversion to Islam*, Proceedings of a seminar held at the SOAS, University of London, 1973, forthcoming.

56. See Turner, *Weber and Islam*.

57. On the special position of Shii Islam see D. Sourdel, "The Abbasid Caliphate," in Holt et al., *Cambridge History of Islam*, 1:104–139; and B. Spuler, "The Disintegration of the Caliphate in the East," in ibid., pp. 143–174.

58. This is more fully elaborated in S. N. Eisenstadt, "Convergence and Divergence of Modern and Modernizing Societies: Indications from the Analysis of the Structuring of Social Hierarchies in Middle Eastern Societies," *International Journal of Middle East Studies*, 8, no. 1 (1977): 1–27; and I. M. Lapidus, "Hierarchies and Networks: A Comparison of Chinese and Islamic Societies," in Wakeman, *Conflict and Control in Late Imperial China*, pp. 26–42.

59. On these constellations in general see E. Gellner, "A Pendulum Swing Theory of Islam," in R. Robertson (ed.), *Sociology of Religion* (Baltimore: Penguin, 1969), pp. 127–141. On the constellations in the Maghreb see, for instance, E. Gellner and C. Micaud (eds.), *Arabs and Berbers: From Tribe to Nation in North Africa* (London: Duckworth, 1973); and C. C. Stewart, *Islam and Social Order in Mauritania: A Case Study from the Nineteenth Century* (Oxford: Clarendon, 1973). On more recent developments see A. S. Ahmed, *Millennium and Charisma among the Pathans: A Critical Essay in Social Anthropology* (London: Routledge & Kegan Paul, 1976).

60. See, in addition to the materials cited in note 53 above, M. G. S. Hodgson, *The Order of Assassins* (The Hague: M. Nijhoff, 1955); M. Laouste, *Les Schismes*, op. cit.; H. A. R. Gibb, "Government and Islam under the Early Abbasids: The Political Collapse of Islam," in *L'Elaboration de l'Islam*, pp. 115–127; and M. A. Shaban, *The Abbasid Revolution* (Cambridge: At the University Press, 1970). Ahmed, *Millennium and Charisma*, deals especially with contemporary developments.

61. For a general background on European society see S. L. Thrupp (ed.), *Early Medieval Society* (New York: Appleton-Century-Crofts, 1967).

62. See, on this, F. Heer, *The Intellectual History of Europe*, vol. 1, *From the*

Beginnings of Western Thought to Luther (Garden City: Doubleday, Anchor, 1968); O'Dea et al., *Religion and Man*, pp. 111 ff.; the various articles on "Christentum" in *Die Religion in Geschichte und Gegenwart*, 3d ed. (Tübingen: Von Mohr, 1957), 1:1685–1721; A. von Harnack, *The Mission and Expansion of Christianity in the First Three Centuries*, 2d ed., 2 vols. (New York: Putnam, 1908); and E. Troeltsch, *The Social Teaching of the Christian Churches* (New York: Macmillan, 1931).

63. On the structural organization and pluralism of European society see M. Bloch, *Feudal Society*, trans. L. A. Manyon (Chicago: University of Chicago Press, 1961); and Thrupp, *Early Medieval Society.*

64. On feudalism and representation in European society see Bloch, *Feudal Society;* J. Prawer and S. N. Eisenstadt, "Feudalism," in D. L. Sills (ed.), *The International Encyclopedia of the Social Sciences* (New York: Macmillan and Free Press, 1968), 11:393–403. O. Brunner, *Neue Wege der Verfassungs- und Sozialgeschichte*, rev. ed. (Göttingen: Vandenhoeck & Ruprecht, 1968), pp. 128–159; H. M. Cam, "Mediaeval Representation in Theory and Practice," *Speculum*, 29 no. 2 (1954): 347–355; E. Lousse, *La Société d'Ancien Régime: Organisations et représentations corporatives* (Paris: Louvain, 1943); and H. E. Hallam, "The Medieval Social Picture," in E. Kamenka and R. S. Neale (eds.), *Feudalism, Capitalism, and Beyond* (London: Edward Arnold, 1975), pp. 28–50.

65. See on this Bloch, *Feudal Society;* Brunner, *Neue Wege*, pp. 213–241; see also P. Anderson, *Passages from Antiquity to Feudalism* (London: New Left Books, 1974); and idem, *Lineages of the Absolutist State* (London: New Left Books, 1974, and New York: Humanities Press, 1974).

66. The analysis of strata formation in Europe follows that in Eisenstadt, *Social Differentiation*, pp. 109–114.

67. Ibid., chap. 6; and R. Mousnier, *Les Hierarchies sociales de 1450 à nos jours* (Paris: Presses universitaires de France, 1969).

68. See J. O. Lindsay, "The Social Classes and the Foundations of the State," in Lindsay, *New Cambridge Modern History*, 7:50–65.

69. On the special characteristics of European cities see M. Weber, *The City* (London: Collier Macmillan, 1957); and Brunner, *Neue Wege*, pp. 213–241.

70. For some special discussions of patterns of change in Europe and some illustrations see C. Tilly (ed.), *The Formation of National States in Western Europe* (Princeton: Princeton University Press, 1975). Especially of interest in this volume are: C. Tilly, "Reflections on the History of European State-Making," pp. 3–83; and S. Rokkan, "Dimensions of State Formation and Nation-Building: A Possible Paradigm for Research on Variations within Europe," pp. 562–600. See also J. N. Gott (ed.), *Hérésies et Sociétés dans l'Europe préindustrielle, 11–18e siècles* (Paris: Mouton, 1968); R. Forster and J. Greene (eds.), *Preconditions of Revolution in Early Modern Europe* (Baltimore: Johns Hopkins Press, 1970); A. L. Moote, "The Preconditions of Revolution in Early Modern Europe: Did They Really Exist?" *Canadian Journal of History*, 3, no. 3 (1972): 212–225. Compare M. Mollat and P. Wolff, *Ongles Bleus, Jacques, et Ciompi: Les Révolutions populaires en Europe aux XIVe et XVIe siècles*

(Paris: Calmann-Levy, 1970); V. Rutenburg, "Révoltes ou révolutions en Europe aux XIVᵉ–XVᵉ siècles," *Annales Economies-Sociétés-Civilisations*, 27, no. 3 (1972): 678–683; N. Cohn, *The Pursuit of the Millennium: Revolutionary Messianism in Medieval and Reformation Europe and Its Bearing on Modern Totalitarian Movements*, 2d ed. (New York: Harper, 1961). An attempt at a general interpretation of the development of European society from a Marxist point of view is Anderson, *Passages from Antiquity to Feudalism;* and idem, *Lineages of the Absolutist State.*

71. On Japanese traditional society see Reischauer and Fairbank, *East Asia;* J. W. Hall, *Japan from Prehistory to Modern Times* (London: Weidenfeld & Nicolson, 1970); C. Nakane, *Japanese Society* (London: Weidenfeld & Nicolson, 1970); H. Passin, "Japanese Society," in D. L. Sills (ed.), *The International Encyclopedia of the Social Sciences* (New York: Macmillan and Free Press, 1968), 8: 236–249; and R. N. Bellah, "Japan's Cultural Identity," *Journal of Asian Studies*, 24, no. 4 (1965): 573–594.

72. R. N. Bellah, *Tokugawa Religion* (New York: Free Press, 1956); idem, "Intellectual and Society in Japan," in S. N. Eisenstadt and S. R. Graubard (eds.), *Intellectuals and Tradition* (New York: Humanities, 1973), pp. 89–116; idem, "Japan's Cultural Identity"; idem, "Values and Social Change in Modern Japan," *Asian Cultural Studies*, Studies on the Modernization of Japan, no. 3 (Tokyo, October 1972), pp. 13–57; and R. Huntsberry, "Myth and Values in Japanese Society," rev. ed., mimeographed (Ohio: Wesleyan University, 1975; originally submitted as a doctoral dissertation to the Harvard Divinity School in 1969).

73. On the place of the Emperor in the Japanese system see Huntsberry, "Japanese Society."

74. On the Japanese status system see Nakane, *Japanese Society;* J. W. Hall and M. B. Jansen, *Studies in the Institutional History of Early Modern Japan* (Princeton: Princeton University Press, 1968); and J. W. Hall, and P. J. Mass (eds.), *Medieval Japan: Essays in Institutional History* (New Haven: Yale University Press, 1974).

75. See, for illustrations, Hall and Mass, *Medieval Japan,* chaps. 4–11; and Hall and Jansen, *Early Modern Japan,* chaps. 1, 2, 17, 18, 19, 20.

76. See H. Nakamura, *Ways of Thinking of Eastern Peoples: India, China, Tibet and Japan* (Honolulu: East-West Center Press, 1964), chaps. 34, 35.

77. S. N. Eisenstadt, "Sociological Characteristics and Problems of Small States," *Jerusalem Journal of International Relations,* 2, no. 2 (1977): 35–50.

78. T. Parsons, *Societies: Evolutionary and Comparative Perspectives* (Englewood Cliffs: Prentice-Hall, 1966), esp. chap. 6.

Chapter 6. Modern Revolutions and the Revolutionary Premises and Symbolism of Modern Civilization

1. CHARACTERISTICS OF MODERN REVOLUTIONS

Modern revolutionary symbolism and movements, as well as associated processes of change, stand in sharp contrast to the traditional patterns we have been discussing. The unique symbolic and organizational characteristics of modern revolution first appeared in the great European revolutions: the Revolt of the Netherlands,[1] the Great Rebellion and the Glorious Revolution in England,[2] the American Revolution,[3] and the French Revolution.[4] Out of these emerged the image of the real, or pure, revolution analyzed in Chapter 1. These revolutions did not differ from the processes of rebellion, conflict, and change in traditional societies merely in the scope or intensity of the rebellions, heterodoxies, highly articulated political movements, and interelite struggles associated with them. The major distinctive characteristics of these revolutions were the connections among the various associated movements of protest and between them and the central political struggle; their basic symbolism and its structural implications; and their structural consequences.

The diverse types of movement of protest and political struggle that crystallized in the great revolutions were rooted in the tradition of chiliastic outbursts, of rebellions, and of the more central movements of reform and heterodoxy. The central political struggle that marked European societies thorughout their history, further fueled these movements.

Structurally the great revolutions were characterized by a very close connection among heterodoxies, rebellions, central political struggle, and institution building. The linkages that they forged were closer than any others in history. In these revolutions, religious heterodoxies and intellectual movements—above all, the various Protestant sects—became inter-

173

twined with rebellions, central political struggles, and interelite contests. They also became closely linked to reconstruction of the symbols and boundaries of political and cultural collectivities and to patterns of institutional innovation in the economic, educational, and scientific spheres.[5]

These great revolutions were carried by numerous coalitions or countercoalitions of elites and institutional entrepreneurs, coalitions more heterogeneous than any preceding situation of change had witnessed. These coalitions comprised primary and secondary economic and political elites, as well as articulators of the solidarity of the different collectivities and of the models of cultural order.

Consequently, the movements of rebellion, protest, and intellectual antinomianism that crystallized into the great revolutions tended strongly to combine themes and orientations of protest with relatively realistic orientations toward the formation of centers and collectivities and toward institution building. Indeed, this connection with concrete institution building and with the formation and institutionalization of centers distinguished these revolutions from all other movements of protest.

The institutional linkages among diverse movements of protest and struggle and the multiplicity of coalitions were in the modern revolutions closely related to new developments in the symbolic field. Changes occurred both in the imagery of the legitimation of the social and political orders and in the more intellectual conceptions of the nature of these orders. (The latter went beyond the conceptions of alternative social and political orders that earlier societies produced.) These symbolic developments derived from the cultural models of antiquity and from European political images and symbols; however, they went far beyond their sources,[6] becoming universalistic and missionary.

In the elaboration of the symbolism of political legitimation the crucial step was, as Michael Walzer has amply illustrated, transition from regicide to revolution. That is, the tendency to substitute one (good) ruler for another (bad) ruler and to condone rebellions against bad rulers gave way to the notion (latent in the Greek, Hebrew, and to a lesser extent medieval traditions) of reconstruction by the legitimate representatives of the community of the entire sociopolitical order, its bases, and premises.[7]

This radical change in the pattern of legitimation became connected in most of the great revolutions, as Hannah Arendt has shown,[8] first with the active quest for reconstruction of the social order—above all, abolition of its hierarchical aspects and promotion of equality, solidarity, and political and social freedom—and second with the tendency, analyzed by J. L. Talmon, toward the ideological formulation of prescriptions of the new, proper social order.[9] These developments were closely related to changes in the more intellectual conceptions of nature and of social life, primarily, with the combination of two elements, "that of change by movement and that of a motion which returns to its starting point. In the modern concept of revolution (as it crystallized in the times of the French revolution) the element of change effecting a forward movement ('progress') prevails." [10]

The organizational and symbolic breakthroughs that characterized the modern revolutions began to occur in the Revolt of the Netherlands and intensified in the Great Rebellion in England. They were more fully elaborated in the ideology of the American Revolution and they crystallized in the French Revolution. It was within the latter revolution that the element of legitimation by violence was added to the new conception of social life and nontraditional patterns of legitimation. This conception and imagery are central to modern political symbolism and thought.

These developments were connected also with basic changes in the parameters of the dominant intellectual traditions, most notably, with the perception of the fundamental problems of social order that emerged from the philosophical discussions of the sixteenth, seventeenth, and eighteenth centuries and the modern scientific outlook. These modern intellectual orientations dated from the Renaissance; they crystallized during the Enlightenment around the ideas of progress and reason.[11] Finally, these developments were associated with the transformation of religious orientations, especially during the Reformation, the mustering of secular opposition to these orientations, and the fullest expression of different tendencies of the Enlightenment. All these changes and movements impinged directly on the central symbolic and institutional spheres of European societies, thus creating a new social and cultural order.[12]

2. RESTRUCTURING OF THEMES OF PROTEST IN MODERN REVOLUTIONS. THE MODERN REVOLUTIONARY *ERLEBNIS*

I

The unique organizational and symbolic dimensions of the modern revolutions shaped the symbols of protest that they employed—symbols that became basic components of the social and political symbolism of modern societies.

Here, as in other situations of change, the institutional foci around which the most important themes of protest converged were those of authority, especially as vested in the various centers; the system of stratification and the symbolic dimensions of hierarchy; and the family as the primary locus of authority. Here, as in other societies, the different themes of protest became articulated in a great variety of ways—in millenarian movements, in intellectual heterodoxies, and in movements of rebellion and political struggle. Nevertheless, the orientations and movements of protest that crystallized in the early revolutions exhibited unique characteristics out of which revolutionary symbolism emerged.

Let us look at modern revolutionary imagery and its structural implications. Note that for the first time in history a conscious attempt was made to change the political and social orders. This innovation was manifest in several different ways. First, there was the call to return to a Golden Age (an orientation common in movements of protest), which paradoxically was combined with a strong emphasis on novelty and on discontinuity with the past.[13] Second, and in close relation to the emphasis on novelty and reconstruction of the social and political orders, was the convergence of these orientations on the ground rules of social interaction, especially principles of distributive justice, meanings of institutions, legitimation of the social order, and, above all, principles of access to power. There was a tendency also to focus on the reconstruction of the relations of individuals and communities to ultimate societal and cultural values. Third, the combination of these foci of protest made the imagery of authority, social hierarchies, and class symbols central to modern revolutionary movements and imbued them with transcendental, religious, universalistic, and missionary dimensions.

The combination of these organizational and symbolic aspects of the great modern, pure revolutions sheds light on the phenomenology of the modern revolutionary *Erlebnis,* of the daily experiences of these revolutions. The *Erlebnis* of religious millenarian or utopian movements is marked by religious fervor—the feeling of the boundless, charismatic moment, of the directness of relations between the transcendental and the mundane; of the release of all the constraints of the social order; the limitless expansion of solidarity and participation. The modern revolutions exhibit a similar sort of fervor but they are socially and politically this-worldly; that is, oriented toward the capture and reconstruction of the centers of the society; toward the merger of the real and double images of society. (Such capture and reconstruction imply personal and moral purification.) Hence, the modern revolution tends to embrace those symbols that by virtue of their reference to the spiritual qualities of human nature (however conceived in a given culture) transcend social organization and in some ultimate sense contradict it. These symbols embody the pure essence of human relations and the modern revolution combines them with orientations toward reconstruction of the societal centers and toward establishment of a new institutional order. Concomitantly, it tends to legitimize violence as a means to attain these ends.[14]

II

The symbolic and organizational characteristics of the modern revolutions rested on a combination of the symbolic premises of the Hebrew, Greek, and medieval political and ideological traditions; on orientations

toward reconstruction of the social order; on the concomitant incorporation of the major themes and movements of protest into the central
spheres and symbolism of society; on the concrete problems of structural
change these movements entailed; and on the specific characteristics of
the modern revolutionary *Erlebnis*. Thus, the image or symbolism—and
to a degree the reality of the true, or pure, revolution, with its strong
emphasis on violence, novelty, and totality, arose.

Changes in the themes and orientations of protest, together with
changes in the very bases of legitimation of the social and political orders,
profoundly affected the symbolic and structural tendencies of the modern
revolutions—tendencies incorporated into the basic characteristics of modern societies. The first effect was the development of the possibility of
combining different movements of protest, heterodoxy, and central political struggle as a natural part of the modern political process even if, needless to say, such a combination would stand apart from the routine workings of political institutions.[15] The second effect (a feature peculiar to the
modern revolutions and postrevolutionary societies) was the continual
incorporation of movements and symbols of protest into the central
spheres and symbols of the society. In these revolutions and in postrevolutionary societies the essential dimensions of protest gradually became
incorporated into the central components of the sociocultural order in
ways that greatly transcended the incorporation of heterodoxy in traditional settings. The basic orientations of protest were no longer purely
intellectual orientations or manifestations of diffuse dissatisfaction but
crucial components of the symbols of collective identity and referrents
of the cultural order. This tendency had manifold institutional derivatives, the most important of which was transformation of the relations
among centers in the direction of reconciling their symbolic differences
and increasing their mutual impingement.[16]

The full force of these symbols and movements of protest was felt
when they became connected with the complex of structural changes
attendant on the development of modernity and modern civilizations,
which we subsequently analyze in greater detail.[17]

3. OUTCOMES OF MODERN REVOLUTIONS.
MODERN SOCIAL STRUCTURES.
THE CIVILIZATION OF MODERNITY

Out of these processes of revolution there developed unique types of
societal transformation and ultimately a new civilization: the civilization
of modernity.

The modern revolutions pushed the societies in which they took place
in the direction of modernization in its organizational and symbolic as-

pects. All postrevolutionary societies experienced growing structural differentiation and specialization, the establishment of universalistic organizational frameworks; the development of an industrial or semi-industrial market economy; the atriculation of relatively open, nontraditional systems of stratification and mobility in which criteria of achievement in general and of economic, occupational, and educational criteria in particular became predominant; and the rise of centralized, strongly bureaucratic political systems.

These organizational changes were intimately connected to the basic premises of modernity—initially the premises of European modernity and later those of modernity in general—which developed out of revolutionary symbols, ideologies, and movements. Indeed, these revolutionary symbols and tendencies are fundamental to the notion of modernity.

Social transformation in these directions of course occurred all in modern and modernizing societies. What distinguished the processes of social transformation in revolutionary societies was not only that they took place through violent upheaval but also that these changes and transformations were effected in specific constellations. They entailed, as we have seen some convergence of changes in at least some of the major ground rules of social interaction (the principles of distributive justice; the meaning of institutional activities; the legitimation of the social order) and, above all, convergence of such changes with changes in the restructuring of access to power and in the reconstruction of the center, its symbols, and patterns of legitimation. Finally, these features were associated with a progressive, universalistic, missionary ideology.

Changes in the political sphere itself crytallized in a certain pattern; that is, into a combination of changes in the symbols and patterns of legitimation of regimes; in the composition of the ruling class; in the bases of access to the center; and in center-periphery relations.

These revolutionary developments heralded tendencies toward farreaching transformation of crucial aspects of the parameters of the social order. First of all, these developments gave rise to the breakdown of the premises of traditionality; to the undermining of the traditional legitimation of the centers of the society; to the weakening of the traditional normative limitations on the contents of the symbols of the social and cultural orders; and to the growing demand for participation of broader groups in the formulations of the society's central symbols and institutions.[18] Second, these orientations were closely connected with a growing tendency toward secularization of the central societal symbols and with nonacceptance of the givenness of the existing cultural tradition, of the sanctity of the cultural centers and symbols and their guardians. With the breakthrough to modernity, traditional legitimation of these symbols and centers was weakened; the principal social groups tended to develop a critical attitude toward the premises of the social order and to become involved with and participate in the formation of cultural traditions. Thus, there arose the possibility of acceptance of an actively critical stance with regard to political, social, and cultural traditions and organizations.

These orientations were based on certain fundamental assumptions about the formation of the central aspects of the social, cultural, and natural orders by conscious human activity, particularly, formation of a new sociopolitical order positively oriented toward change and founded on concepts of universality and equality and of the social order as an autonomous secular entity.

Initially, the central focus or theme of this European order was the exploration and direction (even mastery) of a steadily expanding human and natural environment and destiny. The fullest expression of this attitude was in the premise that the exploration of nature by man is an open enterprise that creates a new cultural order, that the expansion of scientific and technological knowledge could transform both the cultural and social orders and create new external and internal environments to be explored by man and at the same time used to satisfy his intellectual vision and technical needs.[19]

Accordingly, the revolutions and revolutionary conceptions that ushered in the modern political orders were, unlike the processes of change or rebellion in traditional societies, more or less consciously oriented toward changing the basic contours of the societal orders and toward far-reaching transformation of the fundamental premises of the social and cultural orders. The most important structural derivatives of these orientations were restructuring of the relationship between the center and the periphery and growing impingement of the periphery on the center in the name of the ideals or symbols of equality, solidarity, freedom, and participation.[20]

4. REVOLUTIONARY PREMISES OF MODERN CIVILIZATION

The combination of the structural and symbolic dimensions of modernity generated one of its essential characteristics; namely, modern societies, as contrasted with traditional systems, have always faced the crucial problem of the ability of their central frameworks to expand.[21] The demands or expectations of such expansion may develop in several different but interrelated directions. First are the aspirations—mostly of the elites—for the creation or maintenance of new, wider political frameworks. Second are the aspirations or demands for economic and/or administrative development or modernization. Third is the hope that the center will respond to the demands of various new social groups—especially demands for new principles of distribution. Fourth are the demands of these groups in general and of new elites in particular for incorporation into the center, for possible redefinition of the boundaries and symbols of the collectivity, as well as for more active participation in the political process and more direct access to the center.

Closely related to these tendencies was the changing format of political struggle that developed within the framework of modern political institutions—the most pervasive aspect of which was to be found in the structure of political demands in modern political systems.[22]

The concrete contents of such demands of course varied greatly according to structural conditions such as urbanization, change in the agrarian sector, and educational expansion, yet modern societies tended to develop fairly systematic, general patterns of demands. One pattern was the sheer increase in the quantity of demands, which was closely related to the increase in the number of possible channels of access to resources (e.g., the relatively widespread pressure on educational channels of access to bureaucratic or political positions) and to the wider range of groups and strata becoming politically articulate and making demands on the center. This quantitative difference aside, broader groups in modern societies not only made segregated claims for concrete benefits based on differential membership in diverse ascriptive, closed subcollectivities but also demanded access to the center by virtue of membership in the society. These demands on the center derived from the participatory and consensual orientations inherent in the very premises of modernity and were incorporated into the political process. The impingement of these demands on the centers of the social and political orders was evident in the structuring of the major types of political organizations in modern societies and in the tendency toward coalescence among them (coalescence reminiscent of, and related to, the coalescence of rebellions, intellectual heterodoxies, protest movements, and central political struggle that crystallized in the great revolutions).[23]

Among the specific types of organization through which political demands are articulated in modern societies of special importance are interest groups, social movements, public opinion, and political parties. The first three may to some extent be regarded as components of the last; that is, parties are the most articulate form of modern political organization. There may be considerable overlap among these four, too.

The interest or pressure group usually is oriented to gaining concrete goals (economic, religious, cultural, or political) and is interested in the broader political machinery of the party or of the state only insofar as the latter can promote its goals. Of course, there are many types of interest groups, and their specific concerns may vary greatly from situation to situation.

The second type of organization through which political orientations and demands are articulated in modern political systems is social movements. Several types of social movements can be distinguished. First is the relatively restricted movement oriented to the attainment of a general goal that is not directly related to the concrete interest of any articulated group but represents the application of a wide principle of justice; for example, movements against capital punishment, for improving the lot of deprived groups of people (unmarried mothers, delinquents), or for abolition of slavery. The second type is the reform movement, which aims at change in the central political institutions; for instance, extending suffrage to a particular group. (These two types of social movements often constitute important ingredients of public opinion, to be discussed shortly.) The third and most extreme type of social movement is the ideological, totalistic one, which usually aims at development of an entirely new society or polity. It attempts to infuse inclusive and diffuse values or goals into a given institutional structure or to transform this structure according to these values and goals. It usually has a strong future orientation and tends to depict the future as greatly different from the present and to fight for the realization of this change. Very often such movements are apocalyptic or millenarian. Finally, they tend to demand total obedience or loyalty on the part of members and to distinguish sharply friends from foes.

The third channel through which political demands are articulated in modern political systems can be identified as general, diffuse, intelligent interest in public issues and in the public good. By this is meant people or groups that have a rather flexible attitude toward both specific interests and all-embracing ideas and claims, that are not firmly attached to any given interest group, movement, or organization, and that are impelled primarily by concern for the public good and accordingly evaluate political programs in terms of broad values as well as concrete possibilities.

Each of these forms of articulation of political interests and orientations existed in traditional systems. However, with the partial exception of petitions or entreaties by interest groups or cliques, the representation of the political activities and orientations of broad social groups was not, in those societies, fully legitimized within the central political institutions, while social or social-religious movements were largely apolitical or illegitimate from the point of view of the existing political institutions.

Moreover, these groups were concerned with petitioning the rulers for concrete benefits, not with setting major political goals or selecting rulers. Finally, only in the modern political systems have these different interest groups and movements become integrated, even if only to a small extent, into the framework of political activity and organization; for example, political parties or other bodies that mobilize support and coordinate political demands. Such integration is effected by political parties (or partylike organizations) through the development of specific party organs, leadership, and programs; through the subsumption within the party of various concrete interests under broad rules or aims attractive to a wider public; and through the translation of the inclusive, diffuse aims of different social movements into concrete political goals, issues, and dilemmas articulated through party or partylike organizations and activities.

The conjunction of these structural and ideological trends made the symbolism of protest a basic component of modern civilization. Political radicalism thus became part of the central core of the modern political process, imbuing it with a sharp missionary dimension.

Truly enough, the prevalence and spread of revolutionary movements and symbols have prompted strong opposition to them, but such opposition itself—the term "counterrevolution" attests—has tended to be rooted in the premises of the revolutionary concepion of social order.[24]

5. EXPANSION OF MODERN CIVILIZATION. THE INTERNATIONAL SYSTEMS

The civilization of modernity began in Europe and in North America. In Britain, France, the Netherlands, and the United States, revolutionary symbolism and attitudes first became part and parcel of the social and political orders. The internal dynamics and the political-economic expansion of Western European societies were responsible for the spread of this civilization throughout the world. This process was unique in that it combined the most far-reaching undermining of traditional legitimation that ever occurred with the creation of new international systems marked by continual shifts in power, influence, and centers of cultural model building.[25]

Thus, from the sixteenth century on, more and more parts of the world were incorporated into the international economic system, first into the commercial capitalist system, later into the industrial capitalist system, and still later into a highly complex international industrial system that embraced different types of economic regimes—capitalist and communist, for instance. (These economic regimes interact continuously and given the international nature of the economic system they have experienced very interesting and unpredictable shifts of economic and political power.) It was not, however, only an economic international system that developed. Side by side there arose new international political and ideological systems with strong missionary orientations.

Whereas all these systems are ever expanding and closely interconnected, they are not coterminous or identical—each has a dynamic of its own—and often they are in conflict. All these systems have experienced continual shifts of power and influence along with extensive changes in the cultural, social, and political spheres: the interaction of these shifts and changes constitute part of the dynamics of the new international setting and encourage further change. Thus, the type of international systems that developed is unique, approximating neither an Imperial international system, directed from one center and seeking to control the economic, political, and ideological spheres, nor the Islamic pattern of expansion, which rested on at least the ideal of a unified community.[26]

6. REVOLUTIONARY SYMBOLISM IN MODERN CIVILIZATION. THE SPREAD OF SOCIALISM

I

As we indicated above, the symbols of protest, of radicalism, derived from the revolutionary premises of the first European revolutions became incorporated into the basic orientations of the civilization of modernity. In this continuous process fundamental notions of that civilization are ever being reshaped.

The strength of revolutionary symbols in modern civilization can be seen above all in the spread throughout the world of revolutionary and radical movements in general and of socialist and communist symbols and movements (in which the symbolism and ideology of revolution are most fully crystallized and intellectually most fully articulated and elaborated) in particular.[27]

Socialism and communism were initially movements of protest or of intellectual heresy that combined political programs and ideologies with a scientific or philosophical Weltanschauung. As movements of protest, socialism and communism joined orientations of rebellion, protest, and intellectual antinomianism with strong tendencies toward center formation and institution building.[28] In these characteristics as well as the following, socialism and communism owed a debt to the European tradition that brought together rebellions and heterodoxies, on the one hand, and movements of protest and center formation, on the other. Socialism and communism combined the characteristics of movements of protest with the central symbols of various traditions and civilizations, a unique achievement attributable to the fundamental premises of modern civilization and their institutional derivatives.[29] Thus, socialism and communism shared several broad cultural orientations.

1. A strong future orientation, a concerted effort to relate the future to the present, with concomitant missionary orientation.
2. a heavy emphasis on the primacy of the collectivity and on social justice, coupled with the negation of individualistic approaches;
3. an emphasis on close relations among the social, political, and cultural orders and on attempts to construct a new social order and

to justify it according to transcendental criteria and ideals inherent in the basic cultural model;

4. a profoundly this-worldly orientation, stressing not acceptance of the existing order but evaluation of it in terms of transcendental values.

5. socialism and communism tended to emphasize the possibility of active participation of social groups in the formation of a new social and cultural order, as well as a high level of commitment to this order.

6. socialism and communism had a strongly universalistic orientation—in theory negating the significance of political or national boundaries but at the same time attempting to define a new sociopolitical order with broad, yet relatively definite boundaries. These boundaries were identified as those of the workers and the intellectuals—a classification capable of embracing those parts of humanity willing to accept socialism's basic premises and to define themselves in terms of them.

7. socialism and communism developed a specific—and notably modern—mode of legitimation of the social and cultural order it sought to establish.

Socialism and communism incorporated into their traditions and symbols some of the eschatological elements of Christianity—its vision of the course of history and of redemption, the division between the City of Man and the City of God. The earliest socialist movements followed the general ideological trend of European modernity, with its emphasis on the nation-state, on the one hand, and on the tension between state and society and the importance of class society, on the other. This tradition greatly influenced the development of certain important themes of socialism, especially the socialist and communist view of history; its strong emphasis on the temporal dimension of human existence; its activist orientation; and its specifically scientific and missionary components.

Finally, the socialist emphasis on class society derived from the European tradition (analyzed in Chapter 5)—especially the autonomy of the estates and the active participation of broader groups and strata in the formation of the society.

II

Of course, socialism and communism did not represent simple extensions of this tradition. Both were ambivalent toward the great intellectual movements of modern Europe—the Enlightenment and the scientific revolution—accepting many of their orientations and premises but at the same time developing a strongly antinomian tendency.

To contrast socialist movements to the great religions and traditions, on the one hand, and to the great revolutions, on the other, should prove illuminating. Like the great religions and like the revolutionary movements that ushered in modernity in Europe and in contrast to other movements of rebellion, heterodoxy, or millenarianism, the socialist movements connected protest, rebellion, and heterodoxy with active political institution building and center formation. Organized political protest was joined with more elaborate intellectual heterodoxy. Unlike, however, the great religions, socialism was concerned solely with this-worldly activity. The mundane order served as the focus and source of socialism's transcendental orientations—usually undermining the otherworldly legitimation of these orientations. And unlike the English, French, or American revolutions or the Enlightenment, for example, socialist movements were the first modern movements of protest oriented not only against the premises of traditional systems of authority but also against the modern institutional systems—political, economic, and ideological—that developed in the earliest phase of modern European society.

7. CONTRADICTIONS OF MODERN CIVILIZATION AND THE SPREAD OF SOCIALISM

I

The spread of socialism attests to the fact that the development of modernity created a propensity for the continual reconstruction of revolutionary symbols and tendencies, and to the fact that these symbols and tendencies became a basic component of modern civilization—that new, nontraditional great tradition that spread from Europe throughout the world.

The ubiquity of revolutionary symbols and movements in modern societies and the strength of the propensity for reconstruction derived from the internal dynamics of the development of modern civilizations. In most general terms, this propensity was due to the imperfect realization of the initial premises of modernity, especially of the tendencies toward rational expansion in all aspects of cultural and social life. Actual developments in Europe and in other parts of the world did not support the assumptions about the possibility of seemingly automatic expansion in all aspects of human (social and cultural) creativity; many contradictions arose as the civilization of modernity matured. Expansion in one sphere of social life neither necessarily assured parallel expansion in other fields or the growing participation of various groups and strata in the social and the cultural order nor necessarily provided these groups with full access to participation in all spheres of life.

Development, while steady and successful, turned out to be much more problematic than indicated by the initial assumptions of European modernization. Contradictions marked this process—rooted in the fact that all such processes of expansion were connected with constant changes in the distribution of power and in the structural organization of different institutional spheres, as well as in the modes of access to them; and hence with structural dislocation and with differential inclusion, in the social and cultural centers, of social groups, dimensions of human existence, and attributes of human endeavor.

Thus, the early development of socialism in its several forms in Europe was predicated on specific aspects of the development of European modernity and on the development of certain contradictions on that continent. George Lichtheim and Eugene Kamenka maintain that the most important of these features was the specific reaction to the tension between the premises of the French Revolution and the realities or problems created by the Industrial Revolution: between the ideals of universal brotherhood, justice, and participation in the social and cultural orders and the realities of class division and social and economic dislocation created by the Industrial Revolution. In other words, socialism was a reaction to the unique problems and contradictions created by the great structural and symbolic upheavals of modernity that occurred in Europe. The structural and symbolic orientations that spawned the first socialist movements included the premises of European modernity—the strong universalistic tendency, the combination of protest and center formation, the quest for broadening the scope of participation in the center, the tendency to use this participation for effecting changes in the formation of the center and for concrete institution building.

II

The spread of socialism beyond Europe was predicated on the expansion of the civilization of modernity and the recognition of the fundamental contradictions that crystallized as this civilization expanded. Within the framework of expansion and contradictions, the symbolism of protest and revolution evolved, becoming most fully elaborated in the export of socialist movements and symbols.

Of all traditions, ideologies, or movements that originated in Western and Central Europe, socialism spread furthest and endured longest. No other movement entailed such broad participation in the organizational and symbolic frameworks.

The clue to the spread of socialism and communism is to be found in unique features of the encounter of the non-Western, non-European societies with modernity as it spread from Europe.[30] In this process a symbolic parallel was drawn between the position of the working class in Europe vis-à-vis the capitalists and that of the new nations in the modern international systems vis-à-vis Europe (and later the United States). In this sense, those who claim that class struggle is now international rather than intranational and that the Third World constitutes the proletariat in this new international struggle have indeed put their finger on a crucial point—a point that is, contrary to their view, not a concrete structural or organizational feature, but rather a symbolic structural feature of this process and of these relations.[31]

The exact structure of the relations among different countries in the world is of course entirely different from that of classes within one society; the foci of protest are related essentially to international ideological and political stances not to the internal division of labor. Hence, the dynamics of the spread of revolutionary symbolism and changes in general and of socialism in particular differ across countries.

These differences aside, there has indeed taken place a symbolic transposition of the conditions behind the development of socialism in Europe into the situation in which many non-European societies found themselves as a result of the spread of modernity. This symbolic transposition explains the attraction to the socialist tradition among non-European countries. The socialist tradition is the one modern international tradition in which protest against any concrete constellation of modernity may be worked out in terms of the premises of the modern world itself.

The unique attraction of socialism in general lies in the fact that it has proved to be the best means through which active participation in the new, modern (i.e., Western) universal tradition can be combined with negation of selected aspects of modernity—of the West in particular. Socialism has made it possible, especially for the elites of many non-European societies, to incorporate universalistic elements of modernity in their new collective identity without necessarily abandoning either specific components of their identity or their pervasive negative attitude toward the West.

This symbolic transposition of the initial ideology of socialism from European to non-European settings has been greatly reinforced by the combination, in the socialist tradition, of the orientations of protest with those of institution building and center formation. Thus, elites and other groups outside Europe could orient themselves according to their own traditions of protest and center formation and cope with the problems of reconstruction of their own centers and traditions in terms of the new setting in which they found themselves.

8. CARRIERS OF MODERN REVOLUTIONARY SYMBOLS

The multitude of revolutionary symbols was articulated and carried by special institutional entrepreneurs who were crucial also in the crystallization of revolutionary movements throughout the world. Of special importance in this context were the various modern intellectuals who, as Raymond Aron so brilliantly pointed out, were especially attracted to the myth of the revolution, elaborated it, and encouraged its diffusion.[32]

The growth of the international systems of modernity, the shifts of power they experienced, and the institutionalization in most modern societies of certain revolutionary demands and symbols were accompanied by the development of autonomous, specialized revolutionary groups no longer entirely bound to their society of origin but constituting independent international entities and the development of some states as centers or protectors of these revolutionary groups.

From the very beginnings of European modernity, many of the more revolutionary groups such as the Puritans or the various intellectual groups of the Enlightenment were international in character, and international contacts, propaganda, and subversion were part and parcel of their activities.[33] Similarly, the French Revolution pointed up the possibility of a revolutionary state whose mission was to spread the revolution and to encourage revolutionary groups in other activities as a basic ingredient of the European system (later on, of the world-system). This situation was reminiscent of the spread of Christianity and Islam. As the civilization of modernity spread, revolutionary movements became more and more international in character—witness the ties between communist insurgents and foreign political centers.

These developments were connected with far-reaching changes in radical socialist ideology and tactics in general and in Marxist ideology in particular. The most important change was the growing Leninist emphasis on revolutionary organization and on activities by special revolutionary groups versus the natural or spontaneous, working out of social forces—above all, class contradictions.[34] This shift removed Marxist ideology from the experience of Western Europe and related it to internal developments in societies structurally and historically distinct from those in which the true revolutions developed. The combination of these historical circumstances and the rise of autonomous international groups influenced, in many interesting and surprising ways, the process of change in these societies, most notably, the potentialities of revolution. It gave rise to a continuous process of selection by different societies and groups diverse constellations of the major revolutionary premises and symbols.

9. DIFFERENTIAL SPREAD OF RADICALISM, SOCIALISM, AND REVOLUTIONARY IMAGERY

This process selection indicated that despite great appeal, socialism did not spread in the same way throughout the world. In societies like Japan, it has little broad symbolic hold (although it attracted small groups of intellectuals). Even more important is the very well known fact that in one of the great revolutionary societies, the United States, socialism was never central in radical movements.[35] Subsequently we offer an explanation of these developments. Suffice it to say here that even in those societies in which radical tendencies became closely interwoven with socialist imagery, in different societies and in different historical situations the crystallization of these patterns of socialist symbolism involved selection of various socialist orientations and symbols, a process clearest in the manifold images and symbolizations of the true revolution. Within all socialist movements the image of the pure, true revolution (which evolved out of the first European revolutionary experiences and was refined in socialist ideology) became an important symbol—indeed, the basic revolutionary model. The original European revolutions aside, only in the Russian and Chinese and to some extent the Turkish, the Vietnamese, the Yugoslavian, and the Mexican [36] revolutions did the processes of social transformation attendant on the spread of modernity become crystallized through processes exhibiting the features of classical revolutions. Yet, as we have already suggested and as we shall see in greater detail later, most such transformations occurred in ways greatly differing from this image.

Hence, the explanation of the tendency toward revolution in terms of the general premises of modernity although loosely correct does not account for the differential reception of revolutionary symbolism—particularly, the diversity of ways in which the many aspects of revolutionary symbolism and activities became related to different patterns of transformation throughout modern (including European) societies.

Thus, we are back to our original question about the unique conditions behind the development of the modern revolutions as well as behind their differential spread worldwide. We have accordingly to inquire into these conditions within the broad framework of the spread of modern international systems, which generated the development in some societies of processes of change close to the image of pure revolutions, and to determine the similarities between them and the specific conditions behind the development of the initial, true revolutions.

NOTES

1. For some basic data on the Revolution of the Netherlands and on the problems of its interpretation see I. Schöffer, "De Nederlandse Revolutie," in I. Schöffer (ed.), *Zeven Revoluties* (Amsterdam: J. H. de Bussy, n.d.), pp. 9–29; J. W. Smit, "*The Netherlands Revolution*," in R. Forster and J. P. Greene (eds.), *Preconditions of Revolution in Early Modern Europe*

(Baltimore: Johns Hopkins Press, 1970); pp. 19–54; J. E. Ellemers, "The Revolt of the Netherlands: The Part Played by Religion in the Process of Nation-Building," *Social Compass,* 14, no. 2 (1967): 93–103; H. Schilling, "Der Aufstand der Niederlande: Bürgerliche Revolution oder Elitenkonflikt?" in H. U. Wehler (ed.), *200 Jahre Amerikanische Revolution und moderne Revolutionsforschung* (Göttingen: Vandenhoeck & Ruprecht, 1976), pp. 177–231; J. J. Woltjer, "De Vrede-makers," *Tijdschrift voor Geschiedenis,* 89 (1976): 299–321; G. Griffiths, "The Revolutionary Character of the Revolt of the Netherlands," *Comparative Studies in Society and History,* 2 (July 1960): 452–472; G. Nadel, "The Logic of the Anatomy of Revolution, with Reference to the Netherlands Revolt," ibid., pp. 473–484; and I. Schöffer, "The Dutch Revolt Anatomized: Some Comments," ibid., 3, no. 4 (1961): 470–479.

2. For basic data on, and interpretation of, the English Revolution see E. W. Ives (ed.), *The English Revolution, 1600–1660* (New York: Harper & Row, 1968); I. Schöffer, "De Engelse Revolutie," in I. Schöffer (ed.), *Zeven Revoluties,* pp. 29–51; L. Stone, *The Causes of the English Revolution, 1529–1642* (London: Routledge & Kegan Paul, 1972); idem, *Social Change and Revolution in England, 1540–1640* (London: Longmans, Green, 1965); H. C. Schroder, "Die amerikanische und die englische Revolution in vergleichender Perspektive," in Wehler, *200 Jahre Amerikanische Revolution,* pp. 9–37; L. Stone, "The English Revolution, in Forster and Greene, *Preconditions of Revolution,* pp. 55–108; and P. Zagorin, "The English Revolution, 1640–1660," in H. Lubasz (ed.), *Revolutions in Modern European History* (New York: Macmillan, 1966).

3. For some basic data on, and interpretation of, the American Revolution see F. Gentz, *The French and American Revolutions Compared,* transl. J. Q. Adams (Chicago: Gateway, 1955); B. Bailyn, *The Ideological Origins of the American Revolution* (Cambridge: Harvard University Press, Belknap, 1967); R. M. Weir, "Who Shall Rule at Home: The American Revolution as a Crisis of Legitimacy for the Colonial Elite," *Journal of Interdisciplinary History,* 6, no. 4 (1976): 679–700; J. W. Schulte Nordholt, "De Amerikaanse Revolutie," in I. Schöffer (ed.), *Zeven Revoluties,* pp. 51–77; J. K. Martin, *Men in Rebellion: Higher Government Leaders and the Coming of the American Revolution* (New York: Free Press, 1976); Wehler, *200 Jahre Amerikanische Revolution;* R. B. Morris, *The American Revolution Reconsidered* (New York: Harper & Row, 1967); and J. P. Greene, "The Social Origins of the American Revolution: An Evaluation and an Interpretation," *Political Science Quarterly,* 88, no. 1 (1973): 1–22.

4. On the French Revolution see C. Brinton, *A Decade of Revolution, 1789–1799* (New York: Harper & Row, Harper Torchbooks, 1934); Gentz, *French and American Revolutions Compared;* P. Geyl, "De Franse Revolutie," in I. Schöffer (ed.), *Zeven Revoluties,* pp. 77–103; H. G. Koenigsberger, *Estates and Revolutions* (Ithaca: Cornell University Press, 1971), chap. 9; J. Kaplow (ed.)., *New Perspectives on the French Revolution: Readings in Historical Sociology* (New York: Wiley, 1965); G. Lefebvre, *The Coming of the French Revolution* (Princeton: Princeton

University Press, 1941); idem, "The French Revolution in the Context of World History," in Lubasz, *Revolutions in Modern European History,* pp. 74–86; idem, *The Great Fear of 1789* (New York: Pantheon, 1973); G. F. E. Rudé, "The French Revolution and Participation," in E. Kamenka (ed.), *A World in Revolution?* (Canberra: Australian National University Press, 1970), pp. 15–25; E. Schmidt, "Die französische Revolution," in T. Schieder (ed.), *Revolution und Gesellschaft* (Freiburg im Breisgau: Herder, 1973), pp. 65–96; and A. de Tocqueville, *The Old Regime and the French Revolution* (Garden City: Doubleday, 1955). See also A. Barnave, "Theorie der französischen Revolution," *Neue Politische Literatur,* 19, no. 3 (1974): 400–403; and E. Schmitt (ed.), *Die französiche Revolution* (Cologne: Kiepenheuer & Witsch).

5. The problem of the place of Protestantism and its impact on modernity is discussed in S. N. Eisenstadt (ed.), *The Protestant Ethic and Modernization: A Comparative View* (New York: Basic Books, 1968), esp. pp. 3–40; G. Lewy, *Religion and Revolution* (New York: Oxford University Press, 1974), pp. 102–154; H. Lüthy, "Once Again: Calvinism and Capitalism," in Eisenstadt, *Protestant Ethic,* pp. 87–109; M. Walzer, "Puritanism as Revolutionary Ideology," in ibid., pp. 109–134; O. C. Watkins, *The Puritan Experience* (London: Routledge & Kegan Paul, 1972); T. Nipperdey, *Reformation, Revolution, Utopie: Studien zum 16. Jahrhundert* (Göttingen: Vandenhoeck & Ruprecht, 1975); E. Voegelin, *Order and History,* vol. 5, *The Protestant Centuries* (Baton Rouge: Louisiana State University Press, 1975); on the earlier premises of revolution in Europe see Forster and Greene, *Preconditions of Revolution.* See also J. B. Russell, *Dissent and Reform in the Early Middle Ages* (Berkeley: University of California Press, 1965); and J. Le Goff (ed.), *Hérésies et sociétiés dans l'Europe preindustielle, 11e–18e siècles* (Paris: Mouton, 1968).

6. On models of antiquity see A. Fuks, "Patterns and Types of Social-Economic Revolution in Greece from the Fourth to the Second Century B.C.," *Ancient Society,* 5 (1974): 51–81; and A. Heuss, "Das Revolutionsproblem im Spiegel der Antiken Geschichte," *Historische Zeitschrift,* 216 (1973): 1–72. On the background of classical European political thought see G. H. Sabine, *A History of Political Thought* (London: Harray, 1949); L. Kolakowsky, *Chrétiens sans église* (Paris: Gallimard, 1965); and E. R. A. Seligman and A. Johnson (eds.), *Encyclopaedia of the Social Sciences,* 15 vols. (New York: Macmillan, 1930–1935), vol. 1: The Development of Social Thought and Institutions, pp. 3–228, and especially: H. J. Laski, "The Rise of Liberalism," pp. 103–124; C. Brinton, "The Revolutions," pp. 125–144; and for later developments C. A. Beard, "Individualism and Capitalism," pp. 145–164; and C. Brinkmann, "Nationalism," pp. 164–183. See also O. von Giercke, *Political Theories of the Middle Age* (Cambridge: At the University Press, 1958); and C. H. McIlwain, *The Growth of Political Thought in the West from the Greeks to the End of the Middle Ages* (New York: Macmillan, 1959).

7. M. Walzer, *Regicide and Revolution* (Cambridge: At the University Press, 1974); idem, "Puritanism"; and Kolakowsky, *Chrétiens sans église.*

8. H. Arendt, *On Revolution* (New York: Viking, 1963).

9. J. L. Talmon, *The Origins of Totalitarian Democracy* (London: Secker & Warburg, 1952).

10. F. Gilbert, "Revolution," in P. Wiener (ed.), *Dictionary of the History of Ideas* (New York: Scribner's, 1973), pp. 152–167.

11. E. Voegelin, *From Enlightenment to Revolution*, H. Hallowell (ed.), (Durham: Duke University Press, 1975); idem, *Order and History*, vols. 5, 6; and P. Gay, *The Enlightenment: An Interpretation*, 2 vols. (New York: Knopf, 1967).

12. See the references cited in note 6 above; and also the discussion in S. N. Eisenstadt, *Modernization, Protest, and Change* (Englewood Cliffs: Prentice-Hall, 1967), chap. 1.

13. On the theme of a return to the Golden Age see G. van der Leeuw, "Primordial Time and Final Time," in *Man and Time: Papers from the Eranos Yearbooks* (New York: Bollingen Foundation, 1957), pp. 324–353. The emphasis on discontinuity with the past in modern revolution is most fully elaborated in Gilbert, "*Revolution*"; M. J. Lasky, "The Novelty of Revolution," in *Science et conscience de la société: Mélanges en l'honneur de Raymond Aron*, J. C. Casanova (ed.), (Paris: Calmann-Lévy, 1971), pp. 251–291; and idem, *Utopia and Revolution* (Chicago: University of Chicago Press, 1976); see also J. Taubes, *Abendländische Eschatologie* (Bern: Franke, 1947).

14. On the cult of violence see Walzer, *Regicide and Revolution;* Talmon, *Origins of Totalitarian Democracy;* Gilbert, "*Revolution*"; Lasky, *Utopia and Revolution;* and C. Leiden and K. M. Schmitt (eds.), *The Politics of Violence* (Englewood Cliffs: Prentice-Hall, 1968).

15. This is more fully discussed in Eisenstadt, *Modernization, Protest, and Change*, chap. 1.

16. See on this E. Shils, *Center and Periphery: Essays in Macro-Sociology*, esp. pts. 1, 4; Eisenstadt, *Modernization, Protest, and Change*, chap. 2; M. Halpern, "The Revolution of Modernization in National and International Society," in C. J. Friedrich (ed.), *Revolution: Yearbook of the American Society for Political and Legal Philosophy*, Nomos 8 (New York: Atherton, 1967), pp. 178–216; and C. Tilly, "Does Modernization Breed Revolution?" *Comparative Politics*, 5, no. 3 (1973): 425–447.

17. This point is elaborated upon in S. N. Eisenstadt, *Tradition, Change, and Modernity* (New York: Wiley, 1973), pt. 3; and in S. N. Eisenstadt and Y. Azmon (eds.), *Socialism and Tradition* (New York: Humanities, 1975); see also Shils, *Center and Periphery*, pt. 5.

18. L. A. Fallers, *Inequality* (Chicago: University of Chicago Press, 1973); K. Mannheim, *Man and Society in an Age of Reconstruction* (London: Routledge & Kegan Paul, 1944); Shils, *Center and Periphery;* and Eisenstadt, *Tradition, Change, and Modernity*.

19. See, for instance, Voegelin, "From Enlightenment to Revolution"; Mannheim, *Man and Society;* J. Habermas, *Towards a Rational Society* (Boston: Beacon, 1970), pp. 50–62; C. Kerr, *Marshall, Marx, and Modern Times: The Multi-Dimensional Society* (Cambridge: At the University Press,

1969); and E. G. Mesthene, *Technological Change: Its Impact on Man and Society* (Cambridge; Harvard University Press, 1970).

20. See the references cited in notes 17 and 19 above.

21. This point is elaborated upon in Mannheim, *Man and Society;* Shils, *Center and Periphery,* pt. 1; Kerr, *Marshall, Marx, and Modern Times;* and Eisenstadt, *Modernization, Protest, and Change,* pt. 1.

22. This follows Eisenstadt, *Modernization, Protest, and Change,* pt. 1; see also G. Almond and G. B. Powell, *Comparative Politics* (Boston: Little, Brown, 1966), esp. chap. 10.

23. On the coalescence of these different activities see G. Lewy, *Religion and Revolution;* and the materials presented in notes 1–4 above about the revolutions in different countries. The ideological dimension is developed in Arendt, *On Revolution;* and Talmon, *Origins of Totalitarian Democracy.* See also S. Neumann, *Permanent Revolution,* 2d ed. (New York: Praeger, 1965).

24. A. Meusel, "Revolution and Counter-Revolution," in Seligman and Johnson, *Encyclopaedia of the Social Sciences,* 13:367–375; and A. Mayer, *The Dynamics of Counter-Revolution in Europe, 1870–1956* (New York: Harper & Row, 1971), pp. 2, 22–23, 45.

25. On the concept of world-system see I. Wallerstein, *The Modern World-System* (New York: Academic Press, 1974–), vol. 1; and see also S. N. Eisenstadt, "European Expansion and the Civilization of Modernity," Lecture given at the University of Leiden, May 1975, in a symposium on the Expansion of Europe organized in connection with the celebration of the 400th Anniversary of the University, to be published in the Proceedings.

26. F. Braudel, *The Mediterranean and the Mediterranean World in the Age of Philip II,* 2 vols. (London: Fontana-Collins, 1966); B. Lewis, "Islamic Concepts of Revolution," in P. J. Vatikiotis (ed.), *Revolution in the Middle East* (London: George Allen Unwin, 1972), pp. 30–40; and M. Hodgson, *The Venture of Islam: Conscience and History in a World Civilization* (Chicago: University of Chicago Press, 1974).

27. On the spread of socialism see S. N. Eisenstadt, "Socialism and Tradition," in Eisenstadt and Azmon, *Socialism and Tradition,* pp. 1–21, and the bibliography presented therein; see also D. N. Jacobs (ed.), *The New Communism* (New York: Harper & Row, 1969).

28. See on this C. E. Black and T. P. Thornton (eds.), *Communism and Revolution* (Princeton: Princeton University Press, 1964); Kamenka, *A World in Revolution;* M. Drachkovitch (ed.), *Marxism in the Modern World* (Stanford: Stanford University Press, 1965); idem, *Marxist Ideology in the Contemporary World* (New York: Praeger, 1966); G. Lichtheim, *The Origins of Socialism* (London: Weidenfeld & Nicolson, 1968); and idem, *A Short History of Socialism* (London: Weidenfeld & Nicolson, 1970).

29. The discussion here follows Eisenstadt, "Socialism and Tradition."

30. See Chapter 5 (pages 155–61); on the spread of socialism and nationalism see J. Kautsky (ed.), *Political Change in Underdeveloped Countries: Nationalism and Socialism* (New York: Wiley, 1962); and M.

Watnick, "The Appeal of Communism to the Underdeveloped Peoples," in B. F. Hoselitz (ed.), *The Progress of Underdeveloped Areas* (Chicago: University of Chicago Press, 1952), pp. 152–172.

31. S. Neumann, "The International Civil War," *World Politics*, 1, no. 2 (1949), 332–350, and idem, *Permanent Revolution*.

32. R. Aron, *The Opium of the Intellectuals* (London: Secker & Warburg, 1957; and A. Gella (eds.), *The Intelligentsia and the Intellectuals: Theory, Method, and Case Studies* (Berkeley: Sage, 1976).

33. Walzer, "Puritanism as Revolutionary Ideology"; and H. J. Benda, "Intellectuals and Politics in Western History," *Bucknell Review*, 10, no. 1 (1959): 1–14.

34. V. I. Lenin, *State and Revolution* (New York: International Publishers, 1969); Black and Thornton, *Communism and Revolution;* and E. Kamenka, "The Relevance—and Irrelevance—of Marxism," in Kamenka, *A World in Revolution,* pp. 53–71.

35. W. Sombart, *Warum gibt es in den Vereinigten Staaten Keinen Sozialismus?* (Tübingen: J. C. B. Mohr, 1906).

36. See for works on these revolutions notes 3–14 to Chapter 7 and notes 19–54 to Chapter 8.

Chapter 7.   The Social and Historical Conditions of the Modern Revolutions

1. CONDITIONS BEHIND THE DEVELOPMENT OF MODERN REVOLUTIONS. THE DIFFERENT APPROACHES

I

Following the analysis in Chapter 6, we shall now turn to the problem of the specific conditions that may explain the development of the modern revolutions and their specific characteristics and outcomes. What concrete conditions in Europe and in the American colonies spawned the revolutionary processes of change? The vast sociological literature on this question identifies a common factor in these contexts: intensification of external pressures on the existing, traditional regimes, which signaled their ultimate downfall.[1]

The most important external factors were wars, interstate competition, and pressures from the emerging political and economic international systems. The internal pressures stemmed primarily from the development of politically articulated elites or social forces that arose in the wake of far-reaching economic change and dislocation connected with the broadening of markets, technological innovation, the development of new (capitalist) modes of production, and the enunciation of new ideologies. All these created, especially among the middle classes a strong sense of frustration with respect to participation in the social and political centers and frameworks. Moreover, both external and internal pressures were closely connected with intensive intraelite and interelite struggle as well as with broad, popular (especially peasant) uprisings and with religious and intellectual movements.

Nevertheless, some of the most important conditions we have identified (rifts within elites and the connections between these struggles and broader social conflicts) fostered the decline or change of traditional

195

regimes without resulting either in revolutions or in far-reaching structural transformations.

II

Hence, we are back to the question of what specifically directed these processes in a revolutionary direction. A natural starting point for answering this question is the identification of unique characteristics of the participants, characteristics that distinguished them from participants in other societies. A common pattern can be discerned.

In all these societies the principal participants were traditional but potentially modernizing monarchs with strong Absolutist tendencies who tried to generate and control broad social and economic processes and who variously combined traditional closure with certain modernizing tendencies; diversified upper and middle landed and urban groups moving in the direction of a capitalist market economy; heterogeneous peasant groups (in the United States, farmers) caught between dislocation caused by the new economic forces and possibilities of gaining access to and control of the new markets; traditional urban groups and the beginnings of a new urban proletariat; new intellectual and religious sects, groups, and movements; and more diversified institutional entrepreneurs, especially new political elites (which we describe later).[2]

In all societies in which the modern revolutions developed—the Netherlands,[3] England,[4] the American colonies,[5] and France,[6]—it was the combination of external pressures stemming primarily from the emergence of the modern state system and the modern international capitalist economy, on the one hand, and internal pressures and conflicts among these different developments, on the other, that gave rise to the decline of the regime. In Barrington Moore's words, these forces created a situation in which

the whole intellectual and emotional structure that makes the prevailing order seem a mixture of the natural, the legitimate and the inevitable— even to those who derive minimal benefits from that order—begins to crumble in face of questions for which the prevailing orthodoxies gradually cease to have answers that seem satisfactory.[7]

Ultimately, the result was revolution and revolutionary transformation.

Of course, societies differed significantly with respect to the strength of these different groups and the connections among them. But even in the Revolt of the Netherlands and the American Revolution (and much later the Turkish Revolution)—whose focus on restructuring the symbols and boundaries of the political collectivity has called into question the importance of social causes—this pattern obtained.

Specification of the participants brings us a step closer to identification of the unique historical conditions under which these revolutionary processes unfolded. The former task has been tackled most notably by Theda Skocpol and Kay Trimberger.[8] Let us quote Skocpol.

> The French Revolution was remarkably similar to the Russian and the Chinese in its basic causes—failure of old regime officials to mobilize sufficient national resources to promote national economic development and/or counter military competition or threats from more developed nations abroad—and in its structural dynamics—peasants and marginal political elites against a traditional landed upper class.
>
> . . . Let me sum up what this essay has attempted to do. To explain the great historical social revolutions, I have first, conceptualized a certain type of society, the agrarian bureaucracy, in which social control of the lower strata (mainly peasants) rests with institutions locally and regionally controlled by landed upper classes, together with administrative and military machineries centrally controlled, and second, I have discussed differences between agrarian bureaucracies which did and those which did not experience social revolutions in terms of (a) institutional structures which mediate landed upper class relations to state apparatuses and peasant relations to landed upper classes and (b) types and amounts of international political and economic pressures [(]especially originating with more developed nations) impinging upon agrarian bureaucracies newly incorporated into the modernizing world. According to my analysis, social revolutions occurred in those modernizing agrarian bureaucracies—France, Russia and China—which both incubated peasantries structurally prone to autonomous insurrection and experienced severe administrative and military disorganization due to the direct or indirect effects of military competition or threats from more modern nations abroad.[9]

III

Even the preceding specifications leave several very important questions unanswered. One question is why these historical processes gave rise not merely to far-reaching changes and restructuring in the direction of modernization (as happened in a number of societies) but rather to specific revolutionary experiences and to the modern revolutionary process. (Indeed, Sweden, Denmark, and Switzerland[10] experienced extensive symbolic structural transformation without experiencing the *process of revolution* as it evolved in the revolutionary societies; it is interesting, however, that the transformation of their social structures was similar to the outcomes of pure revolutions.)

A more important unanswered question for us concerns the failure of many societies both to achieve the breakthrough to modernity *through this process* and to effect revolutionary-type social and cultural transformations. Indeed, with the exception of Russia,[11] China,[12] and possibly Turkey,[13] Yugoslavia, and Vietnam,[14] Western European societies like Germany[15] and Italy,[16] many Eastern European societies,[17] Asian societies like Japan,[18] and most South and Southeast Asian, Middle Eastern, and

Latin American societies [19] underwent the transformation from traditional to modern nation in a nonrevolutionary manner. While the breakthrough to modernity in these countries partook of many of the symbols and processes of the modern revolutions (and all of them experienced revolutionary movements), it differed both in processes as well as in outcomes from the revolutionary pattern.

Hence, specification either of the general conditions of decline of regimes or of the specific historical conditions and constellations related to the modern setting, important as it is, does not explicate the development of revolutions. To do so requires identification of some combination between the structural and cultural characteristics of the societies in which the modern revolutions took place on the one hand, and the specific historical conditions that served as the framework within which the potentialities for revolution and concomitant social transformation became actualized.

2. THE SOCIOCULTURAL SETTING OF MODERN REVOLUTIONS

I

Of crucial importance from the point of view of our analysis is the fact that the modern revolutions occurred within the framework of European civilization—which as a traditional civilization envinced (1) a very high degree of convergence among movements of protest and between them and more central political struggle and (2) a concomitant tendency toward a relatively high degree of convergence among changes in the major institutional spheres. As we have seen, these changes were closely related to a high degree of distinctiveness of the centers, of mutual impingement of center and periphery, and of strata autonomy and consciousness and to a relatively strong emphasis on this-worldly foci for overcoming the tension between the transcendental and mundane orders.

Truly enough, even within these societies the first true, pure, modern revolutions constituted a sort of mutation, an entirely new type of process of change. But this mutation was produced by the intensification of those very processes of change that could be found in medieval Europe. First, there was the intensification of the activities of a multiplicity of secondary elites—new political and economic elites, new types of articulators of cultural models as well as of the solidarity of different ascriptive collectivities—each with relatively autonomous bases and with strong connections both to the periphery and to the center. Second, there was the growth of linkages among these groups and elites and the centers of societies.

The tendencies toward such linkages were reinforced in early modern Europe primarily by three general social processes: (1) the continual reconstruction of political centers and boundaries and the growing mutual impingement of centers and peripheries; [20] (2) the crystallization of new international frameworks that cut across political boundaries but at the same time very strongly impinged and depended on them [21] and the rise of new economic forces usually subsumed under the term "capitalism"; and (3) the transformation of Protestantism from a collection of closed sects into a broad social, political, and cultural movement and its incorporation into the centers of the societies, along with the political, ideological, and intellectual reactions throughout Europe to this process—especially the Counterreformation and the Enlightenment. [22] These three processes profoundly contributed to the reconstruction of the social and political orders of Europe. [23]

Intensification of the processes of change that marked traditional European civilization combined with Protestantism and rising technology to generate those characteristics of the European revolutions that distinguished them from the movements of protest and change other societies and other periods experienced.

II

The potentialities of Protestantism as an ideological and institutional solvent were rooted in some of its basic cultural orientations—above all, its great stress on the tension between the transcendental order and the sociopolitical order, on their mutual relevance, on the possibility (even necessity) of resolving this tension through this-worldly activity, and on the direct, unmediated access of individuals and communities to the major attributes of the transcendental and sociopolitical orders.

The emergence of Protestant symbolism may be viewed as a mutation (similar to the genesis of the other great religions) but only under the structural and historical conditions outlined earlier could this system become institutionalized. The impact of Protestantism was far-reaching. [24] First, in the formation of centers we can identify the incorporation of orientations of protest and of heterodoxy as they developed in the Reformation, into central symbols of the society. Second (also as regards center formation), we see the fundamental cultural premises of European society recast in a secular mode. Third, in the sphere of institution building, Protestantism heightened commitment to economic, scientific, and political activities and encouraged the sanctification and legitimation of institution building in terms of Protestant symbolic-religious premises. Fourth, in the crystallization of the institutional derivatives of these orientations, we note the emergence of political-intellectual entrepreneurs who combined the functions of political activists and articulators of models of cultural order and who were disembedded somewhat from other social units but maintained strong solidary relations with them, attempting even to restructure the bases of their solidarity with the center. The first version of this new type of entrepreneur developed, as Michael Walzer and Herbert Lüthy have shown,[25] among the Protestant activists.

Protestantism was so potent a force because it evinced all the characteristics of other European movements of heterodoxy and rebellion and maintained close relations between secondary elites and broader strata and combined orientations toward the restructuring of centers with a strong emphasis on institution building.

III

These potentialities of Protestantism and later on of the Enlightenment tended to become actualized primarily in settings in which certain key aspects of structural pluralism inherent in the European tradition were most developed. Such settings were most conducive to the crystallization of this type of political entrepreneur. Hence, the transformative potentialities of Protestantism were not actualized in John Calvin's Geneva,[26] or John Knox's Scotland,[27] or the Netherlands in the sixteenth and seventeenth century,[28] or early in the colonization of America.[29] In these settings the Protestants enjoyed a political monopoly and were able to impose their totalistic socioreligious orientations.

In England, the Netherlands, Switzerland,[30] to a smaller degree Scandinavia,[31] and initially France[32]—where Protestantism became interwoven in a pluralistic context—Protestantism was crucial in transforming European society in line with Europe's basic cultural and institutional characteristics and in this way transcending the traditional (medieval) setting.

In many of the German principalities, Protestantism served initially at least to legitimate a strong warrior, Absolutist state and its expansionist tendencies.[33] In France, Protestantism and reactions to it deepened cleavages among different segments of the elite. In the Catholic states—especially Austria, Spain, and Portugal—the initial Counterreformation reaction to Protestantism was to strengthen the Absolutist structure.[34] As Stein Rokkan's analysis demonstrated,[35] the impact of Protestantism was crucial in the further development of all these societies, most notably, in the pattern of the incorporation of new strata into the emerging modern systems.

The powerful influence of Protestantism throughout Europe attests to the fact that it was a specific combination of unique conditions that gave rise to modern revolutionary symbolism and movements, as well as to the different types of structural transformations with which the early revolutions were connected. But these transformations could develop only in specific historical circumstances.

3. THE HISTORICAL SETTING OF
MODERN REVOLUTIONS

What characteristics distinguished those circumstances that generated revolutions? First, three major aspects of the breakthrough from traditional to modern civilization converged. These aspects were: (1) transition from a traditional, or closed, pattern of legitimation of political authority (perhaps also from a traditional definition of the symbols of collective identity) to an open pattern; (2) transition from a traditional to an open system of stratification (class system) rooted in or connected with movement toward a market economy in general and an industrial economy in particular; [36] and (3) creation and/or incorporation of societal units into a series of continually changing international economic-capitalist, political-cultural systems.[37]

Second, the convergence of these aspects presented traditional centers and groups with a series of problems that called for redefinition of almost all the major ground rules of social interaction and their basic institutional derivatives—above all, the ground rules and their derivates associated with access to power and the structure of the political centers.

Third, growing socioeconomic differentiation provided movements of protest, political struggle, and innovation with a large number of groups ready for social mobilization; while the intensification of processes of change resulted in the emergence of a large number of elites—of institutional entrepreneurs who could serve as agents of such mobilization and linkages among themselves and among the relatively closed centers and broader strata of traditional society.

Hence, under these conditions the potentialities for symbolically and organizationally linking movements of protest, rebellions, heterodoxies, central political struggle, and institution building became actualized and focused on reconstruction of the social order.

4. SOCIAL, CULTURAL, AND HISTORICAL
CONDITIONS BEHIND LATER REVOLUTIONS

I

It is appropriate to ask whether our analysis applies not only to the first modern revolutions but also to later ones.

We noted earlier that within the framework of modern civilization—above all, in Russia, China, and possibly Turkey, Vietnam, and Yugoslavia [38]—phenomena similar to the initial, true revolutions have been rare. Truly enough, these phenomena differed in many ways from early revolutions: they were proletarian rather than bourgeois; they were more violent; and they were purposefully guided by revolutionary groups. Some radical scholars maintain that these revolutions were more real than the early ones and better embodied the image and premises of the true revolution.[39] Other scholars, even radicals like Moore, hold that their strong elements of destruction and particularly the coerciveness they entailed betrayed the emancipatory premises of the revolutionary image.[40]

Subsequently we analyze in detail some of the most important differences among the various revolutions. Nevertheless, we assert that these differences notwithstanding, all these revolutions share basic characteristics.

As regards the revolutionary process, they all combined movements of rebellion, central political struggle, and religious or intellectual heterodoxy. They all witnessed the rise of the new type of political-intellectual entrepreneur—in the later revolutions he often was the professional revolutionary (to use Bruce Mazlish's term, the ascetic revolutionary).[41] In terms of outcomes, they all moved not only in the same general direction —toward modernization, structural differentiation, market economics, political centralization, and restructuring of the nature and contents of the centers and the relations between center and periphery—but also manifested the same constellations through which such institutional changes were effected. Given these similarities, we naturally have to ask whether the conditions that made the later type of revolutionary process possible were similar to those that engendered the earlier revolutions.

II

A closer look at the conditions under which the later revolutions took place does indeed point up marked similarities.

First, these societies belonged to the world's great traditions or high civilizations—all of which were based on highly articulated cultural models (carried by distinct groups and special institutional enclaves) that made universal claims in principle transcending national, regional, and political boundaries and containing missionary elements.[42]

As we have seen, these traditions and civilizations shared several basic cultural orientations or codes. They were characterized by a high level of autonomy and distinctiveness of the cosmic (religious) and social orders but at the same time acknowledged their mutual relevance and the necessity of bridging the gap between the transcendental and the mundane order through a variety of this-worldly activities; by a relatively high level of commitment among the different sectors of the population to the social order; and by relatively autonomous access of at least some societal strata to the major attributes of the social order. Above all, they shared the very important feature of identifying this-worldly activity as the most important means of overcoming the tension between the transcendental-cosmic and the mundane order.

Second, these societies were Imperial or Imperial-feudal systems. Accordingly, they were characterized by a high level of distinctiveness of the centers and of the permeation of the periphery by the center; by the autonomous access of certain strata to various attributes of the cosmic and social orders; and by tendencies toward the impingement of at least part of the periphery on the center or centers.

In connection with these characteristics there developed (as we saw in Chapters 4 and 5) common features of the structuring of social hierarchies and strata formation. These features encouraged the autonomous articulation of strata as distince from but related to the political sphere.

Finally, as we saw earlier, Imperial and Imperial-feudal societies exhibited the pattern of coalescent change and this pattern provided the basis for true revolutionary transformation.

Striking similarities in historical circumstances can also be identified in all revolutionary societies. The conditions under which revolutionary tendencies intensified were shaped by incorporation of the society into the international frameworks of modernity, into the new international political, economic, and cultural systems, which were characterized, on the one hand, by relatively open markets and, on the other, by potentially great inequalities within these markets. Such incorporation involved both early and later revolutionary societies, in the transition from a traditional, or closed, to an open pattern of legitimation of political authority and possibly parallel changes in the definition of the symbols of collective identity; along with the transition from a traditional to an open system of stratification. And, as we pointed out in our discussion of European revolutionary societies, these developments led to far-reaching socioeconomic dislocations; the threatening of traditional centers; the emboldening of broader groups that demanded participation in the centers; and the availability of these groups for social mobilization.

III

Thus, the preceding analysis indicates that the combination of internal cultural and structural characteristics and historical circumstances conducive to the development of revolution, while not necessarily consequent upon the spread of modern civilization, may arise in different societies and in different eras. This possibility is perhaps best attested in the case of North Vietnam [43]—the only postcolonial revolutionary society to exhibit some of the major features of a pure revolution. Other cases that we discuss at length in later chapters indicate that it is only the unique combinaion of internal characteristics and historical circumstances identified in this chapter that generates the potentialities of true revolutions. Thus, the Japanese case (see Chapter 8) reveals that Imperial-feudal structures unconnected to the perception of tension between the transcendental and the mundane order may experience far-reaching structural transformations but not full-scale revolutions. The various Islamic states show that the presence of appropriate cultural orientations in the absence of an Imperial or Imperial-feudal structure is insufficient to produce a true revolution.

The process of social transformation attendant on the breakthrough to modernity in patrimonial societies (see Chapter 9) is distinct from the pattern of revolutionary transformation, as are the patterns of radicalism and social transformation (analyzed in Chapter 10) that accompany late modernization (not the breakthrough to modernity). We analyze these processes after examining in Chapter 8 the outcomes of revolutions.

5. SOCIAL, CULTURAL, AND HISTORICAL FRAMEWORKS. PRECONDITIONS OF REVOLUTION

Thus we come back to a point made earlier; namely, that it is only within the context of the interaction between the structural and the cultural characteristics of the societies and historical frameworks analyzed above that the preconditions of revolution may become linked with one another and lead to the outbreak of a real revolution and to its concomitant changes. (To review, these preconditions are: intraelite and interelite competition; the interweaving of elites with broader social movements; and the political articulation of the feeling of relative deprivation among broader groups.)

In other historical conditions, as well as in other types of societies, the various preconditions may give rise to the demise of regimes or to internal war but not to revolution and revolutionary social transformation. Moreover, revolutions do not necessarily result from the combination of structural and historical conditions most conducive to their development because various elites, subelites and broader groups may become deadlocked, impeding far-reaching transformation. (Still, such deadlocks are least likely if these preconditions obtain.)

Given that the proper conditions exist, whether or not a revolution actually occurs depends greatly on the cohesiveness of would-be revolutionary groups and on the power and solidary relations between them and broader groups and between them and incumbent rulers and/or other contenders for power.

Only insofar as potential revolutionary groups can overpower these groups or form effective coalitions with them are the chances for revolutionary transformation good.[44] In England, the Netherlands, the United States, and to some degree France, relatively open solidary relations existed among the various revolutionary contenders and between them and broader social groups. In Russia, China, and North Vietnam, revolutionary groups were small, cohesive, and relatively closed; they tended to develop more power-oriented and coercive relations with other actors.

6. FIRST AND LATER REVOLUTIONS. SIMILARITIES AND DIFFERENCES

These common characteristics notwithstanding, crucial differences separated the earlier and the later revolutions. In Chapter 8 we analyze some of these differences and their impact on the outcomes of revolution. At this stage, however, it might be worthwhile to pose one question closely related to Weber's classical problem about the relationship between Protestantism and the rise of capitalism: is the fact that the first revolutions took place in Europe and the later ones occurred only under the impact of European expansion but historical accident? Could the early revolutions and the breakthrough to modernity have occurred in societies like Russia or China?

Our analysis indicated that the Imperial systems—for example, the Russian, Chinese, and Ottoman empires—that unlike the Byzantine Empire survived until modern times did so by successfully minimizing (in ways we analyzed above) the potentially transformative tendencies that evolved in them, especially the tendency toward coalescence among movements of rebellion, heterodoxy, central political struggle, and institution building. There is no reason to assume that the segregative policies of the rulers would not have continued to succeed in the face of a development like Protestantism or formidable external threats of the traditional type.

The reason why the potentially transformative tendencies of mutations like Protestantism, if not necessarily their emergence, became actualized in Europe lies in the special European mixture of Imperial and feudal elements; most significantly, the multiplicity of continual changing centers and collectivities within the relatively broad but flexible framework of European civilization and the concomitant multiplicity of more or less autonomous elites. Thus, the implications of Weber's analysis about the uniqueness of the initial Western push to modernity stand. Going beyond these implications, however, our analysis of the similarities between the earlier and later revolutions indicated that once the breakthrough was achieved, its expansion could evoke in some societies responses similar to actual revolutionary ones. But this could happen only insofar as the combination of internal characteristics and historical circumstances created conditions similar to those we identified for Europe as conducive to revolution.

But, as we suggested earlier, even these conditions do not, of course, assure that some type of revolutionary transformation will take place nor do they specify what kind of transformation will take place.

Here two questions arise. First, why did Sweden, Denmark, Switzerland, and (according to those who deny the revolutionary nature of the Revolt of the Netherlands) the Netherlands experience the emergence of a postrevolutionary symbolic and institutional order very much like that which developed in the revolutionary European and American countries but not undergo the process of revolution? The second question refers to a possibility seen in different ways in Germany,[45] Koumintang China,[46] and in a marginal way Spain.[47] That is, despite the appropriate internal and external conditions, why did no revolutionary transformation take place or become institutionalized? In Chapter 8 we look more closely at some of these problems.

NOTES

1. See, for instance, J. R. Gillis, "Political Decay and the European Revolutions, 1789–1848," *World Politics*, 22, no. 3 (1970): 344–370; H. Lubasz (ed.), *Revolutions in Modern History* (New York: Macmillan, 1966); P. Zagorin, "Prolegomena to the Comparative History of Revolution in Early Modern Europe, "*Comparative Studies in Society and History*, 18 April 1976): 151–174; T. Skocpol, "France, Russia, China: A Structural Analysis of Social Revolutions, ibid., pp. 175–210; M. Kossok (ed.), *Studien über die Revolution* (Berlin: Akademie, 1969); idem (ed.), *Studien zur vergleichenden Revolutionsgeschichte, 1500–1917* (Berlin, Akademie, 1974); and see the works cited in notes 21 and 49 to Chapter I.

2. See, for instance, Skocpol, "France, Russia, China."

3. On the Revolt of the Netherlands in this context see especially I. Schöffer, "De Nederlandse Revolutie," in I. Schöffer (ed.), *Zeven Revoluties* (Amsterdam: T. H. de Bussy, n.d.), pp. 9–29; and J. W. Smit, "The Netherlands Revolution," in R. Forster and J. P. Greene (eds.), *The Preconditions of Revolution in Early Modern Europe* (Baltimore: Johns Hopkins Press, 1970), pp. 19–54; see also G. Griffiths, "The Revolutionary Character of Revolt of the Netherlands," *Comparative Studies in Society and History*, 2 (July 1960), pp. 452–472; G. Nadel, "The Logic of the Anatomy of Revolution, with Reference to the Netherlands Revolt," ibid., pp. 473–484; I. Schöffer, "The Dutch Revolt Anatomized: Some Comments," ibid., 3, no. 4 (July 1961): 470–479; H. Schilling, "Der Aufstand der Niederlande: Bürgerliche Revolution oder Elitenkonflikt?" in H. U. Wehler (ed.), *200 Jahre Amerikanische Revolution und moderne Revolutionsforschung* (Göttingen: Vandenhoeck & Ruprecht, 1976): pp. 177–231; J. J. Woltjer, "De Vrede-makers," *Tijdschrift voor Geschiedenis*, 89 (1976): 299–321; and J E. Ellemers, "The Revolt of the Netherlands: The Part Played by

Religion in the Process of Nation-Building," *Social Compass*, 14, no 2 (1967): 93–103.

4. On the English Revolution and its causes see especially C. Hill, "The English Revolution and the Brotherhood of Man," in Lubasz, *Revolutions in Modern European History*, pp. 39–55; I. Schöffer, "De Engelse Revolutie," in I. Schöffer (ed.), *Zeven Revoluties*, pp. 29–51; L. Stone, *The Causes of the English Revolution, 1529–1642* (London: Routledge & Kegan Paul, 1972); idem, "The English Revolution," in Forster and Greene, *Preconditions of Revolution*, pp. 55–108; P. Zagorin, "The English Revolution, 1640–1660," in Lubasz, *Revolutions in Modern European History*, pp. 24–39; P. S. Seaver (ed.), *Seventeenth-Century England: Society in an Age of Revolution* (New York: New Viewpoints, 1976).

5. On the American Revolution see especially R. M. Weir, "Who Shall Rule at Rome: The American Revolution as a Crisis of Legitimacy for the Colonial Elite," *Journal of Interdisciplinary History*, 6, no. 4 (1976): 679–700; R. B. Morris, *The American Revolution Reconsidered* (New York: Harper & Row, 1967); and J. P. Greene, "The Social Origins of the American Revolution: An Evaluation and an Interpretation," *Political Science Quarterly*, 88, no. 1 (1973): 1–22.

6. On the French Revolution see P. Geyl, "De Franse Revolutie," in I. Schöffer (ed.); *Zeven Revoluties*, pp. 77–103; G. Lefebvre, *The Coming of the French Revolution* (Princeton: Princeton University Press, 1941); idem, *The French Revolution* (New York: Columbia University Press, 1962), 1:47–49; idem, *Etudes sur la révolution française* (Paris: Presses universitaires de France, 1963); E. Schmitt, "Die französische Revolution," in T. Schieder (ed.), *Revolution und Gesellschaft* (Freiburg im Breisgau: Herder, 1973), pp. 65–96; A. Soboul, "Classes and Class Struggles during the French Revolution," *Science and Society*, 17, no. 3 (1953): 238–257; idem, *La France à la veille de la Révolution: Aspects économiques et sociaux* (Paris: Centre de documentation universitaire, 1960), chap. 6; G. Rudé, *Interpretations of the French Revolution*, rev. ed., American Historical Association General Series, no. 47 (London, 1972); A. Cobban, *A History of Modern France, vol. 1, 1715–1799* (Baltimore: Penguin, 1963); idem, *The Social Interpretation of the French Revolution* (Cambridge: At the University Press, 1968), chaps. 4, 5; C. B. A. Behrens, *The Ancien Régime* (New York: Harcourt, Brace, 1967); and G. Taylor, "Noncapitalist Wealth and the Origins of the French Revolution," *American Historical Review*, 72, no. 2 (1967): 487–488.

7. B. Moore, *Reflections on the Causes of Human Misery and upon Certain Proposals to Eliminate Them* (Boston: Beacon, 1970), pp. 170–171.

8. T. Skocpol, "Explaining Revolutions: In Quest of a Social-Structural Approach," in L. A. Coser and O. N. Larsen (eds.), *The Uses of Controversy in Sociology* (New York: Free Press, 1976), pp. 155–178; E. K. Trimberger, "A Theory of Elite Revolutions," *Studies in Comparative International Development*, 7, no. 3 (1972): 191–207; and idem, *Revolution from Above*.

9. Skocpol, "France, Russia, China," pp. 208–210.

10. Moore, *Reflections*.

11. From among the innumerable works on the Russian Revolution see E. H. Carr, "The Background of the Russian Revolution," in Lubasz, *Revolutions in Modern European History*, pp. 112–119; R. V. Daniels, "The Russian Revolution Runs Its Course," in ibid., pp. 128–136; Z. R. Dittrich, "De Russische Revolutie," in I. Schöffer (ed.), *Zeven Revoluties*, pp. 103–127; J. Laloy, "1789 et 1917, ou de la fin des révolutions," *Science et conscience de la société;* L. Schapiro, "The Bolsheviks and Their Rivals," in Lubasz, *Revolutions in Modern European History*, pp. 119–128; H. Seton-Watson, *Nationalism and Communism: Essays, 1946–63* (London: Methuen, 1964), pp. 68–76; I. Turner, "The Significance of the Russian Revolution," in E. Kamenka (ed.), *A World in Revolution?* (Canberra: Australian National University Press, 1970), pp. 25–39; I. Berlin, "Russia and 1848," in Lubasz, *Revolutions in Modern European History*, pp. 92–112; Carr, "Background of the Russian Revolution"; F. Venturi, *Roots of Revolution: A History of the Populist and Socialist Movements in Nineteenth Century Russia* (New York: Knopf, 1960); A. B. Ulam, *The Bolsheviks: The Intellectual and Political History of the Triumph of Communism in Russia* (New York: Macmillan, 1965); R. Pipes (ed.), *Revolutionary Russia* (Cambridge: Harvard University Press, 1968); and D. Geyer, "Oktoberrevolution," in Schieder, *Revolution und Gesellschaft*, pp. 117–163.

12. Of the major works on the Chinese Revolution see J. Gardner, "Revolution in China," in P. J. Vatikiotis (ed.), *Revolution in the Middle East* (London: George Allen & Unwin, 1972), pp. 211–232; M. Meisner, "Utopian Socialist Themes in Maoism," in J. W. Lewis (ed.), *Peasant Rebellion and Communist Revolution in Asia* (Stanford: Stanford University Press, 1974), pp. 207–252; M. B. Rankin, *Early Chinese Revolutionaries: Radical Intellectuals in Shanghai and Chekiang, 1902–1911* (Cambridge: Harvard University Press, 1971); K. A. Wittfogel, "Social Revolutions in China," in Kamenka, *A World in Revolution*, pp. 39–53; E. Zurcher, "De Chinese Revolutie," in I. Schöffer (ed.), *Zeven Revoluties*, pp. 145–167; B. I. Schwartz, *Communism and China: Ideology in Flux* (Cambridge: Harvard University Press, 1968); F. Schurmann and O. Schell (eds.), *Republican China: Nationalism, War, and the Rise of Communism, 1911–1949* (New York: Random House, Vintage, 1967); D. Milton, N. Milton, and F. Schurmann (eds.), *People's China: Social Experimentation, Politics, and Entry onto the World Scene, 1966 through 1972* (New York: Random House, Vintage, 1974); Ping-ti Ho and Tang Tsou (eds.), *China's Heritage and the Communist Political System: China in Crisis*, 2 vols. (Chicago: University of Chicago Press, 1968); J. Gray (ed.), *Modern China's Search for a Political Form* (New York: Oxford University Press, 1969), pp. 41–65; F. Michael, "State and Society in Nineteenth Century China," *World Politics*, 7, no. 3 (1955): 419–33; and M. C. Wright (ed.), *China in Revolution: The First Phase, 1900–1913* (New Haven: Yale University Press, 1968), pp. 24–26.

13. The best single piece on the Turkish Revolution is S. Mardin, "Ideology

and Religion in the Turkish Revolution," *International Journal of Middle East Studies*, 2, no. 3 (1971): 197–211.

14. Regarding the Yugoslavian and Vietnamese cases see B. Denitch, "Violence and Social Change in the Yugoslav Revolution," *Comparative Politics*, 8, no. 3 (1976): 465–478; idem, *The Legitimation of a Revolution* (New Haven: Yale University Press, 1976); J. T. McAlister, Jr., and P. Mus, *The Vietnamese and Their Revolution* (New York: Harper & Row, Harper Torchbooks, 1970); J. R. McLane, "Archaic Movements and Revolution in Southern Vietnam," in N. Miller and R. Aya (eds.), *National Liberation: Revolution in the Third World* (New York: Free Press, 1971), pp. 68–101; G. Modelski, "The Viet Minh Complex," in C. E. Black and T. P. Thornton (eds.), *Communism and Revolution* (Princeton: Princeton University Press, 1964), pp. 185–215; S. L. Popkin, "Corporatism and Colonialism: Political Economy of Rural Change in Vietnam," *Comparative Politics*, 8, no. 3 (1976), 431–464; p. Mus, "Buddhism in Vietnamese History and Society," *Jahrbuch des Südasien Instituts*, 1 (1967): 95–115; and C. P. White, "The Vietnamese Revolutionary Alliance: Intellectuals, Workers, and Peasants," in Lewis, *Peasant Rebellion*, pp. 77–95.

15. On Germany see V. Ritterberger, "Revolution and Pseudo-Democratization: The Formation of the Weimar Republic," in G. A. Almond, S. C. Flanagan, and R. J. Mundt (eds.), *Crisis, Choice, and Change* (Boston: Little, Brown, 1973), pp. 285–391; G. Mann, *The History of Germany since 1789*, transl. M. Jackson (London: Chatto & Windus, 1968); and V. Valentin, *Geschichte der deutschen Revolution von 1848–49* (Berlin: Ullstein, 1930).

16. On Italy see A. W. Salomone (ed.), *Italy from the Risorgimento to Fascism* (Garden City: Doubleday, Anchor, 1970); and H. Seton-Watson, *Italy from Liberalism to Fascism, 1870–1925* (London: Methuen, 1967).

17. On East European social changes and revolutions see R. V. Burke, "Eastern Europe," in Black and Thornton, *Communism and Revolution*, pp. 77–116; H. Seton-Watson, *The East European Revolution* (London: Methuen, 1952); and idem, *Nationalism and Communism*, pp. 163–172.

18. On Japan see J. W. White, "State Building and Modernization: The Meiji Restoration," in Almond et al., *Crisis, Choice, and Change*, pp. 499–559; Trimberger, "Theory of Elite Revolutions"; and the literature cited in notes 82–87 to Chapter 8.

19. For relevant material on South and Southeast Asia see R. E. Agpalo, "Revolution and the Philippine Political System," *Solidarity*, 4 (July 1969): *Rebellion*, pp. 151–168; J. Gerassi, *Towards Revolution, vol. 1, China, India, Asia, the Middle East* (London: Weidenfeld & Nicolson, 1971); Lewis, *Peasant Rebellion*; J. H. A. Logemann, "De Indonesische Revolutie," in I. Schöffer (ed.), *Zeven Revoluties*, pp. 127–145; R. T. McVey, "The Southeast Asian Revolts," in Black and Thornton, *Communism and Revolution*, pp. 145–185; R. Mortimer, "Traditional Modes and Communist Movements: Change and Protest in Indonesia," in Lewis, *Peasant Rebellion*, pp. 99–124; on the Middle East see Vatikiotis, *Revolution in the Middle East*.

For a bibliography on Latin America see H. J. Puhle (ed.), *Revolution und Reformen in Lateinamerika: Geschichte und Gesellschaft* (Göttingen: Vandenhoeck & Ruprecht, 1976); and the literature cited in notes 2, 4, 7, 11, 16–17, 20–32, 35, 38–39, 42, 49, 51, 53, 56–59, 61–66, and 69–72 to Chapter 9.

See in general K. Kumar, "Le rivoluzioni del ventesimo secolo in perspettiva storica," in L. Pellicani (ed.), *Sociologia delle rivoluzioni* (Naples: Guida, 1976), pp. 45–94; idem, *Revolution* (London: Weidenfeld & Nicolson, 1971); F. Castiello, "Le rivoluzioni del Terzo Mondo: Il caso dell' Africa portoghese," in Pellicani, *Sociologia delle rivoluzioni,* pp. 95–122; and T. Schieder, "Das Problem der Revolution im 19. Jahrhundert," *Historische Zeitschrift,* 170, no. 2 (1950): 233–271.

20. On the European society in the Age of Absolutism see M. Beloff, *The Age of Absolutism* (London: Macmillan, 1966); T. O. Lindsay (ed.), *The New Cambridge Modern History* (Cambridge: At the University Press, 1957), vol. 7; C. Tilly (ed.), *The Formation of National States in Western Europe* (Princeton: Princeton University Press, 1975); I. Wallerstein, *The Modern World-System* (New York: Academic Press, 1974–), vol. 1; O. Hintze, "The Formation of States and Constitutional Development: A Study in History and Politics," in F. Gilbert (ed.), *The Historical Essays of Otto Hintze* (New York: Oxford University Press, 1975), pp. 157–177; H. G. Koenigsberger, *Estates and Revolutions* (Ithaca: Cornell University Press, 1971), chap. 9; G. Clark, *The Seventeenth Century,* second ed. (Oxford: Clarendon Press, 1950); idem, *Early Modern Europe, 1450–1720* (New York: Oxford University Press, 1957); B. Barber and E. G. Barber (eds.), *European Social Class: Stability and Change* (New York: Macmillan, 1965); Behrens, *Ancien Régime;* Cobban, *Social Interpretation of the French Revolution,* chaps. 4, 5; and Taylor, "Noncapitalist Wealth."

21. See Tilly, *Formation of National States;* E. Kamenka and R. S. Neale (eds.), *Feudalism, Capitalism, and Beyond* (London: Arnold, 1975); F. Braudel, *Capitalism and Material Life, 1400–1800* (New York: Harper & Row, Harper Colophon, 1975); L. Pellicani, "Capitalismo, modernizzazione, e rivoluzione," in Pellicani, *Sociologia delle rivoluzioni,* pp. 11–44; J. H. Elliot, "Revolution and Continuity in Early Modern Europe," *Past and Present,* no. 42 (1969): 35–56; Forster and Greene, *Preconditions of Revolution;* and Zagorin, "Prolegomena."

22. On the development of Protestantism and its impact on modernity see S. N. Eisenstadt (ed.), *The Protestant Ethic and Modernization: A Comparative View* (New York: Basic Books, 1968), and the bibliography given therein.

23. E. Voegelin, *Order and History,* 6 vols. (Baton Rouge: Louisiana State University Press, 1954–1974), vols. 5, 6; idem, *From Enlightenment to Revolution,* J. U. Hallowell, ed. (Durham: Duke University Press, 1975). On the Counterrevolution see R. B. Wernham (ed.), *The New Cambridge Modern History* (Cambridge: At the University Press, 1968), vol. 3.

24. The diverse impacts of Protestantism are discussed in Eisenstadt, *Protestant Ethic;* see also J. C. Brauer, "Puritan Mysticism and the Develop-

ment of Liberation," *Church History*, 19, no. 3 (1950): 151–170; W. Haller, *The Rise of Puritanism* (New York: Harper & Row, 1939); idem, *Liberty and Reformation in the Puritan Revolution* (New York: Columbia University Press, 1955); G. C. Mosse, "Puritan Radicalism and Enlightenment," *Church History*, 29, no. 4 (1960): 424–437, reprinted in S. A. Burrell (ed.), *The Role of Religion in Modern European History* (New York: Macmillan, 1964), pp. 65–76; M. Walzer, "Puritanism as Revolutionary Ideology," in Eisenstadt, *Protestant Ethic*, pp. 109–134; and idem, *The Revolution of the Saints* (Cambridge: Harvard University Press, 1965). A very good recent collection is C. Webster (ed.), *The Intellectual Revolution of the Seventeenth Century* (London: Routledge & Kegan Paul, 1974).

25. M. Walzer, *Regicide and Revolution* (Cambridge: At the University Press, 1974); idem, *Revolution of the Saints;* and H. Lüthy, "Once Again, Calvinism and Capitalism," in Eisenstadt, *Protestant Ethic*, pp. 87–109.

26. N. Birnbaum, "The Zwinglian Reformation in Zurich," *Past and Present*, no. 15 (1959): 27–47; R. Hauri, *Die Reformation in der Schweiz im Urteil der neueren schweizerischen Geschichtsschreibung* (Zurich: Universitäts Verlag, 1945); A. Sayous, "Calvinisme et capitalisme à Genève," *Annales d'histoire économique et sociale*, 7 (1935): 225 ff.; idem, "La Banque à Genève pendant les XVIe, XVIIe, et XVIIIe siècles," *Revue économique internationale*, 34 (September 1934): 1–25; and O. Vasella, "Die Ursachen der Reformation in der deutschen Schweiz," *Zeitschrift für schweizerische Geschichte*, 27, no. 4 (1947): 401–424.

27. G. Donaldson, "The Scottish Episcopate at the Reformation," *English Historical Review*, 60, no. 238 (1945): 349–369; J. Highet, "The Protestant Churches in Scotland: A Review of Membership, Evangelistic, and Other Aspects," *Archives de sociologie des religions*, 4, no. 8 (1959): 97–104; and H. R. Trevor-Roper, "Scotland and the Puritan Revolution," in H. E. Bell and R. L. Ollard (eds.), *Historical Essays, 1600–1750, Presented to David Ogg* (London: Black, 1963), pp. 78–130.

28. E. Beins, "Die Wirtschaftsethik der Calvinistischen Kirche der Niederlande, 1505–1650," *Nederlandsch Archief voor Kerkgeschiedenis*, n.s., 24 (1931): 81–150; P. Geyl, *The Netherlands in the Seventeenth Century*, 2d ed., 2 vols. (London: E. Benn, 1961–1965); H. Hauser, "Calvinism and Capitalism in the Dutch Netherlands," *Journal of Modern History*, 10, no. 4 (1938): 321–343; J. E. C. Hill, "The Ruling Classes in Holland in the Seventeenth Century," in J. S. Bromley and E. H. Kossmann (eds.), *Britain and the Netherlands* (London: Macmillan, 1968), 2:109–132; A Hyma, "Calvinism and Capitalism in the Netherlands, 1555–1700," *Journal of Modern History*, 10, no. 3 (1938): 321–343; D. Nauta, *Het Calvinisme in Nederland* (Franeker: T. Wever, 1949); I. Schöffer, "Protestantism in Flux during the Revolt of the Netherlands," in Bromley and Kossmann, *Britain and the Netherlands*, pp. 67–84; and H. Smitskampf, *Calvinistisch Nationaal Besef in Nederland voor het Midden der XVIIe eeuw* (The Hague: M. Nijhoff, 1947).

29. P. A. Bruce, *Economic History of Virginia in the Seventeenth Century* (New York: Macmillan, 1896); A. H. Hirsch, *The Huguenots of Colonial*

South Carolina (Durham: Duke University Press, 1928); W. S. Hudson, *American Protestantism* (Chicago: University of Chicago Press, 1961); E. A. J. Johnson, *American Economics Thought in the Seventeenth Century* (London: Allen & Unwin, 1932); G. Kolko, "Max Weber on America: Theory and Evidence," *History and Theory*, 1, no. 3 (1961): 243–260; J. J. Loubser, "Puritanism and Religious Liberty: Change in the Normative Order in Massachusetts, 1630–1850" (Ph.D. dissertation, Harvard University, 1964); R. L. Means, "American Protestantism and Max Weber's Protestant Ethic," *Religious Education*, 25 (March-April 1965): 90 ff; idem, "Weber's Thesis of the Protestant Ethic: The Ambiguities of Received Doctrine," *Journal of Religion*, 45, no. 1 (1965): 1–11; P. Miller, *The New England Mind: The Seventeenth Century*, vol. 1 (Cambridge: Harvard University Press, 1954); idem, *The New England Mind: From Colony to Province*, vol. 2 (Cambridge: Harvard University Press, 1953); idem, *Errand into the Wilderness* (Cambridge: Harvard University Press, 1956); A. Simpson, *Puritanism in Old and New England* (Chicago: University of Chicago Press, 1955); and J. Winthrop, "Model of Christian Charity," in P. Miller and H. Johnson (eds.), *The Puritans*, 2 vols. (New York: Harper & Row, 1938), 1:195–199.

30. On Holland and Switzerland see the works cited in notes 26 and 28 above. On England see J. C. Brauer, "Reflections on the Nature of English Puritanism," *Church History*, 23 (June 1954): 98–108; J. S. Flynn, *The Influence of Puritanism on the Political and Religious Thought of the English* (New York: Kennikat, 1920); C. H. George, "A Social Interpretation of English Puritanism," *Journal of Modern History*, 25, no. 4 (1953): 327–342; idem, "English Calvinist Opinion on Usury, 1600–1640," *Journal of the History of Ideas*, 18, no. 4 (1957): 455–476; C. H. George and K. George, "Protestantism and Capitalism in Pre-Revolutionary England," *Church History*, 27, no. 4 (December 1958): 351–372; idem, *The Protestant Mind of the English Reformation 1570–1640* (Princeton: Princeton University Press, 1961); C. Hill, *Puritanism and Revolution: Studies in Interpretation of the English Revolution of the Seventeenth Century* (London: Secker & Warburg, 1958); idem, *Intellectual Origins of the English Revolution* (Oxford: Clarendon, 1965); M. M. Knappen, *Tudor Puritanism* (Chicago: University of Chicago Press, 1939); Simpson, *Puritanism in Old and New England;* L. B. Wright, *Religion and Empire: The Alliance between Piety and Commerce in English Expansion, 1558–1625* (Chapel Hill: University of North Carolina Press, 1943); and P. Zagorin, "The Social Interpretation of the English Revolution," *Journal of Economic History*, 19, no. 3 (1959): 376–401.

31. E. H. Dunkley, *The Reformation in Denmark* (London: S.P.C.K., 1949); J. G. H. Hoffmann, *Les Fondements historiques des églises du Nord: Danemark, Irlande, Norvège, Suède, et Finlande* (Geneva: Editions Labor, n.d.); H. Holmquist, "Kirche und Staat im evangelischen Schweden," *Festgabe für Karl Müller* (Tübingen: J. C. B. Mohr, 1922), pp. 209–277; J. C. Kjoer, *History of the Church in Denmark* (London: S.P.C.K., 1945); and H. H. Schrey, "Geistliches und weltliches Regiment in der schwedischen Reformation," *Archiv für Reformationsgeschichte*, 42 (1951): 146–159.

32. *Revue de théologie de la faculté de théologie d'Aix-en-Provence,* a special
    issue on "Calvin et la Réforme en France," 1944; H. Hauser, *La Mod-
    ernité du XVIe siècle: Cahiers des annales* (Paris: A. Colin, 1963), 2:69–
    104; E. G. Léonard, *Problèmes et expériences du protestantisme français*
    (Paris: Albin Michel, 1940); idem, "Le Protestantisme français au XVIIe
    siècle," *Revue historique,* 72 (October-December 1948): 153–179; idem,
    Le Protestant français (Paris: Albin Michel, 1953); idem, *Histoire générale
    du protestantisme,* 3 vols. (Paris: Presses universitaires de France, 1961);
    and R. Nürnberger, *Die Politisierung des französischen Protestantismus
    und die Anfänge des protestantischen Radikalismus* (Tübingen: J. C. B.
    Mohr, 1948).

33. On Germany see N. Birnbaum, "Social Structure and the German Reforma-
    tion" (M.A. thesis, Harvard University, 1958); A. L. Drummond, *Ger-
    man Protestantism since Luther* (London: S.P.C.K., 1951); J. Hashagen,
    "Kalvinismus und Kapitalismus am Rhein," *Schmollers Jahrbuch,* 47
    (1924): 49–72; C. R. Kayser, "Calvinism and German Political Life"
    (Ph.D dissertation, Radcliffe College, 1961); G. Ritter, "Why the Reforma-
    tion Occurred in Germany," *Church History,* 27, no. 2 (1958): 99–106,
    reprinted in Burrell, *Religion in Modern European History,* pp. 28–36;
    and O. Hintze, "Calvinism and Raison d'Etat in Early Seventeenth Cen-
    tury Brandenburg," in Gilbert, *Historical Essays of Otto Hintze,* pp. 85–
    156.

34. On the Counterreformation in Catholic countries see Wernham, *New Cam-
    bridge Modern History,* vol. 3.

35. S. M. Lipset and S. Rokkan, "Cleavage Structures, Party Systems, and
    Voter Alignments," in S. M. Lipset and S. Rokkan (eds.), *Party Systems
    and Voter Alignments: Cross-National Perspectives* (New York: Free Press,
    1967), pp. 1–65; and S. Rokkan, *Citizens, Elections, Parties: Approaches
    to the Comparative Study of the Processes of Development* (Oslo: Uni-
    versitetsforlaget, 1970).

36. This aspect of modern class and strata formation is analyzed more fully
    in S. N. Eisenstadt, *Social Differentiation and Stratification* (Glenview:
    Scott, Foresman, 1971), chaps. 7, 8; see also S. Ossowski, *Class Struc-
    ture in the Social Consciousness* (London: Routledge & Kegan Paul,
    1963); and R. Bendix, *Nation-Building and Citizenship* (New York:
    Wiley, 1964).

37. The concept of a world-system has been recently addressed by Waller-
    stein, *Modern World-System,* who acknowledges a debt to F. B. Braudel,
    The Mediterranean and the Mediterranean World in the Age of Philip II,
    2 vols. (London: Fontana-Collins, 1966). It has also been stressed, of
    course, by Marxist scholars. See Kossok, *Studien über die Revolution;* and
    idem, *Studien zur vergleichenden Revolutionsgeschichte.*

    Some of the aspects of the spread of international systems are analyzed
    in S. N. Eisenstadt, "Socialism and Tradition," in S. N. Eisenstadt and
    Y. Azmon (eds.), *Socialism and Tradition* (New York: Humanities, 1973);
    and in S. N. Eisenstadt, *The Expansion of Europe and the Civilization
    of Modernity.*

38. On the transformation of class interests into class- and status-oriented activities see L. A. Fallers, *Inequality* (Chicago: University of Chicago Press, 1973); Eisenstadt, *Social Differentiation;* Ossowski, *Class Structure;* and J. Galtung, "Feudal Systems, Structural Violence, and the Structural Theory of Revolutions," in International Peace Research Association, *Studies in Peace Research* (The Hague: Van Gorcum, 1970), 1:110–188.

39. This is of course first of all true of Marxist and radical scholars. See, for instance, Miller and Aya, *National Liberation;* and the two collections Kossok edited that are cited in note 1 above.

40. Moore, *Reflections.*

41. B. Mazlish, *The Ascetic Revolutionary* (New York: Basic Books, 1975); V. C. Nihirny, "Some Observations on Ideological Groups," in R. S. Denisoff (ed.), *The Sociology of Dissent* (New York: Harcourt, Brace, Jovanovich, 1974), pp. 1–22; and idem, "The Russian Intelligentsia: From Men of Ideas to Men of Conviction," *Comparative Studies in Society and History,* 4 (July 1962): 403–435.

42. The basic materials on these civilizations are presented in Chapters 4 and 5.

43. Concerning North Vietnam see McAlister and Mus, *The Vietnamese and Their Revolution;* and White, "Vietnamese Revolutionary Alliance"; on traditional Vietnam see W. F. Vella (ed.), *Aspects of Vietnamese History,* Asian Studies at Hawaii, no. 8 (Honolulu: University Press of Hawaii, 1973); Le Thanh Khoi, *Le Viêt Nam: Histoire et civilisation* (Paris: Editions de Minuit, 1955); J. Buttinger, *The Smaller Dragon* (New York: Praeger, 1958); A. B. Woodside, *Vietnam and the Chinese Model* (Cambridge: Harvard University Press, 1971); P. Mus, *Vietnam: Sociologie d'une guerre* (Paris: Seuil, 1952); and idem, "Buddhism in Vietnamese History and Society," *Jahrbuch des Südasien Instituts Heidelberg,* vol. 2 (1967): 95–115.

44. J. Race, "Toward an Exchange Theory of Revolution," in Lewis, *Peasant Rebellion,* pp. 169–207; see also J. M. Maravall, "Subjective Conditions and Revolutionary Conflict: Some Remarks," *British Journal of Sociology,* 27, no. 1 (1976): 21–34.

45. On Germany see the references cited in note 15 above.

46. On the first phase of the Chinese Revolution in general and on Kuomintang China see Wright, *China in Revolution;* Z. Schiffrin, *Sun Yat-sen and the Origins of the Chinese Revolution* (Berkeley: University of California Press, 1968); M. J. T. Shieh, *The Kuomintang: Selected Historical Documents* (New York: St. John's University Press, 1970); and Schurmann and Schell, *Republican China.*

47. On Spain see J. H. Elliot, *Imperial Spain, 1469–1716* (New York: New American Library, Mentor, 1963); R. Carr, *Spain, 1808–1939* (New York: Oxford University Press, 1966); and E. E. Malefakis, *Agrarian Reform and Peasant Revolution in Spain: Origins of the Civil War* (New Haven: Yale University Press, 1970).

Chapter 8.   Variability of Revolutionary Patterns and Outcomes

PART 1.   MODERNIZATION, DISCONTINUITY, VIOLENCE, AND INSTITUTIONAL EXPANSION

1. APPROACHES TO THE STUDY OF OUTCOMES OF REVOLUTIONS

Our analysis identified the combination of structural and cultural characteristics of societies, on the one hand, and historical circumstances or conditions on the other, that is most conducive to the occurrence of revolutions and of revolutionary transformation as the major mode of social change. This analysis stressed the common features of these societies and historical circumstances, suggesting that in other societies and in other types of sociohistorical circumstances, processes of change in general and modernizing transformation in particular may arise in a different manner. However, before attempting to analyze some of these different patterns of change and social transformation we have to address ourselves to a prior problem; namely, the variability of both the true, or real, revolutions and their outcomes.

Let us recapitulate some of the common characteristics of revolutionary processes and outcomes. The modern revolutions pushed the societies in which they took place in the direction of modernization in its organizational and symbolic aspects alike. All postrevolutionary societies experienced growing structural differentiation and specialization; the establishment of international organizational frameworks and markets; the development of market economies and of modern institutional frameworks (industrial or semi-industrial ones in the economic field); the elaboration of relatively open, nontraditional systems of stratification and mobility in which criteria of achievement—specifically, economic, occupational, and educational criteria—became relatively predominant; and the weakening

215

of traditional strata formation and its replacement by more open class formation in the structuring of social hierarchies and political systems.

These organizational changes were closely associated with the basic premises of the revolutionary image—that is, the premises of equality, freedom, and solidarity—and with their institutional derivatives—the undermining of traditional legitimation, the restructuring of center-periphery relations, the growing impingement of the periphery on the center in the name of revolutionary premises; and far-reaching transformation of the nature and contents of societal centers and of the rules of access to them.

Social transformation took place in varying degrees in the modern and modernizing societies. In revolutionary societies such transformation occurred by means of violent upheavals, and this process incorporated certain elements of change in specific constellations. Revolutionary transformation entailed considerable convergence among changes in the ground rules of social interaction (principles of distributive justice, the meaning of institutional activities, the legitimation of the social order, and delineation of the boundaries and symbols of membership in the collectivity, as well as convergence of these changes with the restructuring of access to power, the center, its symbols, and its patterns of legitimation.

Changes in the political sphere itself crystallized in a certain pattern. Thus, changes in the symbols and patterns of legitimation of regimes, in the composition of the ruling class, in the bases of access to the center, in center-periphery relations, and in positions of control over resources coalesced.

The push toward modernization along with the changes in the ground rules of social interaction and in the political sphere (analyzed above) combined to produce those far-reaching transformations of the symbolic and institutional structures of these societies that constituted the essence of revolution.

Accordingly, it is in the diverse constellations of these changes that some of the major differences among revolutionary societies should be identified, and some efforts in this direction have indeed been made in the literature. Postrevolutionary societies have been held to vary with respect to the scope and intensity of their developmental, or modernizing, outcomes in most of the institutional spheres but most notably the economic and the political. The major differences in the economic sphere emphasized in the literature are the degree and institutional contours of development, especially the degree of development in general and of industrialization in particular, and related differences in the composition of occupational groups (the peasantry, professional groups, and the like). In the political sphere, differences are noted in the degree of unification and centralization of the political system, on the one hand, and of the symbolic and actual participation of broader strata in the new political system, on the other. The major distinction has usually been made between the capitalist, industrially more developed societies (Europe and the United States) and the socialist or communist societies (the Soviet Union, China, and Vietnam.) [1]

But this distinction is just a starting point for more detailed analysis of the various dimensions of institutional change connected with revolutionary transformation. Two closely related dimensions of change emphasized by classical students of revolution—Tocqueville and to some extent Marx—but somewhat neglected subsequently are of great importance.

First, there are qualitative differences among postrevolutionary societies. As we have seen, the revolutionary process and symbolism has built into itself certain ideological and symbolic goals—liberty, progress, and solidarity. The upheaval and violence connected with revolutions often are justified in the name of the attainment of these goals. Crucial in this context is the degree to which the postrevolutionary institutional frameworks are capable of incorporating new social groups that develop due to the continual changes inherent in modern, particularly industrial, societies. Hence, it is important to analyze the degree to which various revolutionary societies have been able to realize these goals.

Second, there are differences in how these goals have been achieved in postrevolutionary societies. The very notion of revolution connotes upheaval, rapid change, discontinuity, and violence. Thus, it is important to analyze the implications of the degrees of rupture and discontinuity that marked the modern revolutions—specifically as regards changes in the major institutional spheres and the realization of the emancipatory goals of revolution.

The common foci of these changes are the degree and type of discontinuity between prerevolutionary and postrevolutionary societies and their symbols and institutional structures. In this chapter we identify criteria that will help us analyze the differences among the modern revolutions and their outcomes. We distinguish systematically the most important aspects of such discontinuity, which is not usually done in the literature.

2. CRITERIA OF INSTITUTIONAL CHANGE IN POSTREVOLUTIONARY SOCIETIES

The following seems to us to be the most important dimensions of continuity-discontinuity in postrevolutionary society.

1. On the most general level of analysis, postrevolutionary societies differ first of all with respect to the relative importance of changes in the ground rules of social interaction and in the structural and organizational derivatives of these ground rules. While all combine changes in the rules of access to power and in the legitimation of the political system with

changes in other ground rules, the actual combination of changes differs. In America, the Netherlands, and to some degree Turkey, the symbols and boundaries of collectivities and the meanings of institutional complexes changed along with the rules of access to power; in France, Russia, and China, the meaning of institutions and the rules of distributive justice changed together with access to power and the symbols of legitimation.

2. The degree of discontinuity in institutional premises and structures between prerevolutionary and postrevolutionary societies also differs. Two dimensions of this discontinuity merit consideration.

a. First, there is the degree of discontinuity in the composition of the ruling elite or class and in the holders of the power and prestige positions in the various institutional spheres. Such discontinuity and change range from complete (violent or nonviolent) elimination of the previously uppermost groups to their assimilation.

b. Second, there are changes in the structuring of the major institutional spheres. Here several aspects have to be distinguished.

i. Organizational changes in the scope of the principal units of the various spheres; for instance, the transition from small-scale cliques to organized parties or from narrow to broad markets.

ii. Changes in the meanings of the major institutional spheres, in their mode of legitimation, and in the articulation of new roles. In the economic sphere such changes are manifest in what Marxists call the mode of production.[2] In the political sphere, there occur changes in the type of regime, in the pattern of political articulation, in center-periphery relations, in the symbols and bases of political legitimation, and in the boundaries and symbols of the political and national communities.

The dimensions of discontinuity outlined in points 2a and 2b generate changes in structural principles; namely, in the criteria of evaluation of activities and positions; in the principles of allocation of resources and of access to them; in the principles of allocation of power and of control over resources—in the control over the access of societal groups to the major markets and over the conversion of resources—and in the degree of dislocation of different groups from their base of power and from their control over the use of resources.

3. Postrevolutionary societies differ in the degree of change in the symbolic sphere, especially in the symbols of collective identity and in the legitimation of regimes, on the one hand, and in basic cultural orientations and codes on the other.[3]

4. Fourth, these societies differ in the amount of violence and violent institutional and symbolic disruption with the past that their revolutions entailed and in the degree to which such violence was symbolically upheld.

The preceding detailed distinctions (in contrast to the more general distinctions typical of the literature) are crucial because very often changes in one dimension of transformation did not accompany changes in other dimensions and because the manifold combinations of changes and discontinuities that account for the major differences in the outcomes of the modern revolutions shaped the specific response of each revolutionary society to the challenge to modernity and their contours as modern societies.

3. CONDITIONS BEHIND DIFFERENT REVOLUTIONARY OUTCOMES. EXISTING APPROACHES. ECONOMIC BACKWARDNESS. CLASS STRUCTURE

How can these differences in the processes and outcomes of revolutions be explained? Differences in the degree of modernization of economic development as well as in some of the major organizational aspects of such development (the tendency to establish highly concentrated financial and industrial complexes) can be explained, Alexander Gerschenkorn showed long ago,[4] in terms of the institutional starting point—the economic position of the prerevolutionary society—and the identity of a society as a pioneer or latecomer vis-à-vis the international economic (initially capitalist) system. The validity of Gerschenkorn's explanation aside, two critical points should be made.

First, as Gerschenkorn fully illustrated, his scheme applies to revolutionary and nonrevolutionary societies alike. Granted, the revolutionary experience adds new dimensions,[5] especially those of discontinuity and rupture, which were discussed above. Gerschenkorn's own comparison of various societies points out that some of the most crucial aspects of the outcomes of the process of development (for instance, whether certain features of economic backwardness will be preserved after economic backwardness itself has disappeared) can be understood only in terms of the political orientations of the ruling traditional or revolutionary groups. The importance of these old and new ruling groups necessarily bring us to some of the variables that might explain the variations in the institutional and symbolic outcomes of revolutions as they are related to different constellations of continuity, discontinuity, and violence attendant on the revolutionary process.

In the literature on revolution there of course have been many attempts to explain variations in the institutional and symbolic outcomes of revolutions. Most of these explanations emphasize the relations among different classes—the aristocracy, the bourgeoisie, the workers, the peasants—and coalitions among them. This approach, best exemplified by Barrington Moore's seminal work *The Social Origins of Dictatorship and Democracy*,[6] has been systematically developed by John Kautsky. Kautsky already stressed, following some earlier studies of modernization, the importance, in addition to classes, of the revolutionary elites themselves.[7] Somewhat similar although less precise explanations couched in rather more metaphysical, orthodox Marxist terms have been advanced by contemporary Marxist scholars of comparative revolutions.[8]

4. CRITICISM OF EXISTING APPROACHES

Moore's work has received much criticism. Many reviews have shown that his analysis in terms of different class coalition does not do justice to the variability of the dynamics of the processes of modernization.[9]

For instance, Moore fails to distinguish systematically between those societies in which modernization was attained through a revolutionary upheaval and those in which it was attained without such an upheaval; similarly, by implication all societies that became fascist did not undergo revolutions. Moore's designation of Japan in the thirties as a fascist state seems to miss some of the essential aspects of Japanese development and smacks of ethnocentrism.

Finally, his explanation in terms of patterns of coalition among classes does not account for other crucial aspects that differentiate outcomes of revolutions (e.g., structural and symbolic discontinuity) and only touches on the emancipatory results of revolutions.

As we suggested in Chapter 2, Stein Rokkan and Seymour Martin Lipset's analysis[10] (as well as some of Rokkan's later works)[11] of coalitions not only among classes but also among political, religious, and national leaders seems to be more fruitful and to point up certain analytical weaknesses of Moore's approach.

These various concrete criticisms of Moore converge around two major analytical weaknesses in his work. First, Moore neglected the importance of the state as a potentially autonomous element in the dynamics of a society and accordingly overlooked the importance of relations between the state and other societal groups (in our parlance, center-periphery relations). Second, Moore failed to note the great variability in the internal structuring of classes across societies as well as in their relations with other social actors, including the center, which may be of crucial importance from the point of view of social change and transformation.

An important step forward in this type of analysis was made by Theda Skocpol and Kay Trimberger.[12] Both scholars have stressed the significance of the state as a potentially autonomous agent, which in some cases cannot be subsumed under class analysis. Skocpol's analysis has also emphasized the importance of different modes or types of relations among social classes, especially between the aristocracy and the peasantry, in influencing the outcomes of revolution.

But these refinements of Moore's approach and of the classical Marxist approach do not go far enough. The line drawn between societies in which the state is viewed primarily as an instrument of, or in close relation to, upper landed groups and in which a genuine social revolution occurs (Russia and some Western European countries) and those in which the state, in the guise of the military, becomes disembedded and relatively autonomous and in which the disembedded (military) elite generates a revolution from above (Japan, Turkey, Peru, and Egypt) fails to explain adequately some of the important characteristics that distinguish these different revolutions.

Thus, it is obvious that important differences separated the European revolutions, differences that cannot be fully explained by their common denominator: close relations between the state and the aristocracy. Nor can the relations between the aristocracy and the peasantry account for differences in the modern revolutions; such an approach ignores the origins of the diverse structuring of class relationships and the place of the state therein. (A close relation between the state and landed groups existed in many Southeast Asian and Latin American countries but did not generate conditions conducive to revolutionary transformation.)

The same criticism applies to Trimberger's analysis of revolutions from above engendered either by a relatively autonomous, disembedded state or by a similarly characterized political (especially military) elite.[13] The outcomes of revolutions thus spearheaded, as Trimberger realizes, varied greatly. The Japanese and to a degree the Turkish revolutions,[14] which produced new institutional complexes and restructured center-periphery relations (both characteristic achievements of so-called real revolutions) stand in contrast to the Egyptian and Peruvian. In the latter cases,[15] important changes occurred in the composition of the ruling class, in the legitimation of the regime, and in the distribution of resources (see Chapter 10) as a result of revolution; however, these changes were not accompanied by far-reaching restructuring of institutions or center-periphery relations.

Neither international standing nor economic development account for the presence or absence of such restructuring. However, they can explain some of the features of the new institutions that emerged in the post-revolutionary societies; for example, the emphasis on industry as against agriculture and the importance of the state in the financing of development.

To sum up, while Skocpol and Trimberger recognize the importance of the state as a relatively autonomous unit, they do not envisage the existence of a great variety of relations between the state and the broader strata. The emphasis on the relative strength of similar classes or on the relations among them in different countries does not sufficiently recognize the great variability in their internal structuring and in their relationship to other social actors (including the center). This variability may be critical in terms of the dynamics of social change and transformation in general and of the outcomes of revolutions in particular.

As was indicated above, all these do not belittle the importance of class interests. Rather, they indicate that such interests may be structured in a great variety of ways that are greatly influenced by variables in no way fully catalogued by traditional or even "corrected" class analysis.

5. STRUCTURE OF CENTERS AND ELITES. SOLIDARY RELATIONS IN REVOLUTIONARY SOCIETIES

In other words, most explanations focus on various components of the organizational division of labor (such as degree of structural differentiation or class conflicts) and do not take into account the major institutional derivatives of the symbolic orientations and their institutional derivatives such as, of human activities or the ground rules of social interaction, the structure of centers, center-periphery relations, the structure of markets, and so on. Nor do they take into account, among the principal actors in the revolutionary processes, the major carriers of such orientations; that is, the institutional entrepreneurs and elites that shape the institutional contours through which seemingly similar concrete interests are molded in different ways. We have seen the importance of such carriers in regard to crucial aspects of the dynamics of traditional civilizations (Chapters 4 and 5) and the development of modern revolutions (Chapters 6 and 7). Accordingly, a full explanation of the variability of revolutionary processes and outcomes (as well as the processes of social transformation attendant on modernization achieved outside the classical revolutionary pattern) must add the variables we have identified to an analysis focused on economic backwardness, international dependency, and different class coalitions.

To account for the different outcomes of coalescent revolutions we shall take for granted that in all such revolutions autonomous institutional entrepreneurs oriented to this-worldly activity were active in the restructuring of centers and institutional spheres. We shall inquire into the variables that possibly explain differences in revolutionary outcomes.

The most important variables are the internal structure of centers, their cohesion and solidarity, and their solidary relations with other groups in society. We begin our analysis with the impact of several aspects of the rigidity of the center. The first such aspect is the center's tactical rigidity in the face of new demands. The second is its structural rigidity; that is, the degree to which the center is based on the denying other groups autonomous access to it. The third such aspect is the heterogeneous composition of the center—a feature that implies potentially solidary relations with some elites and groups in society. Another important structural variable is the relationship among groups in the center as well as among those aspiring to access and between these groups and other social actors (secondary elites, social classes, broad ascriptive collectivities). The importance of such variables as the structure, cohesion, and solidarity of the center and its relationships with other parts of society has been noted in microsocietal studies of leadership; yet they have been applied but rarely to macrosociological orders.[16]

These various aspects of the structure of the center and of its relations with other groups influence the center's ability to mobilize the resources needed for coping with the problems attendant on the transition to modernity, its ability to incorporate new claimants (or potential claimants) to participation in it, and its ability to establish links with the broader strata in order to effect institution building and in this way also to influence the outcomes of revolutions.

PART 2. COMPARATIVE CASE STUDIES OF THE OUTCOMES OF REVOLUTIONS

1. THE REVOLUTIONARY PROCESS AND OUTCOMES IN EUROPE

As we saw earlier, seventeenth-century European societies were characterized by (1) a multiplicity of centers; (2) a high degree of permeation of the periphery by the center and of impingement of the periphery on the center; (3) a comparatively high degree of autonomy of societal groups and strata and of their access to the center; (4) a multiplicity of cultural and functional (economic or professional) elites, a high degree of crosscutting among them, and close relationships between them and broader collectivities and strata; (5) highly developed and autonomous institutional entrepreneurs in general and secondary political, religious, and economic elites in particular; (6) a relatively close relationship between these secondary elites and the broader social strata and hence between the former and movements of rebellion; and (7) a predisposition on the part of these elites and groups to pursue activities oriented toward center formation and to combine such activities with institution building in the economic, cultural, and educational spheres.[17] All these characteristics influenced the rigidity of the different centers that developed in Europe in the Age of Absolutism.

These Absolutist tendencies were most successful where pluralistic elements were weakest (Spain and many German principalities); they were least successful in England, France, and Sweden. The rigidity of the early Stuart and Bourbon centers was manifest above all in their inability to cope with groups and strata that in principle had access to the center. Indeed, this access constituted a basic aspect of the construction of these centers.

The rigidity of the English center was manifest in the short-lived attempt of the Stuarts to limit the scope of autonomous participation of these groups without however denying their right to participation. Consequently, England experienced a temporary exclusion from the center of relatively strong, autonomous classes closely linked to autonomous, solidary secondary elites.[18]

In France the attempt to establish an Absolutist regime was, after the Counterreformation, much more successful. Nevertheless, it, too, contravened inherent premises of the French polity. Hence, while the French center itself appeared to be more closed and exclusive than the English one, it was in fact quite diversified. The French center incorporated somewhat autonomous bureaucratic and autocratic groups in close although ambivalent relations with many relatively new economic and cultural autonomous entrepreneurs; and in relatively close relation—sometimes leading up to almost total embedment—within broader especially landed and middle, strata.[19]

I

The outcomes of the European (and American) revolutions were closely associated with the characteristics of the structure of the centers of the prerevolutionary societies. The English revolutionary process— from the Great Rebellion to the Glorious Revolution—generated a relatively small degree of discontinuity in the symbols of the political community although there took place a rather marked shift in the bases of legitimation. This shift was connected during the Great Rebellion with considerable violence (granted, the later European and Asian revolutions were far more violent).[20]

The revolutionary outcomes in England included major shifts in the importance and power of different segments of the ruling class. The new elements—landed and urban middle groups, lower echelons of the aristocracy, and especially the professional, religous, and independent political entrepreneurs (closely related to but not identical with both aristocratic and middle-class rural and urban strata) [21]—were incorporated into the center without extensive symbolic or physical destruction of the more traditional aristocratic and court groups. At the same time there occurred far-reaching though gradual changes in the basic principles of hierarchization of the social structure and in the criteria of access to resources and to the bases of power from which use of these resources was controlled. Criteria of economic standing slowly became more important, more closely identified with criteria of social status and political power. This development was connected with the increasing strength and autonomy of urban and rural agricultural, commercial, and semi-industrial middle classes and economic activities. The growing control these groups exercised over use of their resources was bound up with the new autonomy of the legal system and with the legal emphasis on private property and of civil rights.

The ascendance of the rule of law was connected with the broadening of access among various, but especially middle, groups to the major markets, as well as with their growing control over the flow of resources among markets. The stress on private property and civil rights was instrumental initially in the dissociation of many of the lower (particularly rural) groups from the bases of their resources and in the creation of an urban proletariat.

But such dissociation was only partial or temporary. The institutionalization of civil rights, the rule of law, and the sovereignty of Parliament later became starting points for the political organization of these groups and for the crystallization of their own rights of access to the center. Thus, access to markets and to control over them, so closely related to the legal system, was extended to the proletarian groups that emerged in the wake of the dislocations caused by capitalistic development in agriculture and later by the Industrial Revolution.[22]

Concomitantly, England experienced an intensification of changes in the meaning of institutions and in the restructuring of roles. In the economic sphere, this meant the capitalist mode of production constituted not only an organizational framework but also a new, self-legitimating system with new, autonomous roles and symbols.[23] In the political field there took place, as indicated above, shifts in the principles of legitimation; seemingly constant restructuring of relations between the socioeconomic and political orders in the direction of differentiation; and growing articulation of the autonomous access of socioeconomic groups to the center.

This restructuring generated far-reaching changes in center-periphery relations in two closely interconnected ways. First, symbolic center-periphery relations were redefined in the direction of autonomy of access to the center and the possibility of its reconstruction by broader strata. Second, ascriptive and traditional controls over such access were gradually weakened. Both of these were greatly reinforced by the development of the conception and practice of citizenship and by the increased autonomy of the legal system.

In England, the combination of these changes in center-periphery relations and the patterns of dislocation generated the possibility of relatively constant incorporation of new social groups into the center, an incorporation closely related to the extension of control over the use of resources.

The outcomes of the revolutions in England came closest to the social transformations that took place in those societies like Sweden, Switzerland, and the (post-Revolt) Netherlands in which no political revolution occurred.[24]

II

France displayed a much greater degree of discontinuity and rupture between prerevolutionary and postrevolutionary society, and the French Revolution was more violent than the English. Indeed, in the French Revolution the cult of violence became part of the revolutionary myth and agenda.

The high level of discontinuity was evident first of all in the violent change of the principles and symbols of legitimation;[25] in the almost total political disablement of the former ruling class and in the execution of many of its members; and in the exile or execution of members of the aristocracy. Concomitantly, there occurred a shift in the principles and activities of recruitment of the ruling class; that is, a growing emphasis was placed on intellectual, professional, and professional political elements of middle-class backgrounds. Unlike England, France saw a deep rift separate its traditional and newer elements.

Far-reaching changes also occurred in the bases of social hierarchies, a pattern most evident in the abolition of the legal and economic privileges of the aristocracy; in the upgrading of the criteria of economic standing; and in the restructuring of formal and informal access to resources and their uses (the latter change meant the institutionalization of private property and the alterations of the differential access of various groups to these resources). All these changes fostered the growth of the urban and rural bourgeoisie and the dislocation of lower groups out of which the new proletariat developed. As in England, in France this dislocation was connected with attaining political and legal rights through which the dislocated–newly created groups might compensate for the results of dislocation by the capture of positions of control over resources. But given the rift that the French Revolution created in the body politic, this struggle was naturally more violent than any England experienced.

The various processes of structural change that developed as the process of modernization continued to dislocate groups on the periphery gave rise to constant confrontations among different social units about the rights and control of access to resources as well as about the legitimation of the postrevolutionary regime. Like England, France saw the broadening and opening up of markets, access to them, and the flow of resources among them, partial shift in the meaning of institutional complexes in the direction of a capitalist order. But because of the rift between the older and the newer groups this process was not as fully legitimized as it was in England.

A parallel process took place in the political sphere and in structuring of relations between the socioeconomic and the political order. The political elites as well as the more independent social forces and elites crystallized in the relatively autonomous yet antithetic forces of state and society. These forces continually fought over their relative importance in the formation of the center of the nation-state, in the regulation of access to it, and in the articulation of the symbols and bases of legitimation of the regime.

2. THE AMERICAN REVOLUTION AND THE REVOLT OF THE NETHERLANDS

Of special interest from the point of view of our analysis is the pattern of discontinuity in two early revolutions that have baffled revolutionary theorists, namely, the Revolt of the Netherlands and the American Revolution.[26] In both these cases, in contrast to the English and French revolutions, the main revolutionary outcome was the reconstruction of the boundaries of the new political community and the symbols of its national (and not only political) identity. In both these cases the definition of new boundaries centered not on ethnic, regional, or other primordial attachments but rather on the construction of civil symbols of a new polity.[27] Such construction was evident above all in the American Revolution, in which a political community was founded on a new political ideology that focused on what Robert N. Bellah has called "civil religion."[28] A similar pattern of legitimation developed in the Netherlands.[29]

While the new civil symbols stressed the separation from the mother or conquering country in the American case they were actually derived from the premises of the English political system. Legitimation of the Revolt of the Netherlands was explicitly related to the common, traditional ideological bases of European polities.

In both the Netherlands and the colonies, far-reaching transformations occurred in other social spheres. In both cases displacement of the "alien" ruling class was connected with change in the composition of the local upper classes and social and political elites. Indeed, as research has abundantly illustrated for both the Netherlands and America, different competing elites, especially the relatively new types of political entrepreneurs, activated and to a degree structured the more specific class and economic interests and conflicts that were important causes of these revolutions.[30] Accordingly (and contrary to the literature, which generally does not define the Dutch and American revolutions as true revolutions), these developments gave rise to rather far-reaching changes in the structure of social hierarchies.

Both these societies experienced extensive upgrading of the criteria of economic achievement and professional attainment; broad changes in the control of access to markets; the most far-reaching institutionalization of private property; and steady expansion of access to the center. Closely connected developments were the opening up and broadening of markets, the redefining of institutional spheres, and the fostering of new institutional and role complexes. These changes were manifest in the rise of capitalist systems in the economic sphere, in the ideal of a free citizenry with full access to the center, and in the autonomy of the legal sphere— all more profound changes, especially in the United States, than England witnessed.[31]

3. THE REVOLUTIONARY PROCESS AND OUTCOMES IN CHINA

In the Chinese case we find a different initial structure and a different pattern of revolutionary process and outcome. The Chinese Imperial system was, as we have seen, characterized by a relatively unified, absolutist center defined both in terms of political power and in terms of cultural tradition, each of which constituted an independent basis of access.[32] The political as well as the cultural components of the center had certain solidary ties with the periphery although they controlled the periphery's orientations to the center. The Imperial center, with its strong Confucian orientation and legitimation, was the sole distributor of prestige and honor, and the various social groups or strata did not develop autonomous status orientations except on the purely local level. The major orientations were bound to the political-religious center.

Of crucial importance here was the structure of the major stratum linking the Imperial center to the broader society—the literati. This group combined in itself the functions or characteristics of political elites and of articulators of models of cultural order and maintained good relations with the articulators of the solidarity of collectivities. As indicated earlier, the literati virtually monopolized access to the macrosocietal order—a monopoly based largely on solidary ties with the periphery and on close class relations to the gentry. The linkages between the solidarity of the broader groups and that of groups in the center were, however, almost entirely controlled by the literati, allowing but little autonomy of access to the center.

Thus in China's prerevolutionary stage, there existed a monopolistic center with some internal diversification. This center enjoyed close ties with broader strata but controlled the access of these groups to itself. The broader groups were internally very solidary but had little autonomy with respect to their orientations to the center and their interelations.

The Chinese Revolution in its two phases—the Kuomintang and the

Communist—resulted in different (partly continuous, partly discontinuous) patterns of restructuring of the sociopolitical order.

The first phase involved a violent break with the legitimation and symbols of the political regime.[33] Concomitantly, in the first phase of the Chinese Revolution the former ruling class—the Confucian literati—was displaced; this group lost control over the access of the broader groups and strata to the center and over the conversion of resources. China also experienced a marked discontinuity in the structuring of social hierarchies. This discontinuity, which began in the first phase of the Chinese Revolution and grew in the second phase, meant that China abandoned traditional criteria for modern, open criteria of achievement or service to the community.[34]

In the first phase of the Chinese Revolution these developments were not connected with far-reaching changes in the composition and standing of the other upper socioeconomic groups—the local gentry, the warlords, and the merchants.[35] Indeed, the opening up of markets and the weakening of central control over them increased the relative strength of these groups with respect to the lower social classes—primarily the peasantry. No new linkages were established between the emerging political leadership and these lower groups that could expand their access to new resources.

These developments ultimately produced the first modern Chinese center: a closed, monopolistic center highly embedded in the stronger strata groups, especially the upper gentry. This center was more closed than the Imperial one and had even fewer links with the periphery.[36]

While center-periphery relations in China were in principle restructured according to the basic tenets of modernity, actual access to the center came under the control of the stronger groups of gentry and warlords; within this center a perpetual search for new principles of legitimation took place. However, the new ruling groups were unable either to redefine the old, or to establish new, premises and frameworks; to structure new levels of political articulation; or to establish new linkages with the broader groups—above all, the peasants. Likewise, the new ruling groups were not able to establish fully their own autonomous identity as distinct from the higher local groups of the gentry. Whatever attempts were made in this direction were cut short by the war with Japan and the reaction to the Communist rebellion. Both these events strengthened the more conservative, rigid elements or orientations of the new ruling groups.

In the first phase of the Chinese Revolution there occurred far-reaching organizational changes in the economic sphere in the direction of a semidependent, capitalist order. But this order did not crystallize into an autonomous institutional complex and gave rise but rarely to new, autonomous roles and role complexes.[37]

The Communist phase of the Chinese Revolution brought even farther reaching ruptures and discontinuities.[38] First of all a clean break was made with the symbols and bases of legitimation of the political system and regime. Second, once in power, the Communists achieved, as indicated above, extensive restructuring of many aspects of the institutional framework. The ruling class was almost totally displaced and many of its members executed; a new, autonomous ruling group rooted in the revolutionary movement emerged.

This new ruling class was the second in history (the first was Russia) to be composed totally of revolutionary professionals; subsequently it incorporated strong party and bureaucratic elements and still later it added entrepreneurial groups from within the local leadership. The new ruling class was disembedded from any social class even if it presented itself as representing, maintaining, or establishing solidary linkages with the proletariat and the peasantry.[39]

China's total displacement of the ruling class in the second phase was closely associated with the displacement and destruction of the upper rural and urban classes, with the emergence of a new social hierarchy or organizational (party and bureaucratic) ruling groups, and with the restructuring of agrarian relations in a mixed pattern of land distribution and communal land ownership.[40]

Far-reaching changes simultaneously occurred in the meaning of institutions, epitomized in the establishment of a new, centralized, socialist mode of production and revolutionary polity under whose direction the gradual modernization of the agricultural structure took place. All these developments were connected with the opening up of markets and the restructuring of the access of different groups to them, with the growing symbolic participation of all groups in the society and in its center, and with the extensive redistribution of resources (especially, as we have seen, land).

Still, centralized control over the use of resources was maintained. The actual access to both markets and centers was tightly regulated by the center, which relied on coercion to a high degree. Yet the center itself was torn by tensions and conflicts. Fierce struggles erupted among different elements of the ruling group: the more radical, antibureaucratic, party elements versus the organizational cadres (the army played a crucial role here). At issue were ideological emphases on power, solidarity, and community as against economic growth.[41] These struggles were connected with a very high degree of symbolic activization of the masses in which the solidary-communal aspects of their participation in the new center were stressed or upheld without allowing them any actual access to centers of power.[42]

To sum up, with few exceptions the control of access was in the hands of the various groups in the centers and their representatives in the periphery. Only in the economic sphere did a degree of decentralization exist. Still, local or regional autonomy was ultimately limited by the cadres.

4. THE REVOLUTIONARY PROCESS AND OUTCOMES IN RUSSIA

The greatest discontinuity from the point of view of restructuring the sociopolitical order, changing the symbolic and political legitimation of the regime and restructuring social hierachies took place in Russia.

Of all Imperial systems, Russia had a traditional center that was the most exclusive and monolithic,[43] with very weak ties among secondary elites and among broader groups and movements. The Russian center was in pricinple autonomous and distinct from other groups and strata, allowing no access to itself. Accordingly, as we have seen, Russia experienced but minimal institutionalized impingement on the center and little autonomous participation in it. The attempts of broader groups to gain access to the political center, as well as their attempts to form autonomous status units, were unsuccessful. At the same time, the center permeated the periphery to a relatively high degree in order to mobilize resources and to control societywide activities. Consequently, its policies were mainly regulative and coercive. There developed in Russia a growing dissociation between the political power elite and other elites (the various institutional elites as well as the articulators of the models of cultural order), and between the central political elites and the articulators of the solidarity of the major ascriptive collectivities. Above all, the access of the secondary elites to each other and to the center came under the control of the upper political elite. As one might suspect, there developed but very few links among relatively solidary but closed broader strata beyond those created by the center. At the same time, however, fairly strong orientations to the center did evolve among the secondary elites, most of which were cohesive but few of which enjoyed autonomous solidary relations with broader groups. Hence, despite their official programs and serious attempts, few secondary elites managed to incorporate in their activities the representatives of the solidarity of broader ascriptive groups or to involve themselves in the concerted efforts at institution building that were being made under the aegis of the the traditional elite, as well as by various secondary economic entrepreneurs.[44]

Under the Bolsheviks Russia broke totally with the past in terms of the structuring of the sociopolitical order.[45] Such a break took place first in the symbols of the polity and in its legitimation. Concomitantly, the ruling class was totally displaced—and almost exterminated—by the new, revolutionary party elite, which constituted a unique type of modern ruling class, and by new upper (usually party and bureaucratic) social and economic groups. Even if these groups sometimes came from older, nonproletarian elements they were organized according to entirely new principles of hierarchization focused on the political dominance of the new ruling elite. Russia also witnessed the almost complete displacement of lower groups, especially the peasants, who lost whatever limited control they once had over their own resources.[46]

Changes also occurred in the meaning and structuring (although not necessarily in the organization) of the major institutional spheres. Movement was away from a partially capitalist economy regulated by the social strata and vaguely defined or legitimized in terms of contributing to the modernization of the collectivity and toward a centralized, collectivist economy placing very strong emphasis on heavy industrialization and controlled by the new party bureaucracy.[47]

Restructuring of the Russian economy was based on expansion of markets and of the flow of resources among them and on determined efforts on the part of the ruling class to control, through coercion, access to the markets and the flow of resources. Similarly, while center-periphery relations were theoretically restructured according to the basic tenets of modernity (which emphasize participation of the broader strata in the center and the accountability of the center), actual access to the center was narrowly restricted by coercive measures. The postrevolutionary center, unlike the traditional one, continuously mobilized the periphery without allowing it autonomous organizations or access to the center (in this following the traditional pattern).

A similar pattern of discontinuity seemed to develop in the case of Vietnam.[48]

5. THE REVOLUTIONARY PROCESS AND OUTCOMES IN TURKEY

The Kemalist Revolution gave rise to a different pattern of transformation.[49] The Ottoman center represented a mixture of Imperial and patrimonial elements. The Imperial element was rooted in the ideology of Islam, subscribed to by certain groups in the center; the patrimonial element was evident (to some degree) in the organization of the center, in the composition of periphery, and in center-periphery relations.[50]

The onset of modernization intensified the development within the center of a plurality of elements: the rulers, different groups of bureaucrats, semiprofessional groups, and the military.[51] Some of these elements established solidary relations with upper groups of the rural periphery and in a sense provided an important link between some of the stronger and internally solidary elements of the periphery with the center.

Accordingly, the Kemalist Revolution resulted in a pattern of transformation distinct from that found in other revolutionary societies. It was connected first of all with a shift in the bases of political legitimation and in the symbols of the political community; together with redefinition of the boundaries of the collectivity. Redefinition of the political community took place in a unique way. The society withdrew from the Islamic framework into that of the newly defined Turkish nation. While this process appears similar to the path followed by the European nation-states, it in fact involved the negation of a universal framework, Islam, which was not the case in Europe.

Thus, Turkey's revolution rejected completely the religious (Islamic) basis of legitimation, attempted to develop a secular, national basis of legitimation as the major ideological parameter of the new collectivity, little emphasizing social components. This shift was connected with an almost total displacement of the former ruling class—political as well as religious—by members of secondary (bureaucratic and intellectual) elites.[52] A parallel development was the broadening of markets and the opening up of the flow of resources among them. However, markets were initially controlled by the ruling elite. Moreover, attempts were made to crystallize new economic institutions modeled on the capitalist system but imbued with a strong étatist orientation.

The displacement of the ruling group was not connected with displacement of the stronger elements of the traditional social and economic spheres. In urban and rural settings displacement occurred in two seemingly contradictory directions. First, the elitist establishments and bureaucracy became stronger, formulating étatist policies. Second, there was movement toward more autonomous class formation based partly on the links between the bureaucratic elements and the stronger, socioeconomic ones.[53]

These shifts in the principles of legitimation and the symbols and boundaries of community, together with the change in the ruling class, were connected with the ideological restructuring of center-periphery relations in the direction of modernity. Concomitantly, political participation was in principle extended to broader strata although in the early years of the revolutionary regime this participation was entirely controlled by the ruling group.[54]

6. CONTINUITY IN CULTURAL CODES, SYMBOLS OF IDENTITY, AND INSTITUTIONAL STRUCTURES

The preceding analysis points out the rather well known fact that the Chinese and Russian (and Vietnamese) postrevolutionary societies showed much greater discontinuity with prerevolutionary symbols of legitimation and institutional systems than Europe or America did. A closer look at the data indicates a more complex picture. China and Russia maintained continuity with the past in certain aspects or dimensions of their contours—dimensions of continuity or discontinuity that have been neglected in the literature on revolution with the exception of Tocqueville's classic work.[55] We refer to the basic cultural orientations and codes, the fundamental conceptions of the cultural and social orders, and their major institutional derivatives (analyzed at length in this volume). Especially important in this regard is the access of the different groups in the society to the principal attributes of the cultural and social orders and their derivatives—evident above all in the structuring of center-periphery relations and the structuring of hierarchies.

I

Truly enough, such continuity can be found in *all* postrevolutionary societies.[56] Thus, to give a few examples, Russia exhibited a very high degree of continuity of cultural codes, center-periphery relations, and patterns of stratification. Before and after the Russian Revolution, this society was characterized by a relatively high degree of permeation of the periphery by the center in order to mobilize the former's resources and to control its societywide activities (a pattern especially evident in modern regimes). Similarly, the policies pursued by traditional and modern Russian centers alike were mainly regulative and coercive.

The pattern of political struggle and organization in both prerevolutionary and postrevolutionary Russia revealed a relatively high degree of organized political activity directed by the center and dominated by the executive or by the party. In the postrevolutionary setting, the party has used its organs to identify demands on it and to mobilize political support. At the same time it has allowed only minimal possibilities either for the autonomous expression of demands or for activity that might result in extremist political, ideological, or religious movements of rebellion.

Continuity in several basic aspects of social stratification also was maintained in Russia. Thus, we find a great similarity in the nature of the principal attributes of status; in the functional contributions to the center and to attributes and symbols monopolized by it; in the segregation of the life-styles and patterns of participation of different local, occupational, territorial, and kinship groups; in the attempts of the elites to minimize the status or class components of family or broader kinship group identity and the autonomous standing of the family in the status system; and in the attempts of the elites of Tsarist and Soviet Russia to establish a uniform hierarchy of evaluation of the major positions especially with regard to access to the center.

Structural continuity is closely associated with continuity in cultural orientations. The fundamental orientations we identified in traditional

Russia were evident in postrevolutionary Russia; that is, the center's monopoly over access to the major attributes of the cultural and social orders and to this-worldly foci, as well as the predominance of the state over society.

II

The basic discontinuity between the Communist regime and the traditional Chinese order manifested itself in the attempt of the Communist regime to destroy most of the concrete traditional symbols, strata, and organizations, to forge new social and political goals, and to create new types of social organizations. However, continuity in certain values and in their institutional derivatives can be identified.

The Chinese Communist regime has tended to perceive the fundamental problems of social and cultural order in broad terms (for example, emphasizing a combination of power and ideology), problems not very different from those of the traditional order. Moreover, the Communist elite and its Confucian-Legalist predecessors similarly viewed the use of different institutional settings and their relative predominance (witness the continuous predominance of state service and centralized bureaucracy). The modern regime has tended to use traditional personnel know-how, and organizational settings but to remove them from their traditional context and deny them any autonomous identity.

III

Postrevolutionary Europe also exhibited continuities with the past. The basic cultural orientations survived the European revolutions as did the principles of center-periphery relations. Thus, modern Europe has displayed a high degree of commitment on the part of centers and peripheries alike to common ideals or goals; a high level of permeation of the peripheries by the centers in attempts to mobilize support for the latter's policies; and constant impingement of the relatively autonomous forces of the peripheries on the centers.

Similarly, postrevolutionary Europe has shown continuity in the pattern of policies of the rulers, which have been not only distributive or allocative but also promotive (that is, oriented toward the creation or promotion of new types of activities and organizations and toward the establishment of facilities for the implementation of new goals represented in an autonomous way by various strata).

All these aspects of political systems are closely connected with continuity in the patterns of political organization and struggle that characterized Western Europe. This continuity has manifested itself in the development of relatively autonomous political groups such as parties and organs of public opinion and in the rise of highly autonomous political movements directed at gaining access to the resources of the center and at influencing the symbols, contexts, and structure of the centers—thus asserting the autonomy of broader groups in the society as the bearers of those values and attributes that the center claims to represent.

Finally, Europe has exhibited continuity with the past in patterns of stratification and in perceptions of social hierarchy. Such continuity is evident in the emphasis on various cultural and social attributes to which different groups have autonomous access; in the combination of orientations toward power and cultural, social, and economic prestige; as well as in the development of a multiplicity of status hierarchies and patterns of status incongruity, along with a very strong tendency toward country-wide strata consciousness and organization.

IV

A somewhat similar pattern of continuity can be found in Turkey. Imperial-patrimonial orientations and structures, along with their control mechanisms, survived the Kemalist Revolution. However, the content of these orientations and structures enabled the development of greater institutional flexibility and autonomy.

The continuity of codes and their structural derivatives was connected with the continuity of certain basic characteristics of the major institutional entrepreneurs active in these societies. This continuity was clearest in terms of their autonomy or embedment in broader ascriptive strata and in the nature of the solidary relations among them and between them and the broader strata. Although all postrevolutionary societies manifested such continuity, some very important differences can be discerned.

7. RESTRUCTURING OF TRADITION

Thus, as our preceding analysis indicates, these societies evinced different rates of discontinuity, that is, discontinuity in the symbols of collective identity, on the one hand, and discontinuity in key aspects of the institutional structure, on the other. It is not just that different degrees of discontinuity in these dimensions of the institutional structure can be correlated with *similar* degrees of continuity in cultural codes and their structural derivatives. A closer look at the various revolutionary societies reveals that a high level of discontinuity in the symbols of legitimation and in the restructuring of institutional spheres seemed to be associated with a high degree of continuity in the major cultural codes—especially their main structural derivatives; with a high degree of control and coerciveness in the reorganizing of the institutional structure; and hence with a smaller ability to absorb the ever developing symbols and movements of protest inherent in the process of modernization.

Conversely, a smaller degree of discontinuity in the symbols of the political regime and collective identity tended to be connected with greater continuity of codes and their institutional derivatives and with a smaller degree of structural coercion (as against simple violence) in the process of restructuring of the institutional framework of postrevolutionary societies.[57]

These differences between more and less coercive revolutionary elites and societies are perhaps best seen in the ways in which traditional orientations were used in prerevolutionary societies and in the ways in which cultural orientations and symbols were restructured in the new settings.[58]

Common to all revolutionary societies were attempts to forge new goals, symbols, and centers; to establish new political and cultural orders; to widen at least symbolically the participation of broader strata in these orders; and to include these orders in new institutional activities. In all such situations a tendency arose toward differentiation of various layers of tradition, toward segregation of traditional and nontraditional (religious and nonreligious) spheres of life, and toward reassessment of the relevance of different symbols and traditions to different spheres of life.

This pattern was unlike that found in situations structured by groups or elites relatively resistant to change. Specifically, segregation of the various spheres of social life was less thorough and rigid. There tended to be greater continuity between institutional and symbolic spheres, with greater overflow and overlap, although this continuity did not as a rule become fully formalized or ritualized.

Thus, unlike their prerevolutionary counterparts these societies did not alternate between total withdrawal of traditional symbols from the new institutional spheres on the one hand, and attempts to impose rigid religious principles on them, on the other. Rather, there developed a predisposition toward a new symbolic order, under which the social spheres, which had developed a degree of autonomy, could be brought together, and within which prerevolutionary symbols and traditions could be incorporated at least partially.

Closely related to these modes of continuity and transformation of tradition, there developed in revolutionary situations a relatively high degree of internal differentiation and diversification of roles and tasks; a growing incorporation of such new roles and tasks into the major social groups; and a greater readiness on the part of members of these groups to undertake new tasks outside their groups and to participate in various new groups. Furthermore, these new roles, tasks, and patterns of participation become interwoven according to highly differentiated principles of integration, exhibiting a greater degree of receptivity to new structural possibilities and to new goals and symbols of collective identity. Finally, the symbols of broader groups were incorporated into the new center.

Most revolutionary societies were predisposed to closer and more positive connections between the personal identity of the members of component groups or the society itself and the symbols of new political, social, and cultural orders. The members of revolutionary sects and parties largely accepted the new symbols as the major collective referents of their personal identity, guiding participation in the social and cultural orders and giving meaning to many new institutional activities.

These similarities aside, important differences distinguished the revolutionary societies especially with respect to power orientations and coerciveness. These differences are most clearly seen in a comparison of the European (and American) postrevolutionary societies, on the one hand, with the Russian, Chinese, and Vietnamese, on the other.

In Europe attempts were repeatedly made to redefine the major problems of social and cultural order and to broaden the scope of solutions to them. This broadening took place without total rejection of traditional symbols; rather, they tended to be incorporated into the new symbolic order. Consequently, Europe experienced the development of both new groups and collectivities and of new types of institutional goals. Moreover, the continuity of cultural orientations encouraged the rise of a great variety of new, relatively autonomous institutions and groups and the easing of controls over them; possibly, these changes (as we see later) resulted in the abandonment of certain of the earlier premises of European modernity.

Hence, the continuity of tradition was maintained mostly in terms of commitment to the central symbols of the social and cultural orders and in terms of general orientations to these orders but not in terms of the content of these orders, which in such situations continually changed.

In Russia, China, and Vietnam, the situation was more complex. On the one hand, their revolutionary elites destroyed most of the concrete symbols and structures of the existing traditions, strata, and organizations and emphasized new social and cultural goals and new types of social organization. Yet at the same time they evinced a greater continuity than the solidary elites with regard to basic modes of symbolic and institutional orientation.

They tended to pose some of the fundamental problems of social and cultural order, and of their interrelations, in broad terms (e.g., emphasis on power) that were not very different from those their predecessors used. Of course, the specific formulation of these problems (e.g., how to establish an autocratic society as against a totalitarian industrial one) and their concrete solution differed greatly from those of the preceding order.

In Russia, China, and Vietnam the revolutionary elites retained traditional orientations but changed their concrete contents and their identification with and connection to the old order. That is, they attempted to control in a new way the fundamental motivational orientations inherent in the earlier system but to alter their contents and context.

A parallel process took place with regard to the incorporation of old societal symbols. On the one hand, we find an almost total negation of these symbols. On the other hand (because of the similarity of problems posed), we find attempts to use or uphold such symbols or general symbolic orientations removed from their context.

Similar differences appeared in the attitudes of the various revolutionary societies with respect to regulating relations between personal and collective identities. The educational policies formulated in Russia and China sought to submerge personal identity in a new collective identity, to minimize personal and subgroup autonomy, and to make the collective symbols and their bearers the principal controllers of the personal superego. They increasingly stressed the solidarity of the total collectivity—symbolically and organizationally defined as the major focus of the individual's superego.

In contrast, Europe and the United States developed a different type of orientation and policy. These societies place strong (albeit flexible) emphasis on personal commitment to the community and institutional activities, but this very flexibility has encouraged or at least tolerated the expression of personal identity—an identity only loosely bound up with the collective identity.

Thus, in all these cases we witness a rather paradoxical relationship between continuity in the symbols of legitimation, the premises of legitimation, and the meanings of institutions, on the one hand, and the composition of ruling groups, the degree of control and coerciveness, and the premises underlying the sociopolitical order, center-periphery relations, and the social hierarchy, on the other. It is this combination of dimensions of control that bears most closely on the problem of the realization of the emancipatory premises of the revolutionary image.

Thus, noncoercive elites tended to permit more pluralistic institutional framework and to broaden the types and dimensions of orientations of protest, thereby creating the perception of incompleteness of the revolution. The coercive elites allowed such developments to a much smaller degree; they focused above all on the dimensions of solidarity, the attributes of which they strove to monopolize, claiming to have fully realized the emancipatory premises of the revolution.[59]

PART 3.   ANALYTICAL CONCLUSIONS

1. STRUCTURE AND CLOSURE OF CENTERS. PATTERNS OF REVOLUTION AND OF SOCIAL TRANSFORMATION. DISCONTINUITY AND DISLOCATION

What conclusions can we draw, on the basis of the material presented in the preceding section, about the relation among the major variables outlined: the structure of the center, its rigidity and composition, and the nature of solidary relations between the central and secondary elites and between them and the broader strata, on the one hand, and various outcomes of revolutions and the emergence of distinct types of postrevolutionary societies (different in terms of the dimensions of modernization, the discontinuity in the social structure, and potential emancipatory results), on the other.

As we indicated, the crucial intervening variable that explains the relations between the structure of centers and the outcomes of revolutions is the ability of the center, first, to mobilize the resources needed for coping with the problems attendant on the transition to modernity; second, to incorporate new or potential claimants to participation in it, and third, to establish links with the broader strata in order to attempt institution building.

It is a common assumption that the greater the center's ability to perform these tasks, the smaller the degree of violence, discontinuity, rupture, and dislocation between the prerevolutionary and the post-revolutionary structure; conversely, the smaller this ability, the greater the violence, discontinuity, rupture, and dislocation. The relation between the center's lack of ability to cope with these problems and a high level of discontinuity and rupture in the revolutionary process is explained partially by the fact that the greater this inability, the stronger the center's tendency to undertake coercive and repressive measures, which in turn often will give rise to extreme reactions from would-be contenders for participation in power and often will result in institutional and symbolic discontinuity between the prerevolutionary and postrevolutionary society.

How, then, do the various aspects of the structure of the center— especially its rigidity, and composition—influence the center's ability to cope with new problems and to incorporate new strata as well as to shape the process of revolution and its outcomes. As we have seen, rigidity on the part of the center has several dimensions. First is tactical rigidity in the face of new demands. Second is structural rigidity, the degree to which the center is based on the denial to other groups of autonomous access to it. Third is the monolithic or pluralistic composition of the center—a pluralism that may imply solidary relations with some elites and groups of the periphery.

The materials presented earlier indicated that in most general terms the rigidity and closure of the center are highly conducive to the development and intensification of the conditions leading to revolution; that is, interelite strife, increasing frustration among the major strata, and so on. Furthermore, the more rigid the center, the more it will engage in coercive measures; accordingly, the more violent the ensuing revolution will be and the stronger its emphasis on breaking with the bases, symbols, and patterns of political legitimation, as well as other major aspects of the institutional structure of the prerevolutionary regime.

Thus, among the prerevolutionary centers, the English was the least rigid (certainly less so than the French); the English and French centers were less rigid than the Russian, Chinese, or the late colonial Vietnamese. Consequently, the degree of violence, as well as the denial of the symbols and premises of legitimation of the preceding regimes, were also much greater in the latter than in the former cases.

The importance of the rigidity of centers in shaping the revolutionary processes is also borne out by a comparison of societies in which the processes of social transformation leading to modernization were not revolutionary. The centers of these societies—the Scandinavian countries and Switzerland, for example—were characterized by great flexibility and a high degree of readiness to incorporate new groups of contenders. This flexibility was rooted in the fact that in Scandinavia and Switzerland, the more autonomous, pluralistic elements of the European tradition either were relatively stronger than elsewhere in Europe or became stronger because of propitious internal and external circumstances.

But even if the rigidity of the center explains in a rough way the degree of actual or symbolic violence that characterizes a given revolution, other aspects of discontinuity and rupture between prerevolutionary and postrevolutionary societies are related to specific dimensions of the center's rigidity and closure. Insofar as the rigidity of the center was only (or mainly) tactical or personal, as in England and to a smaller degree France, rather than based on the principled denial of the access of broader groups to it, discontinuity tended to develop primarily in the symbols of political regimes and in certain premises of their legitimation and secondarily in the composition of the ruling class and the other upper classes. Discontinuity was least evident in the structuring of the access of different groups to resources and to positions of control.

Thus, in England, the American colonies, and to some degree the Netherlands, and France, where the broader strata enjoyed some access to the center, there was relatively little discontinuity in the symbols and premises of political legitimation as well as in the composition of the ruling class. Note that in France the closure of the center was greatest, which gave rise to far-reaching dislocations in all the major dimensions of the institutional structure.

Of special interest from the point of view of this analysis is the pattern of discontinuity of political legitimation in the two cases of early revolution that have baffled revolutionary theorists: the Revolt of the Netherlands and the American Revolution. Both these cases manifested as their central outcome reconstruction of the boundaries of the new political community and generation of the symbols of their national (and not only political) identity accompanied by—especially in America—relatively little violence. This pattern is understandable if we consider that the rigidity of the Spanish and even more so the English center was less felt because of distance. These centers were also weakened in that the revolution was undertaken by groups and elites that were initially accepted—even if secondary—parts of the existing center and that revolted in the name of the premises of the center.

However, in Russia, China, Vietnam, and Turkey, where the distinctiveness of the center was based largely on denying broader groups access to the center, there developed a much farther reaching pattern of discontinuity. Not only did rupture and discontinuity occur in the symbols and legitimation of the political regime to an extent unknown in the preceding cases, but also these trends were connected with the displacement and even execution of the ruling class and the upper classes, with the dislocation of other classes, and with drastic changes in most principles of the distribution of resources.

Still, in terms of outcomes these societies displayed important differences. Here the most crucial variable was the degree to which the center was monolithic, specifically, the degree to which the center developed, in the process of encounter with modernization, relatively autonomous subelites and tolerated access to the center on the part of broader strata. Let us consider Russia, China, and Turkey in this regard.

The Russian center was structurally the most exclusive, a trait that became more pronounced as Russia modernized. Accordingly, Russia experienced the most violent discontinuity and rupture in institutional structures and in the symbols of the political regime and the most extensive destruction of the upper classes in general and the ruling class in particular.

The Chinese and Turkish centers were more pluralistic and this tendency grew stronger as they responded to modernization. In the first phase of the Chinese Revolution, as well as in the Kemalist Revolution, discontinuity in the symbols of political legitimation and removal of the former ruling group were not connected with drastic changes in the composition of the principal upper groups, with far-reaching dislocations of other groups, or with marked shifts in their access to the center.

As we have seen, the first phase of the Chinese Revolution produced a center that was rigid, exclusive, inefficient and unable to institutionalize itself. In the second phase, reaction against this center generated discontinuity in all the major aspects of institutional life.

Thus, the more pluralistic the center and the more politically open it is to at least certain broader groups, the greater the chance that the tendency toward restructuring the principles of political legitimation as well as the principles of access to the center will not be connected with total restructuring of the basic principles of the major institutional spheres.

2. CLOSURE OF CENTERS. SOLIDARITY, DISLOCATION, AND COERCION IN THE RESTRUCTURING OF POSTREVOLUTIONARY SOCIETIES

Another crucial dimension of the process of restructuring in post-revolutionary societies was the degree to which changes in the composition of ruling and other classes were connected not only with changes in the relative position of these groups but also with their loss of access to and/or control over resources, access to bases of power, and to the center, as well as with the degree to which restructuring was connected with coercive measures.

These aspects of the restructuring of revolutionary societies were most closely associated with the rigidity, closure, and composition of the center and with the nature of the solidary relations among the major and secondary elites and the principal groups in the society. Where the pre-revolutionary center was composed of relatively autonomous articulators of models of cultural order, political and economic elites, and articulators of the solidarity of ascriptive collectivities (enjoying solidary relations among themselves and with the principal groups in the society), both the exclusion of major groups from the postrevolutionary center and from upper social positions and the loss of power and bases of control on the part of lower groups were less severe. In such cases there arose a strong tendency toward broadening access to the center and to the major positions of control in the principal spheres of the society.

Conversely, the greater the rigidity and closure of the center, the stronger the tendency toward the exclusion of such groups and social categories from access to the center and to the major channels of advancement; the greater also the tendency toward displacing lower and middle groups from their bases of power and minimizing their control over access to resources; and the more coercive the measures used to effect all these transformations.

Thus, we see that what determines the coerciveness and dislocation that may characterize postrevolutionary societies is the degree of isolation of the ruling political elite from other elites and the degree to which it monopolizes or attempts to control their functions and/or solidary relations with the broader strata. The greater the isolation, the greater the structural coerciveness (and not only the degree of violence) connected with restructuring institutions and the greater the discontinuity and dislocation of strata.

This broad pattern of course varies in actual situations. A detailed analysis of such variations and their impact on the restructuring of the institutional frameworks of postrevolutionary societies is beyond the scope of our analysis. We shall confine ourselves to considering briefly three types of isolated elites.

First are traditional modernizing elites, the most important illustration of which Russia offers. Second are the extreme revolutionary elites that may in principle develop in any modern or modernizing society but that tend to be most successful in societies with closed traditional centers.[60] Third are the extreme revolutionary elites—either indigenous or foreign— that are imposed on a society through the impact of outside revolutionary forces and revolutionary states.[61]

Common to these three types is their merger of the functions of political elites with the articulation of models of cultural and social order; their subjugation of other elites—both articulators of the models of cultural and social order and articulators of the solidarity of ascriptive collectivities; and their but minimally open solidary relations with the broader strata.

Of course, the variables we have been discussing may combine in unusual ways. The most outstanding such combination is a relatively closed and secluded center enjoying solidary relations with the broader strata. The example of Yugoslavia is instructive here.[62] This regime was similar to other Eastern European countries in the post–World War II period in that revolutionary transformation was imposed on it mainly from the outside (namely, by the victory of the Russian army). Thus, Yugoslavia did not experience a pure revolution. This is, however, only part of the picture. Yugoslavia, unlike its neighbors (Albania perhaps excepted), played an active role in establishing its postwar regime. It waged a civil war, both sides of which were aided by external forces. Even more important, this civil war took place in the context of a war of national liberation (as happened in China). Moreover, and again in marked contrast to the pattern in other Eastern European countries,[63] this combination of civil war and national liberation did not give rise to a new revolutionary group isolated from the rest of society. Rather, it helped to forge some new links with the broader strata—especially with the urban workers and to a smaller degree the peasantry. Thus, total change of the symbols and premises of the political regime and of its legitimation, as well as of the ruling class, was connected in Yugoslavia with the incorporation of the older upper class into the secondary echelons of the new state. Moreover, there was less displacement of the lower groups (especially the peasantry) from their bases of power and control and less coerciveness with respect to restructuring the institutional framework than either Russia or other Eastern European countries manifested.

France exhibited still a different variant: relative openness or plurality of the center combined with a high degree of antagonism among some of the components of the center (predominantly along the traditional revolutionary axis), which was reflected in the development of the post-revolutionary French system.[64]

3. AUTONOMY AND SOLIDARITY OF ELITES. RESTRUCTURING OF INSTITUTIONAL COMPLEXES

The extent of organizational change and of the crystallization of new meanings of institutions was influenced principally by another combination of variables mentioned above; namely, the autonomy of the major elites, an autonomy that was associated with varying degrees of closure and with different types of solidary relations with other elites and with broader strata.

The more autonomous and disembedded the major elites, the more they tended to generate new meanings of institutions and to promote far-reaching symbolic and organizational restructuring of institutional spheres and center-periphery relations. Witness the early European revolutions, the American, Russian, Chinese, Vietnamese, and to a lesser extent the Turkish revolutions.

The more embedded these elites, the less they were able to generate new meanings and crystallize new, stable institutional complexes and promote or maintain extensive organizational changes in institutional spheres.

Of course, the concrete example of these two general patterns show important differences that reflect the revolutionary society's orientation to change and modernization. Comparison of traditional, cohesive elites with revolutionary elites is very useful in this regard.

Traditional elites—for instance, the Tsarist government—were able only to uphold far-reaching organizational frameworks; that is, given their basic social orientation such elites had to retain old meanings and systems of control, tending indeed to become more fully committed to the status quo. They espoused the notion of service to the state, which tended to lose its appeal in the postrevolutionary setting.

The lack of such an ability was perhaps more glaring in the case of highly embedded elites; for example, those that developed in the first phase of the Chinese Revolution and that were unable to generate pervasive organizational changes. When such an elite becomes more autonomous, more development oriented (despite adherence to traditional values and authoritarian orientations), it may be able to promote not only extensive organizational changes but also new institutional meanings and structures (consider the case of Taiwan).

The nature of the control mechanisms on which the new institutional complexes are based and according to which they are restructured and, above all, the degree to which they are based on the relatively autonomous access of broader groups to the position of control depends primarily on the variables analyzed above (the nature of the solidary relations among the ruling elites, subelites, and broader groups); that is, on the degree to which political elites enter into relatively free coalitions with articulators of models of social and cultural order as well as with articulators of the solidarity of ascriptive collectivities.

The more autonomous such elites are, lacking close solidary ties to other elites or groups, and the more antagonistic they are to the major social strata, the more the new institutional complexes will be coercively restructured and the smaller the extent of autonomous access of other groups to positions of control. The more autonomous such elites are, enjoying either adaptive or solidary relations with broader groups, the more they will be able to develop coalitions with other relatively autonomous elites, as was the case in Europe and to some degree in Turkey; likewise, the more restructuring of institutional meanings and complexes is combined with the broadening of access to positions of control, the less coercive it will be.

4. RESTRUCTURING OF RULING CLASSES. TRANSFORMATION OF TRADITIONS AND OF ORIENTATIONS OF PROTEST

The various tendencies of discontinuity and reconstruction in post-revolutionary society were correlated with the nature of the emerging ruling elite and the degree of coercion exercised by this class in controlling the broader groups and their participation in the political regime.

Rigidity and closure of the center (especially in combination with the isolation of the actual or potential ruling group and its nonsolidary relations with other elites and broader groups) were connected to the development of a ruling class based on internal closure; on monopolistic control of the social and cultural orders; on minimization of the autonomy of other elites; and on upholding the criteria of service to the collectivity as interpreted by this class. In other words, such an elite obstructed autonomous strata or class formation.

Of course, ruling classes varied in terms of composition—in particular, in the degree of plurality. The more solidary the ruling group with other elites and with broader groups—as was the case in Yugoslavia and China—the more flexible or open the ruling class even at the expense of giving up some cohesion to permit the participation of broader groups in the political system. In contrast, the combination of openness of the centers and solidary relations with broader groups encouraged—as in most of the European cases—attempts to reinforce the solidary links between the center and the periphery. The result was an atmosphere conducive to pluralistic and open systems that permitted incorporation of new classes into the centers and extended the range of their participation in the political system.

The more solidary, autonomous, and innovative the revolutionary elites were at least initially, the more flexible they were vis-à-vis the reconstruction of tradition. Such elites tended to promulgate broad guidelines for reconstruction and to maintain continuity in cultural codes. They generally were flexible with respect to the incorporation of old symbols of identity into new symbols and favored both institutional flexibility and the incorporation of new dimensions of personal and social activities into the institutional frameworks they established.

Autonomous but nonsolidary, coercive elites were as a rule much more rigid in regard to the process of reconstruction of tradition. They permitted little incorporation of old symbols into new but at the same time maintained a much higher degree of continuity in the perception of the basic problems of the social order as well as in its institutional derivatives. Hence, they prevented development of pluralistic orientation toward protest.

To sum up, the solidary, transformative elites tolerated a greater plurality of institutional developments and broadened the scope of participation in the society and in its centers. But for this very reason they tended to diffuse their social orientations and indirectly to encourage the articulation of manifold protest orientations. The coercive elites did not allow pluralism and stressed the symbols of collective solidarity, attempting to monopolize them both internally and externally rather than permitting their articulation in the internal processes of their societies. Thus, we see that the nature of elite structure and of the solidary relations between elites and broader groups determine the relationship between the processes of dislocation, discontinuity, and rupture, which revolutions engender to varying degrees, and the restructuring of institutional complexes and symbols of traditions, which modernization entails.

5. AN ILLUSTRATION.
THE CHINESE REVOLUTION

This broad pattern varied not only across revolutionary societies but within them as well over time. While systematic analysis of all such variations is beyond the scope of this book, we illustrate the feasibility of this type of approach by a brief analysis of the Chinese case.[65]

In the prerevolutionary period, China had a monopolistic center that showed some internal diversification and enjoyed close links with the broader strata. Still, access to the center was regulated by the center itself, and the center controlled the status orientations of the broader groups. The latter were internally very solidary but had little autonomy with respect to linkages among themselves.

These characteristics greatly influenced the Chinese response to modernity. Under the impact of modernity, Chinese intellectuals and bureaucrats initially faced certain problems stemming from the fact that their cultural symbols were embedded in the existing political structure. Any political revolution or reformation necessarily entails rejecting or destroying the cultural order. Similarly, the strong ideological emphasis on upholding the social-political status quo permitted few centers for the crystallization of new symbols to legitimize new social institutions relatively independent of the preceding order.

Accordingly, intellectuals and bureaucrats revealed an ambivalent and rather inflexible attitude toward their tradition and its relation to modernity. They tended to oscillate between utterly rejecting Chinese tradition in favor of Western values, on the one hand, and rejecting Western values and attempting to subordinate Western technology to the traditional Chinese center and its basic orientations, on the other

Looking at the social sphere, we find few points of internal strength, cohesion, and self-identity among groups on which new institutional frameworks could be founded or which could support institutional changes. Hence, China's various reform and national movements were characterized by a certain closure, a ritual emphasis on specific and very limited types of local status. They were mostly composed of groups alienated from the existing elites and from the broader groups and strata of the society.

Thus, we can understand the weakness of these movements in their attempts at institution building and their difficulty in creating new interlinking mechanisms between the center and the periphery. We can also see their potential attraction to neotraditionalism with its manifold implications for policymaking and institution building.

Against this picture stands the success of the Chinese Communists. Two sets of conditions explain their success. First, they were able to forge out of certain elements of the preceding social and cultural orders a cohesive revolutionary elite capable of seizing and maintaining power. Second, this elite was able to select from among the features of modernity ideological and social orientations, elements, and symbols that could serve as foci of its own revolutionary, transformative orientations, of the new sociopolitical and cultural orders, and of the new political-ideological center.

More specifically the Chinese Communists brought together two different threads of Chinese reformist and rebellious tradition by uniquely linking the more idealistic tendencies of the literati and the gentry with the tendencies of the secret societies and peasant rebellions. Thus, various segments of Chinese society—warlords, gentry, and peasants, for example—could go beyond their own restricted social orientations and find a wider basis on which to create new, broader orientations.

Another factor that helped the Chinese Communist movement was the war of national liberation. Thus, the Communists did not have to face the problem of reconciling the transformation of the symbols of the national order and of the social order. The context of national liberation also greatly influenced the nature of the symbols and orientations selected by the Chinese Communists from among the impinging international forces—symbols and orientations that served as foci of the new cohesive elite and its transformative tendencies.

In postrevolutionary China we can see how the Communists' background and orientations shaped the constant struggle between the more radical, seemingly antibureaucratic party elements and the more organizational cadres as we noted earlier. This struggle was at heart ideological. Each ideological camp differently interpreted the new meanings of postrevolutionary institutional complexes, and ideological differences within the party predisposed China to continual internal conflicts—a tendency most vividly expressed in the Cultural Revolution. As the Cultural Revolution demonstrated, masses were extensively mobilized by different elements in the ruling group; the latter explicitly stressed the solidary or communal aspects of the former's participation in the new center.

What precipitated China's ideological rift? Its origin probably was the unusual combination of gentry-literati and peasant-warlord orientations out of which the solidarity of the Communist leadership was forged. And its result is the troubling persistence of traditional loyalties. The regime must therefore control the new motivations or orientations that are being created through its attempts to break down these loyalties and channel them not only into expressions of permanent revolutionary solidarity but also into secondary daily processes of modern institution building. Compounding the difficulty of this task is the low level of trust between the components of the elite and the emerging institutional structures. This distrust may be attributable to both ideological and social structural factors. First, it may be related to the ideological struggle we have been discussing. Second, it is probably rooted in the fact that the unique social linkage effected by the Communist regime did not give rise to new, autonomous, intermediate institutions or organizations; that is, there did not develop new, autonomous social groups, organizations, and bases of social status.

6. THE INTERNATIONAL SETTING AND REVOLUTIONARY OUTCOMES

The analysis of the Chinese case illustrated how structural variables such as the rigidity and exclusiveness of centers; the autonomy of broader groups; the nature of the solidary linkages among them; and the concrete coalitions between different groups at the center and broader social groups are not entirely predetermined by the prerevolutionary past. These variables may be powerfully affected by the revolutionary situation itself; that is, by the impact of international forces on the centers of both prerevolutionary and postrevolutionary societies and by the very process of revolution. Thus, we must now consider how various aspects of the sociohistorical situation impinge on the outcomes of revolutions.

It has often been claimed that the greater the impact of international political and economic forces on the center, the stronger the tendency to increase its rigidity and exclusiveness. This argument is supported to a degree by the data. For instance, the rigidity of the French and above all the Russian and Chinese centers was greatly enhanced by constant threats.

This increase of the rigidity of the center under the impact of external and internal threats influenced the degree to which the various types of groups that emerged out of the processes of change were successful in establishing autonomous linkages among themselves and with different incumbent and contending elites. In general, the more severe the external threats, the smaller the chance for the continual crystallization of pluralistic groups and elites with potentially autonomous access to power and with autonomous linkages among themselves. (Hence, China, for example, manifested patrimonial tendencies and embedment of incumbent elites in broader groups and ascriptive collectivities.) In such situations, the tendency to isolate both ruling and contending elites became stronger as did the propensity of these elites for coercive—whether neotraditional or revolutionary—transformation.

The efforts of liberal groups toward the end of the Chinese and Russian empires are very instructive on this point. In both China and Russia external threats weakened the political class to the extent that it was unable to absorb new elements or make attempts at reform. This led to the establishment of weak coalitions of various liberal groups and increased the fragmentation of the society. Hence, the road to reconstruction lay open to revolutionary groups that were dissociated from autonomous classes or strata and that constructed new, coercive centers in which the weaker or secondary units of the revolutionary coalitions were ultimately destroyed. The result of this was total transformation: continuity was preserved only on the more subtle level of the criteria of codes and of their structural derivatives.

However, in some situations (the later phases of the revolutions in China and Yugoslavia) the very intensity of external forces facilitated the forging of solidary relations between the new (traditionalist or revolutionary), isolated elites and the broader strata. This pattern is most likely when revolutionary upheaval takes place in the context of a war of national liberation and when the internal struggle is engaged in by contending groups that all have actual or potential bases of support.

The impact of international forces on revolutionary situations is also evident in the different loci of impingement of the forces of modernity and in the major problems and possibilities of discontinuity that emerge therefrom. Factors to consider here are the mode of incorporation of a society into the international setting and the relative importance within the society of the major elites and articulators of cultural models and of the solidarity of the principal collectivities. From this point of view two major types of revolutionary society can be distinguished. In the first, changes in the political regime are connected with continuity in the articulators of the solidarity of the national unit (for example, England, France, Russia, Vietnam, and China). In such cases, reconstruction of the boundaries of the major political and national collectivities was not a focus of revolutionary reconstruction, which addressed itself primarily to other ground rules of social interaction. In the second, the articulators of solidarity are not incorporated into the existing center; hence, reconstruction of the boundaries of the political community constitutes the central focus of revolutionary activities, activities connected in different ways with reconstruction of the other ground rules of social interaction (for example, the American colonies, the Netherlands, Turkey, and many Central and Eastern European societies). Significantly, these two types are continuously susceptible to international forces.

Thus, our brief discussion indicates that the ultimate outcomes of any revolution are not necessarily given in the prerevolutionary structure of the society but are the product of interaction among prerevolutionary characteristics, the forces of change—most notably, international forces—and the revolutionary process itself. Only through such interaction do coalitions of broad classes and coalitions between them and the major types of institutional entrepreneurs arise and change. The study of the crystallization of such coalitions constitutes a major challenge to students of revolution.

PART 4.   COMPARATIVE EXCURSUS

1. REVOLUTIONARY TENDENCIES IN NINETEENTH- AND TWENTIETH-CENTURY EUROPE

The variables that we identified as influencing the outcomes of revolutions can explain patterns of transformation of modern or modernizing societies that have perplexed students of revolution: the German case of

1848, as well as the various nationalist movements in Central and Eastern Europe in the nineteenth and twentieth centuries.[66] (The German case in particular shared with the true revolutions certain conditions conducive to revolutionary transformation.) All these societies belonged to Imperial systems that placed strong emphasis on this-worldly resolution of tension between the transcendental and the mundane order. Moreover, some of these societies entered the modern international system in a manner similar to that of the pure revolutionary societies (granted, the Eastern European societies found themselves from the outset in relatively dependent positions). Yet among this group, no true revolution succeeded.

In some cases, however, a pattern developed similar to that of the true revolution in one of its variants studied above. Germany, our central example, witnessed the establishment of a new political system having very strong industrializing and modernizing tendencies. This system was connected with widespread change in the structure of markets and in the organizational aspects of the economic sphere, with the development of a new capitalist and bureaucratic pattern, and with the establishment of a new political entity. The system did not, however, increase the autonomy of the bourgeoisie or markedly alter its access to political centers and positions of control. The push to industrialization and the establishment of a new polity was led by a traditionally based though strongly modernizing elite. This group, while extending the scope of industrial economy, also promoted the interests of the traditional landed groups and limited political access and participation of the broader strata to the center although in principle restructured center-periphery relations in a modern, nationalistic direction.

In Austria, Hungary, and other parts of the Austro-Hungarian Empire, the failure of the 1848 revolution was the direct result of repression. Initially this did not give rise to far-reaching transformation; later, however, there occurred extensive changes in the social and political spheres (e.g., reconstruction of the boundaries of political communities), as well as changes in the political elite and in the class structure.

In some of these countries the establishment of new national units had several results: restructuring of the boundaries of political units; disappearance of the older (Ottoman and/or Austro-Hungarian) ruling class; and to a much smaller degree either restructuring of institutional complexes and class relations or establishment of a new civil polity (as in the Revolt of the Netherlands and in the American Revolution).

A detailed analysis of these nationalist and social revolutions would examine first the degree to which these societies exhibited the cultural and structural characteristics of Imperial or Imperial-feudal systems (as was indeed the case in most Eastern European societies) as well as the mode of their incorporation into the new international frameworks; and second the rigidity of their centers and the relationship between the centers and different elites and broader strata as these dimensions affected the construction of new institutional patterns.

Such an analysis is not our intention. However, we do wish to point out a crucial aspect that distinguishes all these cases from the pure revolutions. To wit, the construction of a new national political center and boundaries constituted the central focus of the movements of protest and of revolutionary activity in these societies. Ultimately, such construction took place under the aegis of the traditional political elite. This elite dissociated itself both from the emerging autonomous articulators of the social order and from the more autonomous strata but attempted to combine its political and modernizing activities with a very strong emphasis on the articulation of a traditionally legitimized order. This elite was relatively autonomous vis-à-vis to the more traditional aristocratic elements from which its members were in the main recruited and with which it continued to enjoy solidary relations.

In the German empire there took place an establishment of new national political collectivities and centers by traditionally oriented elites and the partial (nonrevolutionary) transformation of power and class relations. (The unification of Italy was similar to the German experience in several respects. However, both the newly emerging elite and the upper classes were far less autonomous and far more divided between traditional and modernizing elements.) [67]

A digression on fascism might be appropriate here. From the point of view of our analysis the fascist regimes of Europe could be described as having had an autonomous political elite concerned primarily with articulation of the solidarity of collectivities and dissociated from other elites—autonomous articulators of models of cultural order and functional elites, most notably. This combination of characteristics generated a strongly coercive orientation that resulted in the dislocation or physical destruction of the ruling class and to some extent the upper classes without either changing the bases of social hierarchies or extensively transforming institutional complexes. This phenomenon is a worthy subject for the comparative analysis of revolutions—a challenge lately taken up by Ernest Nolte, Gino Germani and others.[68]

2. TRANSFORMATIVE AND REVOLUTIONARY TENDENCIES IN JEWISH TRADITION AND SOCIETY

I

We pause here briefly to analyze the processes of social change and transformation in an exceptional society and to see whether we can explain them in terms of the variables proposed above or compare them with the revolutionary processes analyzed above. Our example of the Jewish people poses a problem. Given the basic political fact of the Diaspora (which deprived the Jews of an independent political existence and center of power), it is impossible to talk about revolution in the usual sense of the term. However, Jewish tradition manifested seemingly strong revolutionary elements, components, or tendencies. Thus, the independent Jewish states of preexilic times—the First and Second Commonwealths—crystallized out of one of the strongest examples of an exceptional tribal federation.[69] Recall that such tribal federations (along with exceptional city-states) exhibited the most coalescent pattern of change and approached the modern revolutionary vision in certain symbolic aspects.

Fairly early, the Jewish community displayed some of the major cultural codes and orientations and their institutional derivatives specific to Jewish tradition. This tradition most fully articulated during the Second Temple period and shaped the destiny of the Jews as a unique society and polity.[70] Three cultural orientations are crucial from the point of view of our analysis. First, there was a strong emphasis on the tension between the transcendental and the mundane order combined with a profound commitment to a higher moral order and a sharp tension between universalistic and particularistic moral orientations. Second, there developed a powerful this-worldly emphasis on the resolution of the tension between the transcendental and the mundane. (So strong was this emphasis that otherworldly foci were actively negated except in the Second Commonwealth. These foci were very closely related to the development of the messianic concept in Jewish tradition, in which spiritual elements were identified with national political ones. Moreover, otherworldly activity became an important focus of the tension between the universalistic and particularistic orientations in Jewish tradition.) [71] Third, there was emphasis on the autonomous access of the whole community to the major attributes of salvation as well as on the elaboration of the semicontractual elements between God and the Jewish people. This orientation became most fully elaborated in the time of the Second Commonwealth and in the exile periods through the work of the Sages and through the crystallization of the Law—Halacha (the latter developed in opposition to the more ascriptive and ritual emphases of the priesthood). Thus, there arose that unique combination of national (ethnic), political, and religious components of identity that distinguished the Jewish people from other collectivities in antiquity.[72]

All these cultural orientations entailed a very high level of problematization of the data of human existence. The derivatives of this problematization were manifest in a high level of symbolic articulation of the combination of political, religious, and national collectivities. They also generated a high level of symbolic articulation of the major institutional spheres—a high level of distinction between center and periphery but continuous interaction between them, as well as a very high level of ideological political struggle and a multiplicity of movements of heterodoxy and rebellions that were very closely related to each other and to central political struggles.[73]

The persistence of these special characteristics constituted the crucial difference between ancient Israel and neighboring tribal federations and patrimonial societies. They resulted in a very high level of continuity in the symbols of collective political, religious, and national identity in Jewish society and also in the instability of Jewish political regimes. This instability first manifested itself in the division of the Salomonic Kingdom and culminated in the two exilic periods: the relatively short Babylonian Captivity (587–539 B.C.) and the Diaspora, which followed the destruction of the Second Temple in A.D. 70.

These characteristics were reinforced by the peculiar mixture of tribal, city-state, communal, and sectarian tendencies that distinguished the Second Jewish Commonwealth—tendencies carried by a multiplicity of relatively autonomous institutional elites. The most fully articulated and ultimately the most influential of these elites were the sages, who acted as political elites, articulators of collective solidarity, and articulators of the models of cultural order. This group maintained strong solidary relations with the community and emphasized the predominance of the Law.[74] (In the Second Commonwealth, the struggles that divided elite groups attested to the high level of ideological conflict among numerous movements of heterodoxy and rebellion that were very closely related to each other and to central political struggles and further undermined the political system.)

II

These tendencies toward heterodoxy and rebellion were checked when the Jews lost their political independence, and the Sages became predominant and the Law (*Halacha*) provided the framework of Jewish existence.

The *Halacha*, in both its legal and religious aspects, held the Jewish people together, providing the institutional framework for the continuity of their cultural identity. (However, the *Halacha* did not in itself necessarily furnish the major symbols of Jewish cultural identity. Rather, it provided the framework within which the religious, national, kinship, and political dimensions of Jewish identity manifested themselves.

This complex of Jewish identity and traditions was a response to basic dilemmas of Jewish existence and self-conception that arose very early in Jewish history. The dilemma between the universalistic and particularistic orientations was resolved by locating the realization of the universalistic elements in an indefenite future. Jewish reality was particularistic in essence, and Judaism's universalistic orientations could not be given concrete expression because of the relations between Jews and the broader societies in which they lived.

Because Jews were a persecuted minority in the second exilic period, Judaism had to be less tolerant than other monotheistic religions of internal heterodoxy. Granted, mysticism, philosophical speculation, and messianic yearnings were accorded a certain segregated, secondary position, but no alternative interpretations of the *Halacha* or alternative definitions of the major components of Jewish identity were permitted.[75]

III

The transformative and revolutionary tendencies of Judaism broke forth as historical circumstances changed.[76] In this regard two movements in modern Jewish history are of central importance from the point of view of our discussion. (The second of these is discussed in the next section.)

The first movement—the false Messianism of Sabbatai Zevi (1626–1676), the last and greatest of the false Messiahs—was analyzed at length by Gershon Scholem.[77] Sabbatai's conversion to Islam, while revealing him to be a false Messiah to most Jews, nevertheless gave rise to numerous sects founded on the belief that the Messiah had only hidden himself and would return. These sects developed unorthodox beliefs and practices, emphasizing the unimportance of external observances as against inner faith.

Gradually, many members of these sects, people with strong ideological and semireligious motivations, were absorbed into the emerging, open, European society of the late eighteenth and nineteenth centuries. Many of them participated in the more radical intellectual groups of that age.

This phenomenon exhibits parallels with the transformative tendencies and activities of certain radical Protestant groups. Among these similarities are a strong transcendental orientation and commitment, widespread nonacceptance of any mediation between God and people, and the position of these groups as secondary elites or marginal segments within their own societies.

The outcomes of this movement revealed the strong transformative and revolutionary tendencies of Jewish tradition. They indicated also that these tendencies were focused on the carriers, symbols, and frameworks of internal communal power: the Rabbis and the Law. They were aimed at the reconstruction of various components of Jewish identity, the boundaries of membership in this collectivity in relation to other collectivities, and the relations between the particularistic and universalistic orientations of Jewish tradition. At the same time, these groups preserved the major characteristics and cultural codes of traditional Jewish society and its elites.

The assimilationist ideology assumed that integration of the Jews into their respective European societies would require that they give up many aspects of Jewish identity.[78] This assumption derived from contemporary nationalistic rhetoric. The latter appealed strongly to historical and even primordial elements, denying minorities the right to become assimilated as long as they retained their own cultural identity.

Some Jews—above all, intellectuals, liberals, atheists, and socialists— believed or hoped that by abandoning historical (national) and primordial elements of Jewish identity and preserving only the religious or ethical aspects of their tradition, they would be able to become assimilated and in addition resolve the old dilemma between universalistic and particularistic orientations of Judaism. Moreover, it was argued that the political frameworks into which Jews were assimilated would be significantly affected by the infusion of Jewish ethical, rational, and social elements.

IV

The second movement in modern Jewish history in which the transformative and revolutionary tendencies inherent in Jewish tradition became evident were the various Jewish national movements in general and Zionism in particular. In common with the assimilationist, or emancipatory, movements, the Jewish nationalist movements (especially Zionism) focused on restructuring the components of Jewish identity and the boundaries of the collectivity in opposite ideological and concrete directions.

The nationalist view accepted the basic premises of the assimilationists with respect to the conditions of integration into the broader society although it had grave doubts about the latter and about the possibility of the movement's ultimate success. It claimed that within any modern framework the Jews would suffer both from spiritual and cultural annihilation—the undermining of traditional communal life by modern economic, political, and cultural forces—and from the inability of modern society to incorporate them. Thus, the Zionists reasoned that only in Palestine could a new, modern, viable Jewish society be established and only in Palestine could a new synthesis of Jewish tradition and universal human culture be achieved.[79]

Hence the nationalist and Zionist movements aimed at providing the opportunity for cultural and social creativity of universal significance within a free, modern, self-supporting Jewish society. It was this combination that accounted for the tremendous emphasis both movements placed on sociocultural transformation.

Here the transformative and revolutionary tendencies of Jewish tradition were channeled in a new direction. These tendencies were revolutionary in the sense that they aimed at restructuring the boundaries of the collectivity and the major contours of Jewish institutional structures. However, they were aimed not at overthrowing the existing political center but at the establishment through migration and colonization of a new political framework and center.

V

These orientations were carried by the earliest Jewish settlers in Palestine. For the most part these pioneers were young intellectuals rebelling against the traditions and life-styles of their parents. (A large number were Eastern and Central European Jews.) Thus, they created the Yishuv (the Jewish community in Palestine) [80] as a society whose collective identity was formulated in ideological terms and the image of the pioneer (halutz), which stressed the attempt to develop a society wherein social values would be closely linked with the national effort and would be conceived not in utopian terms but rather as essential elements for building the new nation. The attempt to realize this vision in a small and undeveloped country generated the concrete problems and institutional features of the Yishuv.

Responses to these problems were influenced primarily by the nature of the institutional structure formed in the early years of the Yishuv (especially during the first three waves of immigration). A unique feature was the formation of societal and cultural centers before the appearance of a periphery composed of broader groups and social strata not as important as the centers in terms of social and cultural innovation.

These centers were thought capable of instructing, absorbing, and shaping the periphery, which was to grow through ever increasing migration. As a result, most of the institutions created by the centers were aimed not at meeting the needs of the contemporary population but rather at those of the future population. Consequently, they generated very strong future orientations.

The initial encounter between these centers and the institutions they created with the concrete problems they faced determined the development of the social structure of the Yishuv and that of the state of Israel as well as certain fundamental characteristics of modern Israeli society.

Among these characteristics was a high degree of economic centralization: the concentration of public capital in the main sectors of economic development alongside the constant growth of the private sector and the coexistence of public and private sectors in what has been called a pluralistic economic system.

Another was the unique Israeli socioeconomic organization: the kibbutzim and the moshavim (cooperative settlements); the development of cooperative enterprises in the urban sector; and, most important, the integration of these cooperative enterprises and settlements within a unified framework—the *Histadrut*. This integration made possible the transformation of the pioneering groups' agrarian orientations and facilitated the development of the major characteristics of the urban social structure of the *Yishuv*.

Another key aspect of the developing social structure of the *Yishuv* was a strong emphasis on egalitarianism and marked opposition to occupational specialization. These orientations found expression in (1) attempts to reduce status differences between occupations and to minimize displays of social standing and (2) in the assumption that transition from one profession or occupation to another was easy.

The *Yishuv* also developed special characteristics with respect to the relation between tradition and modernization. Two phenomena are of special importance here: the revival of Hebrew and the relationship between nonreligious and religious spheres. Because Hebrew was able not only to serve as a medium of daily communication but also to meet the demands of science and technology, its revival had important implications for the cultural structure of Israeli society. The fact that this ancient and for centuries mostly religious language could serve as an adequate means of communication in a modern society reduced the possibility of differences between traditionalists and modernists centered on linguistic identity and of cultural dependence on foreign centers as exclusive sources of cultural innovation.

In order to understand better the development of the specific characteristics of the Jewish community in Israel, a comparison with other modern revolutionary and immigrant societies is in order.

Israeli society shared important features with such non-Imperial, immigrant societies as the United States and the British dominions: (1) a strong emphasis on equality, at least among the earliest settlers, and the consequent absence of a hereditary, feudal, aristocratic, or landowner class; (2) a concentration of various types of economic and administrative activities within broad, unified, organizational frameworks; and (3) a strong emphasis on the reclamation of the land through work. But the concrete combination of these features within the *Histadrut* was unique. It can be explained by the *Histadrut*'s political character and outlook, by its being the creation of the revolutionary movement.

Unlike many other immigrants, the Palestine pioneers saw themselves from the outset as architects of a modern society and therefore committed themselves to institutional frameworks and organizations that served to promote such development and through which the broader groups of Jewish society could participate in the economic, ideological, and political life of the *Yishuv*. Unlike other modern social and nationalist movements, however, they did not plan for the immediate seizure of power and for a new, unitary political framework. Their primary emphasis was on large-scale rural and urban colonization, which weakened the political implications of their totalistic orientations. Only at the end of the British Mandate, with the intensification of the external political struggle, did the conception of a self-governing polity develop.

The sectarian and social movement elements of the *Yishuv* gave rise to a strong elitist ideology aimed at the creation of a new society through the implementation of an ideological program. In this, Israel was like postrevolutionary nations such as Russia, Yugoslavia, or Mexico, which attempted to mold relatively traditional societies into specifically modern patterns. However, the ideologies that developed within the Zionist movement contained more heterogeneous elements than those either of closed religious sects or of revolutionary political movements. This ideological diversity was greatly reinforced by the inclusion of many different groups within the *Yishuv*, creating new institutional nuclei with orientations toward universalistic cultural and social values.

Israeli society also shared numerous features and problems with other countries that experienced large-scale immigration. It had to deal with wave after wave of immigrants and had to integrate them into the emerging institutional framework. Still, Israel exhibited unique characteristics reflecting the motivations and orientations of the immigrants, especially their strong emphasis on national and social goals.

The revolutionary experience of the Zionist movement as manifest in the colonization of Palestine and later the state of Israel is closest to the experience of the American colonies. Their transformative and revolutionary tendencies were rooted in parallel cultural orientations. In both cases a new community (to become a new polity) was established by ideological religious sects rebelling against their society of origin. And in both cases, the revolutionary impetus resulted in the establishment of a new collectivity and polity. Finally, the institutional derivatives of their transformative orientations were carried in America and in Palestine by religious or ideological pioneers and were focused mainly on this-worldly economic activity, creating new institutional structures.

Of course, several important differences distinguish the American and the Zionist revolutionary experience. In America, the new polity centered on a new civil religion; primordial and traditional elements were represented only weakly; and the universalistic element inherent in the revolutionary experience focused on the components of the civil religion. In Israel, the new political element was closely related to primordial and traditional ones, which perpetuated the tensions between these elements as well as between the universalistic and the particularistic aspects of Jewish tradition. Consequently, the political framework that developed in Israel was not as imbued with revolutionary symbolism as that in the United States. Moreover, in Israel institutional—particularly economic—activities were imbued with a strong collective orientation.

3. JAPAN. THE MEIJI RESTORATION AND NONREVOLUTIONARY TRANSFORMATION

The preceding analysis sought to explain the variability among outcomes of pure revolutions. We also looked briefly at modern and modernizing societies in which the transformation to modernity did not take place according to the image of the pure revolution. Let us now consider an interesting, non-European case of nonrevolutionary transformation: the Meiji Restoration and the subsequent modernization of Japan.[81]

In terms of its ultimate sociopolitical effects, the Meiji Restoration very closely approximated a true revolution. It changed the political regime in Japan from a traditional, centralized, semibureaucratic state built on a petrified feudal structure into a modern, centralized, oligarchic, bureaucratic polity. It also changed the bases of legitimation of the regime. Traditional legitimation of the *shogunate* system in the name of a noneffective Emperor was abandoned and the Emperor became the traditional symbol under whose aegis numerous piecemeal changes in daily life and institutions were legitimized.[82]

The Meiji Restoration also altered the composition and structure of the ruling class. The traditional warrior class ruling over a domesticated feudal group was transformed into an oligarchical, political, bureaucratic elite within which there developed, especially in the twenties, a class of professional party politicians. Although there was some continuity between the new rulers and the secondary officials of the older ruling class, the overall result was a far-reaching change in the composition of the ruling class.

The old social hierarchy in Japan was based on criteria of contribution of the collectivity. This orientation was retained but the criteria themselves were made more modern under the Meiji Restoration. Consequently, the composition of the upper echelons of the major social classes was profoundly altered.

Finally, the Meiji Restoration changed the legal bases of ownership of resources and of their uses, legalizing private property in general and private land ownership in particular. This made possible the development of a capitalist system and an urban proletariat. It also weakened the cohesion of the older, wider (especially village) solidary groups (undermined by internal developments in the earlier, Tokugawa period) but did not destroy the solidarity of family and vertical kinship groups.

All these processes were connected with the extensive restructuring of markets—that is, their opening and widening. Control over access to them was initially vested in the bureaucracy and only later in the economic elite itself. Nevertheless, the importance of families and corporate groups in determining access to these markets was not diminished.

The institutional complex that developed in Japan was capitalist in terms of its organization. A very high concentration of large-scale entrepreneurs in the central banking and industrial complexes was combined with a very wide dispersal of smaller units. But this organizational complex was not legitimized, as in Europe, in terms of a search for transcendental salvation through this worldly activities but rather in terms of its contribution to the well-being, strength, and expansion of the collectivity.

A parallel development took place in the political realm. Japan evolved a unified, centralized, modern bureaucratic state based on universal citizenship and representative or semirepresentative institutions. But the new regime was legitimized, as we indicated above, in terms of the Emperor system, which limited the access of the periphery to the center and vested this control in the Emperor or his representatives.[83]

The peculiar combination of transformation and change that developed in Japan failed to follow the true revolutionary model because Japan lacked a progressive revolutionary ideology or even potentially counterrevolutionary or antirevolutionary ideologies like Germany had. The ideology of the Meiji Restoration was wholly restorative, emphasizing the continuity of the Emperor symbolism. Hence, this movement minimized the symbolic reconstruction of the center and the possibility of symbolic participation of the periphery in it.[84]

How, then, can we explain Japan's combination of transformative outcomes in terms of the variables used in our preceding analysis? The strong transformative tendencies of Japanese society were rooted in the structural characteristics of its Imperial-feudal system (in this, Japan was similar to the European societies that experienced true revolutions): distinctiveness of the center, a very strong mutual impingement of center and periphery, a relatively high degree of articulation of strata formation in terms of status and political orientation, and a tendency toward a relatively wide scope of strata identity (the latter tendency was not entirely suppressed even by the Tokugawa regime and it served as one of the bases of the overthrow of this regime).

The crucial difference between the European and the Japanese experience, as we have seen in Chapter 5, manifested itself in the nature of the coalitions that implemented modernizing changes in these societies. It was most evident in the almost total lack of participation in the processes of modernization in Japan by religious sects or heterodoxies. Somewhat later, with the onset of modernization, this difference showed up in the weakness of autonomous religious groups which became absorbed in the European system. This absorption was reminiscent of the pattern of earlier absorption of Buddhist and even Confucianist groups and orientations in Japan which were allowed, so long as they did not impinge on the basic premises and ground rules of the system, to lead a segregated existence in the intellectual and aesthetic fields.

NOTES

1. See, for instance, B. Moore, *The Social Origins of Dictatorship and Democracy* (Boston: Beacon, 1966); J. H. Kautsky, *The Political Consequences of Modernization* (New York: 1972); idem, *Patterns of Modernizing Revolutions: Mexico and the Soviet Union*, Sage Professional Papers in Comparative Politics, vol. 5, no. 01–056 (Beverly Hills, 1975); M. Kossok (ed.), *Studien über die Revolution* (Berlin: Akademie, 1969); and idem, *Studien zur vergleichenden Revolutionsgeschichte, 1500–1917* (Berlin: Akademie, 1974), esp. pp. 1–15.

2. On the mode of production see K. Marx, *Pre-Capitalist Economic Formation*, edited by E. J. Hobsbawn (New York: International Publishers, 1972); B. Hindess and P. Q. Hirst, *Precapitalist Modes of Production* (London: Routledge & Kegan Paul, 1975); and R. S. Warner, "The Methodology of Marx's Comparative Analysis of Modes of Production," in I. Vallier (ed.), *Comparative Methods in Sociology* (Berkeley: University of California Press, 1971), pp. 49–75. Of special interest is the debate on the Asian mode of production. See F. Tokei, *Sur le mode de production asiatique*, Studia Historica Academiae (Budapest: Scirentarum Hungarica, 1966); D. Gion (ed.), *Sul modo di produzione asiatico* (Milan: Franco Angeli, 1972); and R. Garaudy (ed.), *Sur le mode de production* (Paris: Centre d'Etudes et de Recherches Marxistes, 1969).

3. On the differences among these aspects of the construction of tradition see S. N. Eisenstadt (ed.), *Post-Traditional Societies* (New York: Norton, 1972).

4. A. Gerschenkorn, *Economic Backwardness in Historical Perspective: A Book of Essays* (Cambridge: Harvard University Press, Belknap, 1962); and idem, *Continuity in History and Other Essays* (Cambridge: Harvard University Press, Belknap, 1968), pp. 257–343.

5. Gerschenkorn, *Economic Backwardness;* and idem, *Europe in the Russian Mirror: Four Lectures in Economic History* (Cambridge: At the University Press, 1970), esp. chap. 4.

6. Moore, *Social Origins;* and idem, *Reflections on the Causes of Human Misery, and upon Certain Proposals to Eliminate Them* (Boston: Beacon, 1970).

7. Kautsky, *Political Consequences of Modernization*.

8. Kossok, *Studien über die Revolution;* and idem, *Studien zur vergleichenden Revolutionsgeschichte*.

9. J. M. Wiener, "Review of Reviews: *Social Origins of Dictatorship and Democracy*, by Barrington Moore, Jr.," *History and Theory*, 15, no. 2 (1976): 146–175.

10. S. M. Lipset and S. Rokkan (eds.)) *Party Systems and Voter Alignments: Cross-National Perspectives* (New York: Free Press, 1967); and S. Rokkan, *Citizens, Elections, and Parties: Approaches to the Comparative Study of the Processes of Development* (Oslo: Universitetsforlaget, 1970).

11. See Rokkan, *Citizens, Elections, and Parties;* and idem, "Dimensions of State Formation and Nation-Building," in C. Tilly (ed.), *The Formation of National States in Western Europe* (Princeton: Princeton University Press, 1975), pp. 562–600.

12. T. Skocpol, "Explaining Revolutions: In Quest of a Social-Structural Approach," in L. A. Coser and O. N. Larsen (eds.), *The Uses of Controversy in Sociology* (New York: Free Press, 1976), pp. 155–179; idem, "A Critical Review of Barrington Moore's *Social Origins of Dictatorship and Democracy," Politics and Society,* 4, no. 1 (1973): 30–33; E. K. Trimberger, "A Theory of Elite Revolutions," *Studies in Comparative International Developments,* 7, no. 3 (1972): 191–207; and idem, *Revolution from Above* (New Brunswick: Transaction Press, 1977).

One of the most sophisticated recent analyses of class structure that explains the diversity of seemingly similar class structures is R. Brenner, "Agrarian Class Structure and Economic Development in Pre-Industrial Europe," *Past and Present,* no. 70 (1976): 30–75.

13. See Trimberger, *Revolution from Above.*

14. On the Turkish and Japanese revolutions see ibid.; and the references cited in notes 54 and 82–87 below.

15. On Egypt see P. T. Vatikiotis (ed.), *Egypt since the Revolution* (London: George Allen & Unwin, 1968); and idem (ed.), *Revolution in the Middle East* (London: George Allen & Unwin, 1972). On Peru see D. S. Palmer, *Revolution from Above: Military, Government, and Population Participation in Peru, 1968–1972* (Ithaca: Cornell University, Latin American Studies Program, 1973); and K. J. Middlebrook and D. S. Palmer, *Military Government and Political Development: Lessons from Peru,* Sage Professional Papers in Comparative Politics, no. 01–054 (Beverly Hills, 1975).

16. See for a good summary and analysis C. A. Gibb, "Leadership," in G. Lindsey and E. Aronson (eds.), *The Handbook of Social Psychology,* 2d ed. (Reading: Addison-Wesley, 1968), 4:204–282.

17. See Chapter 5.

18. On the general characteristics of the European revolutionary process and outcomes see C. Tilly, "Reflections on the History of European State-Making," in Tilly, *Formation of National States,* pp. 3–83; Rokkan, "Dimensions of State Formation;" and idem, "Cities, States, and Nations: A Dimensional Model for the Study of Contrasts in Development," in S. N. Eisenstadt and S. Rokkan (eds.), *Building States and Nations,* 2 vols. (Beverly Hills: Sage, 1973), 1:73–99.

19. On the outcomes of the English Revolution see J. H. Plumb, *The Growth of Political Stability in England, 1675–1725* (New York: Macmillan, 1967); D. Little, *Religion, Order, and Law: A Study in Pre-Revolutionary England* (New York: Harper & Row, 1969); H. C. Schröder, "Die amerikanische und die englische Revolution in vergleichender Perspektive," in H. U. Wehler (ed.), *200 Jahre amerikanische Revolution und moderne Revolutionsforschung* (Göttingen: Vandenhoeck & Ruprecht, 1976), pp.

9–37; and D. W. Hanson, *From Kingdom to Commonwealth: The Development of Civil Consciousness in English Political Thought* (Cambridge: Harvard University Press, 1970).

20. On the shift in the ruling class in England see L. Stone, *The Causes of the English Revolution, 1529–1642* (London: Routledge & Kegan Paul, 1972).

21. C. Wilson, *England's Apprenticeship, 1603–1763* (London: Longmans, Green, 1965).

22. On the general trend of postrevolutionary development in England see Plumb, *Growth of Political Stability;* H. Berkin, *The Origins of Modern English Society, 1780–1880* (London: Routledge & Kegan Paul, 1969); and D. A. Baugh (ed.), *Aristocratic Government in Eighteenth Century England: The Foundation of Stability* (New York: New Viewpoints, 1975).

23. E. Kamenka and R. S. Neale (eds.), *Feudalism, Capitalism, and Beyond* (London: Arnold, 1975); and F. Braudel, *Capitalism and Material Life, 1400–1800* (New York: Harper & Row, 1973).

24. R. R. Palmer, *The Age of the Democratic Revolution: A Political History of Europe and America, 1760–1800* (Princeton: Princeton University Press, 1959); T. K. Derry, "Scandinavia," in *The New Cambridge Modern History,* C. W. Crowley (ed.) (Cambridge: At the University Press, 1965), 9:480–494; J. A. van Houtte, "The Low Countries," in ibid., pp. 462–480; A. Cobban, *Aspects of the French Revolution* (New York: Norton, 1970); and G. Rudé, *Revolutionary Europe, 1783–1815* (New York: Harper & Row, 1975).

25. On the specific characteristics of the French regime see, in addition to the references cited in note 4 to Chapter 6 and in note 6 to Chapter 7, P. Goubert, *The Ancien Regime: French Society, 1600–1750* (New York: Harper & Row, 1974); and F. L. Ford, *Robe and Sword* (New York: Harper & Row, 1965). From among the many discussions of the processes and outcomes of the French Revolution see the literature cited in note 4 to Chapter 6; see also J. McManners, "The Historiography of the French Revolution," in *The New Cambridge Modern History,* A Goodwin (ed.), (Cambridge: At the University Press, 1965), 8:618–652; A Goodwin, "Reform and Revolution in France: October 1789–February 1793," in ibid., pp. 680–713; J. Kaplow (ed.), *New Perspectives on the French Revolution: Readings in Historical Sociology* (New York: Wiley, 1965); G. Ziebura (ed.), *Wirtschaft und Gesellschaft in Frankreich seit 1789* (Cologne: Kiepenheuer & Witsch, 1971); G. E. Rudé, "The Outbreak of the French Revolution," in *New Cambridge Modern History,* 8:653–679; D. Thomson, *Democracy in France* (New York: Oxford University Press, 1946); G. Dupeaux, *French Society, 1789–1970* (New York: Harper & Row, 1976); S. Hoffmann, C. Kindleberger, L. Wylie, J. Pitts, J. Doreselle, and F. Gogvel, *In Search of France* (Cambridge: Harvard University Press, 1963); and H. Luethy, *France Against Herself: A Perceptive Study of France's Past, Her Politics, and Her Unending Crises* (New York: Praeger, 1955).

26. On the American Revolution see the works cited in note 3 to Chapter 6 and in note 5 to Chapter 7; see also B. Bailyn, *The Ideological Origins of the American Revolution* (Cambridge: Harvard University Press, Belknap, 1967); Schröder, "Die amerikanische und die englische Revolution"; H. Gerstenberger, "Revolution und Staatsgrundung," in Wehler, *200 Jahre amerikanische Revolution,* pp. 38–58; and H. Wellenreuther, "The Wisdom to Secure the Entire, Absolute, and Immediate Dependency of the Colonies: Überlegungen zum Verhältnis zwischen der Krone und den englischen Kolonien in Nordamerika, 1689 bis 1776," in ibid., pp. 59–75. On the Revolt of the Netherlands see H. Schilling, "Der Aufstand der Niederlande: Bürgerliche Revolution oder Elitenkonflikt?" in ibid., pp. 177–231; and J. E. Ellemers, "The Revolt of the Netherlands: The Part Played by Religion in the Process of Nation-Building," *Social Compass,* 14 (1967): 93–103.

27. See Bailyn, *Ideological Origins;* and Palmer, *Age of the Democratic Revolution.*

28. R. N. Bellah, *Beyond Belief* (New York: Harper & Row, 1970), pp. 168–193; idem, "Religion and the Legitimation of the American Republic," mimeographed (Berkeley, Calif., 1976), pp. 1–21; S. M. Lipset, *The First New Nation* (New York: Basic Books, 1963); and idem, *Revolution and Counterrevolution: Change and Persistence in Social Structures* (New York: Basic Books, 1968), esp. pp. 31–117.

29. See, in addition to the literature cited in note 1 to Chapter 6 and in note 3 to Chapter 7, A. Lijphart, *The Politics of Accommodation: Pluralism and Democracy in the Netherlands* (Berkeley: University of California Press, 1968); and H. Daalder, "Building Consociational Nations," in Eisenstadt and Rokkan, *Building States and Nations,* 2:4-32.

30. Schilling, "Der Aufstand der Niederlande"; J. J. Woltjer, "De Vredemakers," *Tijdschrift voor Geschiedenis,* 89 (1976): 299–321; Ellemers, "Revolt of the Netherlands"; and R. Saage, "Probleme der Sozialgeschichte der amerikanischen Revolution," *Neue politische Literatur,* 19, no. 3 (1974): 310–339.

31. See, for instance, D. Hoerder, "Vom korporativen zum liberalen Eigentumsbegriff: Ein Element der amerikanischen Revolution," in Wehler, *200 Jahre amerikanische Revolution,* pp. 76–100; and a more critical work, R. N. Bellah, *The Broken Covenant.*

32. On the structure of the traditional Chinese center and society see Chapter 5.

33. On the first phase of the Chinese Revolution see especially F. Wakeman, Jr., *The Fall of Imperial China* (New York: Free Press, 1975); F. Schurmann and O. Schell (eds.), *Imperial China: The Decline of the Last Dynasty and the Origins of Modern China, the Eighteenth and Nineteenth Centuries* (New York: Random House, Vintage, 1967); idem, *Republican China: Nationalism, War, and the Rise of Communism, 1911–1949* (New York: Random House, Vintage, 1968); M. C. Wright (ed.), *China in Revolution: The First Phase, 1900–1913* (New Haven: Yale University

Press, 1968); J. K. Fairbank, E. O. Reischauer, and A. M. Craig, *A History of East Asian Civilization*, vol. 2, *East Asia, the Modern Transformation* (Boston: Houghton Mifflin, 1965), chaps. 5, 8; and M. B. Rankin, *Early Chinese Revolution: Radical Intellectuals in Shanghai and Chekiang, 1902–1911* (Cambridge: Harvard University Press, 1971).

34. On the whole cycle of Chinese Revolution see, in addition to the works cited in note 33 above: Ping-ti Ho and Tang Tsou (eds.), *China's Heritage and the Communist Political System: China in Crisis*, 2 vols. (Chicago: University of Chicago Press, 1968); and D. Milton, N. Milton, and F. Schurmann (eds.), *People's China: Social Experimentation, Politics, and Entry onto the World Scene, 1966–1972* (New York: Random House, Vintage, 1974).

35. On this phase see L. W. Pye, *Warlord Politics* (New York: Praeger, 1971); Z. Schiffrin, *Sun Yat-sen and the Origins of the Chinese Revolution* (Berkeley: Univ. of California Press, 1968); Wright, *China in Revolution;* and F. Wakeman, Jr., and C. Grant (eds.), *Conflict and Control in Late Imperial China* (Berkeley: University of California Press, 1975). In this collection see especially F. Wakeman, Jr., "Introduction: The Evolution of Local Control in Late Imperial China," pp. 1–25; idem, "Localism and Loyalism during the Ch'ing Conquest of Kiangnan: The Tragedy of Chian-yin," pp. 43–85; and J. Dennerline, "Fiscal Reform and Local Control: The Gentry-Bureaucratic Alliance Survives the Conquest," pp. 86–120.

36. See Schurmann and Schell, *Republican China;* M. J. T. Shieh, *The Kuomintang: Selected Historical Documents* (New York: St. John's University Press, 1970); and Ho and Tsou, *China's Heritage*, esp. 1: chap. 3.

37. See M. Elvin, "The Gentry Democracy in Chinese Shanghai, 1905–14," in J. Gray (ed.), *Modern China's Search for a Political Form* (New York: Oxford University Press, 1969), pp. 41–65; J. Chesneaux, "The Federalist Movement in China, 1920–3," in ibid., pp. 96–137; P. Cavendish, "The 'New China' of the Kuomintang," in ibid., pp. 138–186; and J. E. Sheridan, *China in Disintegration: The Republican Era in Chinese History, 1912–1949* (New York: Free Press, 1975).

38. On the general course of the Chinese Communist Revolution see the references cited in notes 33–37 above. See also D. W. Treagold (ed.), *Societ and Chinese Communism: Similarities and Differences* (Seattle: University of Washington Press, 1967); J. M. H. Lindbeck (ed.), *China: Management of a Revolutionary Society* (Seattle: University of Washington Press, 1971); and T. H. E. Chen (ed.), *The Chinese Communist Regime: Documents and Commentary* (New York: Praeger, 1967).

39. On this aspect of Chinese revolutionary movements see M. Selden, *The Yenan Way in Revolutionary China* (Cambridge: Harvard University Press, 1971); D. Wilson, *The Long March, 1935* (New York: Avon, 1971); W. Hinton, *Fanshen: A Documentary of Revolution in a Chinese Village* (New York: Random House, Vintage, 1968); R. C. North and I. de Sola Pool, "Kuomintang and Chinese Communist Elites," in H. D. Lass-

well and D. Lerner (eds.), *World Revolutionary Elites* (Cambridge: MIT Press, 1966), pp. 319–455; J. MacDonald, "The Performance of the Cadres," in Gray, *Modern China's Search,* pp. 268–298; and E. Friedmann, *Backward toward Revolution: The Chinese Revolutionary Party* (Berkeley: University of California Press, 1974).

40. J. W. Lewis (ed.), *Party Leadership and Revolutionary Power in China* (Cambridge: At the University Press, 1970); R. A. Scalapino (ed.), *Elites in the People's Republic of China* (Seattle: University of Washington Press, 1972); and F. Schurmann, *Ideology and Organization in Communist China,* 2d ed., enl. (Berkeley: University of California Press, 1968); "Two Billion People: A Survey of Asia," *The Economist* (London), May 7, 1977.

41. On the basic ideological concepts of the cultural revolutions see F. Wakeman, Jr., *History and Will: Philosophical Perspectives of Mae Tse-tung's Thought* (Berkeley: University of California Press, 1973); J. B. Starr, "Conceptual Foundations of Mao Tse-tung's Theory of Continuous Revolution," *Asian Survey,* 11, no. 6 (1971): 610–628; and R. MacFarquhar, *The Origins of the Cultural Revolution* (New York: Columbia University Press, 1974). On the continuity between Confucian and Maoist thought, see T. A. Metzger, *Escape from Predicament: Neo-Confucianism and China's Evolving Political Culture* (New York: Columbia University Press, 1977).

42. See Lewis, *Party Leadership,* and "Two Billion People."

43. The outcomes of the Russian Revolution are discussed in E. J. Simmons (ed.), *Continuity and Change in Russian Soviet Thought* (Cambridge: Harvard University Press, 1955); R. Pipes (ed.), *Revolutionary Russia* (Cambridge: Harvard University Press, 1968); C. E. Black (ed.), *The Transformation of Russian Society: Aspects of Social Change since 1861* (Cambridge: Harvard University Press, 1960); E. H. Carr, *A History of Soviet Russia: The Bolshevik Revolution, 1917–1923,* 3 vols. (New York: Macmillan, 1950–1953); idem, *A History of Soviet Russia: The Interregnum, 1923–1924* (New York: Macmillan, 1965); A. Inkeles, *Social Change in Soviet Russia* (Cambridge: Harvard University Press, 1968); and A. Inkeles and K. Geiger (eds.), *Soviet Society: A Book of Readings* (Boston: Houghton Mifflin, 1961).

44. About the vicissitudes suffered by different revolutionary groups in Tsarist Russia see A. Yarmolinsky, *Road to Revolution: A Century of Russian Radicalism* (New York: Macmillan, 1959); R. Wortman, *The Crisis of Russian Populism* (Cambridge: At the University Press, 1967); M. Raeff, *Origins of the Russian Intelligentsia: The Eighteenth-Century Nobility* (New York: Harcourt, Brace, 1966); J. L. H. Keep, *The Rise of Social Democracy in Russia* (Oxford: Clarendon, 1963); G. Fischer, *Russian Liberalism: From Gentry to Intelligentsia* (Cambridge: Harvard University Press, 1958); E. Lampert, *Sons Against Fathers: Studies in Russian Radicalism and Revolution* (Oxford: Clarendon, 1965); and idem, *Studies in Rebellion* (London: Routledge & Kegan Paul, 1957).

45. See the references cited in note 43 above.

46. Z. K. Brzezinski, *Ideology and Power in Soviet Politics* (New York: Praeger, 1962); L. Schapiro, "The Bolsheviks and Their Rivals," in H. Lubasz (ed.), *Revolutions in Modern European History* (New York: Macmillan, 1966), pp. 119–128; and T. H. von Laue, *Why Lenin? Why Stalin?* (Philadelphia: Lippincott, 1964), pp. 76ff.

47. On the structure of the Communist party and the economy see L. Schapiro, *The Communist Party of the Soviet Union* (New York: Random House, 1960); J. A. Armstrong, *Ideology, Politics, and Government in the Soviet Union* (New York: Praeger, 1962); and A. Nove, *Was Stalin Really Necessary? Some Problems of Soviet Political Economy* (London: Allen & Unwin, 1964).

48. On Vietnam see the references cited in notes 14 and 43 to Chapter 7; see especially W. F. Villa (ed.), *Aspects of Vietnamese History*, Asian Studies at Hawaii, no. 8 (Honolulu: University Press of Hawaii, 1973).

49. On the Kemalist Revolution see S. Mardin, "Ideology and Religion in the Turkish Revolution," *International Journal of Middle East Studies*, 2, no. 3 (1971): 197–211.

50. On the structure of the Ottoman Empire see H. Inalcik, *The Ottoman Empire: The Classical Age, 1300–1600* (London: Weidenfeld & Nicolson, 1973); idem, "The Nature of Traditional Society: Turkey," in R. Ward and D. Rustow (eds.), *Political Modernization in Japan and Turkey* (Princeton: Princeton University Press, 1964), pp. 42–63; S. Mardin, "Power, Civil Society, and Culture in the Ottoman Empire," *Comparative Studies in Society and History*, 11 (June 1969): 258–281; C. Keydar, "The Dissolution of the Asiatic Mode of Production," *Economy and Society*, 5, no. 2 (1976): 178–197; and K. H. Karpat (ed.), *The Ottoman State and Its Place in World History* (Leiden: E. J. Brill, 1974).

51. On the modernization process in Turkey see Ward and Rustow, *Japan and Turkey*; M. Ma'oz, *Ottoman Reform in Syria and Palestine, 1840–1861* (New York: Oxford University Press, 1968); Keydar, "Dissolution of the Asiatic Mode of Production"; S. Mardin, *The Genesis of Young Ottoman Thought* (Princeton: Princeton University Press, 1962); and idem, "Ottoman Empire."

52. See Mardin, "Ideology and Religion."

53. M. Heper, "Political Modernization as Reflected in Bureaucratic Change: The Turkish Bureaucracy and a 'Historical Bureaucratic Empire' Tradition," *International Journal of Middle East Studies*, 7 (1976): 507–521; idem, "The Recalcitrance of the Turkish Public Bureaucracy to 'Bourgeois Politics': A Multi-Factor Political Stratification Analysis," *Middle East Journal*, 30, no. 4 (Autumn 1976), pp. 485–500; and idem, "Transformation of Charisma into a Political Paradigm: Ataturkism in Turkey," mimeographed (Bogazici University, Istanbul, 1976).

54. See K. Karpat, *Turkish Politics: The Transition to a Multi-Party System* (Princeton: Princeton University Press, 1952); and I. Sunar, *State and Society in the Politics of Turkey's Development* (Ankara: Ankara University, Faculty of Political Sciences, 1974).

55. A. de Tocqueville, *The Old Regime and the French Revolution* (Garden City: Doubleday, 1955).

56. These concepts, as well as the concept of codes, are developed in S. N. Eisenstadt, "Post-Traditional Societies and the Continuity and Reconstruction of Tradition," in Eisenstadt, *Post-Traditional Societies*, pp. 1–29; see also Chapter 4.

57. This paradoxical relation among different aspects of the reconstruction of traditions is analyzed in ibid.

58. The dynamics of traditions are more fully analyzed in S. N. Eisenstadt, "Some Observations on the Dynamics of Tradition," *Comparative Studies in Society and History*, 11, no. 4 (October 1969), 451–475; and idem, *Tradition, Change, and Modernity* (New York: Wiley, 1973), chap. 14.

59. The different constellations of incorporation of symbols of protest by coercive and noncoercive elites are analyzed in S. N. Eisenstadt and Y. Azmon (eds.), *Socialism and Tradition* (New York: Humanities, 1975). The relation among revolution, coerciveness, and totalitarianism is discussed in A. Cavicchia Scalamonti, "Rivoluzione e totalitarismo," in L. Pellicani (ed.), *Sociologia delle rivoluzioni* (Naples: Guide, 1976), pp. 155–180; and E. V. Trapanese, "'Rivoluzione e despotismo burocratico," in ibid., pp. 233–254. See also E. Allardt, "Revolutionary Ideologies as Agents of Cultural and Structural Change," in N. Hammond (ed.), *Social Science and the New Societies: Problems in Cross-Cultural Research and Theory Building* (East Lansing: Michigan State University, Social Science Research Bureau, 1973), pp. 149–171; and P. Worsley, "The Revolutionary Party as an Agency of Social Change (or the Politics of Mah jong)," in ibid., pp. 217–245.

60. See pages 231–32 for an analysis of the Russian case.

61. A very good case study analysis of one such elite is K. Jowitt, *Revolutionary Breakthroughs and National Development: The Case of Romania, 1945–1965* (Beverly Hills: University of California Press, 1971).

62. On the Yugoslav Revolution see the references in B. Denitch, "Violence and Social Change in the Yugoslav Revolution," *Comparative Politics*, 8, no. 3 (1976): 465–478; and idem, *The Legitimation of a Revolution* (New Haven: Yale University Press, 1976).

63. On other Eastern European revolutions see H. Seton-Watson, *The East European Revolution* (London: Methuen, 1952); and idem, *Nationalism and Communism: Essays, 1946–63* (London: Methuen, 1964).

64. See the references cited in notes 24 and 25 above; see also R. J. Mundt, "The Republic Which Divides Us Least: The French Crisis of 1870–75," in G. A. Almond, S. C. Flanagan, and R. J. Mundt (eds.), *Crisis, Choice, and Change* (Boston: Little, Brown, 1973), pp. 224–284.

65. See the literature on the Chinese Revolution cited in notes 33–42 above.

66. On Germany in and after 1848 see the references cited in notes 15 and 33 to Chapter 7; see also L. B. Namier, *1848: The Revolution of the Intellectuals* (Garden City: Doubleday, Anchor, 1964); H. U. Wehler (ed.), *Moderne deutsche Sozialgeschichte* (Cologne: Kiepenheuer & Witsch,

1968); A. Dorpalen, "Die Revolutionen von 1848," in T. Schieder (ed.), *Revolution und Gesellschaft* (Freiburg im Breisgau: Herder, 1973), pp. 97–116; A. Gerschenkorn, *Bread and Democracy in Germany* (New York: Fertig, 1966); W. O. Henderson, *The State and the Industrial Revolution in Prussia, 1740–1870* (Liverpool: Liverpool University Press, 1958); G. Mann, *The History of Germany since 1789*, trans. M. Jackson (London: Chatto & Windus, 1968). On other Eastern European revolutions see Seton-Watson, *East European Revolution;* R. L. Wolff, *The Balkans in Our Time* (New York: Norton, 1967), chaps. 5–15; and S. Fischer-Galati (ed.), *Man, State, and Society in East European History* (New York: Praeger, 1970), chaps. 26, 43.

67. On Italy see A. W. Salomone (ed.), *Italy from the Risorgimento to Fascism* (Garden City: Doubleday, Anchor, 1970).

68. On the analysis of fascism see S. J. Wolf (ed.), *The Nature of Fascism* (New York: Random House, Vintage, 1969); E. Nolte, *Three Faces of Fascism* (New York: Holt, Rinehart & Winston, 1966); idem (ed.), *Theorien über den Fascismus* (Cologne: Kiepenheuer & Witsch, 1970); H. A. Turner, Jr. (ed.), *Reappraisals of Fascism* (New York: New Viewpoints, 1975); A. J. Gregor, "Fascism and Comparative Politics," *Comparative Political Studies*, 9, no. 2 (1976): 207–223; and see also B. Hagfvet and S. Rokkan, "Preconditions of Fascist Victory: Towards a Geoeconomic Model for the Explanation of Violent Breakdowns of Competitive Mass Politics," mimeographed draft (Bergen, 1976); G. Germani, Autoritarismo, Faschismo e Classi Sociali (Bologna: Il Molino).

69. On ancient Jewish history see R. de Vaux, *Ancient Israel* (London: Downton, Longman & Todd, 1961); and H. H. Ben-Sasson (ed.), *A History of the Jewish People* (Cambridge: Harvard University Press, 1976), pt. 1. For a general analysis of Jewish history see ibid.; idem (ed.), *Jewish Society through the Ages* (London: Mitchell, 1971); and V. Nikiprowetzky, "Ethical Monotheism," *Daedalus*, Spring 1975, pp. 69–90.

70. On the period of the Second Temple see Ben-Sasson, *History of the Jewish People*, pt. 3; S. Safrai and M. Stern (eds.), *The Jewish People in the First Century* (The Hague: Van Gorcum, 1974), vol. 1; and A. Momigliano, "Greeks, Jews, and Romans from Antiochus III to Pompey," in A. Momigliano (ed.), *Alien Wisdom, The Limits of Hellenization* (Cambridge: At the University Press, 1975), pp. 97–122.

71. On the Messianic elements in Jewish tradition see G. Scholem, *The Messianic Idea in Judaism and Other Essays on Jewish Spirituality* (New York: Schocken, 1971); idem, *Major Trends in Jewish Mysticism* (New York: Schocken, 1941); and Momigliano, "Greeks, Jews, and Romans."

72. On this special characteristic of the Jewish nation see J. Kaufman, *Gola ve nechar* [Diaspora and exile] (Tel Aviv: Dvir, 1935).

73. On the pattern of struggle in Jewish society see Safrai and Stern, *The Jewish People in the First Century*, vol. 1; and Momigliano, "Greeks, Jews, and Romans."

74. On the Sages and the Law see Ben-Sasson, *History of the Jewish People,*

pt. 4; and E. E. Urbach, *The Sages, Their Concepts, and Beliefs,* 2 vols. (Jerusalem: Magness, 1975).

75. On medieval Jewish society see Ben-Sasson, *History of the Jewish People,* pt. 5; and J. Katz, *Tradition and Crisis* (New York: Free Press, 1962).

76. On Jewish emancipation see Ben-Sasson, *History of the Jewish People,* pt. 6; and J. Katz, *Emancipation and Assimilation: Studies in Modern Jewish History* (London: Gregg, 1972).

77. See G. G. Scholem, *Sabbatai Sevi: The Mystical Messiah* (Princeton: Princeton University Press, 1973); and idem, *Major Trends.*

78. See J. Katz, *Out of the Ghetto: The Social Background of Jewish Emancipation, 1770–1870* (Cambridge: Harvard University Press, 1973); and idem, *Emancipation and Assimilation.*

79. On the origins of Zionism see D. Vital, *The Origins of Zionism* (New York: Oxford University Press, 1975); and S. N. Eisenstadt, *Israeli Society* (New York: Basic Books, 1968), chap. 1.

80. On the Yishuv and its development see Eisenstadt, *Israeli Society;* and D. Horwitz and M. Lissak, "Ideology and Politics in the Yishuv," *Jerusalem Quarterly,* no. 2 (1977): 12–27.

81. On the Meiji Restoration see P. Akamatsu, *Meiji 1868* (New York: Harper & Row, 1972); H. Norman, *Japan's Emergence as a Modern State* (New York: Institute of Pacific Relations, 1940); A. M. Craig, *Choshu in the Meiji Restoration* (Cambridge: Harvard University Press, 1961); and H. Kohachiro Takahashi, "Die Meiji-Restauration in Japan und die französische Revolution; Ein historischer Vergleich unter dem Gesichtspunkt der Agrarfrage und der Bauernbewegung," in Kossok, *Studien über die Revolution,* pp. 303–312.

82. On the outcomes of the Meiji Restoration see Akamatsu, *Meiji 1868;* Norman, *Japan's Emergence;* R. A. Scalapino, "Japan between Traditionalism and Democracy," in S. Neumann (ed.), *Modern Political Parties* (Chicago: University of Chicago Press, 1965), pp. 305–353; Fairbank et al., *East Asia,* pp. 408–442; R. P. Dore (ed.), *Aspects of Social Change in Modern Japan* (Princeton: Princeton University Press, 1967); R. Ward (ed.), *Political Development in Modern Japan* (Princeton: Princeton University Press, 1968); and W. W. Lockwood (ed.), *The State and Economic Entrepreneurs in Japan* (Princeton: Princeton University Press, 1965).

83. M. Earl, *Emperor and Nation in Japan* (Seattle: University of Washington Press, 1964); and M. Maruyama, *Thought and Behavior in Modern Japanese Politics* (New York: Oxford University Press, 1964).

84. See R. Huntsberry, "Myth and Values in Japanese Society," rev. ed., mimeographed (Wesleyan University, 1975; originally submitted as a doctoral dissertation to the Harvard Divinity School in 1969); and R. N. Bellah, *Tokugawa Religion* (New York: Free Press, 1956). On the ideology of the Meiji see Akamatsu, *Meiji 1868;* K. D. Magarey, *Emperor and Nation in Japan: Political Thinkers of the Tokugawa Period* (Seattle: University of Washington Press, 1964); and Maruyama, *Modern Japanese Politics.*

Chapter 9. Beyond Classical Revolutions—Processes of Change and Revolutions in Neopatrimonial Societies

1. INTRODUCTION

The preceding analysis attempted to explain the outcomes of real revolutions. But, as we saw in Chapters 6 and 7, the processes of social change and transformation attendant on modernization, as well as revolutionary ideologies, symbols, and movements, were not confined to the societies we analyzed: they could characterize any society given the right conditions. In most societies, however, patterns of transformation of the social and political structures as well as movements of protest and would-be revolutions have not followed the true revolutionary model.

It is beyond the scope of this book to analyze patterns of transformation and all such different movements even to the limited extent that we analyzed the true revolutions. We wish, however, to make some broad comparisons of these patterns of transformation and movements of protest or rebellion. Thus, in this chapter we analyze briefly those modern and modernizing societies whose basic cultural orientations and structural characteristics differed from the Imperial or Imperial-feudal patterns and in many of which the impact of modernization or the breakthrough to modernity occurred under conditions different from those in the societies that experienced true revolution. (In Chapter 10 we analyze selected revolutionary movements in relatively mature postrevolutionary societies.)

Our procedure is first to analyze the processes of change in nonrevolutionary societies or situations and to compare them to processes of change in pure revolutionary societies. Second, we analyze how such variables as the structure of centers and the solidarity of elites shaped the contours of the processes of change in the former group of societies. We also address ourselves to the problem of whether conditions ever arise in these societies that are conducive to phenomena similar to the so-called true revolutions. In this context we analyze briefly the Mexican, Bolivian, and Cuban revolutions, as well as the recent overthrow of Portugal's authoritarian regime.

2. INCORPORATION OF PATRIMONIAL SOCIETIES IN THE MODERN INTERNATIONAL SYSTEMS

Let us consider at the outset the modernizing, potentially revolutionary experiences of those societies whose basic structural characteristics and cultural orientations differed significantly from the Imperial and Imperial-feudal pattern: Spain and Portugal;[1] most Latin American countries;[2] the majority of Middle Eastern societies; as well as most of the colonial societies of South Asia and Africa.[3] All these societies were in their traditional or early modern periods much closer to the patrimonial than to the Imperial or Imperial-feudal model. (In Africa the tribal model predominated.) Indeed, very few colonial societies originally exhibited an Imperial or Imperial-feudal pattern—Vietnam is one exception, and as we noted above this Imperial society generated a pattern of change very close to that of the true revolution. India, with its unusual pattern of change in a traditional setting, constitutes a special case. Still, its political structure was essentially patrimonial.

By virtue of their patrimonial or semipatrimonial nature, these societies manifested a lack of structural distinction between center and periphery; a high degree of status segregation—weak countrywide status consciousness and little political articulation of strata; a low level of organizational and symbolic articulation of, and linkages among, movements of rebellion, protest, and central political struggle; as well as a relatively low level of symbolic articulation of the various collectivities. They were also characterized by a relatively low level of symbolic and institutional autonomy on the part of major secondary elites, by a high degree of embedment of these institutional enterpreneurs within ascriptive groups; and by weak autonomous linkages among these elites and between them and the centers.

The variations these patrimonial systems developed reflected their historical circumstances. Spain and Portugal were of course located within the European tradition. Latin America had a mixed Spanish and Indian heritage.[4] The colonial societies of the Middle East, South Asia, and

Southeast Asia were profoundly affected, as we shall see later, by several aspects of the colonial experience.[5]

Despite different historical and cultural backgrounds, these societies shared two characteristics of crucial importance from the point of view of our analysis. First—and in contrast to the traditional patrimonial regimes of the past—they all felt the impact of modernity; that is, they were all incorporated into the modern international systems. Within all of them there developed some variant of modern political and social processes— for instance, modern legitimation and accountability of the ruler and more differentiated social and economic structures. But, on the other hand, the patterns of these processes, the responses to the problems they generated, and the specific manner in which modernity was assimilated differed greatly from the modern European (and American), Russian, or Chinese revolutionary and postrevolutionary experiences (however much the latter served as models).

Truly enough, all these societies underwent far-reaching changes under the impact of incorporation into the emerging international systems and of revolutionary movements and ideology, many of which, like the wars of independence in Latin America and much later in other colonial countries, were designated as revolutions by their architects.[6] Internal changes of regime were often depicted as revolutionary by both their carriers and opponents. And postcolonial regimes like Algeria [7] defined themselves as revolutionary. In many of these societies there developed strong predilections to revolutionary symbolism, which were susceptible to the influence of international revolutionary movements as well as to the power politics of revolutionary states. In Eastern Europe,[8] so-called revolutionary communist regimes were forcefully imposed and sustained— with Yugoslavia and possibly Albania the only qualified exceptions.[9]

Solely in the cases of Mexico, Bolivia and Cuba [10] did revolutionary efforts approach the pure revolutionary pattern: most of the other societies discussed in this chapter developed a variant of what may be called the neopatrimonial pattern. This pattern did not manifest itself in the initial phases of modernization. It became apparent as these societies were gradually incorporated into the new, continually shifting, modern international systems and as they transformed themselves into modern societies. In most Latin American countries the neopatrimonial mode predominated despite the attraction of models of European and North American modernity.[11] In Spain and Portugal this pattern was hidden for a long time under the rhetoric of Western European ideologies, movements, and symbolism.[12] In postcolonial societies outside Latin America the neopatrimonial pattern crystallized upon the dissolution or breakdown of the ideological and/or institutional models inherited from the colonial period and from the struggle for independence.

3. STRUCTURAL CHARACTERISTICS OF NEOPATRIMONIAL SOCIETIES. CENTER-PERIPHERY RELATIONS AND THE POLITICAL PROCESS

The most important characteristics of neopatrimonial society were to be found in the structure of centers and in center-periphery relations.[13] In the majority of cases the center increasingly came to monopolize power and political resources, allowing little independent access by broader groups to such resources and to the positions controlling them. Such growing monopolization was associated with only minimal attempts by the centers to restructure the periphery (above all, center-periphery relations) or to create social institutions based on new constellations of ground rules and new structural principles.

Truly enough, in most neopatrimonial societies there tended to develop new types of modern, open centers. Nevertheless, this openness and the mutual impingement of center and periphery were coupled with relatively little structural and symbolic permeation or transformation of the periphery by the center. The distinctiveness of the center did not become connected—especially after the initial and relatively unsuccessful phase of attempting to institutionalize a nation-state or a revolutionary type of modern regime—with efforts to transform structurally and ideologically the periphery or to effect far-reaching changes in the periphery's conception of social order and relations to the center. The crystallization of the center generated neither a high degree of commitment to the social order nor new motivations for assuming more differentiated roles and developing the discipline necessary for their fulfillment. Thus, the distinctiveness of the center and of its relations to the periphery was very similar to that characteristic of traditional patrimonial regimes.

Concomitantly, most neopatrimonial societies experienced progressive weakening of autonomous access by different groups and strata to the formation of the symbols of the social and moral orders; conversely, the perception of the center as the sole or major repository of such—albeit given—values or symbols was strengthened. The conception of the social order as being created or formed by free, autonomous activities on the part of social groups (a conception implicit in the revolutionary and nation-state models) tended to lose ground and to be upheld only by marginal intellectual elites or revolutionary groups.

The importance of paternalistic distributive, accumulative, and extractive policies steadily increased in these societies.[14] The paternalistic orientation of such policies was evident in the fact that the center controlled most of the resources and mechanisms necessary for economic development. The center attempted to manipulate other sectors and accordingly monopolized the formulation of policies of welfare and distribution. Even when these policies paid lip service to development and even in Brazil, Tunisia, and Peru, where this orientation was not entirely nominal, they strongly stressed the extraction and distribution of resources and the increase of productivity within existing institutional frameworks rather than the creation, either by the center or by peripheral groups, of new types of resources and activities or the restructuring of economic and social units and their interrelations. Whatever restructuring occurred usually took place without the direct involvement of the centers.

Closely related to these characteristics of the center and of center-periphery relations were special features of the internal structure of the centers, of the channels of political struggle, and of political organization and processes. There was a growing movement away from more representative or constitutional types of political institutions and universalistic, bureaucratic, legal, and parliamentary frameworks (the heritage of the colonial period) and toward the executive branch of the government in general and within it to bureaucratic, army, or political cliques, to pressure groups, and to volatile populist parties or movements.[15] The rules that developed within these political frameworks tended to emphasize co-optation by, or denial of access to, the center and sources of distributive policies and bureaucratic positions. They tended to emphasize the center's mediation among the different cliques, and there was but little leeway for the development of autonomous access, by these or other broader groups, to such resources and positions.

Within these frameworks and coalitions, the major means of political struggle were increasingly co-optation or alteration of clientele and factional networks or corporatist, hierarchical arrangements. All of these were often coupled with populist appeals in the name of ascriptive symbols or values representing different ethnic, religious, or national communities. Such appeals frequently were especially vocal outbreaks that served to signal the inadequacy of existing patterns of co-optation.[16]

Whatever the organizational details, these shifts in the scope and channels of political struggle denoted changes in the meaning or functioning of many institutions—parliaments, parties, bureaucracies, and the judiciary—that dated from the colonial period or had been patterned after European or North American models.

Parliaments tended to become primary arenas of symbolic representation of the polity, or political socialization, and arenas of contest among various cliques not forums for autonomous representatives of different groups and strata. Parties tended more and more to be instruments for the forging of symbols of a collective identity and battlegrounds for the struggle over positions controlling the distribution of resources and patronage networks.

Voting and mobilization into parties usually served the function of broadening the base of access to such distributive positions; of creating new clientele and patronage systems, factional networks, or corporatist arrangements; or of signaling adherence to the symbols of polity represented by the center. Only to a lesser degree did voting or mobilization into parties serve to work out new principles of social distribution, to change the rules of access to the center, or to influence the center from independent power bases advocating a specific ideological orientation. Parties, the administration, and the army competed to perform these functions and to control the central resources.

These developments gave rise to the crystallization of unstable centers of power within which the army often occupied a strategic position as holder of actual power and as preserver of the fundamental symbols of the sociopolitical order. Often this strategic position of the army was reinforced by its crucial role as one of the major avenues of social mobility in general and mobility into the center in particular.[17] At the same time, mobile or uprooted marginal groups that could not gain access to existing channels of power and patronage became pockets of violence and insurgency.[18]

The broader groups of neopatrimonial societies were dependent upon the center in terms of regulating their own internal affairs that somehow bore on the wider societal framework. This dependence can be most clearly seen in the nature of the political demands that were made in these societies. The spread of the civilization of modernity engendered and intensified demands for the broadening of access to the center as a distributive agency; for control of the center and for effecting changes in its contents and symbols; and for creation of new types of social and cultural orders.

Even in the most modern areas of life these demands generally were based on ascriptive assumptions about rights of access to the center and/or of distribution of resources from the center. The claims to these rights were couched either in terms of actual power position (like those made by various bureaucratic or oligarchic groups) or in terms of membership in ethnic, religious, or national communities. They were but rarely related (as was the case in Japan) to the contribution of such groups to the center and its goals. Thus, economic demands and policies commonly focused on access to resources, power positions, and jobs rather than on the development of new types of economic activities and new status and class relations. In the educational field emphasis was increasingly placed on gaining or providing wider access to educational facilities as means of unconditional access to occupational positions. This tendency was closely related to the increase in administrative personnel and to the expansion of bureaucracies as mechanisms for co-opting wider groups into the modern patrimonial center—one of the most striking characteristic of neopatrimonial society.[19] Finally, demands for land redistribution and possibly expropriation became much more insistent while calls for diversification, and change in central economic frameworks lost urgency.[20]

4. PROCESSES OF CHANGE IN NEOPATRIMONIAL SOCIETIES. SOCIAL MOBILIZATION. RESTRUCTURING OF ELITES, INSTITUTIONAL SPHERES, AND SOCIAL HIERARCHIES

The neopatrimonial contours of these societies persisted despite far-reaching social, economic, and political changes within them. Moreover, the neopatrimonial modes of social action influenced crucial aspects of these changes—especially those aspects most closely related to the image of the true revolution.

The processes of social, economic, and political change that occurred as these societies were incorporated into the modern international systems took the form not only of coups, populist outbursts, population dislocations, or urbanization but also of extensive restructuring of the ground rules of social interaction and their major institutional derivatives.

First, all these societies experienced large-scale social mobilization.[21] This process resulted in the diversification of occupational groups, in the growth of middle sectors (especially lower urban and rural strata), and in the crystallization of new economic, political, and social structures (vast industrial complexes, broad bureaucratic organizations, and mass parties, for example). This process also furthered the restructuring of the basic contours of the major institutional spheres in the direction of widening their markets and diversifying units of production.

Second, there arose in these societies continuous processes of replacement and restructuring of elites. Traditional oligarchies gave way to a combination of capitalist, technocratic, and professional elites in the economic sphere and to populist and professional leaders in the political sphere. Beyond simple replacement of elites, increase in the number of elite positions, broadening of the bases of recruitment to these positions, and disembedment of elite members from the broader ascriptive strata took place. The military and portions of the bureaucracy were among the most important groups that became at least organizationally disembedded from ascriptive settings. These changes often were connected, as was the case in Egypt, Peru and Brazil, with the replacement and even physical destruction of older ruling and/or upper groups.[22]

Third, in close association with broadening the scope of the institutional spheres, far-reaching changes were effected in the organization of the economy and in the meanings of institutional complexes (witness the shift from a narrow, distributive, plantation system to an export-oriented, capitalist or state capitalist economy.[23]

Fourth, many of these processes converged in the restructuring of social hierarchies.[24] Social mobilization coincided with the multiplication of groups and strata and encouraged the tendency to adopt modern criteria of status: economic or educational achievement and/or political connections. Parallel to changes in the elite structure were far-reaching shifts in the centers of power that resulted in the dislocation of former upper groups. In many cases, there also took place large-scale redistribution of resources.

5. THE NONCOALESCENT PATTERN OF CHANGE IN NEOPATRIMONIAL SOCIETIES

All these changes were individually and collectively similar to those that took place in societies that experienced revolutionary transformation. Moreover, as the neopatrimonial societies were being incorporated into the modern international frameworks such changes developed along with both the preconditions for revolution and a strong tendency toward radicalism and revolutionary activity and symbolism, as well as yearning for revolutionary transformation. This tendency was reinforced by the importance of international revolutionary groups and leaders and by the emergence of strong revolutionary states.[25]

Nevertheless, none of these societies followed the pure revolutionary pattern. Processes of change within them rarely crystallized into a highly coalescent pattern of change. Thus, changes in many of the ground rules of social interaction did not impinge directly on the political sphere in a way that led to the repatterning of control over access to the center and to the major positions in the society; or the restructuring of the symbols of legitimation of the regime; or the replacement of one ruling group by another. At most, changes in the rules of distributive justice and their derivatives (especially the rules regarding the distribution of resources) sometimes became connected with changes in the access to power or with changes of regimes.

Changes in other ground rules of social interaction, such as restructuring the meaning of institutions and the boundaries of collectivities and their institutional derivatives, were but rarely connected with changes in the principles of the access to power and with the restructuring of the center-periphery relations. Likewise, far-reaching institutional changes in the economic sphere or the restructuring of social hierarchies did not necessarily result in the restructuring of the center even when such activities were initiated by the center. Moreover, when changes in the broader institutional spheres impinged on the center, they affected only one component of the center, usually the structure of elites.[26]

Developments in each institutional sphere were usually carried by different coalitions, and, just as in the traditional patrimonial systems, in the neopatrimonial societies diverse coalitions formed in connection with restructuring various institutional systems. While these coalitions often had close ties, only rarely were they effectively and permanently connected in new structural complexes. They did not always impinge together on the center and above all they did not necessarily give rise to the restructuring of the center. Significantly enough, efforts in this direction were most often initiated by external forces.

6. RESTRUCTURING OF ELITES AND POPULIST INCORPORATION

Changes in the political sphere itself did not always follow the same pattern or direction as political changes in the pure revolutionary situations. Of course, significant restructuring of the political sphere did occur in neopatrimonial regimes; for example, in the boundaries of societies; in the symbols and legitimation of regimes; and in the structure of the ruling class. Equally significant was the tendency toward the disembedment of the center of the state: initially dominated by oligarchic groups, it became an organizationally stronger and symbolically distinct unit although not an ideologically autonomous or (even when employing such rhetoric) a truly mobilizing one.[27]

Moreover, there was the replacement of elites, a process evident not only in the adoption of occupational criteria and the expansion of sources of recruitment but also in the disembedment of elites from broader ascriptive groups and strata. And there was the continual symbolic and, to a degree, institutional incorporation of broader strata into the political system. This incorporation took place by extending formal voting rights and by organizationally and symbolically including broader groups in the central frameworks. The most far-reaching attempts at such incorporation were made by the various populist regimes in Latin America (the Vargas regime in Brazil and the Peronist one in Argentina) and by the Nasserist regime in Egypt. These regimes usually were based on dramatic changes in the symbols of legitimation (commonly couched in revolutionary terms that emphasized greater incorporation and participation in the center); quite often, they were connected with changes in the composition of ruling groups as well as upper social echelons.[28]

Finally, regimes frequently changed. In some cases only the members of the ruling group were replaced; in many others, elite structure and policy changed, too. The most important such policy changes concerned the degree to which the ruling elites saw themselves as active promoters of social and economic transformation; the degree to which they viewed peripheral groups as potentially active participants in this process; and the relative predominance of right and left orientations (orientations that usually were closely related to the social class the elite purported to represent). These orientations greatly influenced the principles and types of social and economic policies—agrarian reform, land redistribution, nationalization of industry—formulated by the elites.

7. CONTINUITY OF PATRIMONIAL CENTER-PERIPHERY RELATIONS

To repeat, the neopatrimonial societies did not follow a pattern of highly coalescent change. Thus, changes in the composition and orientations of elites did not, as in the revolutionary societies, converge. To give a few illustrations, some of the more specialized (military or technocratic) groups—that exhibited internal, professional solidarity but were relatively segregated from the broader strata—formulated expansive policies based on strong development orientations and on co-optative tendencies. Such policies precluded wide participation in the political framework. The populist leaders who emerged in these societies under the pressure of new social forces often broadened the scope of symbolic participation, sometimes implementing new principles of distribution, but usually did not emphasize economic development or restructuring of the economic or educational spheres.

While many new elites called themselves revolutionary and often instituted far-reaching changes in the distribution of resources, they were rarely ready to extend the scope of participation of the periphery in the societal center or to restructure relations between the reconstructed center and the periphery. Accordingly, in such cases incorporation of broader strata into the center usually did not follow the revolutionary or nation-state model. In many cases incorporation was not effected by independent leaders or elites able to organize these broader groups into permanent, autonomous structures. Moreover, such incorporation was rarely connected with far-reaching changes either in the access of the major groups to the positions of control in the main institutional spheres and in the center or in the autonomous political articulation of these groups. More often, this process was connected with changes in the principles of distributive justice and in distributive policies.[29]

Similarly, innovations in the meaning and organizational scope of institutional spheres were infrequently accompanied by the restructuring of access to positions of control and of center-periphery relations. Even the creation of mass parties and wide-scale bureaucracies, or the opening up of new channels of mobility, or the replacement of old elites was generally not paralleled by extensive restructuring of center-periphery relations.

This lack of convergence occurred even in self-proclaimed revolutionary regimes like Algeria and Egypt. Thus, in Algeria the establishment of a new ruling class (itself constantly changing) was connected with the construction of a new, semipatrimonial center. This center was indeed able to establish new economic organizations and to achieve some land redistribution. But the access of broader groups to the center or to the major institutional positions of control was not expanded and new center-periphery relations were not created. In various Peruvian regimes and in Egypt under Nasser,[30] the more autonomous military elites alternated between attempts to mobilize the broader groups and to control the access of these groups to the center. Above all, they tended to extend patronage networks or to create corporatist arrangements rather than to encourage the autonomous organization of these groups. A similar pattern developed in Bolivia, where the elite brought to power by the Revolution of 1952 was unable to establish an organization that could effectively mobilize broader groups.[31]

8. PERSISTENCE OF PATRIMONIAL ORIENTATIONS

How can we explain the perpetuation in these societies of patrimonial characteristics and structures and the closely connected pattern of relatively noncoalescent change? Their patrimonial origins alone do not explain this persistence, which we shall examine in the light of our previous analysis. Note the persistence in the majority of these societies of the basic cultural orientations and models of social order that are associated with patrimonial regimes—in particular, the conceptions of authority and hierarchy and their institutional derivatives. The best studied examples of such continuity are Latin American. These analyses have shown that the corporatist-hierarchical model continues despite changes in regime and despite economic development and influences the pattern of noncoalescent change.[32] Similar continuities have been identified in the Maghreb, in India, and in Indonesia.[33]

The perpetuation of such codes and of their institutional derivatives was greatly facilitated by the fact that both internal processes in these societies and external forces generated conditions that preserved the structural conditions conducive to the maintenance of the patrimonial model. Specifically, these processes sustained the blocking of autonomous access of broader groups to the centers and to positions of power of control over the conversion of resources or weakened such access where it already existed, and sustained or weakened the relatively low level of autonomy of the major entrepreneurs as well as the segregative arrangements among elites.

The most important cases in which the potential access of wider groups to the center was limited are Spain and Portugal. Indeed, Spain and to a smaller degree Portugal best approached in the late fifteenth and sixteenth centuries the image of a strong Imperial center. Nevertheless, they ultimately approximated the patrimonial pattern. A variety of historical processes was at work here: reconquest of the Iberian peninsula, colonization of the Americas, and transformation of Iberian Catholicism by the Counterreformation. All these processes moved Spain and Portugal in a patrimonial direction because they weakened the pluralistic elements in Spanish and Portuguese society and the autonomy of their major institutional entrepreneurs and gave the center control over resources that were beyond the reach of the broader groups—especially after the exile or suppression of active, independent groups like the Jews and the Moors. Finally, because of their growing wealth, the Spanish and Portuguese centers lost their orientations toward mobilization of broader groups. They turned instead to distributive policies through which they could buy off the principal autonomous groups, thus increasing their dependence on the center and minimizing their own autonomy and reinforcing the segregative tendencies between themselves and other strata and among the latter.[34]

The major external factor that reinforced existing patrimonial orientations in many neopatrimonial societies was their mode of incorporation into the modern international systems. What was crucial was whether or not the breakthrough to modernity followed the three-part pattern necessary to the development of revolutionary preconditions: first, transition from a traditional, or closed, pattern of legitimation of political authority to an open one; second, transition to an open system of stratification (a class system); and, third, transition to a market economy in general and an industrial economy in particular.

In most of the societies we have been discussing the three features of the modern system did not arise simultaneously. Such uneven transitions took place primarily in situations of dependence. That is, these societies were incorporated into the international economic markets in a relatively nonautonomous way and without concomitant changes in the political or cultural spheres; conversely, incorporation into the international political system and restructuring of the political sphere were not connected with far-reaching, autonomous changes in the position of these societies in the international economic system.[35]

In their case, the tendencies toward segregation of institutional developments were reinforced. Such tendencies were very strong even in the Imperial or Imperial-feudal societies of China, Japan, or Vietnam. However, in these societies the Imperial pattern prevailed both in the restructuring of institutional arrangements and in the bringing together of different types of protest activities—rebellions, heterodoxies, and central political struggle—as well as in the reassertion by the center of control over responses to the international systems. Yet, even here, as we saw above, this mode of incorporation probably reinforced segregative tendencies. But in countries with patrimonial backgrounds and/or characteristics, as in Latin America or Southeast Asia, this mode of incorporation into the international systems reinforced inherent segregative tendencies without being met by strong countervailing forces.

Within this general pattern of incorporation of these societies into the modern international frameworks the colonial experience held special importance. First, colonial frameworks fostered the structural conditions conducive to the perpetuation of patrimonial regimes by restricting access to power and resources, which were to a very high degree monopolized by colonial rulers; by segregating access to various types of central resources (wealth, prestige, and power); and by controlling all the channels of conversion among them. Second, the colonial and postcolonial settings reinforced patrimonial tendencies by encouraging economic, political, and cultural dependence on the metropolis; these ties all minimized the autonomous access of broader groups to resources and thus weakened their power. Third, under colonialism the educational system served as yet another upholder of patrimonial orientations.[36]

9. STRUCTURE OF ELITES IN NEOPATRIMONIAL SOCIETIES. EMBEDMENT, LACK OF AUTONOMY, AND DISSOCIATION

All these social processes reinforced the institutional characteristics that constituted the most important carrier of the patrimonial modes of structuring social and instrumental activity and organization; namely, the high degree of embedment of institutional entrepreneurs and elites and the major integrative frameworks within ascriptive collectivities, and the low level of symbolic autonomy of such entrepreneurs as well as of their access to the center, to each other, and to the principal social groups. These characteristics persisted or became restructured via the far-reaching changes the neopatrimonial societies experienced. Such persistence or restructuring was most evident in the major social characteristics of the new type of seemingly independent, modern political entrepreneurs and leaders who were so crucial in the crystallization of the revolutionary processes in Europe, Russia, China, and Vietnam. Many years ago Harry Benda [37] pointed out that Southeast Asian elites were often composed of uprooted intellectuals: politicians who combined a relatively high degree of isolation from other groups, a small degree of internal solidarity, a very high degree of symbolic embedment within a broader ascriptive collectivity, and a lack of autonomous identity. Not surprisingly, such elites vacillated between dissociation from the broader groups and political bases, as well as from the representatives of the solidarity of the broader ascriptive collectivities, on the one hand, and embedment in such collectivities and lack of autonomy, on the other. At the same time, they were relatively isolated from the more functional—economic, technocratic, and professional—elites.[38] And the articulators of models of social and cultural order, who were not highly distinct from the articulators of the solidarity of the ascriptive communities, were rarely autonomous or capable of generating new conceptions of such order. The more independent and innovative among them were usually relegated to secondary positions.

The political elites were closely associated with the articulators of models of social and cultural order but attempted to dissociate themselves from them as well as from the functional elites. Moreover, they were inconsistent in relating to broader strata and were unable to establish autonomous, regulative frameworks and stable coalitions among themselves or with other groups.[39] Contact between the political leadership and the functional elites was not institutionalized. It was made either within the frameworks of the different bureaucracies, patronage networks, or corporatist arrangements or on the basis of participation in the broader ascriptive collectivities or populist movements.

10. VARIATIONS IN NEOPATRIMONIAL SOCIETIES

Differences among elites over time and across societies were related to their historical traditions and to their modernizing settings.[40] Of special importance was first the extent to which there existed oligarchic landowner and commercial elements or, as Southeast Asia, patrimonial, aristocratic elements. Second, significant differences existed in the degree to which there occurred, within the middle class proper, independent commercial, industrial, or professional groups, as in Ceylon and Malaysia, as opposed to bureaucratic, administrative elements. Third, variations existed in the degree to which economically independent groups were composed, as in Malaysia, Indonesia, and to some degree in Maghreb and Latin America, of foreign ethnic elements. Fourth, these societies varied in the relative importance and strength of different types (traditional, religious, or modern) of intellectual, professional, and technocratic groups and in their political orientations. Fifth, they differed in the self-conception and cohesiveness of elites and broader strata, especially in terms of modernizing and development goals and social orientations and ideologies, and in the degree of attachment of the population to the frameworks of the polity. Last, they differed greatly in the degree of uprootedness, of dislocation, of rural and urban groups alike.[41]

These characteristics influenced many aspects of social structure. For example, less organized parties and more restricted cliques tended to develop in societies with low levels of social mobilization; more continuous types of political organization in general and better organized parties in particular tended to develop in societies with a higher degree of social mobilization. Similarly, these societies witnessed public outbursts that were sporadic and unorganized (even if recurrent in the less developed societies) at one extreme and sustained, widespread populist movements at the other.

The combination of these characteristics also influenced the overall pattern of political struggle within these regimes. Thus, in societies with a low level of differentiation and a relatively strong traditional center, political struggle often focused on interclique relations, on the one hand, and the placation of groups able to stage ad hoc outbursts, on the other. As a rule, the political issues in these societies were segregated, discrete, and poorly articulated. In societies with higher levels of mobilization, political struggle generally centered on a wide range of problems or claims that were related to broader demands for incorporation into the center.

Similarly, these characteristics influenced coalition formation. Thus, in the less developed societies coalitions were rather similar to those in traditional patrimonial societies: small palace groups, loose cliques of army officers or bureaucrats, and leaders of family and regional groups. In the more developed neopatrimonial societies, coalitions comprised a potentially wider range of elite groups including professional and urban elites, as well as looser parties and populist leaders. Especially where the center was composed of weak and contending groups and the society manifested an unstable institutional framework, the army tended to play a very important role in political struggle.

11. STRUCTURE OF REBELLIONS, MOVEMENTS OF PROTEST, AND POLITICAL STRUGGLE IN NEOPATRIMONIAL SOCIETIES

The prevalence of the neopatrimonial pattern explains specific characteristics of the movements of protest and patterns of conflict that developed in neopatrimonial societies in conjunction with the processes of change analyzed above.

Although the majority of these societies displayed certain preconditions of revolution, none experienced a true revolution. The rebellions, millenarian movements, and religious heterodoxies that developed under colonial rule as well as after independence resembled such phenomena in traditional patrimonial societies in that they were otherworldly in their (institutional) orientations.[42] While many (especially postindependence) heterodox religious movements were *ideologically* this-worldly, this orientation was in essence populist. They focused on the creation or articulation of new symbols of distributive justice or of the political community, without necessarily giving rise to more organized or disciplined this-worldly activities or structures. Truly enough, a number of uprisings in export-oriented, agricultural countries or sectors did develop revolutionary orientations; that is, emphasis was placed on the transfer of power and on altering property relations in the agrarian sector.[43] But even such programs were couched in populist and distributive terms. More important from the point of view of our analysis is the fact that the most radical of these rebellions or movements rarely resulted in more differentiated, self-disciplined activities or organizations.

Despite the fact that the structural conditions attendant on modernization (growing social mobilization, the extension of markets, and the spread of modern media) were seemingly conducive to greater coalescence among the various rebellions, movements of heterodoxy, and central political struggles, such coalescence was uncommon. Needless to say, these different processes of rebellion, heterodoxy, and political struggle reinforced each other, but their effective, permanent merger was rare— and efforts in this direction were usually spearheaded by external revolutionary forces.[44] Analysis of the Indonesian Communist party shows that it was very difficult for this group to effect solid, long-term linkages with broader groups or with the central political struggle although the Communists easily undermined the stability of the regime.[45]

Similarly, institutional entrepreneurs—economic or educational—who established new institutional complexes or restructured old ones did not tend actively and steadily to participate in these movements or in the political processes generated by them or to contribute to the restructuring of political organization and ideology.[46]

Only in the colonial societies in the crucial phase of the struggle for independence did enduring and effective linkages among different movements develop.[47] However, after independence the ruling elites attempted again to segregate these movements. They tried to control and regulate the political process in such a way that it would not threaten their monopoly of central political power and would not enable the development among various groups of independent access to sources of society-wide power. Hence, most of these rulers attempted to minimize the possibility of the development of new political orientations, of demands for new types of political participation, or of new concepts of political symbolism. Insofar as new political concepts and organizations arose, the ruling elites strove to suppress or segregate them. Nevertheless, many of these elites did use revolutionary rhetoric and were sometimes closely allied with autonomous, internationally based revolutionary groups (preferably groups active abroad).

12. FRAGILITY OF NEOPATRIMONIAL REGIMES

The weakness of the leading elites in neopatrimonial societies was often manifest in their inability either to guide, mobilize, and control in a sustained way the groups that were mobilized in situations of upheaval and change or to be able to forge alliances with other elites. Hence, situations of political upheaval often resulted in stalemates among contending elites.

One of the most important outcomes of this pattern was a high degree of regime instability. In more extreme cases, civil wars broke out that had a very strong class and revolutionary ideology and symbolism based on an extreme emphasis on irreconcilable class conflict but unmediated, as in the revolutionary societies, by the activities of relatively autonomous political entrepreneurs who put these conflicts into broader sociopolitical terms and frameworks.[48]

The best illustrations of the combination of such developments can be found in the case of the Spanish Civil War,[49] in the aftermath of the Bolivian Revolution (analyzed later in this chapter),[50] and most dramatically in Chile.[51] Attempts at revolution and far-reaching change were not lacking, of course, in the history of Spain before the Civil War, and these efforts resulted in significant economic and social development. They were not, however, combined with far-reaching restructuring of the center, and the weakness of the Spanish elites fostered the development of a protracted class war. As Henry A. Landsberger and Tim MacDaniel have shown, it was partially the inability of the Allende government to control the highly mobilized masses that generated civil war and repression in Chile.[52]

13. COERCION, REPRESSION, EXPANSION, AND STABILITY IN NEOPATRIMONIAL SOCIETIES

The combination of regime instability and all these processes of change and movements of protest does not imply, as we have emphasized several times, that significant changes did not take place in these societies. What it does mean, however, is that the different dimensions of change did not follow the pattern that has been associated with the classical nation-state and revolutionary types of regimes. Similarly, the various processes of change in these societies took a rather specific direction in terms of the restructuring of institutional spheres, coercion, repression, and incorporation of new groups.

Let us now systematically compare the developments in neopatrimonial and postrevolutionary societies. In both cases such variables as the closure and rigidity of the center and its solidary relations with different groups shaped the institutional outcomes of the processes of change. As in so many other polities in general, and modern polities in particular, the regimes' capacity for expansion was influenced by the degree of its cohesion and autonomy; by its organizational experience; by the extent of its attachment to broader political units; as well as by the continuity of institutional frameworks.[53]

Economically, socially, and politically regressive policies (policies that minimize the expansive capacities of a society) tended to develop in societies with rather weak institutional structures and with ineffective, noncohesive, and relatively isolated elites and few strong nontraditional groups. Similarly, the chance for the development of regressive policies was greater wherever there existed a high degree of conflict among the major groups in the center and between them and broader groups and wherever relatively isolated and noncohesive elites predominated—elites that attempted to strengthen their power by populist appeals—and sought to operate in a weak institutional setting.

Conversely, the capacity for expansion was greater in those cases in which the major elites and strata evinced a relatively high degree of cohesion, some internal autonomy, and general openness toward broader institutional frameworks and had wide organizational experience; important in this regard were a high degree of attachment to, and identification with, broader, national political frameworks and a high degree of continuity in institutional frameworks.

Beyond these conditions common to all modern—and perhaps traditional—regimes, the elements of the outcomes of processes of change tended in the neopatrimonial regimes to be combined in ways that were different from the constellations found in revolutionary regimes.

Thus, changes in coalitions of elites often took place in neopatrimonial societies with or without the incorporation of broader strata in the polity; with or without economic and organizational development; and with or without change in the principles of economic distribution or policy or in center-periphery relations. Similarly, repressive and regressive policies could develop somewhat independently of each other and independently of the inclusion of new elites in the center or of the incorporation of new strata in the polity.

The repression and exclusion of a wide range of elites was coupled, as in Brazil under the recent military regime, with attempts at economic development, with attempts at the incorporation of wider—but politically passive groups into the polity, and with only minimal changes in the control over resources or the principles of their distribution. Regressive policies on organizational and economic development were associated in many populist regimes of Latin America with widening the scope of participation and of incorporation of broader strata into the polity. In such Middle Eastern countries as Syria and Iraq, similar policies were also connected with considerable instability in the composition of central elites. Indonesia provides some fascinating variations of these patterns. Under the economically regressive Sukarno regime Indonesia experienced the incorporation of wider strata into the polity. Under Suharto there occurred a slight shift toward developmental policies and toward greater limitation and regulation of political participation.

Moreover, different policy orientations may influence the stability of regimes in unique ways that contrast with the patterns typically associated with postrevolutionary societies. The key to the stability of modern nation-states has been the ability of rulers to maintain effective links with broader strata. In the neopatrimonial regimes the key has been the ability of the various cohesive and solidary elites to maintain or set up segregative arrangements among different sectors of the population, together with a low level of interelite conflict.

Regressive tendencies and regressive outcomes were connected with the stability of regimes in many Latin American countries in the nineteenth century and in many African countries today. These societies were characterized by relatively weak elites segregated from broader groups and by congruence between the resources available for immediate distribution and the expectations of the broader strata. In such societies political conflicts were confined to relations among elites organized for the most part in small cliques.

In societies in which the intraclique or interclique element predominated, crises of regimes gave rise to a series of political breakdowns and to political stagnation. In Spain, Indonesia, and Argentina, a marked discrepancy between expectations and distributable resources caused the breakdown of segregative arrangements, violent cleavages, and engendered far-reaching regime changes and more repressive policies.

Expansive tendencies or outcomes of regime crises were connected in Malaysia and until recently in the Philippines with regime stability attributable to a low level of conflict among relatively coherent and mutually open elites and groups and relatively stable and long-standing institutions with a tradition of attachment to a common polity. Under such circumstances, demands for expansion do not greatly disrupt existing segregative arrangements. As happened lately in the Philippines, these conditions became weakened, creating a situation conducive to instability and repression. Where the level of conflict is high, expansive tendencies were associated with regime instability, as in many of the more developed, contemporary Latin American societies. Concomitantly, segregative arrangements tended to break down and the major sectors of society tended to become polarized.

To conclude, whatever differences existed in the structures and patterns of change in neopatrimonial regimes, these societies exhibited more of a propensity to combine far-reaching changes with considerable regime instability than did nation-states or revolutionary regimes.

14. REVOLUTIONARY MOVEMENTS IN NEOPATRIMONIAL SOCIETIES

Closely related to the pattern of regime instability and far-reaching change was the continual development of isolated, violent, highly vocal, extremist revolutionary groups (usually recruited from the upper middle sectors). Such revolutionary groups—whether intellectuals, anarchists, or contemporary rural and urban guerrillas—formed in all neopatrimonial societies.[54]

These groups were, however, rarely able to create effective links with broader strata or to restructure central political processes, as the experience of the guerrillas in Colombia, the urban guerrillas in Venezuela, and the Tupamaros in Argentina and Uruguay shows. Only in Mexico and Cuba, where (as we analyze subsequently) semirevolutionary processes developed, or in situations in which civil war was closely related to external pressure, as in Southeast Asia and again in Cuba, did these groups become effective linked with either center political struggles or with broadly based rebellions. But in all cases the activities of such groups greatly influenced the political process, deepening societal cleavages and often ushering in oppressive regimes.

Many of these groups were co-opted into the center as part of the ruling elite or as an accepted opposition (joining the neopatrimonial coalitions). Insofar as they became involved with central political activities they tended to oscillate between the desire for immediate and specific rewards and the desire for rather nebulous transformation of the entire system. They generally articulated demands very much in the patrimonial mode: (1) changing the rules of access to the center; (2) broadening the bases of the collectivity whose prestige the center could represent without fostering new, active commitments to the center or altering the attitudes of the broader groups' center to a broader sociocultural order; and (3) transforming the patterns of resource distribution. The intense ideological and political conflicts that often developed among these groups had little to do with restructuring the center or opening up new avenues of participation in it. But, side by side with the co-optation of revolutionary groups, new, extremist ones continually emerged.

15. INTERNATIONAL FACTORS

The continual emergence of extreme revolutionary groups was facilitated and intensified by the unique combinations of internal developments in these societies and by the impingement of international forces on them. The most important such internal factors were the greater instability of regimes, the constant shifting of centers of power in the international systems, and the improvement of international communications. All these fostered the development of revolutionary groups and ideologies that were offshoots of successful revolutions (such as the Chinese).[55] Whatever success such groups had in effecting the far-reaching social restructuring they advocated, they nevertheless constituted a new, permanent element in the international setting that could affect the processes of change in any society. Such groups could undermine existing foreign regimes without necessarily being able to achieve extensive reconstruction at home.

An alternative—the imposition of coalescent, revolutionary change through external force (as in Eastern Europe or Southeast Asia)—was produced by the segregative mode of these societies' incorporation into the modern international systems, together with the growing strength of international revolutionary movements and revolutionary states and with the increase in the impact of specialized, autonomous revolutionary groups. Obviously, in most instances, this pattern was connected with a high degree of coerciveness, with the displacement of groups and strata, and, in societies in which there was little initial tendency toward mobilization, with the destruction of large numbers of people.

16. REVOLUTIONS AND REVOLUTIONARY REGIMES IN NEOPATRIMONIAL SOCIETIES: MEXICO, BOLIVIA, CUBA, PORTUGAL

International forces could thus generate or reinforce noncoalescent patterns of change. In some cases, however, international forces could affect internal developments in such a way as to create conditions similar to those connected with the development of true revolutions. Mexico, Cuba, Bolivia, and Portugal are interesting examples of this possibility.

In several neopatrimonial societies—Mexico, Bolivia, Cuba, and Portugal—internal and external forces combined to produce situations similar in two crucial aspects to the pattern of the pure revolution. First, extensive contact was established and maintained between processes of rebellion and more central political struggle. Second, these societies (especially Cuba and Portugal) gave birth to movements that defined themselves as revolutionary. Third, the revolutions in these societies (especially Mexico and Cuba) resulted in change in the symbols of the political regime, in certain aspects of access to power, and in the ruling elite. These changes were combined with far-reaching restructuring of the organizational aspects of institutional spheres and sometimes with changes in the pattern of distribution of resources.

These similarities with true revolutions notwithstanding, the Mexican,

Bolivian, Cuban, and Portuguese revolutions differed from the classical pattern in terms of both processes and outcomes.

I

The Mexican Revolution [56] differed in important ways from revolutions in other neopatrimonial societies. More than any other such society, Mexico exhibited a very strong—even if uneasy—linkage between peasant rebellions and more central political struggle. This linkage developed not so much because of the momentum of these movements or because of the presence of autonomous institutional entrepreneurs who aimed at such linkage but rather because of a special conjunction of internal and external factors. First, Mexico had an unusually strong tradition of centralism dating from the colonial period. This tradition was strengthened by the Díaz regime, which pursued economic growth and encouraged the rise of new, somewhat autonomous sectors within the more central elites. These developments, together with the external pressures that generated the overthrow of the Díaz regime, gave rise to the possibility of combining central political struggle with peasant rebellions. [57]

Yet from the very beginning one element central to classical revolution was absent or very weak in Mexico: intellectual or religious heterodoxies and independent political entrepreneurs. Even after the institutionalization of the revolution, autonomous political entrepreneurs (from among the different political actors) were least integrated into the revolutionary party. Accordingly, the linkage between peasant rebellions and central political struggle was unstable, and it did not give rise to a permanent, new coalition or to a new, stable institutional framework. When this framework was institutionalized as the Institutional Revolutionary Party (PRI), the peasants were initially excluded from it (de facto). [58]

Contrary to the view of many revolutionary theorists, the explanation behind Mexico's failure to stage a true revolution is not that conservative and radical elements were irreconcilably split. The existence of such a rift in classical revolutionary situations did not preclude stable coalitions (and countercoalitions) and stable institutional complexes. Rather, what Mexico lacked was a high degree of coalescence among rebellious peasant elements, intellectuals, and both secondary and central autonomous political leaders. [59]

It was the weakness of the connection among these groups that gave rise to a protracted civil war, as well as to Mexico's inability to institutionalize over the long run any cohesive political coalitions or organizational frameworks. The low level of convergence among these groups (especially of the more autonomous, disembedded political and intellectual elements) and the predominance of patrimonial-type coalitions also explain the lack of a highly articulated revolutionary ideology that transcended populist agrarian or peasant or communal symbolism. [60]

The impact of these special characteristics of revolutionary process in Mexico—above all, the nature of the revolutionary coalitions—was most clearly manifest in the outcomes of the revolution: the unique combination of changes in regimes, far-reaching restructuring of institutional complexes in the direction of modernity, and economic development, on the one hand, and strong neopatrimonial features, on the other.

The Mexican Revolution changed the symbols and legitimation of the regime as well as its entire institutional base creating not only a relatively centralized administration but also a new institutional political framework in the form of PRI. It replaced the former ruling groups and some elements of the upper social echelons, especially landowners and the Church, and minimized, paradoxically enough, the power of the military.

Establishment of a relatively centralized state went hand in hand with the establishment of more unified markets. The Mexican Revolution generated one of the highest levels of long-term economic development in Latin America and opened up new channels of social and political mobility. Moreover, there occurred a relatively extensive redistribution of resources—a policy pursued most effectively by the Cárdenas regime.[61]

The Mexican Revolution also resulted in far-reaching restructuring of the organizational aspects of institutions in general (and of economic institutions in particular) in the direction of state capitalism. Such restructuring was paralleled by attempts to give new meanings to institutions—to redefine them in terms of a positive orientation to development and service to the state.

Yet this process differed in several ways from the classical revolutionary pattern. First, the replacement and dislocation of the upper classes was only partial, leaving large segments of this group intact (but allowing an infusion of new members). Second, the whole pattern of control over the principles of recruitment for political activities and of access to power and the basic structure of coalitions did not change greatly despite the shift in the loci of power as well as in the composition of the groups actually contending for positions of power.

Thus, the Mexican Revolution produced a more centralized state (with dynamic central symbols) that was nevertheless neopatrimonial. The structure of center-periphery relations followed the patrimonial pattern essentially. It did not allow for the autonomous participation or access of groups to the centers of power although the scope of mobility to the centers increased greatly. Mobility, along with access to the resources generated by economic development, was largely controlled by the political center.

Postrevolutionary Mexican society was characterized by the demobilization of wider strata and strong control over their political expression.[62] But the regime did not attempt (as totalitarian regimes do) to restructure the broader strata. Instead, it relied on co-optation through a great variety of networks and sectors that found their pivot in the orga-

nization of the PRI.[63] This framework enabled continual expansion as
well as the co-optation of new groups to coexist with movements of
protest in marginal sectors of the society and later on, in the 1960s,
among the students.[64]

II

Developments in Bolivia are even more indicative of the limitations
of revolutionary transformation in neopatrimonial regimes. The so-called
Revolution of 1952 took place first of all because of the breakdown of a
relatively weak regime.[65] It was generated by the economic burden of a
foreign war and by the massive dislocation of groups due to this burden.
International pressures were influential in two ways: in the intensification
of all these internal processes and in the spread of revolutionary socialist
ideology. The combination of external and internal forces explains the
intensity of the struggle that developed in Bolivia and the emergence of
a revolutionary coalition of (mostly middle-class) political leaders, workers (especially miners), and peasants.

During the revolution itself the weaknesses of this coalition became
apparent—and became even more so in the later stages of the institutionalization of the revolution. In both these periods, autonomous political
and/or intellectual elements were very weak. Moreover, unlike Mexico,
which had a tradition of relatively centralized political leadership, Bolivia lacked the element of strong, even if patrimonial, central leadership.[66] Consequently, the ruling elite was unable effectively to coordinate
the activities and demands of its component groups. Because of its
inability to reconcile economic stability or development with demands
from workers and peasants alike, the revolutionary regime ultimately
fell.[67] (Paradoxically, the United States was ready to help the revolutionary regime in order to further the Alliance for Progress.) [68]

III

The Cuban Revolution attests to the combination of two trends—first,
the relatively small chance in patrimonial settings of the internal development of revolutionary transformation and, second, the possibility of
overcoming some of these difficulties through the impingement of international forces and powers as well as the costs of this alternative. According to the literature, the origins of the Cuban Revolution may be
traced to the total breakdown of the legitimacy and efficiency of the
Batista regime (due in no small degree to its internal vagaries) and to
the fact that Cuba was a relatively centralized state with a rather well
developed, even if monolithic export-oriented economy largely dependent
on the United States.[69] These features encouraged the development of
elites and middle-class groups that became alienated from the regime.
Simultaneously, the peasants grew increasingly disaffected. Thus, peasant

groups and disaffected central groups turned to guerrilla activity, but as was the case in Mexico and Bolivia, links among the insurgents were tenuous.

Autonomous intellectual and political elements were very weak in Cuba: the only such independent force, the Communist party, was largely under foreign control.[70] The linkage between the Communist party and the postrevolutionary regime took place not in the process of the revolution itself but only under the impact of external development (the policy of the United States, the Cold War, and the incorporation of Cuba into the Russian orbit). Only at this point did the Cuban revolutionary leadership develop the revolutionary ideology and program that gave rise to executions and social dislocations on a large scale and to extensive changes in social hierarchies and institutional spheres and that emphasized mass education, redistribution of resources, and opening up of channels of mobility.

The violence of these developments was mitigated by the fact that large segments of the middle and upper social echelons migrated to the United States. (Another result of this emigration was that the post-revolutionary society lacked professionals and skilled workers.)

Restructuring of the major institutional spheres took place in the direction of a highly centralized and coercive regime. At the same time, this regime (initially at least) developed strong solidary relations with the broader strata, increasing mobility and raising the level of education and health care. It also encouraged (the controlled) participation of the population in the political and economic frameworks.[71]

Cuba's postrevolutionary economy, which has lately encountered many problems, is highly dependent on subsidies from the Soviet Union. Still, it is too early to tell whether Cuba will develop into a totalitarian regime modeled after either the Soviet or the Yugoslavian pattern or, as some observers believe, into a new variant of the neopatrimonial, authoritarian pattern.

IV

A rather different pattern of development can be identified in the recent Portuguese Revolution.[72] Portugal developed within the framework of European civilization in a patrimonial direction but it did not lose its orientation to the more active elements of the European tradition. Salazar headed an autocratic, neopatrimonial regime that incorporated certain aspects of the nation-state model. This regime was backward in outlook yet modern in terms of its centralization; the latter encouraged the development of cohesive elites and revolutionary tendencies. These tendencies were intensified by economic expansion under Salazar and especially under his successor, Caetano, and by the combination of Portugal's relative marginality and closeness to the principal European centers. All these factors fostered the rise of independent political groups.

Interestingly enough in Portugal it was the army, usually the mainstay of autocratic regimes, that became—by extension of its social bases through compulsory recruitment and specifically the incorporation of students—the core of the new political force. Portugal's more extreme revolutionary tendencies were triggered by the rising costs of retaining the Portuguese Empire.

These features generated the breakdown of the autocratic regime and started the revolutionary process. In this process, there developed (in conjunction with different international forces) a very strong element of autonomous political leaders and intellectuals who could serve as links with popular movements and architects of a highly coalescent pattern of change. These autonomous political elements were the most active members of the coalitions of political revolutionaries. Such coalitions were often closely associated with external forces and broader movements.

The struggle among Portuguese revolutionary elements, closely related to external forces, seems to have moved the regime in a more solidary direction. This tendency may ultimately enable the regime to overcome the weaknesses and conflicts of the first phase of the revolution and to attempt to formulate effective economic policies.

17. SUMMARY

All these revolutionary processes and outcomes in neopatrimonial settings reveal several characteristics of interest from the point of view of our analysis.

First, despite the existence of conditions conducive to the development of some of the structural characteristics of the pure revolution— especially the merger of rebellions and more central political struggles and the seizure of power by relatively disembedded, autonomous elites— these features did not emerge.

Second, all these societies exhibited weak linkages among autonomous political and intellectual leaders.

Third, all these regimes achieved little actual restructuring of center-periphery relations, minimized autonomous access to the center, and emphasized patronage and corporatist arrangements.

These tendencies may be partially overcome by the impact of international forces. Through the activities of foreign elites or the reinforcement and/or financial support of dissociated local elites, far-reaching changes may be coercively effected, the experience of most Eastern European societies demonstrates. But as we indicated above, in such cases the pattern of change will diverge greatly from the classical revolutionary one.

NOTES

1. On Spain see E. E. Malefakis, *Agrarian Reform and Peasant Revolution in Spain: Origins of the Civil War* (New Haven: Yale University Press, 1970); R. Carr, *Spain, 1808–1939* (New York: Oxford University Press, 1966); J. Linz, "Early State Building and Late Peripheral Nationalism against the State," in S. N. Eisenstadt and S. Rokkan (eds.), *Building States and Nations*, 2 vols. (Beverly Hills: Sage, 1973), 2:32–117; J. H. Elliot, *Imperial Spain, 1469–1716* (New York: New American Library, Mentor, 1963); and M. Kossok, "Der Iberische Revolutionszyklus, 1789–1830: Bemerkungen zu einem Thema der vergleichenden Revolutionsgeschichte," in M. Kossok (ed.), *Studien zur Vergleichenden Revolutionsgeschichte* (Berlin: Akademie, 1974), pp. 209–229. On Portugal see A. H. Oliveira Marques, "Revolution and Counterrevolution in Portugal: Problems of Portuguese History," in ibid., pp. 403–418; L. S. Graham, *Portugal: The Decline and Collapse of an Authoritarian Order*, Sage Comparative Politics Series, no. 01–053 (Beverly Hills, 1975); and M. Harsgor, *Portugal in Revolution*, Sage Comparative Politics Series, no. 480032 (Beverly Hills, 1976); "A Revolution Tamed: A Survey of Portugal," *The Economist* (London), May 28, 1977, survey, pp. 1–30.

2. On the trend of development in Latin American society see H. F. Cline (ed.), *Latin American History: Essays on Its Study and Teaching, 1898–1965*, 2 vols. (Austin: University of Texas Press, 1965); and L. Hanke (ed.), *History of Latin American Civilization*, 2 vols. (Boston: Little, Brown, 1967).

3. On South Asia see D. J. Steinberg (ed.), *In Search of Southeast Asia: A Modern History* (New York: Praeger, 1971); W. F. Wertheim, "Southeast Asia," in D. L. Sills (ed.), *International Encyclopedia of the Social Sciences*, 17 vols. (New York: Macmillan and Free Press, 1968), 1:423–438; J. Bastin and H. J. Benda, *A History of Modern Southeast Asia* (Englewood Cliffs: Prentice-Hall, 1968); J. Bastin (ed.), *The Emergence of Modern Southeast Asia, 1511–1957* (Englewood Cliffs: Prentice-Hall, 1967); R. O. Tilman (ed.), *Man, State, and Society in Contemporary Southeast Asia* (New York: Praeger, 1969); V. Purcell, *The Chinese in Southeast Asia* (New York: Oxford University Press, 1951); K. Legge, *Indonesia* (Englewood Cliffs: Prentice-Hall, 1964); and W. Gungwu (ed.), *Malaysia* (New York: Praeger, 1964).

On Africa see T. Turner (ed.), *Colonialism in Africa, 1870–1960* (Cambridge: At the University Press, 1971).

4. See on this M. Sarfatti, *Spanish Bureaucratic-Patrimonialism in America*, University of California, Institute of International Studies, Politics of Modernization Series, no. 1 (Berkeley, 1966); S. Schwartzman, "Back to Weber: Corporatism and Patrimonialism in the Seventies," in J. M. Malloy (ed.), *Authoritarianism and Corporatism in Latin America* (Pittsburgh: University of Pittsburgh Press, 1977), pp. 89–106; see also C. H. Haring, *The Spanish Empire in America* (New York: Oxford University Press,

1947), chaps. 7, 12; J. M. Otis Capdequi, *El estado español en las Indias* (Mexico City: Fondo de cultura económica, 1946), pp. 1–25; and idem, "Instituciones económicas de la América española durante el período colonial," *Anuario de la historia del derecho español*, 9 (1932): 103–128.

5. I. Wallerstein (ed.), *Social Change: The Colonial Situation* (New York: Wiley, 1960); see also references cited in note 30 below.

6. See, for instance, T. Halperin-Donghi, *The Aftermath of Revolution in Latin America* (New York: Harper & Row, Harper Torchbooks, 1973).

7. See A. Humbaraci, *Algeria: A Revolution That Failed* (London: Pall Mall, 1958); M. Lebjaoui, *Vérités sur la révolution algérienne* (Paris: Gallimard, 1965); P. J. Vatikiotis (ed.), *Egypt since the Revolution* (London: George Allen & Unwin, 1968); idem (ed.), *Revolution in the Middle East* (London: George Allen & Unwin, 1972); and M. F. Lofchie, *Zanzibar: Background to Revolution* (Princeton: Princeton University Press, 1965).

8. See H. Seton-Watson, *The East European Revolution* (London: Methuen, 1952); and idem, *Nationalism and Communism: Essays, 1946–63* (London: Methuen, 1964).

9. On Yugoslavia see B. D. Denitch, *The Legitimation of a Revolution* (New Haven: Yale University Press, 1976).

10. See the references cited in notes 57–72 below.

11. See Malloy, *Latin America*, pp. 513–526; and H. J. Wiarda, *Politics and Social Change in Latin America: The Distinct Tradition* (Amherst: University of Massachusetts Press, 1974).

12. See the references cited in note 1 above; see also M. Kossok, "Revolution–Reform–Gegenrevolution in Spanien und Portugal, 1808–1910," in Kossok, *Studien zur Vergleichenden Revolutionsgeschichte*, pp. 134–159.

13. See the literature cited in notes 2 and 3 above; see also R. Scott, *The Politics of New States* (London: George Allen & Unwin, 1970); S. Rose, "Political Modernization in Asia," *France-Asie*, 22, no. 1 (1968): 31–45; R. L. Park, "Second Thoughts on Asian Democracy," *Asian Survey*, 1, no. 2 (1961): 28–31; R. Emerson, *From Empire to Nation: The Rise to Self-Assertion of Asian and African Peoples* (Cambridge: Harvard University Press, 1960); S. Rose, *Socialism in Southern Asia* (New York: Oxford University Press, 1959); idem (ed.), *Politics in Southern Asia* (New York: St. Martin's, 1963); G. J. Pauker, "Political Doctrines and Practical Politics in Southeast Asia," *Pacific Affairs*, 35, no. 1 (1962): 3–11; H. J. Benda, "Decolonization in Indonesia: The Problem of Continuity and Change," *American Historical Review*, 70, no. 4 (1965): 1058–1073; J. M. van der Kroef, "The Changing Pattern of Indonesia's Representative Goverment," *Canadian Journal of Economics and Political Science*, 26, no. 2 (1960): 215–240; W. Schilling, "Der Sturz Sukarnos und Die 'Neue Ordnung' in Indonesien," *Politische Studien*, 21 (March-April 1970): 172–184; J. S. Furnivall, *The Governance of Modern Burma*, 2d ed., enl. (New York: International Secretariat, Institute of Pacific Relations, 1960); J. Grossholtz, *Politics in the Philippines* (Boston: Little, Brown, 1964); and

R. H. Fitzgibbon, "Dictatorship and Democracy in Latin America," *International Affairs*, 36, no. 1 (1960): 48–57.

14. On some of the general characteristics of the economic structure and process in these countries see B. Rivlin and S. Szyliowicz (eds.), *The Contemporary Middle East: Traditions and Innovation* (New York: Random House, 1965). See especially the following selections: United Nations, "Changing Socio-Economic Patterns in the Middle East," pp. 299–313; C. A. O. van Nieuwenhuijze, "The Near Eastern Village: A Profile," pp. 314–324; International Labor Organization, "Employment Prospects of Children and Young People in the Near and Middle East," pp. 359–367; N. Burns, "Planning Economic Development in the Arab World," pp. 368–374; and R. B. Pettengill, "Population Control to Accelerate Economic Progress in the Middle East," pp. 375–387. See also F. H. Golay, R. Anspach, R. Pfanner, and E. Ayal (eds.), *Underdevelopment and Economic Nationalism in Southeast Asia* (Ithaca: Cornell University Press, 1969); J. A. C. Mackie, *Problems of the Indonesian Inflation* (Ithaca: Cornell University, Department of Asian Studies, 1967); H. Schmidt, "Post-Colonial Politics: A Suggested Interpretation of the Indonesian Experience, 1950–58," *Australian Journal of Politics and History*, 9, no. 2 (1963): 176–183; Soedjatmoko, *Economic Development as a Cultural Problem* (Ithaca: Cornell University, Department of Asian Studies, 1968); J. Adams and H. Hancock, "Land and Economy in Traditional Vietnam," *Journal of Southeast Asian Studies*, 1, no. 2 (1970): 90–98; F. H. Golay, *The Philippines: Public Policy and National Economics* (Ithaca: Cornell University Press, 1961); J. Puthucheary, *Ownership and Control of the Malay Economy* (Singapore: Eastern Universities Press, 1960); C. K. Meek, *Land Law and Custom in the Colonies* (New York: Oxford University Press, 1964); and T. H. Silcock (ed.), *Readings in Malayan Economics* (Singapore: Eastern Universities Press, 1961).

15. On developments in administration and bureaucracy see H. J. Benda, *The Pattern of Administrative Reforms in the Closing Years of Dutch Rule in Indonesia*, Yale University, Southeast Asia Studies Reprint Series, no. 16 (New Haven, 1965); R. O. Tilman, *Bureaucratic Transition in Malaya* (Durham: Duke University Press, 1964); idem, "The Bureaucratic Legacy of Modern Malaya," *Indian Journal of Public Administration*, 9, no. 2 (1963): 25–48; O. D. Corpuz, *The Bureaucracy in the Philippines* (Quezon City: University of the Philippines, Institute of Public Administration, 1957); and W. J. Siffin, *The Thai Bureaucracy* (Honolulu: East-West Center Press, 1966).

16. On these processes see J. M. Malloy, "Authoritarianism and Corporatism in Latin America: The Modal Pattern," in Malloy, *Latin America*, pp. 3–19; D. A. Chalmers, "The Politicized State in Latin America," in ibid., pp. 23–46; G. A. O'Donnell, "Corporatism and the Question of the State," in ibid., pp. 47–87; S. Schwartzman, "Back to Weber: Corporatism and Patrimonialism in the Seventies," in ibid., pp. 89–106; and R. R. Kaufman, Corporatism, Clientelism, and Partisan Conflict: A Study of Seven Latin American Countries," in ibid., pp. 109–148.

17. M. Lissak, "Center and Periphery in Developing Countries and Prototypes of Military Elites," *Studies in Comparative International Development*, 5, no. 7 (1969–1970): 139–150; J. E. Miguens, "The New Latin American Military Coup," ibid., 6, no. 1 (1970–1971): 3–15; J. L. Weaver, "Political Styles of the Guatemalan Military Elite," ibid., 5, no. 4 (1969–1970): 63–81; J. Cotler, "Political Crises and Military Populists in Peru," ibid., 6, no. 5 (1970–1971): 95–113; J. H. Badgley, "Burma's Military Government: A Political Analysis," *Asian Survey*, 2, no. 6 (1962): 32–37; and H. Z. Schiffrin (ed.), *Military and State in Modern Asia* (Jerusalem: Jerusalem Academic Press, 1976).

18. On the patterns of revolt and insurgency in these societies see K. Gough and H. P. Sharma (eds.), *Imperialism and Revolution in South Asia* (New York: Monthly Review Press, 1973); N. Miller and R. Aya (eds.), *National Liberation: Revolution in the Third World* (New York: Free Press, 1971); R. L. Solomon, "Saya San and the Burmese Rebellion," *Modern Asian Studies*, 3, no. 3 (1969): 209–233; G. Gobron, *History and Philosophy of Caodaism* (Paris: Dervy, 1949); G. Goulet, *Les Sociétés secrètes en terre d'Annam* (Saigon: C. Ardin, 1926); M. C. Guerrero, "The Colorum Uprisings, 1924–1931," *Asian Studies*, 5, no. 1 (1967): 65–78; Sartono Kartodiridjo, *The Peasants' Revolt of Banten in 1888, Its Conditions, Course, and Sequel: A Case Study of Social Movements in Indonesia* (The Hague: M. Nijhoff, 1966); H. J. Benda and L. Castles, "The Samin Movement," *Bijdragen Tot de Taal-, Land-, en Volkenkunde*, 125, no. 3 (1969): 207–240; H. J. Benda and R. McVey (eds.), *The Communist Uprisings of 1926–1927 in Indonesia: Key Documents* (Ithaca: Cornell University Press, 1960); and J. P. Harrison, *The Communists and Chinese Peasant Rebellions* (New York: Atheneum, 1969).

19. On educational problems and policies in some of these countries see J. W. G. Miller, *Education in Southeast Asia* (Sydney: Ian Novak, 1968), pp. 186–220, 255–284; M. Shamul Hug, *Education and Development Strategy in South and Southeast Asia* (Honolulu: East-West Center Press, 1965), pp. 17–21, 158–161, 192–196; P. Foster, "The Vocational School Fallacy in Development Planning," in C. A. Anderson and M. J. Bowman (eds.), *Education and Economic Development* (Chicago: Aldine, 1965), pp. 142–166; C. A. Anderson, "Technical and Vocational Education in the New Nations," in A. M. Kazamias and E. H. Epstein (eds.), *Schools in Transition: Essays in Comparative Education* (Boston: Allyn & Bacon, 1965), pp. 174–189; and G. Ramanathan, *Educational Planning and National Integration* (London: Asia Publishing House, 1965).

20. On agrarian reform, crises, and demands see H. A. Landsberger (ed.), *Latin American Peasant Movements* (Ithaca: Cornell University Press, 1969); A Quijano Obregón, "Tendencies in Peruvian Development and Class Structure," in J. Petras and M. Zeitlin (eds.), *Latin America: Reform or Revolution?* (Greenwich: Fawcett, 1968), pp. 289–328; G. Huizer, "Peasant Organization in the Process of Agrarian Reform in Mexico," *Studies in Comparative International Development*, 4, no. 6 (1968–1969): 115–145; E. H. Jacoby, *Agrarian Unrest in Southeast Asia*, 2d ed., rev.

and enl. (London: Asia Publishing House, 1961); D. Warriner, *Land Reform in Principle and Practice* (Oxford: Clarendon, 1969); E. Feder, "Social Opposition to Peasant Movements and Its Effect in Latin America," *Studies in Comparative International Development*, 6, no. 8 (1970–1971): 159–189; F. L. Starner, *Magsaysay and the Philippine Peasantry: The Agrarian Impact on Philippine Politics, 1953–1956* (Berkeley: University of California Press, 1961); J. M. Paige, *Agrarian Revolution* (New York: Free Press, 1965); and J. S. Migdal, *Peasants, Politics, and Revolution: Pressures toward Political and Social Change in the Third World* (Princeton: Princeton University Press, 1974).

21. See on this G. Germani, *Política y sociedad en una época de transición de la sociedad tradicional a la sociedad de masas*, 2d ed. (Buenos Aires: Paidos, 1968); and idem, *Sociología de la modernización* (Buenos Aires: Paidos, n.d.).

22. See, for instance, J. L. Horowitz and E. K. Trimberger, "State Power and Military Nationalism in Latin America," *Comparative Politics*, 8, no. 2 (1976): 223–245; and F. Bourricaud, *Power and Society in Contemporary Peru* (New York: Praeger, 1970).

23. See the literature cited in note 14 above and also F. H. Cardoso, *Sociologie du dévéloppement en Amérique latine* (Paris: Anthropos, 1969); idem, *Mundancas Sociais na America Latina: Corpo e alma do Brasil* (São Paulo: Difusao europeia do livro, 1969); idem, *Empresario Industrial e Desenvolvimiento Economico no Brasil: Corpo e alma do Brasil* (São Paulo: Difusao europeia do livro, 1964); and W. Baer, R. Newfarmer, and T. Trebat, *On State Capitalism in Brazil: Some New Issues and Questions*, University of Texas, Institute of Latin American Studies, Technical Papers Series, no. 1 (Austin, 1976).

24. On the structuring of social hierarchies in these societies see M. Sarfatti and A. E. Bergman, *Social Stratification in Peru*, University of California, Institute of International Studies, Politics of Modernization Series, no. 5 (Berkeley, 1969), pp. 43, 52–54; B. G. Burnett and R. F. Johnson (eds.), *Political Forces in Latin America* (Belmont: Wadsworth, 1968). In this volume see especially R. L. Peterson, "Guatemala," pp. 61–80; J. A. Fernandez, "Honduras," pp. 81–94; R. P. Hoopes, "El Salvador," pp. 95–114; K. F. Johnson and P. L. Paris, "Nicaragua," pp. 115–130; J. B. Gabbert, "Ecuador," pp. 284–287; and B. G. Burnett, "Chile," pp. 384–394. See also J. Graciarena, *Poder y Clases sociales en el Desarrollo de América latina* (Buenos Aires: Paidos, 1968); Germani, *Política y sociedad;* D. B. Heath and R. N. Adams (eds.), *Contemporary Cultures and Societies in Latin America* (New York: Random House, 1965), esp. pt. 3; F. Bourricaud, "Structure and Function of the Peruvian Oligarchy," *Studies in Comparative International Development*, 2, no. 2 (1966): 17–31; A. Touraine, "Social Mobility, Class Relations, and Nationalism in Latin America," ibid., 1, no. 3 (1965): 19–25; S. M. Lipset and A. Solari (eds.), *Elites in Latin America* (New York: Oxford University Press, 1967), esp. pp. 242–249; J. López, "Etude de quelques changements fondamentaux dans la politique et la société brésiliennes," *Sociologie du travail*, 7, no. 3 (1965): 238–253; M.

G. Navarro, "Mexico: The Lop-Sided Revolution," in C. Veliz (ed.), *Obstacles to Change in Latin America* (New York: University Press, 1965), pp. 206–229; P. Gonzales-Casanova, "L'Evolution du système des classes au Mexique," *Cahiers internationaux de sociologie*, 39 (1965): 113–136; B. Ryan, "The Ceylonese Villages and the New Value System," *Rural Sociology*, 17, no. 4 (1952): 311–321; F. H. Cardoso, "Le Proletariat brésilien: Situation et comportement social," *Sociologie du travail*, 3, no. 4 (1961): 50–65; O. Sunkel, "Change and Frustration in Chile," in Veliz, *Obstacles to Change*, pp. 116–144; G. A. Dillon Soaves, "The Politics of Universal Development: The Case of Brazil," in S. M. Lipset and S. Rokkan (eds.), *Party Systems and Voter Alignments: Cross-National Perspectives* (New York: Free Press, 1967), pp. 467–498; and A. Touraine and D. Pecaut, "Working Class Consciousness and Economic Development," *Studies in Comparative International Development*, 3, no. 4 (1967–1968): 71–84. A general discussion of these patterns of stratification appears in S. N. Eisenstadt, *Social Differentiation and Stratification* (Glenview: Scott, Foresman, 1971), chap. 12.

25. H. J. Puhle, "Revolution von oben und Revolution von unten in Lateinamerika: Fragen zum Vergleich politischer Stabilisierungsprobleme im 20. Jahrhundert," in H. J. Puhle (ed.), *Revolution und Reformen in Lateinamerika; Geschichte und Gesellschaft* (Göttingen: Vandenhoeck & Ruprecht, 1976), 2:143–159; D. H. Pollock and A. R. M. Ritter (eds.), *Latin American Prospects for the 1970's: What Kind of Revolution?* (New York: Praeger, 1973); H. J. Puhle, "Sehnsucht nach Revolution," in K. Lindenberg (ed.), *Politics in Latin America* (Hanover: Verlag für Literatur und Zeitgeschehen, 1971); O. Paz, *Alternating Current* (New York: Viking, 1973), pp. 192 ff.; and Gough and Sharma, *Imperialism and Revolution in South Asia*.

26. On patterns of political and social change in these societies see, in addition to the references cited in notes 22–25 above, G. Brunn, "Mexico, Brasilien, Argentinien: Aspekte eines Vergleichs," in Puhle, *Revolution und Reformen in Lateinamerika*, 2:234–240; P. Waldmann, "Stagnation als Ergebnis einer 'Stückwerkrevolution': Entwicklungshemnisse und Versäumnisse im peronistischen Argentinien" in ibid., pp. 160–187; W. Grabendorf (ed.), *Lateinamerika: Kontinent in der Krise* (Hamburg: Hoffmann & Campe, 1973); A. J. D. Matz, "The Dynamics of Change in Latin America," *Journal of Inter-American Studies*, 8, no. 1 (1966): 66–76; D. E. Worcester, "The Spanish-American Past: Enemy of Change," ibid., 11, no. 1 (1969): 66–75; K. H. Silvert, "Latin America and Its Alternative Future," *International Journal*, 24, no. 3 (1969): 403–414; H. D. Evers, *Kulturwandel in Ceylon* (Baden-Baden: Lutzeyer, August 1964); E. Sarkisyanz, *Buddhist Backgrounds of the Burmese Revolution* (The Hague: M. Nijhoff, 1965); and J. M. Pluvier, *Confrontations: A Study in Indonesian Politics* (New York: Oxford University Press, 1965).

27. See on this Malloy, "Authoritarianism and Corporatism in Latin America"; Chalmers, "Politicized State in Latin America"; O'Donnell, "Corporatism and the Question of the State"; S. Schwartzman, *São Paulo e o estado*

nacional (São Paulo: Difel, 1975); and X. Stephen (ed.), *Authoritarian Brazil* (New Haven: Yale University Press, 1973).

28. A. E. van Niekerk, *Populisme en politieke ontwikkeling in Latijns Amerika* (Rotterdam: Universiteits Pers, 1972); Wiarda, *Politics and Social Change in Latin America;* O. Ianni, *O colapso do populismo no Brazil* (Rio de Janeiro; Civilizacão brasileira, 1968), available in translation as *Crisis in Brazil* (New York: Columbia University Press, 1970); P. Waldmann, *Der Peronismus, 1943–1955* (Hamburg: Hoffman & Campe, 1974); idem, "Stagnation als Ergebnis einer Stückwerkrevolution"; and R. M. Levine, *The Vargas Regime: The Critical Years, 1932–38* (New York: Columbia University Press, 1970).

29. R. Rogowski and L. Wasserpring, *Does Political Development Exist? Corporatism in Old and New Societies,* vol. 2, Sage Professional Papers in Comparative Politics, no. 01–024 (Beverly Hills, 1971); and Malloy, *Latin America.*

30. On Peru see K. J. Middlebrook and D. S. Palmer, *Military Government and Political Development: Lessons from Peru,* Sage Professional Papers in Comparative Politics, 5, no. 01–054 (Beverly Hills, 1975). On Egypt see Vatikiotis, *Egypt since the Revolution.* On Algeria see E. Hermassi, *Leadership and National Development in North Africa* (Berkeley: University of California Press, 1972), esp. chap. 7; Vatikiotis, *Revolution in the Middle East;* M. Lebjaoui, *Vérités sur la révolution algérienne;* and Humbaraci, *Algeria.*

31. See J. M. Malloy and R. S. Thorn (eds.), *Beyond the Revolution: Bolivia since 1952* (Pittsburgh: University of Pittsburgh Press, 1931).

32. See Wiarda, *Politics and Social Change in Latin America;* Malloy, *Latin America;* and J. Petras (ed.), *Latin America: From Dependence to Revolution* (New York: Wiley, 1973).

33. On the Maghreb see J. Waterbury, *The Commander of the Faithful* (London: Weidenfeld & Nicolson, 1970); A. Laroui, *L'histoire du Maghreb* (Paris: Maspero, 1970); and Y. Lacoste, *Ibn Khaldoun, naissance de l'histoire, passé du tiers-monde,* (Paris: Maspero, 1966). On India see R. Kothari, *Politics in India* (Boston: Little, Brown, 1969). Very good discussions of this problem are found in Tilman, *Contemporary Southeast Asia,* and in the literature cited in note 13 above.

34. Eliott, *Imperial Spain;* A. Castro, *The Structure of Spanish History* (Princeton: Princeton University Press, 1954); and *De economía,* a special issue entitled "Sobre la decadencia económica de España," 6, no. 25–26 (1953); and C. F. Gallagher, "The Shaping of the Spanish Intellectual Tradition," *American Universities Field Staff Reports,* 9 (1976), no. 8.

35. One of the best expositions of the problem of dependence is C. Furtado, *Obstacles to Development in Latin America* (Garden City: Doubleday, Anchor, 1970); see also Cline, *Latin American History,* vol. 2. In this volume see M. Burgin, "Research in Latin American Economics and Economic History," pp. 466–475; and C. Griffin, "Economic and Social Aspects of the Era of Spanish-American Independence," pp. 485–494. See

B. Stallings, *Economic Dependency in Africa and Latin America,* vol. 3, Sage Professional Papers in Comparative Politics, no. 01–031 (Beverly Hills, 1972).

36. On the colonial situation see J. S. Furnivall, *Colonial Policy and Practice: A Comparative Study of Burma and Netherlands India* (Cambridge: At the University Press, 1948); V. Turner (ed.), *Colonization in Africa;* S. N. Eisenstadt, *Essays on Sociological Aspects of Political and Economic Development* (The Hague: Mouton, 1961); and I. M. Wallerstein (ed.), *Social Change: The Colonial Situation.*

37. H. J. Benda, "Political Elites in Colonial Southeast Asia: An Historical Analysis," *Comparative Studies in Society and History,* 7, (April 1965): 233–251; and idem, "Non-Western Intelligentsia as Political Elites" in S. N. Eisenstadt (ed.), *Political Sociology* (New York: Basic Books, 1971), pp. 437–445.

38. On the structure of elites in some of these countries see Benda, "Political Elites"; idem, "Non-Western Intelligentsia"; Eisenstadt, *Essays;* Lipset and Solari, *Elites in Latin America;* C. Veliz (ed.), *The Politics of Conformity in Latin America* (New York: Oxford University Press, 1967); J. A. Fernandez, *The Political Elite in Argentina* (New York: New York University Press, 1970); and M. R. Singer, *The Emerging Elite: A Study of Political Leadership in Ceylon* (Cambridge: MIT Press, 1964).

39. See especially Lipset and Solari, *Elites in Latin America;* see also the other references cited in notes 37 and 38 above.

40. See Chapter 5.

41. This analysis is more fully elaborated in S. N. Eisenstadt, *Traditional Patrimonialism and Modern Neo-Patrimonialism,* Sage Research Papers in the Social Sciences, Studies in Comparative Modernization, no. 90–003 (Beverly Hills, 1973).

42. See, for instance, M. I. Pereira de Queiroz, *La "Guerre sainte" au Brésil: Le Mouvement messianique du "contestado,"* University of São Paulo, Department of Philosophy, Arts, and Sciences Bulletin no. 187 Sociologia I, No. 5, (São Paulo, 1957); idem, *O messianismo no Brasil e no mundo* (São Paulo: Editora da Universidade de São Paulo, 1965); idem, *Messianismo e conflito social: A guerra sertaneja do contestado, 1912–1916* (Rio de Janeiro: Civilizacão brasileira, 1966); H. J. Benda, "Peasant Movements in Colonial Southeast Asia," *Asian Studies,* 3, no. 3 (1965): 420–434; idem, "The Structure of Southeast Asian History: Some Preliminary Observations," *Journal of Southeast Asian History,* 3, no. 1 (1962): 106–138; F. Hills, "Millenarian Machines in South Vietnam," *Comparative Studies in Society and History,* 13 (July 1971): 325–350; B. Dahm, "Leadership and Mass Response in Java, Burma, and Vietnam" (Paper presented to the International Congress of Orientalists, Canberra, January 1971; on file at Kiel University); M. Osborne, *Region of Revolt: Focus on Southeast Asia* (Oxford: Pergamon, 1970); and J. van der Kroef, "Javanese Messianic Expectations: Their Origin and Cultural Context," *Comparative Studies in Society and History,* 1, no. 4 (1959): 299–323.

43. Paige, *Agrarian Revolution;* and Migdal, *Peasants, Politics, and Revolution.*

44. On the impact of external forces see D. Galula, *Counterinsurgency Warfare* (New York: Praeger, 1964); G. K. Tanham, *Communist Revolutionary Warfare,* 2d ed. (New York: Praeger, 1967); and F. N. Trager (ed.), *Marxism in Southeast Asia* (Stanford: Stanford University Press, 1959).

45. See R. Mortimer, "Traditional Modes and Communist Movements: Change and Protest in Indonesia," in J. W. Lewis (ed.), *Peasant Rebellion and Communist Revolution in Asia* (Stanford: Stanford University Press, 1974), pp. 99–125; and T. J. Frijtof, "Stagnatie en beweging, sociaal-historische beschouwingen over Java en Indonesie in Aziatisch verband," Summary in academic dissertation, Amsterdam, *Newsletter* (University of Leiden, Center for the History of European Expansion), 1, no. 3 (1975): 30–71.

46. See Eisenstadt, *Essays.*

47. Ibid.; see also Wallerstein, *Social Change.*

48. Specifically addressed to the problem of instability are J. L. Sorenson, "The Social Bases of Instability in Southeast Asia," *Asian Survey,* 9, no. 7 (1969): 540–545; C. A. Woodward, *The Growth of a Party System in Ceylon* (Providence: Brown University Press, 1969); and Soedjatmoko, "The Rise of Political Parties in Indonesia," in P. W. Thayer (ed.), *Nationalism and Progress in Free Asia* (Baltimore: Johns Hopkins Press, 1956).

49. See Carr, *Spain.* For an analysis of the crises and their outcomes in some of these countries, in addition to the literature quoted above, the reader is referred to W. A. Hanna, *The Indonesia Crisis: Mid-1964 Phase, American University Field Staff Reports,* 14, no. 7 (Washington, D.C., 1966); idem, *Re-Reviving a Revolution,* ibid., 11, no. 4 (1963); idem, *The Indonesia Crisis: Early 1963 Phase,* ibid., no. 8 (1963); A Ravenholt, *A Note on the Philippines,* ibid., vol. 10, no. 8 (1962); W. A. Hanna, *Modes of Modernization in Southeast Asia,* ibid., 17, no. 3 (1969); L. Dupree, *A Note on Pakistan,* ibid., 7, no. 8 (1963); idem, *Pakistan, 1964–1966; Part 1: The Government and the Opposition,* ibid., 10 no. 5 (1966); idem, *Pakistan, 1964–1966; Part 3: The Economy and the Five Year Plans,* ibid., no. 7 (1966); A. W. Horton, *Syrian Stability and the Baath,* ibid., 14, no. 1 (1965); J. Hanessian, Jr., *Iranian Land Reform,* ibid., 12, no. 10 (1963); R. W. Patch, *The Last of Bolivia's MNR?* ibid., 11, no. 5 (1964); idem, *Bolivia's Nationalism and the Military,* ibid., 16, no. 3 (1969); idem, *The Peruvian Agrarian Reform Bill,* ibid., 11, no. 3 (1964); idem, *A Note on Bolivia and Peru,* ibid., 9, no. 4 (1962); idem, *Peru's New President and Agrarian Reform,* ibid., 10, no. 2 (1963); idem, *A Note on Bolivia and Peru,* ibid., 12, no. 2 (1965); K. H. Silvert, *A Note on Chile and Argentina,* ibid., 8, no. 8 (1961); and idem, *Nationalism and the Role of Elites in Latin America,* ibid., 1, no. 2 (1959). See also G. Brenan, *The Spanish Labyrinth: An Account of the Social and Political Background of the Cruel War* (Cambridge: At the University Press, 1960).

50. See Malloy and Thorn, *Beyond the Revolution.*

51. H. A. Landsberger and T. McDaniel, "Hypermobilization in Chile, 1970–73," *World Politics*, 28, no. 4 (1976): 502–542.

52. Ibid.

53. This analysis, based on the materials cited in notes 22–26 above, elaborates upon that in Eisenstadt, *Traditional Patrimonialism*. See also P. C. Schmitter, *Interest, Conflict, and Political Change in Brazil* (Stanford: Stanford University Press, 1971); D. Lehmann, "Political Incorporation versus Political Stability: The Case of the Chilean Agrarian Reform, 1965–70," *Journal of Development Studies*, 1, no. 4 (1971): 365–396; Petras, *Latin America;* Stepan, *Authoritarian Brazil;* K. S. Mericle, "Corporatist Control of the Working Class: Authoritarian Brazil since 1964," in Malloy, *Latin America*, pp. 303–338; K. E. Sharpe, "Corporate Strategies in the Dominican Republic: The Politics of Peasant Movements," in ibid., pp. 339–377; D. S. Palmer, "The Politics of Authoritarianism in Spanish America," in ibid., pp. 377–412; H. A. Dietz, "Bureaucratic Demand-Making and Clientelistic Participation in Peru," in ibid., pp. 413–458; Malloy, "Authoritarianism and Corporatism"; and E. Duff and J. McCamant, *Violence and Repression in Latin America* (New York: Free Press, 1976).

54. On such extremist movements see E. Halperin, *Terrorism in Latin America*, The Washington Papers, vol. 5, no. 33 (Beverly Hills: Sage, 1976); J. Gerassi, *Towards Revolution*, 2 vols. (London: Weidenfeld & Nicolson, 1971); Migdal, *Peasants, Politics, and Revolution;* A. Mack, "Counterinsurgency in the Third World: Theory and Practice, *British Journal of International Studies*, 1, no. 3 (1975): 226–253; Milller and Aya, *National Liberation;* Gough and Sharma, *Imperialism and Revolution in South Asia;* and J. Decornoy, "Ceylon: Naissance d'une révolution," *Le Monde*, June 16 (pp. 1, 5), June 17 (p. 5), and June 18 (p. 6).

55. C. Johnson, *Autopsy on People's War* (Berkeley: University of California Press, 1973).

56. On the Mexican Revolution see J. Reed, *Insurgent Mexico* (New York: Simon & Schuster, 1969); R. E. Quick, *The Mexican Revolution, 1914–1915* (New York: Citadel, 1963); H. F. Cline, *Mexico: Revolution to Evolution* (New York: Oxford University Press, 1962); F. Katz, *Deutschland, Diaz, und die mexikanische Revolution* (Berlin: Deutscher Verlag der Wissenschaften, 1964), chaps. 5, 6; J. Wormack, Jr., *Zapata and the Mexican Revolution* (New York: Random House, Vintage, 1968); J. Meyer, *La Révolution mexicaine* (France: Calmann-Lévy, 1973); and F. Katz, "Zu den spezifischen Ursachen der mexikanischen Revolution von 1910," in Kossok, *Studien zur Vergleichenden Revolutionsgeschichte*, pp. 334–341.

57. On the Díaz regime see Katz, *Deutschland, Diaz, und die mexikanische Revolution*, chap. 2. On the earlier period see ibid., chap. 1; and J. Sierra, *The Political Evolution of the Mexican People* (Austin: University of Texas Press, 1969).

58. On the weakness of this element see Wormack, *Zapata;* F. Katz, "Einige Besonderheiten der mexikanischen Revolution: Kommentar," in Puhle, *Rev-*

olution und Reformen in Lateinamerika, 2:241–243; and Katz, *Deutschland, Diaz, und die mexikanische Revolution*, chaps. 4–6.

59. On the problems of these coalitions see Katz, *Deutschland, Diaz, und die mexikanische Revolution;* Cline, *Mexico;* and H. W. Tobler, "Die mexikanische Revolution zwischen Beharrung und Veränderung," in Puhle, *Revolution and Reformen in Lateinamerika*, 2:188–217.

60. On the ideological bases of the Mexican Revolution see Wormack, *Zapata;* Cline, *Mexico;* and Meyer, *La Révolution mexicaine.*

61. On the reorganizing of the Mexican political and social structures see J. W. Wilke, *The Mexican Revolution: Federal Expenditure and Social Change since 1910* (Berkeley: University of California Press, 1967); Cline, *Mexico;* J. G. Maddox, *Mexican Land Reform* (Washington: J. G. Maddox, 1957), pp. 5–57; S. Eckstein, *The Impact of Revolution: A Comparative Analysis of Mexico and Bolivia*, vol. 2, Sage Contemporary Political Sociology Series, no. 06–016 (Beverly Hills, 1976); R. R. Fagen and W. S. Tuchy, "Aspects of the Mexican Political System," *Studies in Comparative International Development*, 7, no. 3 (1972): 206–220; D. C. Villegas, *Changes in Latin America: The Mexican and Cuban Revolutions* (Lincoln: University of Nebraska Press, 1960); W. P. Glade, Jr., and C. W. Anderson, *The Political Economy of Mexico* (Madison: University of Wisconsin Press, 1963); J. F. H. Purcell and S. K. Purcell, "Mexican Business and Public Policy," in Malloy, *Latin America*, pp. 191–226; and E. P. Stevens, "Mexico's PRI: The Institutionalization of Corporation?" in ibid., pp. 227–258.

62. Tobler, "Die mexikanische Revolution"; and P. Gonzales-Casanova, *La democracia en México* (Mexico City: Era, 1965).

63. J. H. Kautsky, *Patterns of Modernizing Revolutions: Mexico and the Soviet Union*, Sage Professional Papers in Comparative Politics, no. 01–056 (Beverly Hills, 1975).

64. On the movement of protest in Mexico see S. R. Ross (ed.), *Is the Mexican Revolution Dead?* (New York: Knopf, 1966).

65. On the Bolivian Revolution see C. Blasier, "Studies of Social Revolution: Origins in Mexico, Bolivia, and Cuba," *Latin American Research Review*, 2 (1966–1967): 28–64; J. M. Malloy, *Bolivia: The Uncompleted Revolution* (Pittsburgh: University of Pittsburgh Press, 1972); H. J. Puhle, "Tradition und Reformpolitik in Bolivien: Wirtschaft, Gesellschaft und Politik in einem südamerikanischen Entwicklungsland," Forschungsinstitut der Friedrich-Ebert Stiftung, *Vierteljahresberichte*, Probleme der Entwicklungsländer, Special issue no. 5 (Hanover: Verlag für Literatur und Zeitgeschehen, 1970); C. Goodrich, "Bolivia in the Revolution," in Malloy and Thorn, *Beyond the Revolution*, pp. 3–24; and H. S. Klein, "Prelude to the Revolution," in ibid., pp. 25–53.

66. On the leadership of the Bolivian Revolution see Malloy, *Bolivia;* and idem, "Revolutionary Politics," in Malloy and Thorn, *Beyond the Revolution*, pp. 111–157.

67. On these developments see Malloy, *Bolivia;* idem, "Revolutionary Politics."

68. See R. S. Thorn, "The Economic Transformation," in Malloy and Thorn, *Beyond the Revolution*, pp. 157–217; and J. W. Wilkie, "Public Expenditures since 1952," in ibid., pp. 217–233. On the external impact and force see C. Blasier, "The United States and the Revolution," in ibid., pp. 53–111. For a different view see S. Eckstein, "How Economically Consequential Are Revolutions? A Comparison of Mexico and Bolivia," *Studies in Comparative International Development*, 10, no. 3 (1975): 48–62; and idem, *Impact of Revolution*.

69. On the origins of the Cuban Revolution see Blasier, "Studies of Social Revolution"; H. Thomas, *Cuba: The Pursuit of Freedom* (New York: Harper & Row, 1971), chap. 8; R. E. Bonachea and N. P. Valdés (eds.), *Cuba in Revolution* (Garden City: Doubleday, Anchor, 1972); and W. MacGaffey and C. R. Barent, *Twentieth Century Cuba: The Background of the Castro Revolution* (Garden City: Doubleday, Anchor, 1962).

70. On Communist participation in the Cuban Revolution see A. Suárez, *Cuba, Castroism, and Communism, 1959–1966* (Cambridge: MIT Press, 1967).

71. On the restructuring of Cuban society after the Revolution see C. Mesa-Lago (ed.), *Revolutionary Change in Cuba* (Pittsburgh: University of Pittsburgh Press, 1974); T. Draper, *Castro's Revolution: Myths and Realities* (New York: Praeger, 1962); Bonachea and Valdés, *Cuba in Revolution*; M. Zeitlin, *Revolutionary Politics and the Cuban Working Class* (New York: Harper & Row, 1970); and R. R. Fagen, *The Transformation of Political Culture in Cuba* (Stanford: Stanford University Press, 1969).

72. On Portugal see Graham, *Decline and Collapse of an Authoritarian Regime*; Harsgor, *Portugal in Revolution*; N. Poulantzas, *La Crise des dictatures: Portugal, Grèce, Espagne* (Paris: F. Maspéro, 1975); M. Soares, *Portugal: Quelle révolution?* (Paris: Calmann-Lévy, 1976); and "A Revolution Tamed: A Survey of Portugal," *The Economist* (London), May 28, 1977, Survey pp. 1–30.

Chapter 10. Beyond Classical Revolutions— Revolutionary Movements and Radicalism in Late Modern Societies

1. THE EXPECTATION OF REVOLUTION

The pattern of structural change and of revolutionary movements and symbolism that developed in late modern societies—especially in post-industrial societies [1]—differs of course from the pattern in neopatrimonial societies. Yet, because of developments within the latter and because of the fact that both late modern and neopatrimonial societies belong to the same international system, they exhibit certain common features.

First, despite the attraction of revolutionary symbolism, patterns of change within both types of societies diverged from the image of the pure revolution.

This result may seem paradoxical with respect to late modern societies in particular. The strength of the revolutionary tradition and especially of Marxist predictions about the coming proletarian revolution has motivated social scientists and other analysts to try to identify the conditions that brought about revolutions in these societies.[2]

Developments in nineteenth-century European societies made revolution appear highly likely. In the earlier phases of modernization many significant social and political changes (e.g., the acquisition of political rights and citizenship, the extension of social services, the development of the welfare state with its redistributive orientations, and the growing interference of the state in the economy—all implied in the revolutionary premises) were implemented at least partially through the activities of socialist and labor groups, movements, and parties among which revolutionary and especially class symbolism predominated. Concomitantly, class consciousness became a key aspect of the self-identity of many groups in modern European societies.

Some events in the 1960s reemphasized the strength of revolutionary orientations and intensified the search for conditions that might lead to revolutionary change in late modern societies. Among these developments were the revolutionary movements connected with student unrest in Western societies; [3] the multiplicity of international revolutionary groups in general and the resurgence of urban guerrilla and terrorist groups; [4] as well as Czechoslovakian and Polish resistance to Soviet domination. [5]

The analyses that attempted to identify the preconditions of revolution focused on internal developments and contradictions in the later stages of industrialization and on the vulnerability of late capitalist and, to a smaller degree, of communist regimes. [6] This vulnerability was presumably connected with constant, far-reaching structural changes that were going on in all these societies. These changes disturbed basic aspects of the social structure and underlined the contradictions between the premises of the early revolutions and the original vision of European modernity, on the one hand, and the institutional expansion seemingly attendant on these images, on the other—contradictions that originally gave rise to socialism and communism.

Truly enough, the Western world has witnessed a steady, unprecedented increase in the standard of living, in this way realizing the vision of continual institutional expansion. But, as we indicated in Chapter 6, the process of expansion was neither smooth nor unproblematic. Expansion in one social sphere did not necessarily assure parallel expansion in other spheres. Likewise, it did not always entail the growing participation of various groups and strata in the social and cultural orders or provide these groups with a greater sense of participation in different areas of life.

Finally, expansion was connected with continual shifts in the distribution of resources and in the modes of access to them and hence with processes of structural dislocation and with the exclusion or inclusion of different social groups, dimensions of human existence, and attributes of human endeavor in the social and cultural centers.

Some of these contradictory tendencies became most apparent in the later stages of industrialization, and they were connected with basic structural trends in highly developed industrial societies. Among the most important of these trends was first the bureaucratization of economic, educational, scientific, political, and administrative spheres. [7] Second was the growing dissociation between ownership of resources, on the one hand, and control over occupational positions and economic power, on the other, as well as the extension of political rights and actual control over economic and political resources and decisions. [8] Third was the expansion of the educational system, which led or was closely related to changes in occupational and class structure—especially to the increasing predominance of such new groups as service workers, white-collar employees, technicians, bureaucrats, and intellectuals. [9] The sphere that has experienced seemingly steady, unhindered development and expansion—namely science and technology—has had the most problematic impact on other aspects of social life.

The contradictory possibilities inherent in the impact of technology on social life are rooted primarily in the fact that the constant expansion of science and technology and the increase in the importance of information have taken place within the context of the bureaucratization and oligarchization of scientific and technological enterprises. These developments have manifested themselves in far-reaching changes in the structure of the production and above all the administration of knowledge.

The spread of technology and the other processes we have been discussing had important organizational effects in the late industrial societies.[10] The most general and significant effects were the growth of monolithic, monopolistic, or oligopolistic organizations; the accumulation and automation of information; and the limitation of access to knowledge. Within these broad processes we can identitfy the merger of political, administrative, professional, and bureaucratic activities inside the same structure or organization, as well as far-reaching changes in the structure of decisionmaking in bureaucratic (and professional) organizations. Most important here were the coalescence of managers and experts and the tendency to monopolize specialized knowledge—which has indeed become crucial in the exercise of political control—on the part of upper management and technical experts.[11] Such merger and monopolization reduced the access of the lower echelons in organizations as well as the wider public (the clientele of the administrative and bureaucratic organizations) to such knowledge. Consequently, these processes minimized the possibilities of structural pluralism and autonomous access of different groups to the centers of power and enhanced the tendencies toward direct bargaining between various levels of experts and different segments of the public.[12]

The contradictory impacts of technology were very closely related to the inclusion or exclusion of various social groups and domains of human experience in the centers of social and cultural life. Insofar as these processes of dislocation became connected with some of the social structural changes analyzed above, their contradictory impacts tended to be more obvious. As Dermott pointed out,

> the most important such impact seems to be, first, that technological progress requires a continuous increase in the skill levels of its work force, skill levels which frequently embody a fairly rich scientific and technical training, while at the same time the advance of technical rationality in work organization means that those skills might be less and less fully used, thus giving rise to a situation in which the work force in advanced technological systems must be over-trained and under-utilized.
>
> Second, in the economic spheres, there is a parallel process at work.

It is commonly observed that the work force within technologically advanced organizations is asked to work not less hard but more so. This is particularly true for those with advanced training and skills.

Yet the prosperity which is assumed in a technologically advanced society erodes the value of economic incentives (while, of course, the values of draftsmanship are "irrational"). Salary and wage increases and the goods they purchase lose their overriding importance once necessities, creature comforts, and an ample supply of luxuries are assured.

Politically, the advance of technology tends to concentrate authority within its managing groups, but at the same time the increasing skill and educational levels of the population create latent capacities for self-management in the work place and in society. Finally, there is a profound social contradiction between the highly stratified society implicit in, say, Brzezinski's *Meritocracy* and the spread of educational opportunity—each of which appears equally required by advanced technology.[13]

2. STRUCTURAL TRANSFORMATION. INSTITUTIONALIZATION OF REVOLUTIONARY SYMBOLISM. CHANGING RELATIONS AMONG STATE, SOCIETY, AND ECONOMY

Many scholars have seen in the contradictions of late modern society the forces that will generate new revolutionary processes and upheavals in the image of the true revolution. These expectations were reinforced by the fact that these problems and contradictions served as the principal foci of many revolutionary upheavals, especially student revolts, in the sixties.[14] These movements grew out of Europe's revolutionary tradition, and many regarded them as the culmination of that tradition.[15] Yet the 1848 uprising in France, the Paris Commune, and so on, indicated to those who were willing to see—and Marx himself sensed some of these problems although he was not always willing to admit them—that the pattern of social transformation and political radicalism in Western societies had gone beyond the premises and expectations of the image of the pure revolution. This became even more evident in late industrial or postindustrial society.

A closer look at developments in these societies reveals a complex picture. Revolutionary symbols and movements have indeed become a very powerful, seemingly natural force in postindustrial society, a focus of attraction and a model of virtue and of social and personal charisma. At the same time, however, the pattern of change, transformation, and radicalism has assumed peculiar features, pointing less and less at the possibility of pure revolution and instead encouraging the tendency toward the development of *revolts*.[16]

Several processes explain this development. One was the institutionalization of revolutionary premises and class symbolism. Indeed, the fundamental institutional frameworks of modern societies can be seen as the institutionalization of the initial premises of European revolutionary modernity. The basic premises of these political systems imply the possibility of the complete coalescence of central political struggle with movements of protest and intellectual and ideological heterodoxies, which will result in far-reaching and convergent structural, political, social, and economic changes in all the ground rules of social interaction and their institutional derivatives. By the later stages of industrialization, these changes had been effected within institutional frameworks that incorporated revolutionary symbolism and premises and class symbolism in particular. Thus, the classical revolutionary image lost some of its vitality or attraction.

However, this process was not just routinization of revolutionary charisma.[17] It weakened the preconditions of revolution—namely, the denial of the legitimacy of a relatively closed center that limited access to itself and regulated the system of stratification in a traditional way (a denial that touched off the quest for total reconstruction of the center). Hence, all the changes in the political, social, and economic spheres attributable to the original premises of modernity became less and less connected with undermining the bases of political legitimation or the symbols of the political regime and with totally restructuring access to power.

Second, this weakening of the conditions behind revolutionary transformation (in the image of the real revolution) was reinforced by the structural tendencies that developed in all late modern societies. Of special importance in this respect were the structural changes that arose out of the conflicts and contradictions connected with later industrialization, changes (analyzed above) in the patterns of stratification, the ordering of social hierarchies, and the relationships among state, economy, and society.

Altered relations between the state and the impact of this change on social stratification were analyzed brilliantly by Claus Offe and summarized by W. Müller and K. A. Mayer. Offe showed that the basic structure of late capitalism is the contradiction between socialized labor and the private appropriation of surplus value.[18] However, in contrast to traditional class society, in late modern society the economic sector is no longer private because the state constantly intervenes in order to secure full employment and balanced economic growth. The state has to provide sufficient and profitable opportunities for private investment and has to compensate in areas where private investment is lacking. This intervention is held to have far-reaching consequences in terms of inequality and class relations.

Offe maintains that traditional class theory, as best exemplified in

Weber's work, has become inadequate in several respects. While in traditional theory it is assumed that income is determined by the particular supply of labor and capital in markets, now the relationship between individual performance at work and income derived from this work has loosened because the price for labor is determined not by the market but by noneconomic standards of just remuneration and by political regulations like minimum wages, welfare provisions, and income redistribution policies. It is not only that the observable extent of inequality has ceased to be a direct counterpart of the distribution of economic power, but also that this modified distribution of monetary income determines only partially the unequal access to goods and values. More and more needs such as education, health care, and transportation cannot be satisfied by consumer markets but are collectively met and financed as well as politically determined.

Thus, political intervention takes place both between labor and income and between income and actual life chances. Therefore, the new forms of inequality cannot directly be derived from economically determined class relationships between producers and owners of the means of production. The irrational consequences of capitalism now make themselves felt in the differential provision of private and public goods. Although the capitalist mode of production continues to produce inequality of income and therefore of property, this inequality does not lead to class conflict as the major focus of societal change, but is superimposed by horizontal disparities. These changing relations among state, economy, and society in late industrial societies have been reinforced by the bureaucratization of the channels of mobility that developed in capitalist and socialist countries alike, as well as by the growing internationalization of economic markets, corporations, and government activities.[19]

3. SEGREGATION OF POLITICAL STRUGGLE AND NEW PATTERNS OF CONFLICT. FROM REVOLUTION TO REVOLT

The central place of the state as a distributive and regulatory agency —access to which is open to various interest groups—capable of responding to broad demands and pressures gave rise, as Offe pointed out, to the growing segregation of status groups and to the potential depoliticization of class struggle. This trend was encouraged by the fact that in all late industrial societies, the increasing professionalization and institutional specialization of elites, along with the tendencies toward concentration analyzed above and the growth of government planning, promoted the dispersal and segregation of elites (especially articulators of the models of cultural order and the more functional elites).[20] These developments gave rise to new types of coalitions among different political, economic, intellectual, and social elites that to some extent followed a neopatrimonial pattern—greatly emphasizing co-optation and direct negotiation and bargaining.[21]

The changed role of the state, the rise of new coalitions, the institutionalization of the original revolutionary premises, the legitimation of revolutionary symbolism, and the opening of access to the center fostered segregation of political demands related to different ground rules of social interaction. Above all, these developments caused political demands related to changes in the various ground rules to be increasingly dissociated from demands for access to power, the latter becoming increasingly taken for granted.

These tendencies toward the segregation of different issues or levels of political struggle were in turn reinforced by the activities of these coalitions. Concurrently, there developed in late industrial societies a new pattern of social dislocation. Many of the so-called lower groups such as skilled or semiskilled workers were put into positions of power. Both they and white-collar groups came to be relatively isolated from intellectual elites with ideological orientations—as the May 1970 events in France dramatically demonstrated.

All these developments led, as Alain Touraine,[22] Samuel P. Huntington,[23] and Barrington Moore [24] indicated in their analyses of postindustrial societies, to the development of new patterns of conflict. First, different elements of the working class became dissociated, which weakened the class consciousness of potentially revolutionary strata. Second, the working class and intellectuals grew similarly dissociated. Third, the preceding encouraged, as Touraine has shown, the development of new types of group strife—such as intergenerational or interethnic conflict—that differed from classical class struggle.

Thus, the trends that developed in late industrial societies although predicated on the initial revolutionary vision and rooted in the institutional derivatives of that vision created a situation that weakened the structural conditions conducive to full revolutionary transformation, which explains why no new revolutions but only, as Jacques Ellul has put it, revolts have occurred.[25]

4. CHANGING FOCI OF PROTEST

These developments were very closely related to or manifest in the continual shifts in the orientations and loci of protest in the different stages of modernity.

In the earlier stages of modernity the major orientations and foci of protest rested on the assumption that it is through the reformation and reorganization of national political centers that most social problems—especially the problems of meaningful participation in the sociocultural order and the problems generated by industrialization—can be solved.[26] These centers were viewed as the principal frameworks for the charismatic orientations through which the modern social and cultural orders are defined and also as the most important reference points for individuals' cultural and collective identities. They were also conceived as being able, through appropriate social policies or through revolutionary change, to restructure those aspects of the modern economy that were regarded as most conducive to alienation and anomie.

Thus, in the first stages of modernity, most movements of social protest revolved around the revolutionary image of broadening the scope of participation and the channels of access to the centers; changing or reforming their cultural and social contents; solving the problems of unequal participation in them; and finding ways to resolve through the policies of the centers, the crucial problems arising out of industrialization in general and the initial development of the capitalist system in particular. Solution of these problems constituted the major goal of most social and national movements in this period, and this goal was perceived as embodying the most important charismatic dimension of the modern sociocultural order. In other words, it was the sociopolitical center of the nation-state and the quest for access to it and participation in it that constituted the main foci through which orientations of protest could become at least partially institutionalized in emerging social systems. The best illustration of such a movement of protest is the classical class struggle as envisaged by most revolutionary and reformist socialist movements.

However, with the growing legitimation of the centers and institutionalization of revolutionary premises, reconstruction of the centers and the bases of their legitimacy became less and less the central political struggle. The problem of legitimation of the system shifted, as Jürgen Habermas has shown, away from such reconstruction and toward identification with the broad value orientations seemingly implicit in the modern era.[27]

This shift was evident both in the structure of movements of protest and their relationship to political struggle as well as in the symbols and foci of protest that developed in late industrial societies. The most important aspect of these structural characteristics was the growing dissociation of the various extreme movements of protest that arose in all these societies and the more central political struggle—and hence the dissociation between these movements and restructuring of the political center. (Some of these trends were apparent in the French uprising of 1848, the Paris Commune, and the German upheavals of 1918.) [28] The more central (class) political entrepreneurs were interested primarily in broadening access to a relatively open center and not in restructuring class relationships (as extremist groups advocated). Once this goal was attained, the coalition of these different elements—initially weak—broke down, generating new cleavages. Most of the extremists dissociated themselves from the restructuring of the center once the latter was opened, and the concrete struggle for various socioeconomic changes tended more and more to be channeled into the newly established institutional and political frameworks.

These constraints on the possibility of revolutionary change within modern society, brilliantly analyzed by Otto Kirchheimer, were manifest in the German upheavals of 1918. In this case the very transition to an open center not only dampened the pure revolutionary fervor of more extreme groups but also, as Volker Rittberger demonstrated, precluded the possibility of a broader restructuring of this center that would minimize the power of more conservative groups and assure it greater legitimacy.[29]

As it became clearer that the working class in the relatively successful industrial societies and mature democracies tending to be increasingly domesticated (accepting the legitimacy of the system, relating itself to central political struggle, but dissociating itself from intellectual movements and more extreme movements), there occurred the shift in revolutionary tactics and ideology mentioned in Chapter 6. The thrust of that shift was the emphasis on external activities of extreme revolutionary groups as against the spontaneous working out of social forces. This shift is most fully elaborated in Leninism but also characterizes the ideology of Rosa Luxemburg and the latest theories of insurrection and guerrilla warfare.[30] Thus, in the later stages of industrialization it was obvious that the institutionalization of revolutionary symbolism, the opening of centers, and the structural transformations analyzed above had diminished the possibility of that combination of movements of protest with far-reaching structural changes implicit in the image of pure revolution.

A parallel development in modern societies was the shift away from demands for greater participation in national political centers and toward their restructuring. First, there were efforts made to strip these centers of their charismatic legitimacy and perhaps of any legitimacy at all; second, there were repeated searches for new loci of meaningful participation and attempts to create new centers that would be independent of the old; and third, there were efforts to couch the patterns of participation in the centers not so much in sociopolitical or economic terms but rather in the symbols of primordial or direct participation in social institutions.

Many of these new orientations of protest were directed not only against the bureaucratization and functional rationalization connected with growing technology but also against the supposed central (or any) place of science and scientific investigation in the sociocultural order. They all manifested an important aspect of what Weber called the demystification of the world—demystification that here focused on the possibility that gaining participation in the social and cultural centers might be meaningless.[31]

(Interestingly enough, many active political, revolutionary orientations lately have focused on areas such as ethnic identity, relations between the sexes, or esthetic experiences, all of which are beyond the premises of the initial revolutionary image.) [32]

5. REVOLUTIONARY AND RADICAL GROUPS. STUDENT REVOLT

The most vocal revolutionary groups in late industrial societies were the student movements of the 1960s, the various guerrilla and terrorist movements, and the more extreme revolutionary elites and movements that were closely related to, or part of, the growing internationalization of revolutionary activity.

Most of these movements exemplified the shift in the orientations of protest that culminated in the most extreme expressions of antinomianism, as manifested in the university revolts. It was not simply that certain bureaucratic or meritocratic features of postindustrial societies were necessarily more developed in the university than in other organizations and institutions. Rather, the university was perceived as the major locus and symbol of the discrepancies between social reality and the ideal premises of the modern social and cultural orders and as the very place in which the quest for creativity and participation inherent in the modern vision should be institutionalized.

The university was perceived as the principal source of legitimation of the modern social order. Attack on it indicated not only dissatisfaction with the university's internal arrangements or role but also frustration that the existing order had not realized the premises of modernity.

Thus, in the attack on the university the new antinomian dimension of protest—the negation of the premises of modernity and the emphasis on the meaningless of existing centers and symbols of collective identity—became articulated in an extreme way.[33]

(This negative attitude toward the modern centers was shared by more professional revolutionaries—terrorists—bent on their total upset from inside or from outside. In terms of being antinomian, both student and terrorist movements were akin to many earlier intellectual and religious heterodoxies, but they had a much broader impact on society.)

The strong impact made by student protesters was due mainly to their social location.[34] These were no longer, as formerly had been the case, small, closed, isolated intellectual groups; they were groups from within the broader collectivity of aspirants to intellectual status, who constituted a large segment of the educated public. Therefore, such groups impinged on the centers of intellectual creativity and cultural transmission and constituted integral, even if transient, parts thereof. This very closeness to the centers ensured that the student movements would powerfully affect society although not necessarily in keeping with the pure revolutionary image.

The more violent revolutionary or terrorist groups could easily produce deep cleavages in their own societies. Their activities provoked repressive orientations and measures; but they rarely effected the structure of the centers and access to power. They could influence, even if indirectly the principles of distributive justice that dealt with consumption, leisure, and privacy, dimensions to a large degree neglected in the original vision of European modernity. Many of these processes gave rise to important institutional changes.

In close relation with shifts in the meanings of institutions there was movement within the framework of certain bureaucratic organizations toward greater participation on the part of constituent groups as well as broader (community or political) collectivities in the definition of their goals. In some cases this resulted in extensive alteration of organizational goals by the incorporation of new community or societal aims and orientations. Second, many late industrial societies witnessed a growing dissociation between high occupational strata and conservative social attitudes; thus, top level executives espoused politically and culturally leftist views and participated in the counterculture. Third, the political sphere exhibited tendencies toward the redefinition of the roles of the citizen and his obligations and toward redefinition of the boundaries of collectivities. As a result, there occurred growing dissociation between political centers and the social and cultural collectivities and the development of new nuclei of cultural and social identity that transcended existing political and cultural boundaries.

These changes may be instituted in a great variety of ways—legislation, co-optative arrangements among different coalitions, and loose though steady contact among structural enclaves within which new cultural orientations (concerned with the possibility of extending individuality beyond the bureaucratic, meritocratic, occupational, and administrative structures) may be articulated.

These enclaves, in which both permanent and temporary participation is possible, may become centers of subcultures. They may harbor extreme revolutionary groups, or engender new movements, or become allied with more central coalitions.

The development of such enclaves, as well as their different and seemingly contradictory functions or potentialities, is rooted not only in the internal developments of each postindustrial society but also in the structure of intersocietal relations. Of special importance here is the fact that the organizational and informational bases of postindustrial societies—

universities, science-based industries, large, multinational corporations, and mass media—as well as the major loci of protest tend to cluster around certain intersocietal meeting points.

While participants in all these arenas differ as their societies differ, they tend to espouse similar attitudes toward the symbolic premises and promises of modernity and manifest similar perception of relative deprivation with regard to these premises and promises. This phenomenon reinforces the conditions that predisposed modern societies to radicalism and revolutionary symbolism and to the development of revolutionary groups.

6. THE WEAKENING OF REVOLUTIONARY TRANSFORMATION. THE SHIFTING PREMISES OF MODERN CIVILIZATION

To sum up, the legitimation of revolutionary symbols, the opening of centers, and the structural transformations analyzed in this chapter have diminished the possibility that late modern or industrial societies will witness the combination of movements of protest and far-reaching structural changes inherent in the image of pure revolution. Nevertheless, internal developments and international forces may react so as to produce (especially among relatively backward societies such as Portugal, Greece, and even Spain) processes of political struggle and movements of protest that will be connected with questioning the basic premises of political regimes and to promote revolutionary activities and changes.[36] But such a course of events is exceptional. The more general trend is that late industrial and especially capitalist societies do not follow the pattern of transformation envisaged by the revolutionary image.

The preceding analysis does not minimize the importance of the revolutionary vision. It does, however, indicate that in the late modern, postrevolutionary societies there took place a marked shift in the combination of these elements, which are necessarily linked in the image of the pure revolution.

We do not suggest that far-reaching structural changes, overthrows of regimes, conflicts, and violence, on the one hand, and movements of protest based on revolutionary symbols, on the other, will not arise in later industrial—either capitalist or socialist, democratic or totalitarian—societies. Neither does the preceding analysis imply that capitalist democracies may not be led in the direction of social welfare, as took place in Sweden, or their economies undermined through the internal dislocation of elites, as may happen in Great Britain, or their political systems transformed through the incorporation of the left, as may occur in Italy.

Similarly, the upheavals and unrest in communist societies do not seem to move in a direction in which the different aspects of political struggle subsumed under the image of revolution tend to become dissociated from one another. Thus, in these societies the classical revolutionary image has become separated from concrete political processes and struggles. Of course, given the actual even if not the symbolic closure of communist centers, it may well be that there will develop within them tendencies toward the coalescence of different movements of protest, aiming at the opening up of the centers. But such struggle will not be able to undermine political regimes unless it becomes connected with national causes. Accordingly, the tendency to revolt will be much stronger than the possibility of revolution in the communist world.[37]

These new orientations of protest and their structural locations and implications indicate that we may be witnessing the disintegration of some crucial components of the revolutionary tradition, especially the negation or weakening of the assumption of the initial vision of modernity that the fullest expression of the charismatic dimension of life is to be found in the occupational and economic spheres and in the sphere of scientific endeavor, on the one hand, and in political participation in the new national centers, on the other. This development—at odds with the initial premises of the revolutionary vision—would reinforce the tendencies toward segregation of institutional spheres.

But such segregation would necessarily be structured in a way different from that in traditional society. It would be based to a greater extent on the continuous flow of (very often the same) people through various structural and organizational units within which these distinct types of orientations and information would be organized. Hence, tension among institutional spheres would constitute a permanent aspect of the sociocultural scene.

NOTES

1. D. Bell, *The Coming of Post-Industrial Society: A Venture in Social Fore-casting* (New York: Basic Books, 1973); A. Touraine, *La Société post-industrielle* (Paris: Denoël, 1969), available in translation as *The Post-Industrial Society* (New York: Random House, 1971); and F. Bourricaud, "Post-Industrial Society and the Paradox of Welfare," *Survey,* 16, no. 1 (1971): 23–60.

2. See S. Andreski, *Prospects of a Revolution in the U.S.A.* (New York: Harper & Row, Harper Colophon, 1973); R. Aya and N. Miller (eds.), *The New American Revolution* (New York: Free Press, 1969); N. Miller and R. Aya (eds.), *National Liberation: Revolution in the Third World* (New York: Free Press, 1971); B. Moore, Jr., "Revolution in America?" *New York Review of Books,* 12, no. 2 (1969): 6–12; T. Schieder (ed.), *Revolution und Gesellschaft* (Freiburg in Breisgau: Herder, 1973); M.

Halpern, "The Revolution of Modernization in National and International Society," in C. J. Friedrich (ed.), *Revolution: Yearbook of the American Society for Political and Legal Philosophy*, Nomos 8 (New York: Atherton, 1967), pp. 178–216; C. B. Macpherson, *Democratic Theory* (Oxford: Clarendon, 1973), pp. 157–170. See also two collections of Marxist writings: M. Kossok (ed.), *Studien über die Revolution* (Berlin: Akademie, 1969); and idem (ed.), *Studien zur vergleichenden Revolutionsgeschichte, 1500–1917* (Berlin: Akademie, 1974).

3. The literature on student unrest and protest is enormous. Representative collections and works are P. G. Altbach, "Students and Politics," in J. R. Gusfield (ed.), *Protest, Reform, and Revolt: A Reader in Social Movements* (New York: Wiley, 1970), pp. 225–244; P. G. Altbach and R. S. Laufer (eds.), *The New Pilgrims: Youth Protest in Transition* (New York: McKay, 1972); R. Aron, *The Elusive Revolution: Anatomy of a Student Revolt* (London: Pall Mall, 1969); V. L. Bengtson and R. S. Laufer (eds.), "Youth, Generation, and Social Change: Part 1," *Journal of Social Issues*, 30, no. 2 (1974): 1–20; V. L. Bengtson and R. S. Laufer (eds.), "Youth, Generation, and Social Change: Part 2," ibid., no. 3 (1974): 1–209; R. Boudon, "Sources of Student Protest in France," in Altbach and Laufer, *New Pilgrims*, pp. 297–312; E. Brown, "The Black University," in G. R. Weaver and J. H. Weaver (eds.), *The University and Revolution* (Englewood Cliffs: Prentice-Hall, 1969), pp. 141–152; J. D. Douglas, "The Theories of the American Student Protest Movements," in R. S. Denisoff (ed.), *The Society of Dissent* (New York: Harcourt Brace Jovanovich, 1974), pp. 58–79; R. Flacks, "Social and Cultural Meanings of Student Revolt: Some Informal Comparative Observations," in ibid., pp. 161–179; E. S. Glenn, "The University and the Revolution: New Left or New Right?" in Weaver and Weaver, *University and Revolution*, pp. 99–120; R. Kirk, "The University and Revolution: An Insane Conjunction," in ibid., pp. 67–82; J. Newfield, "In Defense of Student Radicals," in ibid., pp. 43–54; J. Habermas, L. von Friedeburg, C. Oehler, and F. Weltz, *Studenten und Politik* (Berlin: Luchterhand, 1969); K. Keniston, *Young Radicals* (New York: Harcourt, Brace, 1968); S. M. Lipset, *Rebellion in the University* (Chicago: University of Chicago Press, 1971); D. Singer, *Prelude to Revolution* (London: Jonathan Cape, 1970); I. Howe and M. Barrington (eds.), *The Seventies: Problems and Proposals* (New York: Harper & Row, 1972); E. E. Ericson, Jr., *Radicals in the University* (Stanford: Stanford University, Hoover Institution, 1975); A. Touraine, *The May Movement: Revolt and Reform* (New York: Random House, 1971); and F. Bourricaud, *Universités à la dérive: France, Etats-Unis, et l'Amérique du Sud* (Paris: Plon, 1971).

4. On international revolutionary groups, urban guerrillas, and terrorist groups see L. Berkowitz, "The Study of Urban Violence: Some Implications of Laboratory Studies of Frustration and Aggression," in J. C. Davies (ed.), *When Men Revolt and Why* (New York: Free Press, 1971); A. Burton, *Urban Terrorism* (New York: Free Press, 1975); R. A. Falk, "World Revolution and International Order," in Friedrich, *Revolution*, pp. 154–177; T. Ali (ed.), *The New Revolutionaries: A Handbook of the Inter-*

national Radical Left (New York: Morrow, 1969); S. Neumann, "The International Civil War," *World Politics*, 1 (1948): 333–350; M. Oppenheimer, *Urban Guerrilla* (Chicago: Quadrangle, 1969); A. Neuberg, *Armed Insurrection*, trans. Q. Hoare (London: New Left Books, 1970); and E. J. Hobsbawm, *Revolutionaries* (London: Weidenfeld & Nicolson, 1973), pp. 163–245.

5. Concerning developments in Eastern Europe see J. Kuron and K. Modzelewski, "Öffener Brief an die polnische Vereinigte Arbeiterpartei," in M. Jänicke (ed.), *Politische Systemkrisen* (Cologne: Kiepenheuer & Witsch, 1973), pp. 364–378; D. Lane, "Dissent and Consent under State Socialism," *Archives, European Journal of Sociology*, 13, no. 1 (1972): 37–44; and P. E. Zinner (ed.), *National Communism and Popular Revolt in Eastern Europe: A Selection of Documents on Events in Poland and Hungary* (New York: Columbia University Press, 1956).

6. On the vulnerability of later capitalist and communist regimes see A. Meyer, "Theories of Convergence," in C. Johnson (ed.), *Change in Communist Systems* (Stanford: Stanford University Press, 1970), pp. 313–341; V. Rouge, "Die Umwelt im kapitalistischen System," in Jänicke, *Politische Systemkrisen*, pp. 329–352; F. W. Scharpf, "Reformpolitik im Spätkapitalismus," in ibid., pp. 353–363; R. Lowenthal, "Social Transformation and Democratic Legitimacy," *Social Research*, 43, no. 2 (1976): 246–275; J. Habermas, *Legitimation Crisis* (Boston: Beacon, 1975); and D. Bell, *The Cultural Contradictions of Capitalism* (New York: Basic Books, 1976). See also Z. Bauman, "Social Dissent in the East European Political System," *Archives européennes de Sociologie*, 12, no. 1 (1971): 25–51; L. Kolakowski, "A Pleading for Revolution: A Rejoinder to Z. Bauman," ibid., 52–60; J. Baechler, "De la fragilité des systèmes politiques," ibid., 61–86; D. Lane, "Dissent and Consent under State Socialism," ibid., 13, no. 1 (1972): 37–44; F. Parkin, "System Contradiction and Political Transformation," ibid., 45–62; and R. Aron, "Remarques sur un débat," ibid., 63–79.

7. On the trends to bureaucratization see S. N. Eisenstadt, "Bureaucracy and Bureaucratization: A Trend Report," *Current Sociology*, 7, no. 2 (1958): 99–124; P. Blau and R. A. Schoenher, *The Structure of Organizations* (New York: Basic Books, 1971); Touraine, *Société post-industrielle*; R. A. Dahl, *After the Revolution* (New Haven: Yale University Press, 1970); and V. Belhoradsky, "Burocrazia carismatica: Ratio e carisma nella società di massa," in L. Pellicani (ed.), *Sociologia delle rivoluzioni* (Naples: Guida, 1976), pp. 181–232.

8. This trend is well summarized in Bell, *Post-Industrial Society*, chaps. 1, 2, 4.

9. On·these broad trends in social stratification in late modern societies see S. N. Eisenstadt, *Social Differentiation and Stratification* (Glenview: Scott, Foresman, 1971), chaps. 9–11; Bell, *Post-Industrial Society*; and S. P. Huntington, "Post-Industrial Politics: How Benign Will It Be," *Comparative Politics*, 6, no. 2 (1974): 163–193.

10. C. Kerr, *Marshall, Marx, and Modern Times: The Multi-Dimensional*

Society (Cambridge: At the University Press, 1969); and E. G. Mesthene, *Technological Change: Its Impact on Man and Society* (Cambridge: Harvard University Press, 1970).

11. See on this Blau and Schoenher, *Structure of Organizations.*

12. See Bell, *Post-Industrial Society;* Huntington, "Post-Industrial Politics"; J. D. Douglas, *Freedom and Tyranny* (New York: Knopf, 1971), pp. 3–33; F. F. Rositi (ed.), *Razionalità sociale e tecnica delle informazione,* 3 vols. (Milan: Di Communità, 1973).

13. J. M. L. Dermott, "Technology: The Opiate of the Intellectuals," *New York Review of Books,* 13, no. 2 (1969): 28.

14. On student revolts in the sixties see the works cited in note 3 above; see also P. H. Partridge, "Contemporary Revolutionary Ideas," in E. Kamenka (ed.), *A World in Revolution* (Canberra: Australian National University Press, 1970), pp. 91–100; and MacPherson, *Democratic Theory,* pp. 157–170.

15. See A. Dorpalen, "Die Revolutionen von 1848," in Schieder, *Revolution und Gesellschaft,* pp. 97–116; S. K. Padover, "Karl Marx as Revolutionist," in K. Marx, *On Revolution,* ed. S. K. Padover (New York: McGraw-Hill, 1971), pp. ix–xxx; R. C. Tucker, *The Marxian Revolutionary Idea* (New York: Norton, 1969); and D. Kramer, *Reform und Revolution bei Marx* (Cologne: Paul Rugenstein, 1971).

16. See J. Ellul, *Autopsy of Revolution* (New York: Knopf, 1971); and J. Ortega y Gasset, *El tema de nuestro tiempo: Ni vitalismo, ni racionalismo; el ocaso de las revoluciones; el sentido histórico de la teoria de Einstein* (Madrid: Revista de occidente, 1956).

17. Concerning the institutionalization of charisma see S. N. Eisenstadt, "Charisma and Institution Building: Max Weber and Modern Sociology," in S. N. Eisenstadt (ed.), *Max Weber: On Charisma and Institution Building* (Chicago: University of Chicago Press, 1968), pp. ix–lvi; Belohradsky, "Burocrazia carismatica."

18. See C. Offe, "Die Herrschaftsfunktionen des Staatsapparates," in Jänicke, *Politische Systemkrisen,* pp. 236–246; W. Müller and K. U. Meyer, "Social Stratification and Stratification Research in the Federal Republic of Germany, 1945–1975 (mimeo), to be published in R. Caporale (ed.), *Classes and Social Structure in Economically Advanced Societies,* forthcoming.

19. See the materials cited in Müller and Meyer, "Social Stratification"; and also Habermas, *Legitimation Crisis;* Jänicke, *Politische Systemkrisen;* and Bell, *Cultural Contradictions of Capitalism.*

20. J. Habermas, *Toward a Rational Society* (Boston: Beacon, 1971), pp. 62–81; Touraine, *Société post-industrielle;* and Rositi, *Razionalità sociale.*

21. See, among the many descriptions, Singer, *Prelude to Revolution;* Touraine, *The May Movement;* and Hobsbawm, *Revolutionaries,* esp. pp. 234–244.

22. See Touraine, *Société post-industrielle;* and idem, "Les nouveaux conflits sociaux," *Sociologie du travail,* 17, no. 1 (1975): 1–17.

23. Huntington, "Post-Industrial Politics."

24. Moore, "Revolution in America"; see also Andreski, *Revolution in the U.S.A.*

25. Ellul, *Autopsy of Revolution.*

26. This follows S. N. Eisenstadt, "Changing Patterns in Modern Political Protest and Centers," in *Science et conscience de la société: Mélanges en l'honneur de Raymond Aron* (Paris: Calmann-Lévy, 1971), 1:473–499.

27. See on this Habermas, *Legitimation Crisis,* and the critical appraisal by Lowenthal, "Social Transformation and Democratic Legitimacy," *Social Research,* 43, no. 2 (1976): 246–276.

28. See Dorpalen, "Die Revolutionen von 1848"; and V. Rittberger, "Revolution and Pseudo-Democratization: The Formation of the Weimar Republic," in G. A. Almond, S. C. Flanagan, and R. J. Mundt (eds.), *Crisis, Choice, and Change* (Boston: Little, Brown, 1973), pp. 285–391.

29. See Rittberger, "Revolution and Pseudo-Democratization"; and O. Kircheimer, "Confining Conditions and Revolutionary Breakthroughs," *American Political Science Review,* 59, no. 4 (1965): 964–974.

30. See V. I. Lenin, "What Is to Be Done," in Gusfield, *Protest, Reform, and Revolt,* pp. 458–472; for more diversified trends see J. P. Nettl, *Rosa Luxemburg on Revolution* (New York: Oxford University Press, 1969), pp. 174–202, 464–465; and L. Basso, *Rosa Luxemburgs Dialektik der Revolution* (Frankfurt am Main: Europäische Verlagsanstalt, 1969), pp. 88–148. For different trends in Marxism see C. Derfler, *Socialism since Marx: A Century of the European Left* (New York: Macmillan, 1973); D. Howard and K. E. Klare (eds.), *The Unknown Dimension: European Marxism since Lenin* (New York: Basic Books, 1972); and J. Gerassi (ed.), *Towards Revolution* (Weidenfeld & Nicolson, 1971). As one illustration of the vicissitudes of the Left in the welfare state see S. Wichert, "Zwischen Klassenkampf und Wohlfahrtsstaat: Grossbritanniens "Linke" im 20. Jahrhundert," *Neue politische Literatur,* 16, no. 2 (1971): 221–241. See also H. Lefebvre, *La survie du capitalisme* (Paris: Editions Anthropos, 1973).

31. For materials on Weber see Eisenstadt, "Charisma and Institution Building."

32. See Aya and Miller, *New American Revolution;* Partridge, "Contemporary Revolutionary Ideas"; Hobsbawm, *Revolutionaries,* pp. 216–219; and N. Glazer, "The Universalization of Ethnicity: Peoples in the Boiling Pot," *Encounter,* 17, no. 2 (1975): 8–17.

33. See the literature on student revolt and on guerrillas cited in notes 3 and 4 above; see especially Burton, *Urban Terrorism;* and Falk, "World Revolution and International Order."

34. On the continuity of the general revolutionary vogue among the intellectuals see R. Aron, *The Opium of the Intellectuals* (London: Secker & Warburg, 1957); and A. Gella, "Revolutionary Mood among the Contemporary Intellligentsia," in A. Gella (ed.), *The Intelligentsia and the Intellectuals: Theory, Method, and Case Study* (Beverly Hills: Sage, 1976), pp. 112–152. See also S. Delany (ed.), *Counter-Tradition* (New

York: Basic Books, 1971), a collection of materials on countertraditions throughout the ages; L. Henny, "Filmmakers as Part of a Revolutionary Intelligentsia," in Gella, *The Intelligentsia and the Intellectuals*, pp. 173–200; H. M. Hodges, Jr., "The Humanistic Intelligentsia," in ibid., pp. 153–172; Hobsbawm, *Revolutionaries*, pp. 245–266; and H. G. Helms, *Fetisch Revolution: Marxismus und Bundesrepublik* (Berlin: Luchterhand, 1976).

35. See S. N. Eisenstadt, "Generational Conflict and Intellectual Antinomianism," in Altbach and Laufer, *New Pilgrims*, pp. 139–154; Bourricaud, *Universités à la dérive;* Rositi, *Razionalità sociale;* and Dahl, *After the Revolution.*

36. N. Poulantzas, *La Crise des dictatures: Portugal, Grèce, Espagne* (Paris: Maspéro, 1975) available in translation as *The Crisis of Dictatorship* (London: New Left Books, 1976).

37. See, for instance, the articles cited in *Archives Européennes de Sociologie* cited in note 6 above. See also Johnson, *Change in Communist Systems.*

Epilogue

1. INTRODUCTION

We have come to the end of our story although the story itself is not ended. Our starting point was that the different components of social action that come under the umbrella of pure revolution constitute a special type of process through which social transformation takes place. In other words, while social conflict, heterodoxy, rebellion, change, and transformation are inherent in societies, the unique combination of elements subsumed under the image of the true revolution is in both traditional and modern systems just one of several avenues of change.

In the preceding chapters we analyzed the conditions that gave rise to the revolutionary process. We also noted that although revolutionary symbolism and movements have become a part of modern civilization, that mixture of symbolic and structural features that is characteristic of the real, classical revolutions arose only in exceptional circumstances. This fact, which we examined in Chapters 9 and 10, is further elucidated by analysis of the differential spread of the most prevalent type of modern revolutionary symbolism: that of socialism and communism.

2. INCORPORATION OF REVOLUTIONARY SYMBOLS IN MODERN SOCIETIES

We shall now analyze this differential spread.[1] Let us consider four points: first, which societies, social groups, or elites are prone to incorporate the symbolism of socialism into the central symbols of their collective (cultural and political) identity; second, is this symbolism accepted in its totality or are certain aspects rejected; third, to what are symbolic and/or institutional and/or organizational aspects of the socialist tradition or programs adopted; fourth, are the reformist, and revolutionary aspects or the harmonious and solidary as well as class aspects of socialist

329

symbolism emphasized? We shall briefly outline the major patterns of incorporation of the symbolism of socialism and communism.

In Western Europe, and to some degree Central Europe, many elites and groups incorporated into the symbols of the collectivities that they created in the nineteenth and twentieth centuries several socialist orientations and symbols. Among these groups only a few secondary or marginal, extremist elites accepted socialist tradition in its entirety: socialism was accepted wholesale primarily in the initial phases of its development by marginal groups. More commonly, with the growing institutionalization of socialism in Europe, its broad social and cultural symbols, as well as its concrete political and social programs, were incorporated into the emerging political and collective symbolism.

At the same time, there was continuity between the symbols of socialism and those of earlier European traditions, both modern and traditional. Specifically, these societies were willing to use their own traditions to find answers to new problems within the social and cultural orders.

In Russia and China, by contrast, the elites that established the revolutionary regimes made socialist symbolism the central component of their political-cultural identity and symbolism. In so doing, these revolutionary elites destroyed most of the concrete symbols and structures of existing traditions, strata, and organizations and emphasized new contents and new types of social organization. Yet, they nevertheless maintained continuity with regard to certain traditional symbolic and institutional orientations.

Thus, in Russia and China the symbols of socialism and communism became part of the central symbols of the collectivity, monopolized by the elites and closely related to socialist policies and institution building (the latter being continuously legitimized by the former). Officially, these symbols could not become symbols of internal protest but only of internal struggle among elites (although sometimes they have been taken up by extreme underground groups as symbols of protest against the regime).

Several Asian countries (Ceylon and Burma, for example), as well as some Moslem (Arab) countries, witnessed the rise of groups that sought to incorporate into the symbolism of their own societies certain socialist symbols. They tended to select socialism's broad cultural orientations and political programs. But only rarely in Asia and in the Arab world was socialism made the predominant element in the symbols of the collective identity.

Moreover, in most of these countries the socialist orientation did not entail, except among extremist elites, a high degree of commitment to its premises or a very high degree of institution building. In these societies emphasis was placed on continuity with existing symbols of collective identity.

The picture of African socialism is more complicated. We find among central elites a very strong tendency to incorporate the symbols of socialism into their own symbols of identity. But such incorporation was mostly symbolic, especially with regard to political symbols. We find also a tendency to accept the ideological-scientific contents and even the political programs of socialism. At the same time, many African countries (among them the Islamic nations) consciously stressed the continuity between socialist symbols—especially those of solidarity and harmony—and indigenous symbols. However, few African countries carried out institution building according to the original socialist pattern.[2]

Latin America presents yet another complicated picture. Originally, only marginal groups there developed a commitment to socialist symbols. Since the Cuban Revolution and during the Allende regime in Chile, however, such symbols moved into more central spheres of society and culture.

India's situation was the obverse of that in many Middle Eastern and African countries. The symbols of socialism were not central to the new symbols of collective identity that were created in the movement toward independence and afterward (even though that symbolism played an important role in the world view of Jawaharlal Nehru). However, many socialist programs were adopted, and socialism informed social policy and institution building.

Finally, in societies like Japan, only extreme groups, which never succeeded in gaining access to the political center, incorporated socialist symbolism into their collective identity.

3. CONDITIONS BEHIND THE INCORPORATION OF REVOLUTIONARY SYMBOLS

The different patterns of incorporation of the socialist tradition can be explained by some of the variables that we previously identified with respect to the specific conditions and outcomes of revolutions, by the combination of internal societal characteristics and position in the international frameworks, and by the society's evaluation of its international standing. Five characteristics of special importance can be discerned.

1. The structure of centers; and the nature of cultural orientations.

2. The degree to which there existed among various groups and elites a strong orientation toward participation in a great tradition—especially universalistic traditions; the degree to which these groups succeeded in incorporating their societies into the new international systems according to their own universalistic premises and/or those of the civilization of modernity.

3. The emphasis on utopian or millenarian orientations.

4. The cohesion and continuity of the centers as well as the continuity of the collective identity of these societies; the degree of impingement of the forces of modernity on the centers; the degree to which these forces undermined certain aspects of the collective identity; the degree to which the centers could espouse components, symbols, or orientations of the civilization of modernity.

5. The evaluation by various groups of the society's prospects for realizing the ideals of modernity. This characteristic was greatly influenced by the cohesiveness of these groups, by their vision of modernity, by the society's social and cultural openness in general and its attitude toward change in particular, as well as by its emphasis on power or prestige as the basic social orientation. Such evaluation was also influenced by the degree of dislocation of these groups within their own societies (caused by the impingement of internal and external social, political, and economic forces) and by their relative place in the emerging international power structure.

How do these variables explain the different patterns of incorporation of socialism and communism? It seems the receptivity to socialist symbols as components of the central symbols of the collective identity is dependent on the degree to which a society's traditions (or those of its elites) contain strong universalistic elements that transcend the tribal, ethnic, or national community, as well as strong utopian elements and orientations. Thus, it was in Western Europe, Russia, China, and to some degree the Middle East where universalistic and utopian elements were predominant (but not in Japan or India, where they were weak or nonexistent), that there developed a marked predisposition to the incorporation of socialist symbols. Moreover, receptivity to the central symbols of socialism is dependent on the degree to which universalistic orientations and elements existed in the society's own great tradition, as well as on its own security and cohesion as its great tradition was challenged in the process of incorporation into the new international systems. It is dependent on the degree to which the process of incorporation gives rise to a discrepancy between a society's aspirations to participate in the universalistic great tradition and its ability to create or preserve this tradition.

Thus, in Europe, such symbols were created as part of the European tradition and part of the processes of Europe's reshaping in the nineteenth and twentieth centuries. Elsewhere it was the manner of incorporation into the new, European-dominated, international settings that influenced the strength of tendencies to adopt socialist symbols. Thus, in Russia and China, where indigenous great traditions were shattered, socialist symbols were most welcome.

The cases of Japan, Latin America, and to some extent Africa reveal a different pattern. As long as cultural identity was maintained in relations with the West and its international systems (either through the society's attainment of a strong position without significantly altering its self-conception, as was the case in Japan, or through the society's acceptance of its own part in the new international frameworks, as was the case for a very long time in Latin America), the predisposition toward the incorporation of socialist symbols into central collective symbols was very small. Indeed, this tendency was limited to extremely marginal elites that were unable to influence the center and/or broader groups: in the sixties, as central Latin American elites grew increasingly disaffected from the European and North American centers, the symbols of socialism became more important.

In most African societies, colonialism drew relatively simple political and cultural units with weak (if any) great traditions into the new international frameworks and predisposed at least the more educated and urbanized elites toward participation in the new, broader setting.

In the central Islam countries it was the weakening of their own great tradition that encouraged certain elites to incorporate into the central societal symbols those of socialism. Especially important was uncertainty over the relations between the new, emerging political centers and the universalistic orientations of Islam. At the same time, given the persistence of this ambivalence, as well as that of Islam as a universalistic tradition, these elites selected some general socialist symbols as well as broad, nationalistic, political programs.

It is significant that the predisposition to the incorporation of socialist symbols was weakest in those African groups or societies that had a strong Islamic identity, which assured them of the possibility of participating in an existing great tradition. At the same time, the fact that these groups stood on the periphery of Islam removed them from the turbulence and problems of the central Islamic countries. In many instances, socialist symbols were simply added to the Islamic symbols of the collectivity.

Among the most important conditions that influenced the acceptance of socialism as a comprehensive system were first, the strength of universalistic and utopian elements in a society's traditions or in its elites' traditions, second, the relative strength of societal centers (the degree to which the centers commanded a high degree of commitment, and third, the nature of the major orientations of these centers and especially the emphasis on prestige and power; and the multiplicity and internal solidarity of elites.

Acceptance of socialism in its entirety was greatest in those societies with the strongest universalistic and utopian orientations and in which the undermining of indigenous traditions impinged on powerful cultural and political centers (that commanded a high degree of commitment) and gave rise to strong, totalistic movements. While such tendencies could develop among almost any elite or group, on the whole, the influence of such elites was greatest insofar as they developed in societies with strong but relatively closed centers (that is, societies that emphasized power and prestige orientations, of which Russia and China provide the clearest illustrations).

Given the strong universalistic elements of its tradition, Europe tended first to incorporate the social and social-political programs of socialism into existing political symbols. Second, given the relatively strong cohesion and solidarity of European elites, they placed a rather heavy emphasis on the institutional and organizational as well as the motivational aspects of socialism. However, Europe's pluralistic traditions combined with strong commitment to the social order to preclude wholesale acceptance of socialism. The more flexible European pattern of incorporation enabled various socialist symbols to serve as constantly changing foci of different dimensions of protest.

In many Southeast Asian countries, where patrimonial centers were prevalent, as well as in Latin America, with its Spanish, patrimonial heritage, the tendency comprehensively to accept socialism was even weaker. Except among marginal groups that attempted to create new, far-reaching symbols of collective identity, it was socialism's broad cultural orientations that were selected. Similarly, given the relatively low degree of elite solidarity, there developed only weak tendencies toward concrete institution building or center formation, while at the same time there developed a strong tendency to emphasize the symbols of the collectivity and center formation.

Emphasis on protest instead of center formation or institution building was most influenced by the position of elite groups vis-à-vis their society and the international power structure and by their perception of this position. Thus, very often (as in Russia or Africa) elites changed their emphasis from protest to center formation when they became ruling elites, and new opposition groups within the society tended to develop a strong protest orientation couched in socialist terms to use against the ruling elites.

4. ANALYTICAL CONCLUSIONS

The preceding analysis of the differential incorporation of socialist symbolism in modern and modernizing societies may help us draw together some of the major threads of our analysis in this book. First, note that the emergence of modern revolutions in Europe from the seventeenth century on should not be seen as a natural, inevitable development but rather as a unique development or mutation. This mutation took place under specific conditions that were to be found in numerous societies. But neither the occurrence of such a mutation nor the crystallization of any of its institutional derivatives was ineluctable.

This point about the nature of modern revolutions applies to the evolutionary perspective as it has informed the comparative analysis of societies: no concrete institutional pattern (e.g., Imperial, patrimonial, or feudal systems; specific modes of production) can be understood only in terms of certain general characteristics or trends of society. Such characteristics or trends—technological development or structural or symbolic differentiation, for example—create potentialities that are indeed similar in diverse societies. But the crystallization of a given institutional and/or macrosocietal complex is, as we stressed in Chapters 5 and 8, the result of continuous interaction between, on the one hand, various collectivities, strata, and coalitions of institutional entrepreneurs who are the carriers of specific cultural orientations and who control or attempt to control different resources, and, on the other hand, distinct ecological settings.

5. ANALYSIS OF REVOLUTIONS AND CRITICISM OF SOCIOLOGICAL THEORY

We reached this conclusion through reexamination of some general problems of sociological theory. First we critically examined the emphasis most contemporary sociological theories place on the organizational aspects of the institutional order, on such features of the social division of labor as level of technology and of structural differentiation as the major explanatory variables of institutional differences, and on the assumption that the norms ensuring maintenance of the social order can be derived directly from broad value orientations and/or from the systemic needs of social groups or of social interactions. Such an emphasis, which its critics charge is strongest in structural-functionalism, is present also in conflict and in exchange theory. Criticism of the assumptions underlying these theoretical models—specifically, of the importance they attach to the preceding societal variables—engendered the unwillingness of most approaches to accept the givenness of any single institutional arrangement in terms of the organizational or systemic needs of the social system to which it belongs. No institutional arrangement—the formal structure of a factory or a hospital, the division of labor in the family, the official definition of deviant behavior, the place of a ritual in a given social setting—is examined in terms of its contribution to the maintenance of a particular group or society. Instead, the very setting up of institutional arrangements is viewed as a problem to be explained. Thus, it is asked what forces beyond the organizational needs of a society explain its institutional arrangements.

The various theoretical models are divided over how to explain concrete institutional orders. The individualistic and conflict models, as well as the symbolic interactionist approach, stress that any institutional order is developed, maintained, and changed through a continuous process of interaction, negotiation, and struggle among those who participate in it. Accordingly, the explanation of institutional arrangements has to be attempted in terms of the power relations, conflicts, and coalitions that arise during such processes. Concomitantly, a strong emphasis is laid on the autonomy of any subsetting—subgroup or subsystem—that can give expression to goals that differ from those of the broader organizational or institutional setting, as well as on the environments within which the social setting operates (in the analysis of any macrosocietal order, this environment is the international systems). The structuralists and the Marxists, however, seek to explain the nature of any given institutional order and especially its dynamics in terms of principles of deep, or hidden, structure. In attempting to identify these principles the structuralists stress the importance of the symbolic dimensions of human activity and of inherent rules of the human mind. In contrast, the Marxists stress a combination of structural and symbolic dimensions such as the contradictions between the forces of production and the relations of production; alienation; and class consciousness as providing the principles of the deep structure of societies.

The very multiplicity of approaches to the study of fundamental sociological issues indicates that a number of key questions remain unanswered. How are cultural orientations or traditions interwoven into the institutional arrangements of a society? Which aspects of such arrangements are influenced and shaped by cultural orientations? Who are the major carriers of such orientations? What are the social mechanisms—the processes of social interaction and struggle—through which the carriers of cultural orientations influence the shaping of institutional arrangements? What processes of change develop within societies?

6. THE NEED FOR FURTHER RESEARCH

In our analysis of revolutions we addressed ourselves to these problems. We identified crucial aspects of institutional structure (e.g., the ground rules of social interaction and their major institutional derivatives such as the structure of centers, center-periphery relations, the ordering of social hierarchies, and processes of change) that are not given in the organizational aspects of the social division of labor and that are influenced by symbolic orientations.

In our comparison of social types—Imperial, Imperial-feudal, patrimonial, city-state, and tribal systems—we demonstrated how cultural codes and their constellations affect institutional spheres as well as patterns of change. It was through the development of these analytical tools that we were able in our analysis of both the causes and outcomes of revolutions to go beyond earlier analyses that focused exclusively on class conflict, interelite struggle, and other factors (without of course denying the importance of these variables).

We also identified the carriers of cultural orientations—the major types of elites, institutional entrepreneurs and elite coalitions—as well as the principal types of regulative institutional frameworks (legal, professional, and so on). We then attempted to show how different types of entrepreneurs and coalitions explain various patterns of institutional building and change.

These indications are preliminary, and we intend to pursue further some of the problems that concerned us in this volume. Thus, we wish to examine the mechanisms of control through which different entrepreneurs and coalitions are able to maintain their specific patterns of institutionalization and to discourage the emergence of new types of enterpreneurs who might challenge these patterns. This problem is closely related to the fact that great continuity of codes and of their basic institutional derivatives can be found in most societies.

Despite the continuity of codes and their institutional derivatives, the emergence of the great religions and the institutionalization of different patterns of political regimes attest to the importance of innovations and mutations in history. Here we come back to a problem mentioned in earlier chapters: is it the emergence of different types of cultural orientations that gives rise to specific elites and collectivities or is it elites and collectivities with certain latent or manifest attributes that create or select consonant orientations? We suggested that through a process of continuous feedback groups or persons with certain structural tendencies select appropriate orientations and that the institutionalization of these orientations reinforces the structural tendencies. We also noted that the interaction of these forces as they shape institutional settings and macrosocietal complexes, the process of feedback, and the mechanism through which feedback is institutionalized poses a crucial challenge for further research. We also stressed the importance of ecological settings both in the process of such feedback as well as in shaping different institutional outcomes of relatively similar orientations.

Our analysis pointed out the systemic nature of societies, the multiplicity of dimensions of social systems and of forces that generate different complexes of these dimensions, as well as the openness of situations of change. This openness was most fully illustrated in our analysis of revolution. To wit, however strong the predisposition to revolution in any given setting, this process constitutes a mutation.

The impact of revolutions was greater than the impact of the establishment of new political centers or the emergence of the great religions because the former process entailed a combination of symbolic and structural characteristics. This combination created the reality and above all the image of coalescent change as the natural and best type of change in human societies, as well as the reality of continually changing international systems through which this image spread worldwide.

Yet, as our analysis showed, even when the spread of international systems produced conditions conducive to coalescent change, in fact the actual pattern of social change and transformation varied according to the conditions analyzed throughout this book. Indeed, the very spread of these international systems of revolutionary imagery gave rise to a paradoxical situation. In contrast to traditional societies, in which special enclaves served as the carriers of innovations, the modern revolutions stressed the image of coalescent change generated entirely through the internal forces of the society as the most natural avenue of change.

Still, in many societies the processes of change attendant on modernization did not follow the revolutionary pattern. This fact, together with the continual expansion of the new international systems and the spread of revolutionary imagery and movements, re-created a situation in which small groups of revolutionaries and intellectuals were very active.

We thus seem to have come full circle. Yet the situation today is different in crucial ways from the traditional setting. First, the growth of international systems resulted in the constant impingement of revolutionary enclaves and movements on all societies. Second, this impingement was strengthened by alliances of such enclaves with different states and by shifts of power in the international systems. Third, we are faced with the intensification of both domestic and international violence, which in turn affects these processes.

The study of revolution indicates another central aspect of social life: the ubiquity of protest; of the search for freedom and community; and of attempts to transcend the existing situation. The study of revolution attests to the urgency of this quest, to the limitations on its fulfillment, and to the costs of different patterns of attempted fulfillment. These limitations and costs will be evaluated in different ways by different people but all of them have to face this problem honestly.

NOTES

1. This analysis follows S. N. Eisenstadt, "The Patterns of Incorporation of Different Dimensions of Socialist Tradition," in S. N. Eisenstadt and Y. Azmon (eds.), *Socialism and Tradition* (New York: Humanities, 1975), pp. 221–227.

2. See on this S. N. Eisenstadt and M. Curelaru, *The Form of Sociology* (New York: Wiley, 1976), chaps. 8, 10.

Index

Abbasside dynasty, 74, 135
Absolutist era, 142, 223–224
Africa, 274
  socialism in, 331–333
Akkad kingdom, 74
Albania, 244, 275
Alexander II, Tsar, 127
Algeria, 275, 283
Alienation, 22, 25, 336
Allende regime (Chile), 289, 331
Alliance for Progress, 296
Almond, Gabriel, 1, 64
American Revolution, 1, 9, 173, 175,
    196, 204, 227–228, 241, 245,
    251, 252, 275
Anarchists, 292
Anomie, 23
Anti-intellectualism, 59
Antinomianism, 59, 174, 183, 320
Antirationalism, 59
Arab countries, 330
Archaic civilizations, 62, 65; see also
    Traditional societies
  major characteristics of, 54–56
  traditional legitimation in, 56–58
Archaic religion, 62–63
Arendt, Hannah, 174
Argentina, 281, 291
Army, 230, 278, 298
Aron, Raymond, 188
Ashoka, Empire of, 122
Assemblies of Estate, 141
Assyrian kingdom, 74
Austria, 200, 252
Austro-Hungarian Empire, 252

Axial Age, 89

Babylonian Captivity, 255
Babylonian kingdom, 74
Baechler, Jean, 6, 7
Batista regime (Cuba), 296
Bellah, Robert N., 2, 61–62, 74, 144,
    227
Benda, Harry, 285
Bendix, Reinhard, 23, 25
Bhakti movement, 121
Blau, Peter, 23
Bloch, Marc, 142
Bolivian Revolution of 1952, 275, 283,
    289, 293, 296
Brahmanic ancestors, 159
Brahmanism, 116–117, 119–120, 122
Brazil, 277, 279, 281, 290
Brinton, Crane, 6
Buddha, 159
Buddhism, 76, 79, 81, 89, 90, 91, 94,
    115–116, 133, 149
Burma, 330
Byzantine Empire, 74, 80, 81, 127–
    128, 133, 139, 205

Caetano regime (Portugal), 297
Capitalism, 182, 195, 196, 205, 216–
    217, 315–316
Castes, 116–121
Center-periphery relations, 56, 57, 65,
    66
  in city-states, 97
  in Imperial societies, 86, 87, 96,
    127, 140, 144, 262

Center-periphery relations (*cont.*)
  modern revolutions and, 179, 180, 199, 202, 203, 216, 220–221, 223, 225, 226, 228, 229, 231–235, 240, 246
  in neopatrimonial societies, 276–277, 282–283, 295
  in patrimonial regimes, 90–91, 117
Centers, structure of, 36–39
  in city-states, 97–99
  in Imperial societies, 86–87, 123–124, 129–130, 136, 140, 144
  modern revolutions and, 179, 180, 199, 200, 202, 203, 222–224, 229–232, 240–243, 246–250
  in neopatrimonial societies, 276–277, 283
  in patrimonial regimes, 90, 116–117
  in tribal regimes, 97–99
Ceylon, 286, 330
Change: *see* Modern revolutions; Traditional societies
Chile, 289, 331
Chinese Empire, 74, 89, 90, 128–134, 150, 151, 205
Chinese Revolution, 1, 189, 197, 201–202, 205, 228–231, 233–235, 238–239, 241, 242, 245, 247–251, 275
Chomsky, Noam, 25
Christian tradition, 89, 90
Cities, development of, 142
Citizenship, 85
City-state regimes, 55, 60
  center-periphery relations, 97
  centers, structure of, 97–99
  cultural orientations of, 99–100
  exceptional change in, 74–75, 84–85, 97–100
  protest, rebellion, and political struggle, 77–79
  segregative change in, 74–80
  strata formation, 98
Civil religion, 260
Civil rights, 225
Civil wars, 6, 244, 289
Class: *see* Strata formation

Class conflict, 2, 22
Class consciousness, 25, 141, 311, 336
Cliques, 287
Coalescent change, 74, 75, 80–84, 133–134, 137, 203, 254, 338
Coalitions, 33–34, 37, 44–45, 77, 78, 220, 281, 287
Codes, 38–41
  institutionalization of, 40–45
Cognitive development, 63
Collective behavior, 6, 7
Collectivities, 20–22, 28, 32–33
  construction of, 36–39
  in Imperial societies, 88–89
  in patrimonial regimes, 92
Collins, Randall, 23, 25
Colombia, 292
Colonialism, 285, 288, 333
Communism, 182, 217, 322–323
  cultural orientations of, 183–184
  incorporation of revolutionary symbolism, 329–334
Communist phase of Chinese Revolution, 229–231
Compact markets, 152–154
Conflict theory of change, 23, 24, 26, 335
Confucianism, 89, 129, 130, 133, 159, 228
Continuity of codes, 234–236
Continuity-discontinuity in postrevolutionary society, 217–219
Coser, Louis, 25
Cosmic and mundane order, tension between, 116, 124, 127, 129, 147–150, 202, 252, 254
Counterreformation, 199, 200, 224, 284
Counterrevolution, 182
Crosscutting markets, 152–154
Cuban Communist Party, 295
Cuban Revolution, 275, 292, 293, 296–297, 331
Cultural orientations, 100–104, 145–146, 337
  of city-states, 99–100
  of communism, 183–184

of Imperial societies, 89–90, 128–
129, 134–136, 139
influencing patterns of change,
147–154
of Jewish tradition, 254–255
of patrimonial regimes, 94, 115
of socialism, 183–184
of tribal regimes, 99–100
Cultural Revolution, 249
Czechoslovakia, 312

Dahrendorf, Ralf, 23, 25
Davis, James, 7
Demographic apathy, 96
Demographic change, 54
Denmark, 197, 200, 206, 241
Dermott, J. M. L., 313–314
Deutsch, Karl, 7
Diaspora, 254, 255
Díaz regime (Mexico), 294
Differentiation, 61–63, 66
Discontinuity, 2–4, 217–219, 224–
227, 229–236, 240–242, 247
Dislocation, 225, 226, 240, 243, 247
Disorganization, 22, 23
Dunn, John, 7
Durkheim, Emile, 22, 23, 60
Dynastic change, 5, 80

Early modern religion, 63
Early modern societies, 62
Eckstein, Harry, 7
Ecological settings, 152–154, 158
Economic activities, 35, 76, 81–84, 87
Edwards, Lyford P., 6
Egypt, 74, 221, 279, 281, 283
Elites, 5, 32–33, 45, 98, 102–104,
136, 146, 147, 152–154, 155,
158, 337
emergence of, 67–68
in Japan, 145
in Jewish tradition, 255
in late modern societies, 317–318
modern revolutions and, 195, 198,
201, 204, 222, 223, 227, 229–
234, 245–48, 250, 253

in neopatrimonial societies, 279,
281–282, 285–286, 288–291
in postrevolutionary societies, 244
Ellul, Jacques, 317
England: *see* Glorious Revolution;
Great Rebellion
Enlightenment, 175, 184, 185, 188,
199, 200
Equality, 179, 216
Erlebnis, 6, 7, 176, 177
Ethnomethodology, 24
European revolutions of 1848, 1, 251–
253, 314, 318
Evolutionary perspective, 60–68, 155–
158
Exceptional change, 75, 84–85
Exchange theory of change, 23, 24,
32, 335
Existential codes, 39
Exploitation, 22
Exploration, 179

Family, 35, 43, 52, 98, 117–118, 130,
141
Fascism, 9, 253
Fatimites, 135
Feudal system, 60; *see also* Imperial
and Imperial-feudal societies
Fishing societies, 61
Fortes, M., 35
France: *see also* French Revolution
postrevolutionary society, 244–245
Protestantism and, 200
uprising of 1848, 314, 318
Freedom, 179, 216
French Revolution, 1, 173, 175, 186,
188, 197, 204, 226–227, 241,
250
Friedrich, Carl, 3

Geertz, Clifford, 101
Geiger, Theodor, 3
Germani, Gino, 9, 253
Germany, 206, 251, 252–253
Protestantism and, 200
upheavals of 1918, 318, 319
Gerschenkorn, Alexander, 219

Gillis, John R., 6, 7, 8
Glorious Revolution, 1, 173, 204, 224–225, 241, 251
Great Rebellion, 1, 173, 175, 204, 224–225, 251
Greece (ancient), 74, 84–85, 159–160, 322
Greek Orthodox church, 81
Greek philosophers, 159
Ground rules of social interaction, 28–34, 37, 156, 178, 201, 216, 222, 279, 280, 336
  institutionalization of, 40–45
Gurr, Ted, 7
Guerrilla movements, 292, 297, 312, 319, 320

Habermas, Jürgen, 63, 318
Hebrew prophets, 159
Henderson, R. N., 67
Herding societies, 61
Heterodoxy, 44, 45, 58–60, 66; *see also* Modern revolutions
  coalescent change and, 82–83
  in Imperial societies, 82–83, 132–133
  in neopatrimonial societies, 288
  in patrimonial, tribal, and city-state regimes, 77–79
  segregative change and, 77–79
Hinduism, 76, 79, 81, 90, 94, 116–122, 149, 153–154
Hinze, Otto, 140
Histadrut, 269
Historic intermediate empires, 62
Historic religion, 63
Historical civilizations: *see also* Traditional societies
  major characteristics of, 54–56
  traditional legitimation in, 56–58
Hittite kingdom, 74
Homans, George C., 23
Horticultural societies, 61
Hoselitz, Bert F., 91
Human activities, symbolic dimension of, 29–31
Hungary, 252
Hunting-gathering societies, 60, 61

Huntington, Samuel P., 4, 6, 8, 317
Hyksos kingdom, 74

Ideological articulation, 77–79, 82–83, 143
Imperial and Imperial-feudal societies, 60, 74, 75
  Byzantine Empire, 74, 80, 81, 127–128, 133, 139, 205
  center-periphery relations, 86, 87, 96, 127, 140, 144, 262
  centers, structure of, 86–87, 123–124, 129–130, 136, 140, 144
  Chinese Empire, 74, 89, 90, 128–134, 150, 151, 205
  coalescent change in, 74, 75, 80–84, 133–134, 137, 203
  collectivities, structuring of, 88–89
  cultural orientations of, 89–90, 128–129, 134–136, 139
  institutional entrepreneurs in, 131–132, 136
  Islamic civilization, 76, 87, 89, 90, 134–139, 150, 151, 153, 232–233, 333
  Japan, 143–145, 147
  Ottoman Empire, 74, 137, 138, 205
  patterns of change, 122–145
  protest, rebellion, heterodoxy, and political struggle, 82–83, 132–133
  Russian Empire, 74, 123–127, 155, 205
  strata formation, 88, 124–127, 130–131, 137–138, 141–144, 160, 262
  Western European civilization, 139–143, 151, 153
India, 74, 116–122, 151, 274, 283, 331, 332
Indonesia, 283, 286, 291
Indonesian Communist party, 288
Industrial Revolution, 186, 225
Industrial societies, 61, 64
Industrialization, 216, 312, 315, 318, 319
Institutional entrepreneurs, 102–105, 118, 145–146, 150, 222, 337

in Imperial societies, 131–132, 136
modern revolutions and, 187–188,
  201
in neopatrimonial societies, 285,
  288
in patrimonial regimes, 118
Institutional Revolutionary Party
  (PRI), Mexico, 294, 295
Institutional structure, 20–21, 100–
  104, 119–120, 156–157, 215–
  219, 225, 228, 230, 232–237,
  245–246
Intellectual antinomianism, 174, 183
Intellectuals, modern, 187–188, 292
Interest (pressure) groups, 180
Internal wars, 6–8
International relations, 54, 55, 58,
  182–183, 249–251, 292–293
Iran, 137
Iraq, 290
Islam, 76, 87, 89, 90, 134–139, 150,
  151, 153, 232–233, 333
Israel (ancient), 74, 84, 254–260
Israel, state of, 258–260
Italy, 253, 322

Jaeggi, Urs, 8
Jänicke, Martin, 8
Japan, 66, 143–145, 147, 203, 221,
  261, 262, 278, 331–333
Jewish tradition, 253–260
Johnson, Chalmers, 4

Kamenka, Eugene, 3–4, 186
Kautsky, John, 219
Kemalist Revolution: *see* Turkish
  Revolution
Kibbutzim, 258
Kinship, 35, 43, 52, 98, 117–118, 130,
  141
Kirchheimer, Otto, 319
Kshatriyas, 118, 121
Kuomintang phase of Chinese Revolu-
  tion, 206, 228, 229, 242

Labor, social division of, 20–22, 27,
  34, 40, 43
Land, redistribution of, 230, 278

Landauer, Gustav, 3
Landsberger, Henry A., 289
Late modern societies, 62, 311–323
Latin America, 274, 275, 285, 286,
  331–333; *see also* names of
  countries
Law (*Halacha*), 254–256
Lederer, Emil, 3
Legal system, 90, 225, 226, 228
Legitimation, 56–58, 174–175
Leninism, 188, 319
Lenski, Gerhard, 61, 74
Lenski, Jean, 61, 74
Lerner, Daniel, 1
Lévi-Strauss, Claude, 23, 25, 29
Levites of Israel, 98
Lichtheim, George, 186
Lipset, Seymour Martin, 8, 33, 220
Literati, Chinese, 131–132, 228, 229
Lüthy, Herbert, 200
Luxemburg, Rosa, 319

MacDaniel, Tim, 289
Macrosocietal order, 20–21, 27, 31, 34
  symbolic articulation of, 36–39
Maghreb, 138, 283, 286
Magic, 94
Malaysia, 286, 291
Mamelukes, 136
Mardin, Sherif, 5, 8
Maritime societies, 60, 61
Markets, 147–155, 195, 225, 226, 228,
  229, 230, 233, 261, 284, 288
Marx, Karl, 3, 22, 23, 60, 217, 314
Marxism, 24, 25, 27, 188, 220, 336
Mayer, K. A., 315
Mazlish, Bruce, 202
Media, 288
Meiji Restoration of 1868, 9, 261, 262
Mesoamerican kingdoms, 74
Messianic concept, 254, 256
Mexican Revolution, 9, 189, 275, 292–
  296
Millenarian protest movements, 44,
  175, 176, 181, 287
Mobility: *see* Social mobility
Modern civilization, 177–187
Modern religion, 63

Modern revolutions, 173–272; *see also*
    Late modern societies; Neo-
    patrimonial societies; specific
    revolutions
  carriers of symbols, 187–188
  center-periphery relations and, 179,
    180, 199, 202, 203, 216, 220–
    221, 223, 225, 226, 228, 229,
    231–235, 240, 246
  centers, structure of, 179, 180, 199,
    200, 202, 203, 222–224, 229–
    232, 240–243, 246–250
  characteristics of, 173–175
  conditions behind development of,
    195–198, 201–204
  discontinuity, 224–227, 229–236,
    240–242, 247
  dislocation, 225, 226, 240, 243, 247
  early, compared to later, 205–206
  elites and, 195, 198, 201, 204, 222,
    223, 227, 229–234, 245–248,
    250, 253
  historical setting of, 201
  institutional entrepreneurs in, 187–
    188, 201
  institutional structure, 225, 228,
    230, 232–237, 245–246
  markets, 229, 230, 233
  modern civilization and, 177–187
  restructuring of protest themes,
    175–177
  socialism, 183–189
  sociocultural setting of, 198–200
  strata formation and, 219–221,
    224–234, 246–248
  symbolic and organizational dimen-
    sions of, 175–177
Mongols, 74
Monistic societies, 67–68
Moore, Barrington, 8, 9, 33, 196, 202,
    219–220, 317
Moral development, 63
Moshavim, 258
Müller, W., 315
Multinational corporations, 322

Nasserist regime (Egypt), 281, 283
National liberation, 244, 249, 251

Natural history approach, 6
Nehru, Jawaharlal, 331
Neoevolutionary approaches, 1–2, 60
Neo-Marxist theory of change, 25, 27
Neopatrimonial societies, 273–298
  Bolivia, 275, 283, 289, 293, 296
  center-periphery relations, 276–277,
    282–283, 295
  centers, structure of, 276–277, 283
  Cuba, 275, 292, 293, 296–297, 331
  elites, 279, 281–282, 285–286, 288–
    291
  fragility of, 289
  institutional entrepreneurs in, 285,
    288
  international relations and, 292–293
  Mexico, 9, 189, 275, 292–296
  noncoalescent change in, 280–281
  persistence of patrimonial orienta-
    tions, 283–285
  Portugal, 293, 297–298
  processes of change in, 279–280
  protest, rebellion, and political
    struggle, 287–288
  revolutionary movements in, 292
  social mobility, 278, 279–280
  stability of, 289–291
  structural characteristics of, 276–
    278
  variations in, 286–287
Netherlands, Revolt of the, 9, 173,
    175, 196, 204, 206, 227–228,
    241, 251, 252
Nolte, Ernest, 253

Offe, Claus, 315, 316
Orthodox church, 126
Ottoman Empire, 74, 137, 138, 205

Palestine, 257–260
Paris Commune, 1, 314, 318
Parliaments, 277
Parsons, Talcott, 2, 25, 61, 62, 74,
    160
Patrimonial regimes, 55, 60
  Buddhist societies, 115–116
  center-periphery relations, 90–91,
    117

centers, structure of, 90, 116–117
collectivities, structuring of, 92
cultural orientations of, 94, 115
Hindu civilization in India, 116–
122
incorporation of, in modern international systems, 274–275
institutional entrepreneurs in, 118
institutional structure, 119–120
patterns of change, 114–122
protest, rebellion, and political
struggle, 77–79
segregative change in, 73–80, 137
social units, incorporation of, 93
strata formation, 92–93, 117–118,
138
Peasant rebellions, 5, 7, 195, 294
Peasantry, 91, 125, 126, 131
Periphery: *see* Center-periphery relations
Peronist regime (Argentina), 281
Persia (ancient), 122
Peru, 221, 277, 279, 283
Pettee, George S., 6
Philippine Islands, 291
Piaget, Jean, 63
Poland, 312
Polanyi, Karl, 91
Political elites: *see* Elites
Political parties, 180, 181–182, 235,
277–278
Political struggle, 44, 45, 58–60; *see
also* Modern revolutions
coalescent change and, 82–83
in Imperial societies, 82–83, 132–
133
in neopatrimonial societies, 287–
288
in patrimonial, tribal, and city-state
regimes, 77–79
segregative change and, 77–79
Populist regimes, 281, 290
Portugal, 200, 274, 275, 284, 322
Portuguese Revolution, 293, 297–298
Post-industrial societies: *see* Late
modern societies
Postrevolutionary societies, 177, 178,
216

criteria of institutional change in,
217–219
restructuring of, 236–245
Primitive religion, 62
Primitive societies, 62, 65
change in, 52–54
Private property, 225, 226, 228
Privatization, 59
Production, 25, 336
Professional revolutionary, 202
Protest, 58–60, 66; *see also* Modern
revolutions
coalescent change and, 82–83
in Imperial societies, 82–83, 132–
133
in neopatrimonial societies, 287–
288
in patrimonial, tribal, and city-state
regimes, 77–79
segregative change and, 77–79
themes of, 43–45
Protestantism, 173, 199–200, 206
Psychological (psychosocial) ap-
proach, 6
Public goods, 34
Public opinion, 180, 181, 235
Pure revolution, 8–9, 68, 173, 298
Puritans, 188
Pye, Lucian, 64

Radicalism, 182, 314, 320–322
differential spread of, 188–189
Reason, 175
Rebellion, 44, 45, 58–60, 66; *see also*
Modern revolutions
coalescent change and, 82–83
in Imperial societies, 82–83, 132–
133
in neopatrimonial societies, 287–
288
in patrimonial, tribal, and city-state
regimes, 77–79
segregative change and, 77–79
Reform movements, 181
Reformation, 199
Regimes, crises of, 6–8
Religion: *see* names of religions
Renaissance, 175

Revolt of the Netherlands, 9, 173, 175, 196, 204, 206, 227–228, 241, 251, 252
Revolts, 314, 317, 320–323
Revolution of 1848, 1, 251–253, 314, 318
Revolutions: *see* Modern revolutions
Rex, John, 23
Rittberger, Volker, 4
Ritual, 94
Rokkan, Stein, 8, 33, 200, 220
Rome (ancient), 74, 84–85, 155, 159–160
Rosenstock-Huessy, Eugen, 3
Runciman, W. C., 8
Russian Empire, 74, 123–127, 155, 205
Russian Revolution, 1, 189, 197, 201–202, 205, 221, 231–235, 238–239, 241, 242, 245, 250, 251, 260, 275

Sabbatai Zevi, 256
Salazar regime (Portugal), 297
Sangha, 115
Scandinavia, 197, 200, 206, 241, 322
Scholem, Gershon, 256
Scientific revolution, 184
Second Jewish Commonwealth, 254, 255
Seedbed societies, 62, 160
Segregative change, 73–80, 137
Service, Elmer, 53–54, 65
Sexual behavior, 35
Shii Islam, 137
Shils, Edward, 37
Simmel, Georg, 23
Skocpol, Theda, 6, 8, 197, 220–221
Smelser, Neil, 4
Social class: *see* Strata formation
Social interaction, 19–20
    ground rules of, 28–34, 37, 40–45, 156, 178, 201, 216, 222, 279, 280, 336
    symbolic and organizational aspects, interweaving of, 34–36
Social mobility, 120, 126, 131, 142, 278, 279–280, 288

Social movements, 180–181
Social Origins of Dictatorship and Democracy (Moore), 33, 219
Social welfare, 322
Socialism, 183–189, 217
    attraction of, 187
    cultural orientations of, 183–184
    incorporation of revolutionary symbolism, 329–334
    spread of, 185–189
    strata formation and, 184
Societal differentiation, dimensions of, 54–56
Solidarity, 179, 216
Solomonic Kingdom, 85, 255
South Asia, 274
Southeast Asia, 74, 275, 285, 286, 334
Spain, 155, 200, 206, 274, 275, 284, 291, 322
Spanish Civil War, 289
Specialization, 62
Srinivas, M. S., 120
State, emergence of, 56
Status incongruency, 141
Stein, Lorenz von, 3
Stone, Lawrence, 6, 8
Strata formation, 35, 55
    caste system, 116–121
    in city-states, 98
    in Imperial societies, 88, 124–127, 130–131, 137–138, 141–144, 160, 262
    in late modern societies, 315–318
    modern revolutions and, 219–221, 224–234, 246–248
    in patrimonial regimes, 92–93, 117–118, 138
    socialism and, 184
    in tribal regimes, 98
Structural differentiation, 54–55, 59, 60, 65, 66, 139, 147, 156, 158, 160, 222
Structural-functional theory of change, 23–27, 335–336
Structural pluralism, 139–140, 144, 200, 313
Student revolt, 312, 314, 320–322
Subjectivism, 59

Sudras, 118
Suharto regime (Indonesia), 291
Sukarno regime (Indonesia), 291
Sunni Islam, 137
Swat, 138
Sweden, 197, 206, 322
Switzerland, 197, 200, 206, 241
Symbolic articulation, 100–105, 145–146
Symbolic dimension of human activities, 29–31
Symbolic-interactionist theory, 23, 32, 336
Symbolic-structuralist theory of change, 23–26, 29
Syria, 290

Taiwan, 245
Talmon, J. L., 174
Taoism, 89, 133
Technological development, 54, 59, 61–63, 65, 195, 313
Temple-cities, 55
Territorial attachment, 52
Terrorist movements, 312, 320
Tilly, Charles, 4, 6, 8, 45
Tocqueville, Alexis de, 2, 3, 217, 234
Tokugawa regime (Japan), 144, 261, 262
Totality of change, 2–4
Touraine, Alain, 317
Traditional legitimation, 56–58
Traditional societies, 52–161
  city-state regimes, 55, 60
    center-periphery relations, 97
    centers, structure of, 97–99
    cultural orientations of, 99–100
    exceptional change in, 74–75, 84–85, 97–100
    protest, rebellion, and political struggle, 77–79
    segregative change in, 74–80
    strata formation, 98
  evolutionary perspective, 60–68, 155–158
  Imperial societies, 60, 74, 75
    Byzantine Empire, 74, 80, 81, 127–128, 133, 139, 205

center-periphery relations, 86, 87, 96, 127, 140, 144, 262
centers, structure of, 86–87, 123–124, 129–130, 136, 140, 144
Chinese Empire, 74, 89, 90, 128–134, 150, 151, 205
coalescent change in, 74, 75, 80–84, 133–134, 137, 203
collectivities, structuring of, 88–89
cultural orientations of, 89–90, 128–129, 134–136, 139
institutional entrepreneurs in, 131–132, 136
Islamic civilization, 76, 87, 89, 90, 134–139, 150, 151, 153, 232–233, 333
Japan, 143–145, 147
Ottoman Empire, 74, 137, 138, 205
patterns of change, 122–145
protest, rebellion, heterodoxy, and political struggle, 82–83, 132–133
Russian Empire, 74, 123–127, 155, 205
strata formation, 88, 124–127, 130–131, 137–138, 141–144, 160, 262
Western European civilization, 139–143, 151, 153
  patrimonial regimes, 55, 60
    Buddhist societies, 115–116
    center-periphery relations, 90–91, 117
    centers, structure of, 90, 116–117
    collectivities, structuring of, 92
    cultural orientations of, 94, 115
    Hindu civilization in India, 116–122
    institutional entrepreneurs in, 118
    institutional structure, 119–120
    patterns of change, 114–122
    protest, rebellion, heterodoxy, and political struggle, 77–79
    segregative change in, 73–80, 137
    social units, incorporation of, 93

Traditional societies (*cont.*)
  strata formation, 92–93, 117–118, 138
  primitive societies, 52–54
  societal differentiation, 54–56
  traditional legitimation, 56–58
  tribal regimes, 55, 60
    center-periphery relations, 97
    centers, structure of, 97–99
    cultural orientations of, 99–100
    exceptional change in, 84–85
    protest, rebellion, and political struggle, 77–79
    segregative change in, 74–80
    strata formation, 98
  variability of societies, 60–65
Transcendental-cosmic and mundane order, tension between, 116, 124, 127, 129, 147–150, 202, 252, 254
Tribal regimes, 55, 60
  center-periphery relations, 97
  centers, structure of, 97–99
  cultural orientations of, 99–100
  exceptional change in, 84–85, 97–100
  protest, rebellion, and political struggle, 77–79
  segregative change in, 74–80
  strata formation, 98
Trimberger, Kay, 6, 8, 197, 220–221
True Believers, 124
True revolutions: *see* Modern revolutions
Tunisia, 277

Tupamaros, 292
Turkish Revolution, 5, 9, 189, 196, 201–202, 221, 232–233, 236, 242, 245, 251

Ulemas, 153
Ummah, 135
Universities, 320–322
Uruguay, 292
Utopian movements, 44, 176

Vaishyas, 118, 121
Vargas regime (Brazil), 281
Venezuela, 292
Vietnamese Revolution, 189, 201–203, 205, 232, 238–239, 241, 242, 245, 251, 274
Violence, 2–4, 45, 226

Walzer, Michael, 174, 200
Weber, Max, 4–5, 22, 23, 31, 60, 67, 90, 205, 316, 319
Western European civilization, 139–143, 151, 153
Wirtschaftsethik, 31
Writing, invention of, 54

Yishuv, 258–260
Yugoslavian Revolution, 189, 201–202, 244, 250, 260, 275

Zionism, 257, 260
Zoroastrianism, 79, 115
Zulu, Kingdom of the, 53